Marc Clement

The Tireless Engine

The Story of the Most Produced Steam Locomotive

The original German edition was published under the title 'Die Unermüdlichen', © 2022 Marc Clement
© 2024 Marc Clement

Produced and published by BoD - Books on Demand, Norderstedt, Germany

ISBN 978-3-7597-8175-8

Contents

         Romanization
         Railway companies
         Locomotive works
         Boiler suppliers for war locomotive production
         References

Foreword

The steam engines discussed in this book were part of an extraordinarily eventful period in history. They were built at a time when it was clear that the future belonged to diesel and electric trains. Enabling travel between major cities at unprecedented speeds, the 'flying trains' of the Reichsbahn were the first sign of the upcoming era. It marked the end of the age of the steam engine, which had shaped the face of the railway for over a century and remains an iconic image to this day.

At the end of the 1930s, the German Reichsbahn put a light freight locomotive into service. As one of the Reichsbahn's many standard engines its purpose was to replace the worn-out units of the past. Interest would typically have been limited to a small group of steam locomotives enthusiasts in Germany, but even they could never have imagined the role it would play in a changing world.

The new machines were developed on the eve of the Second World War. At that time, Adolf Hitler had already told the leaders of the Reich that he intended to start a new war in the foreseeable future and it was natural to predict the involvement of the railways. Already there were indications that its construction was prepared for its use in war.

These new freight locomotives became part of the biggest war in human history, with millions of deaths and an unprecedented genocide. The greatest catastrophe of the 20th century, it engulfed the whole of Europe and destroyed millions of lives as well as centuries-old communities and cultures.

During the war the original design was simplified, giving way to a series of military engines. These not only reflected the raw material shortages caused by the war, but also represented one of the first attempts in Europe to mass-produce locomotives on an industrial scale, assembling them by the thousands from standardised parts provided by different suppliers. Modern division of labour, such as the supply of complete, fully assembled subassemblies were applied on a large scale despite the fact that factories and infrastructure were destroyed by heavy bombing. This was achieved using thousands of slave labourers.

After the war, the same engines that had previously helped with the attempt to subjugate Europe to an insane ideology now played one of the most crucial roles in the reconstruction of the continent.

With this book you are invited to follow the path of this construction whose story encapsulated technology, contemporary history and today's commercial models. Due to the extraordinary nature of the period, the aim was not to write a purely technical book, but to place its design, production and later operation in the historical context of the railways and countries concerned. In order to avoid repeating some of the many illustrations of the engine found in literature and the web, only illustrations of the models of my collection of commercially available models (scale 1:87) were used. These could be standardised in order to draw attention to special features.[1]

Although these locomotives travelled during the uncertain times of war and social upheaval, we know the vast majority of the places where they were operating. For the examples presented in this book, those locations have been included.

Of course, this book would not have been possible without the help of many friends and supporters, in particular Nancy Cunningham, H. G. W. Davie of the University of Wolverhampton, Dave Evans of the PRR Technical & Historical Society, 'Florin' of trains-addicted.ro, Dr. Dirk Forschner of the TU Berlin, Andreas Giller of the Henschel Museum + Sammlung e.V., Jianwei Han, Lars Linde from the Järnvägarnas Museiförening Linköping, Prof. Masami Nagatomo, Robert Schoenberg from rail-fan.net, the service teams of the producers of the commercial models, Egbert von Steuber, the SNCF 'Centre National des Archives Historiques', the Trainworld-museum in Schaerbeek, Karl-Heinz Wunderlich and Ing. Martin Žalmánek. Special thanks also to Pferdi's crew. You both were a great help. Last but not least, I would like to thank my wife for her encouragement for this project.

---

[1] Bastian Königsmann has put together a wonderful collection of photos of originals of these locomotives (Königsmann, 2021).

1 Situation after the First World War

In 1920, the former individual railways of the German States became the property of the Reich, which merged them under the name 'Deutsche Reichsbahnen', later changed to 'Deutsche Reichsbahn', under the direction of the Reich Ministry of Transport. This merger had already been provided for in the Weimar Constitution of 1919, in which the central power of the Reich was strengthened, among other things, by the transfer of sovereignty over train transport.[2] In November 1919, the Government of the Reich therefore decided, on behalf of the German States, to take over the state railways on 1st April 1920, which was affected by a state treaty on 10th March 1920. The length of line taken over was 51,957 km.[3] The ownership of the land holdings was also transferred to the Reich, although any encumbrance or sale of the land holdings was still subject to the approval of the respective States. For the transfer of the railways, the former States were compensated with a one-off payment totalling 39 billion Reichsmarks[4].

At the start of the First World War, the German government had suspended the gold standard (the convertibility of its currency into gold) in order to finance the high costs of the war. The idea behind was to pay off the mounting debts after winning the war by imposing reparations on the defeated Allies, similar to the German victory over France in 1870/71.

But as the war was lost, the idea of passing the burden on to the Allies did not work, and worse, the Reich itself had to pay reparations. So, the government began to print paper money, exacerbating inflation. Although the reparations had to be paid in foreign currency or gold, the state tried to raise the necessary funds through an uncontrolled expansion of its own currency. As a result, money became more and more worthless, and when Germany failed to pay its instalments of reparations on time, the Allies demanded reparations in kind (coal, steel, timber). When it became clear that the Reich was in arrears, Allied troops occupied the Ruhr in 1923.

The occupation provoked an outcry of national indignation in the Weimar Republic. Chancellor Wilhelm Cuno called on the population to engage in 'passive resistance'. Strikes paralysed parts of the administration and transport. Inflation rose to a level of

---

[2] (Baumann, 1931), pages 62f
[3] Track length at the end of the accounting year 1920 (Statistisches Reichsamt, 1923), page 78
[4] (Baumann, 1931), page 63, according to today's purchasing power (2021) around 20 billion € (Deutsche Bundesbank).

a hyperinflation and the economy began to collapse. In September 1923, the new German government under Gustav Stresemann put an end to the resistance and introduced a currency reform. The way was now clear to renegotiate reparations.

At the end of 1923, a committee of the Reparations Commission drew up a plan to link Germany's reparations payments to its economic strength. This stabilised the economic situation of the Weimar Republic.

The Reichsbank received US-loans but was placed under international control. In this way, the US wanted to ensure that Germany could meet its obligations to France and Britain so that they in turn could repay their war loans to the US.

As a further step, it was decided to set up the Reichsbahn as an independent company in the form of a public limited company (Deutsche Reichsbahngesellschaft, DRB) and to issue a bond of 11 billion gold marks (about 200 billion €)[5], secured by a corresponding mortgage on the Reichsbahn's land holdings. The bond should have an interest of 5 % per annum and be paid off at 1 % per annum.[2] In addition, the board of directors had to include foreign members and an international commissioner was appointed. Although this special arrangement ensured the Reich's ownership of the company, it effectively placed the Reichsbahn under international control. The spin-off took place on 11th October 1924.

Carl Oeser, who had previously been the Reich Minister of Transport, was appointed as the first General Director[6] of the new company. To assist him in his duties, the post of a permanent deputy general director was created in 1925 and filled by Julius Dorpmüller. After Oeser's death, Dorpmüller was appointed General Director of the Deutsche Reichsbahngesellschaft by the Board of Directors in June 1926.

In 1930, the Reichsbahn underwent further changes as a result of the so-called Young Plan. This new payment plan was prompted by fears that Germany would soon be over-indebted and unable to repay its reparations. Despite Germany's economic recovery, it was foreseeable that the Reich would be unable to service their debt obligations.[7] The most important change for the Reichsbahn was that the Reichsbahn's debt certificates were cancelled and the foreign members of the board of directors and the commissioner withdrew.[8] With the cancellation the foreign control of the Reichsbahn was removed.

---

[5] The gold mark was the equivalent of a certain amount of fine gold. One gold mark corresponded to the price of 0.358423 g (0.0111482 oz.tr.) of gold. According to today's value (2/2022), this is about 20 €. (Deutsche Bundesbank).
[6] Comparable to today's function of a CEO.
[7] (Pfleiderer)
[8] (Baumann, 1931), page 68

Tab. 1: Situation of the DRB in key figures[9]

	1926	1928	1930	1932	1934	1936[10]
Commercial:						
Operating income [M RM][11]	4.541	5.159	4.570	2.934	3.326	3.985
Operating profit [M RM]	694	865	480	-67	24	472
	15 %	17 %	11 %	-2 %	1 %	12 %
Operational:						
Locomotive density [number per 100 km network length][12]	50	46	45	41	38	38
Network load [1000 tkm/km network length] Freight traffic[13]	1.239	1.391	1.157	841	1.078	1.301

From the mid-1920s, the Reichsbahn became a profitable company. With an operating surplus of around 15 % of revenue, the company was able to invest heavily in a series of technical developments that attracted worldwide attention. New design principles were developed for the construction of standardised steam locomotives – a first step towards the standardisation of rolling stock. Other important developments gained worldwide recognition: the bogie type Görtlitz[14], the road roller[15] (colloquially known as the 'Culemeyer'), the 'Oberbau K'[16] and the construction of the Berlin S-Bahn. However, the Great Depression at the beginning of the 1930s significantly slowed things down.

Until the 1930s, a large part of the Reichsbahn's investment was spent on improving the track. The main focus was on upgrading the tracks so that wagons with higher axle loads could be used. This meant that more tonnage could be carried per wagon on the existing lines, increasing capacity and reducing costs. In 1924, only 64 % of all

---

[9] (Statistisches Reichsamt, 1926), pages 148ff ;(Statistisches Reichsamt, 1930), pages 161ff; (Statistisches Reichsamt, 1932), pages 149ff; (Statistisches Reichsamt, 1934), pages 173ff; (Statistisches Reichsamt, 1936), pages 190ff; (Statistisches Reichsamt, 1938), pages 210ff; Profit: incl. narrow-gauge railways of the DRB and two private railways, which were operated in unseparated operating accounts. Operational: only for DRB mainline railways. Locomotive density: data for 1926 and 1928 include railcars.

[10] incl. Saarland, integration took place on 1st March 1935.

[11] M RM = **M**illion **R**eichsmark

[12] incl. railcars

[13] tkm = **t**on-**k**ilometre: a unit of measurement for the performance of freight transport: kilometres travelled multiplied by the quantity of goods transported in tons.

[14] Initially, railway carriages had only fixed axles, but later the bogie, which can ultimately be understood as a small 'carriage' with two or three axles, mounted movably under the vehicle frame, came into use. In the early 1920s, '**W**aggon-und **M**aschinenbau **AG**' (WUMAG) in Görlitz developed a new bogie type for passenger carriages that used leaf springs arranged lengthwise.

[15] The road roller is a vehicle trailer for transporting railway wagons and heavy loads on the road.

[16] In addition to the rolling stock, the track is of great importance. In this context, the 'Oberbau K' was a special, standardised way of fastening the rails to the sleepers.

lines had a weight of rail of ≥ 40 kg/m. By 1929, investment had increased this to 75 %. This meant that the majority of German main lines could accommodate an axle load of 20 tons.[17]

However, the number of locomotives decreased steadily over the years. This figure should be understood against the background of the organisation of railway traffic in the era of the steam engine. At that time, the machines were assigned to individual depots, where they were maintained and provided with fresh supplies (water, coal). Repairs were also carried out here.

A steam locomotive range was limited by the amount of supplies in the tender. Therefore, they would haul a train from a starting point near their home depot for a certain distance (about 200 - 300 km), then be replaced by another machine with fresh supplies. The previous engine would then return to its home depot. In this way, a train moved on like a relay race, being hauled by different units. This encouraged the construction of terminal stations: When a train entered a station, the 'empty' steam locomotive could be uncoupled at the front, while a 'fresh' engine could be coupled at the rear and took over the train.

It was therefore important that there were sufficient machines on the line to service the train, otherwise the train service was limited by the number of units, even though the line may have had a much higher capacity.

A reduction in the DRB's locomotive density per 100 km of track (cf. Table 1) simply meant that there were fewer engines available than before. Therefore fewer trains could be run. At the same time, the load of freight traffic on the network decreased. This reflects the slowdown in economic development from the end of 1920's and through the Great Depression.

The banking system collapsed as a result of the Great Depression and it became clear that Germany would not be able to meet its reparations obligations even after the Hoover moratorium[18]. A new reparations treaty was needed. In 1932, the Treaty of Lausanne agreed on a final payment to be made in the form of Reich bonds. As a result, the Reichsbahn's outflow of funds for reparations payments ceased. In the following years, however, the Reichsbahn's surpluses were used to finance state projects outside the Reichsbahn.

---

[17] (Mierzejewski, 1999), page 222

[18] The Hoover Moratorium was a promise made by US-President Hoover in 1931 to suspend loan repayments for one year because of the Great Depression. This affected not only German reparations, but also the repayment of war loans from Britain and France to the US.

Tab. 2: Organisation forms and levies of the German railways 1920-1945[19]

	Operation	Owner	Administration	Levies
5.1920-2.1924	Deutsche Reichsbahn	German Reich	Under direction of the Reich	Income and expenditure directly linked to the state budget
2.1924-10.1924	Unternehmen Deutsche Eisenbahn	German Reich	Trust administration by a legal entity, General Director: RVM[21]	Net profit and debt service directly linked to the state budget
10.1924-2.1937	Deutsche Reichsbahn-gesellschaft	German Reich	Trust administration by a legal entity and own organisation, only participation of the Reich	Reparation payments for the Reich until 6.1932; from 7.1932 on: 70 M RM annually
2.1937-2.1939	Deutsche Reichsbahn	German Reich	Special asset, special management by RVM[21]	70 M RM annually
2.1939-4.1945	Deutsche Reichsbahn	German Reich	Special asset managed as an independent institution of the Reich by RVM[21]	min. 100 M RM annually

The fact that the network load increased again in the mid-1930s, with little change in unit numbers, was due to some improvements:[19]

- The change of the maintenance work methods (planned maintenance, more efficient working methods).
- The improvement of marshalling with a reduction in the number of yards required.
- The electrification of lines[20]
- The simplification of operations on secondary lines

The issue of low number of locomotives came up again later, when the length of the network to be served by the Reichsbahn had increased considerably as a result of the war conquests.

---

[19] (Kittel, 1954)

[20] Electric locomotives carry no supplies (other than sand to increase friction between the engine and the track, e.g. when braking), so they can take a train from start to finish without changing the machine.

[21] RVM = Reichsverkehrsministerium (Reich Minister of Transport)

2 Between Hitler's rise to power and start of war

The National Socialists' seizure of power meant that things at the DRB were to change significantly. The 'Gesetz zur Wiederherstellung des Berufsbeamtentums' [22] of 7th April 1933 was quickly adopted by the Reichsbahn, although they were not obliged to do it, as the range of the law did not affect them [23]. As a result, employees who could not prove their 'Aryan origin' were dismissed relatively quickly. Another group affected were members of the KPD [24], the SPD [25] and the trade unions. In the Reichsbahn directorates, 'unreliable' managers were dismissed and replaced by 'old Nazi fighters', with professional qualifications often playing a secondary role. As part of this 'purge', Wilhelm Kleinmann was installed as president of the RBDs [26] and was soon to be promoted to Reichsbahn's board. General Director Julius Dorpmüller himself came under criticism, but this was quelled by Hitler's support. [27]

After Hitler's rise to power, the world economy started to recover. Freight traffic in Germany increased steadily, but revenues and operating surpluses did not increase at the same rate. This was due to the large price reductions imposed on the Reichsbahn by the former Brüning government [28] and the repayment of debts incurred to finance Hitler's job-creation schemes ('Gesetz zur Verminderung der Arbeitslosigkeit' and '2. Gesetz zur Verminderung der Arbeitslosigkeit' [29], both 1933). Of particular note was the 'Gesetz über die Errichtung eines Unternehmens Reichsautobahnen' [30] from 1933, which was set up as a branch of the Reichsbahn and should be financed by it. The Nazis saw the future of mobility in the motorisation of society (not only on land, but also in the air), and this should be financed by the Reichsbahn as a 'cash cow'. The Nazis initially thought that the construction of the 'autobahn' and the promotion of the car industry would help to fight mass unemployment, especially since mass motorisation was a perfect way to portray the attributes of 'dynamism' and 'modernity' with which National Socialism was so fond of adorning itself. [27] The

---

[22] Law for the Restoration of Professional Civil Service
[23] (Gottwaldt, 2009), pages 78f
[24] **K**ommunistische **P**artei **D**eutschlands (Communist Party of Germany)
[25] **S**ozialdemokratische **P**artei **D**eutschlands (Social Democratic Party of Germany)
[26] RBD = **R**eichs**bahnd**irektion. In Germany, the Reichsbahn was disaggregated in railway divisions (Reichsbahndirektionen), which were in charge for the operation and the regional network. Kleimann got head of all RBDs.
[27] (Rinn, 2008), pages 20f, 34ff
[28] Heinrich Brüning served as Chancellor of Germany from March 1930 to May 1932.
[29] Law to Reduce Unemployment and Second Law to Reduce Unemployment
[30] Law on the Establishment of a Reichsautobahn-Company

fact that the Reichsbahn had to finance these investments had negative effects on future development. The Nazi-government did not or was not willing to recognise this. The promotion of the automobile over the railway as the supposed landmark for modernity was a legacy that would have political repercussions in Germany for a long time to come, even till today.

In order to finance these laws, an idea of former Reich-Chancellor Heinrich Brüning[28] was taken up, namely to pre-finance the financial requirements by means of so-called 'Arbeitsbeschaffungswechsel'.[31] At the same time, the Ministry of Finance made clear that the Reichsbahn would have to balance its own budget.[32] In 1935, the Reich Minister of Transport, Paul von Eltz-Rübenach, and Dorpmüller succeeded in raising freight rates, thus easing the financial situation of the Reichsbahn in the second half of the 1930s.

During this period, however, iron and steel were rationed for the armament of the Wehrmacht, so that the maintenance of the tracks could not be carried out to the extent planned. There was also a lack of funds and materials for the (replacement-) procurement of rolling stock.[33] As a short-term measure, from March 1937 the Reichsbahn began overloading its goods wagons by one ton. This practice was criticised by the maintenance departments because it increased wear and tear on cars and tracks. Until December 1939, the overloading of freight wagons was limited to local traffic. Then it was extended to all traffic.[34]

Nevertheless, the shortage of freight engines became increasingly apparent as freight traffic continued to grow during this period. In particular, the locomotive classes G8[1] (55^{25-56}) and G10 (57^{10-35}), which had been purchased in the 1920s, were reached their limits when train speeds were increased. More and more of them broke down and had to be taken out of service.

The standard freight machine classes 43 and 44 developed in the mid-1920s were faster and much more powerful, but their axle loads of around 19 tons meant that they could only be used on the main lines. The universal locomotive classes 41 and 45, developed in the early 1930s, were no great improvement either, as they were not suitable for use on branch lines.

---

[31] The 'Arbeitsbeschaffungswechsel' (Job Creation Bills) were promissory notes first issued by the German government in 1932. They were designed to raise additional funds for public works initiatives and later job creation, cf. (Bastisch, 2000), Chapter 2.2.2..

[32] (Mierzejewski, 2005), page 66

[33] (Kreidler, 2001), page 33

[34] (Mierzejewski, 2005), page 106

Tab. 3: Overview of widely used German freight locomotives with an axle load of about 16 t (1935)[35]

	55[16-22] (G8)	55[25-56] (G8[1])	56[2-8] (G8[1] rebuilt)	57[10-35] (G10)'	58[2-5,10-21] (G12)
Axle arrangement[36]	D h2	D h2	1'D h2	E h2	1'E h3
First production year	1902	1913	1934	1910	1917
Axle load [t]	15,0	17,5	16,4	15,3	16,6
Max. speed forward [km/h]	55	55	70	60	65
Max. speed reverse [km/h]	50	50	50	50	60
Power [hp_i]	1,100	1.260	1.260	1.100	1.540
Inventory[37] Trend	476 ↘	1.928 ↘	85 ↗	2.352 →	1.335 →

As funds were scarce, the first step was to rebuild the G8[1]s in good condition, adding a front axle and moving the boiler slightly forward ('G8[1] rebuilt', see Table 3). The additional axle decreased the axle load to 16 tons and increased the maximum speed to 70 km/h, allowing the locomotive to be used on branch lines and to keep up with the faster and increasing traffic. In principle, however, this conversion, remarkable as it was, could not replace a modern light freight locomotive.

The mid-1930s also saw some important changes:

1. In 1936, in his Memorandum on the Four-Year Plan, Hitler demanded that the German army should be ready for action by 1940 and that the German economy should be ready for war by the same date. He believed that the solution to Germany's problems lay in expanding its 'Lebensraum' in Poland and the Soviet Union.[38] And it had to be clear to everyone that this meant a coming war of expansion in the east against these two states, since it could not be assumed that they would voluntarily make their territory available for the German 'Lebensraum'. In fact, the declaration was also a reaction to the foreseeable economic crisis caused

---

[35] (Wenzel, 1979), pages 12ff; (Ebel, et al., 1988), pages 10ff, (Deutsche Bundesbahn , 1953)
Different maximum speeds for forward or reverse result from the design, braking technology and coupling of the tender then leading. In addition, the engine driver stands on the 'wrong' side of the machine when driving backwards and can only observe the track and signals to a limited extent.
[36] Given according to the UIC-system: The axle arrangement is a characterisation of the axle sequence of a locomotive. This is indicated from front to rear, e.g. 1'D = one movable front running axle (1') and four driven axles (D) or 1'E = one movable running axle and five driven axles (Wikipedia001). The UIC (= Union Internationale des Chemins de Fer (International Union of Railways) with today 200 member companies in 100 countries (UIC, 2017) was founded to improve international transport through standardisation.
[37] (Ebel, et al., 1988), page 10, reporting date: 31.12.1935
[38] (Treue, 1955)

by the forced rearmament by the Nazi government. The idea of Hitler and his men was to stop paying attention to a balanced state budget and to impose the resulting debts on the conquered countries and peoples.[39]

Although the railways were not mentioned at all in this document, it must have been clear to the management of the Reichsbahn that they would also be involved in this war and that it would have to be able to provide adequate transport services by 1940. It must also have been clear to the experts that the existing heavy freight locomotives of the Reichsbahn were of limited use, as the lines in eastern Poland and the Soviet Union were not designed for their heavy axle loads and only the machines from the First World War with their comparatively light weight were available for this purpose.

2. In 1937 Hitler ended the existence of the independent Deutsche Reichsbahngesellschaft (see Table 2). It was brought under direct state administration by the Reich Ministry of Transport. At the relevant cabinet meeting, several ministers, civil servants and officers were awarded with 'golden party badges'. The Reich Minister of Transport, Eltz-Rübenach, refused the award referring to the Nazi 'Kirchenkampf', leading to his resignation and surveillance by the Gestapo[40] until his death in 1943. Julius Dorpmüller was appointed as his successor.[41] In his new position, he retained the title of 'General Director of the Deutsche Reichsbahn'. He was assisted by Wilhelm Kleinmann as Deputy General Director.

As a result of this change, in early 1938 the Reichsbahn ordered a new insignia to be used in place of the 'Deutsche Reichsbahn' emblem, in the form of a right-facing eagle with a laurel wreath and a swastika. This meant that the position of the other plates (incl. previous number plates) on the cabs of the steam locomotives had to be changed.[42]

With Kleinmann as top manager of the Reichsbahn and Nazi-party member demands for steel quotas for a successor for the class G10 (57^{10-35}) engine found a more sympathetic ear. In 1938, higher quotas were granted and an investment volume of 3.5 bn RM was approved. It provided for the procurement of 5,480 units, of which 1,200 were of a new class 50 locomotive. Needless to say, that this plan was significantly altered as a result of the war that followed.[43]

---

[39] (Forstmeier, et al., 1981), pages 163f

[40] Gestapo = **Ge**heime **Staatspo**lizei. The Gestapo was the secret police of Nazi Germany and in German-occupied Europe.

[41] Dorpmüller, however, did not join the NSDAP until 1941.(Gottwaldt, 2009), page 115.

[42] (Diener, 2012), pages 131ff

[43] (Gottwaldt, 1978), page 150

3 Development of the class 50

The description of the development steps and the design of class 50 has already been presented in detail by Mr. Jürgen Ebel[44], so we will not go into them here.

However, I would like to use some simple formulae to show how the main dimensions of the machine can be derived from its specifications. It should be noted that these formulae have not been derived analytically, but are the result of decades of work with steam locomotives. They represent, so to speak, the treasure trove of experience of earlier knowledge expressed in mathematics. They are therefore often to be understood as approximate values, which have always been supplemented by the individual experience of the development engineers. Unfortunately, this knowledge – if not documented – has been lost.

3.1 Specifications for the new freight locomotive

As early as April 1937, the Reich Ministry of Transport commissioned the Reichsbahn-Zentralamt[45] in Berlin to develop a freight locomotive for branch lines. The specifications were as follows: [46]

1. To haul a medium-heavy freight train on level ground at 80 km/h.
2. To haul the same train on a 1:80 gradient at 25 km/h without bank engine[47].
3. To pass through 140 m radius curves and railway switches with 1:7 and H = 140 m.[48]
4. Axle pressure and weight of the locomotive per running metre (weight per metre) must comply with the guidelines for J-tracks given in §98 Appendix 30 of the operation regulations.[49]
5. The locomotive shall be of simple construction and shall require little

---

[44] see (Ebel, et al., 1988)

[45] The 'Reichsbahn-Zentralamt' was responsible for central functions in the area of technical development (especially vehicles and track), procurement, the revision of general technical and accounting regulations. The Reichsbahn had two of these offices located in Berlin and Munich.

[46] (Ebel, et al., 1988), page 13

[47] Bank engine is an additional engine at the head or the end of a train when the power of the single machine is no longer sufficient to move the train, e.g. on a gradient.

[48] The type of switch designation originates from the specifications of the former Prussian State Railway. '1:7' is the angle of the switch, H is the curvature of the branching track, see 'Weiche Nr. 6d, Blatt 83 vom 30.10.1901', available at (Schulz).

[49] This requirement is not understandable, as §93 of the operation regulation from 27.04.1933 regulates the 'Carriage of heavy vehicles' and the Annex 30 the 'Driving instruction for small cars (to § 101 (1))', see (Noßke). Other sources state that for J-tracks, an axle load of 16 t and a weight per metre of 6.54 t/m was valid. (Kommerell, 1925)

maintenance.

(This requirement can be seen as a response to accusations against Richard Wagner, former head of the 'Lokomotiv-Versuchsamt Berlin-Grunewald'[50] and later President of the 'Reichsbahn-Zentralamt', that the locomotives he had helped to design were thought to be too expensive.[51] We shall see later whether this accusation was justified, at least for the locomotive classes 50 and 52.)

6. To burn hard coal, but easily convertible to brown coal briquettes.

7. To have higher reversing speeds than before, i.e. over 50 km/h.

(The reversing speeds of some freight locomotives of the time are listed in Table 3.)

8. To be able to turn on 20 metre diameter turntables

(In 1920, the standard turntables of the former Prussian Railways (K.P.u.G.H.St.E.)[52] had a diameter of 20 metres. From 1938, it was regulated to use the diameters 23 m and 26 m for new installations, with the 23 m turntable being the most common.[53] However, this only applied to the operational area of the Reichsbahn within the borders of 1937.)

9. The rear of the cab should have a solid covering to protect the locomotive crew from rain and wind when driving backward.

The specifications were drawn up by Friedrich Röhrs, an employee of Wagner. The initial work was classified as 'secret' because the German army was involved in drawing up the specifications. However, when it became clear that none of the above requirements had a clear military application, the classification was removed.[54] As for the engineers involved in the design of this machine, it seems that nobody expected that the upcoming war would be a war against the Soviet Union. The expectation was more that it would be a new armed engagement with France.[55]

Initially, the Henschel, Krupp, Schwartzkopff and Borsig locomotive factories[56] were commissioned to produce preliminary designs with axles arrangements 1'D and 1'E. These designs were completed in the summer of 1937. Initially the 'Zentralamt' had opted for an engine with an axle arrangement 1'D in order to achieve a

---

[50] Grunewald Locomotive Research Office
[51] (Gottwaldt, 1978), pages 126, 128
[52] For railway companies and used abbreviations, cf. Annex 'Railway companies'
[53] (Stroner, 2002), page 42
[54] (Gottwaldt, 1978), page 138
[55] (Gottwaldt, 1978), page 126
[56] For company names and used abbreviations, cf. Annex 'Locomotive works'

correspondingly low service weight: By the end of the year it had become clear that the Reich Ministry of Transport preferred a 1'E axle arrangement, so this arrangement was decided on at a meeting of the Locomotive Committee[57] in December 1937.[58]

3.2 The main dimensions of class 50

The following sections may be a little technical because of the many formulae used, but they are intended to show that the main dimensions of a steam engine are relatively easy to understand. This does not mean, of course, that everything is finished, as the designer's job was to combine and coordinate the various parts into a large whole. As with many complex machines, the whole is greater than the sum of its parts. In the calculations that follow, all quantities are generally not expressed in today's SI-units, but in the non-conforming units that were common when steam locomotives were built.

3.2.1 Train resistance and required locomotive power

It should be clarified what a 'medium-heavy freight train' is, as mentioned in the first two specifications. Class 44, a freight machine, which already existed at the time and was designed for heavy goods trains, can be used as a good guide. The performance table of this class gives a wagon weight of 970 tons for a speed of 80 km/h on flat track.[59] Assuming that a medium-heavy goods train weighs about 2/3 of a heavy goods train, the requirement for the new class 50 would be about 600 tons.

Every land vehicle has to overcome a certain amount of resistance in order to start moving. When accelerating or going up a slope, additional forces have to be applied. The forces acting against a vehicle are called rolling resistance. So, let us imagine a train consisting of a class 50 and wagons with a total weight of 600 tons travelling at 80 km/h on a flat track.

The rolling resistance of a train consists of the resistance of the locomotive and the resistance of the attached wagons.

---

[57] After the First World War, the Reichsbahn set up a Committee for the Construction of new locomotives. This committee developed design principles and a programme for the development of standardized classes of new German engines. The first machines were built in 1925 according to these standards. Richard Wagner, then head of the 'Lokomotiv-Versuchsamt Berlin-Grunewald', had a major influence on this development.

[58] (Ebel, et al., 1988), pages 13ff

[59] (Deutsche Bundesbahn , 1953), page 165

For the engine, the resistance can be estimated with 'Strahl's formula':[60]

$$Z_{locomotive+tender} = 2{,}5 \cdot G_0 + c \cdot G_R + 0{,}6 \cdot A \cdot \frac{(v + \Delta v)^2}{100} \qquad [1]$$

where:

G_0	Weight of machine and tender on the non-driving axles, expressed in Megapond (Mp), calculated with a unit and tender with full supplies.
G_R	Weight on the driving axles in Mp.
c	Design value, for engine with 2 cylinders and 5 driving axles the value is 9.3 kp/Mp
A	Surface of the machine exposed to the airstream, which is 10 - 12 m² for standard-gauge locomotives. Here, the average value of 11 m² is chosen.
v	Speed in km/h
Δv	Supplement to the speed in case of cross- or headwind. For this calculation the option 'no wind', i.e. 0 km/h, is chosen.

From the equation above we can already assume that the locomotive has an axle arrangement of 1'E with a maximum of 16 tons on each driving axle. This gives a maximum weight on all the driving axles of G_R = 80 tons.

In addition, the machine should be able to turn on a 20-metre turntable, from which, assuming a maximum overhang of 1 m on each side, a maximum total length of 22 metre can be assumed. Since the weight per metre of the new engine may not exceed 6.54 t/m,[49] the planned machine should have a maximum weight of 144 t. This means that minus the 80 t on the driving axles, the remaining weight on the non-driving axles should be a maximum of G_0 = 64 tons.

If these values are entered in equation [1], the running resistance of the locomotive at a speed of 80 km/h is $Z_{locomotive+tender}$ = 1,326 kp.

The rolling resistance of the wagons can be calculated in a similar way:[60]

$$Z_{wagons} = \left(2{,}5 + \frac{(v + \Delta v)^2}{k}\right) \cdot G_W \qquad [2]$$

where:

k	Design value, which is 2000 for freight trains of mixed composition.
G_W	Load of all wagons, here 600 t

If we use the above assumptions into equation [2], the train resistance of the wagons at a speed of 80 km/h is Z_{wagons} = 3,420 kp.

The total train resistance of our train is now the sum of the locomotive and the wagons:

---

[60] (Schwarze, et al., 1998), pages 321f

$$Z_{total} = Z_{locomotive+tender} + Z_{wagons} \tag{3}$$

and is 4.746 kp.

In order to maintain the required speed of 80 km/h, the new engine must have a tractive force equal to or greater than the train resistance. The following formula can be used to estimate the minimum power that the new machine should have: [61]

$$N_{flat} = \frac{Z_{total} \cdot v}{270} \tag{4}$$

where:

N_{flat} Power in metric horsepower (PS)

Z_{total} Total train resistance to be overcome by tractive power of the locomotive

At a speed of 80 km/h, this results in a minimum machine power of about 1,400 PS.

We are not finished yet, as the specification also demands that the machine should pull our train up a gradient of 1:80 (12.5 ‰) at 25 km/h without support (bank engine). First, we need to calculate the train resistance of our train at 25 km/h. To do this we again use our equations [1] to [3]. These give a running resistance of $Z_{locomotive+tender}$ = 945 kp for the engine and Z_{wagons} = 1,688 kp for the wagons, together only Z_{total} = 2,633 kp.

It is an interesting note that the locomotive accounts for over 35 % of the total train resistance. The energy (coal) consumed by our train is therefore significantly used to move the machine.

When the train travelling up a hill, the so-called climbing resistance Z_S is added to the train resistance, which is calculated according to the following formula: [62]

$$Z_S = f_S \cdot (G_0 + G_R + G_W) \tag{5}$$

where:

f_S Specific climbing resistance in kp/Mp, which is equal to the gradient in ‰

$G_0 + G_R + G_W$ Sum of all the weights of the equations above: 64 t + 80 t + 600 t = 744 t

The gradient resistance is then Z_S = 9,300 kp. Together with the running resistance at 25 km/h, the total running resistance for the gradient is 2,633 kp + 9,300 kp = 11,933 kp. Substituting this into equation [4] shows that running up the hill with 25 km/h the locomotive needs at least 1,105 PS. As this is considerably lower than the 1,400 PS determined earlier, the engine seemed to have enough power to manage the required gradients.

---

[61] (Schwarze, et al., 1998), page 333
[62] (Schwarze, et al., 1998), page 323

The power of the locomotive determined so far is the output that must be available at the engine's draw bar hook (effective power).

However, there are still a number of power losses between the steam cylinder and the draw bar hook: friction losses at the axle bearings and the connecting rods, as well as at the transition from wheel to rail. In order to compensate for these losses, the machine pistons have to generate more power than the effective power at the hook. The power that had to be produced in the pistons is called the indicated power. This value is later important for the dimensions of the locomotive cylinders.

The relationship between effective and indicated power is as follows:[63]

$$N_i = {N_e}/{\eta} \qquad\qquad [6]$$

where:

N_i	Indicated power
N_e	Effective power
η	Mechanical efficiency of the power transmission from cylinder to draw bar hook. This is roughly estimated at 0.85.

This results in an indicated power of 1,650 PS$_i$ which is needed for the new engine. In fact, in the real-world test runs of the class 50 machine gave an indicated power of 1,625 PS$_i$.[64]

3.2.2   Cylinder

After having determined the indicated power of the locomotive, the dimensions for the cylinders can be calculated.

In order to estimate the cylinder stroke, we first have to know the diameter of the driving wheels. Therefore, we take the following formula:[65]

$$D = \frac{v}{0,188 \cdot n} \qquad\qquad [7]$$

where:

D	Driving wheel diameter in m
v	Max. speed in km/h
n	Maximum values for revolutions per minute at maximum speed. A maximal value of n = 300[66] was normally chosen for a five-coupled locomotive.

[63] (Schwarze, et al., 1998), page 326
[64] (Deutsche Bundesbahn , 1953), pages 54f
[65] (Eckhardt, 2009), page 28
[66] (Henschel-Werke GmbH, 1960), page 277, Table 26

If we again take the required maximum speed of 80 km/h, the equation yields a value for the driving wheel diameter of 1.42 m.

In fact, a diameter of 1.40 m was chosen for the locomotive.

The cylinder stroke then results from the following empirical formula:[67]

$$^s/_D = 0{,}45 - 0{,}55 \qquad\qquad [8]$$

where:

s	Cylinder stroke in mm
D	Driving wheel diameter in mm

This should give a cylinder stroke between 630 and 770mm.

Unfortunately, the formula only gives a range which the stroke should have, not a definite number. The Reichsbahn was trying to standardise components and chose to use a stroke of 660 mm which was within the results of the formula.

Tab. 4: Piston dimensions of freight locomotives [68]

Class	First year of production	Axle arrange-ment	Piston stroke	Cylinder di-ameter
44	1925	1'E	660 mm	600 mm
43	1926	1'E	660 mm	720 mm
44	1936	1'E h3	660 mm	550 mm
41	1936	1'D1'	720 mm	520 mm

If we list the cylinder stroke values of the new freight locomotives built by the Reichsbahn to date (see Table 4), we can see that the freight locomotives had already widely been standardised to a piston stroke of 660 mm.

The cylinder diameter d results from the so-called stroke ratio, which for machines with single expansion[69] is given by[67]

$$^s/_d = 1{,}1 \; to \; 1{,}5 \qquad\qquad [9]$$

This results in a cylinder diameter between 440 mm and 600 mm for the new locomotive. In fact, a cylinder diameter of 600 mm was chosen for the new class 50, which also was the diameter of class 44 from 1925.

---

[67] (Schwarze, et al., 1998), page 331

[68] (Wenzel2, 1979), page 12; (Ebel, et al., 1988), page 12; (Deutsche Bundesbahn , 1953), pages 42 and 46; (Deutsche Reichsbahn, 1999)

[69] In a single expansion steam engine, live steam is fed from the boiler to each cylinder where it is expanded. The exhaust steam is then expelled. In machines with double steam expansion, the steam is first fed into so-called high-pressure cylinders and then into low-pressure cylinders before being expelled as exhaust steam. The DRB's standard units had only single steam expansion.

3.2.3 Grate dimension

Now we come to the area of steam generation and boiler design. In order to be able to estimate the boiler design, it is first necessary to establish how much steam the boiler will have to supply.

It was known by experience that two-cylinder superheated steam engines with single steam expansion needed to supply about 6.5 - 7.0 kg of steam per PS$_i$ and hour.[70] If we take an average value of 6.7 kg/PS$_i$h as the basis for the following calculations and consider additional 10 % for auxiliary, steam consuming, units (pumps, heating, etc.) the boiler must be able to deliver a steam quantity of

$$D_h = 1.1 \cdot 6{,}7 \; {}^{kg}/_{PS_ih} \cdot 1{,}625 \; PS_i = 11{,}976 \; {}^{kg}/_h \tag{10}$$

, which is about 12 t per hour at an indicated power of 1,625 PS$_i$.

Of course, this steam supply must be matched by an equivalent amount of water to prevent the boiler from running dry. This means that the feedwater pumps[71] must be installed with the same capacity (plus a certain safety margin).

In fact, the later built locomotive was equipped with two feedwater pumps of 250 l/min each (= 15,000 litres of water per hour, equivalent to 15 t/h).[72] The reason for having two pumps with full capacity was for safety reasons. If one of the pumps failed during a journey, the other pump could take over the full load until the next locomotive change.

A coal fire is maintained in the firebox to evaporate the water. This fire should be able to generate the required amount of steam. So the size of the grate has to be adapted to the steam production. The grate area can be estimated using the following formula:[73]

$$R = \frac{D_h \cdot (Q_{\ddot{U}} - Q_W)}{A \cdot 10^6 \cdot \eta_K} \tag{11}$$

where:

D_h	hourly steam quantity, in our case: 12,000 kg/h
$Q_{\ddot{U}}$	Heat content of the superheated steam in kcal/kg. These values can be derived from tables[74] and is about 750 kcal/kg for superheated steam at a temperature of 350 °C.
Q_W	Heat content or temperature of the feedwater in kcal/kg. According to tests at Reichsbahn,

---

[70] (Schwarze, et al., 1998), page 336
[71] The feedwater pumps pump water from the tender to the boiler, which is used to generate steam.
[72] (Ebel, et al., 1988), page 27
[73] (Schwarze, et al., 1998), page 104
[74] (Henschel-Werke GmbH, 1960), Table 49, page 374.

a clean feedwater heater[75] resulted in a water heating of 80 °C (at a water feeding rate of 15 t/h).[76] For our estimation, we take a value of 80 kcal/kg.

A   The amount of heat developed by 1 m² of grate surface and hour in kcal/m²h. A value of 3 kcal/m²h is assumed for a 'good continuous performance'.[77]

η_K Boiler efficiency, estimated at 0.70.[78]

All the assumptions made in the equation [11] result in a required grate area of 3.8 m², which is nearly the size of grate area that was built (3.89 m²).[64]

Although this value appears to have been derived organically from the existing formulae, the size of the grate was a requirement of the army, who wanted to ensure that low-grade coal could be burned.[79] Without this requirement, the grate area of the locomotive might have been smaller. This had also to do with the different views on the basic design of a locomotive boiler that prevailed within the Locomotive Committee, with Wagner's view on the one hand and Friedrich Witte's[80] on the other.

After the size of the grate area has been clarified, the theoretical fuel consumption can be derived:[81]

$$m_B = \frac{A \cdot R \cdot 10^6}{H_u} \tag{12}$$

where:

A   See eq. [11], estimated at 3 kcal/m²h

R   Grate area in m²

H_u Lower heat value of the fuel in kcal/kg: about 7,000 kcal/kg for hard coal and about 4,500 kcal/kg for brown coal.[77]

This gives a quantity of fuel (m_B) to be burnt for the two types of coal of

- 1,670 kg/h for hard coal
- 2,600 kg/h for brown coal.

These values were important because the fuel has to be shovelled into the firebox by the fireman as the Reichsbahn did not use any mechanical stoker. In normal operation a fireman had to shovel a maximum of two tons of coal per hour in continuous

---

[75] The feedwater heater is used to heat the feedwater with the waste heat from the exhaust fumes. See also Chapter 10.9.2..

[76] (Meineke, et al., 1949), page 53

[77] Guidelines according to (Schwarze, et al., 1998), page 103; (Henschel-Werke GmbH, 1960) uses similar data.

[78] (Meineke, et al., 1949), page 24, Figure 13

[79] (Gottwaldt, 1978), pages 140, 163. The demand was made because the military expected to capture only low-grade coal during its campaign in the Soviet Union.

[80] In 1937, Friedrich Witte became head of the department for the mechanical equipment of the railway facilities at the RBD Berlin. He was also member of Locomotive Committee. In October 1942, Witte succeeded Wagner as head of the department for steam locomotive construction at the 'Reichsbahn-Zentralamt'.

[81] (Henschel-Werke GmbH, 1960), page 266

operation.[82] Above this limit a mechanical stoker would have been provided to feed the grate.

The value of two tons of coal per hours for the continuous operation should not be underestimated. To achieve this quantity a fireman had to scoop two to three shovels of coal per minute into the firebox, a considerable physical effort!

In the case of firing of brown coal, the value is of two tons per hour was exceeded. If only this type of fuel was available, the situation became critical, as the physical limits of the fireman were exceeded and the performance of the engine decreased. On way to solve the problem was to tune the brown coal with oil, if available. This procedure increased the heat value of the fuel and so less material had to be moved.[83]

3.2.4   Heating surfaces

There were three main areas in the boiler of a superheated steam locomotive:

Firebox

This is the part of the boiler's heating surface where heat transfer takes place mainly by very effective heat radiation. It is located mainly at the rear of the boiler.

Fire Tubes (tubes and flues)

After leaving the firebox the flue gases pass through the fire tubes surrounded by water. The boiler tubes run from the firebox front to the front of the boiler. Together with the radiant heating surface, the tube heating surface forms the evaporation surface.

Superheater surface/superheater unit

In this part of the boiler the steam is further heated to increase the efficiency of the steam engine. The superheater unit is located in front of the boiler.

When designing the evaporation area, it is of course necessary to consider how much steam the boiler will have to supply. As we have already determined this, we can use the following formula:[84]

$$H_V = \frac{D_h}{b} \qquad [13]$$

where:

D_h Projected maximum steam production, in our case: 12,000 kg/h

---

[82] (Henschel-Werke GmbH, 1960), page 272
[83] See the procedure of the BDŽ (Chapter 10.3) and CFR (Chapter 10.18) and (Pottgiesser, 1975), page 30. For operation with brown coal and a mechanical stoker, cf. Chapter 10.10.4..
[84] (Schwarze, et al., 1998), page 109

b   Load of the heating surface. This value was set at 57 kg/m²h as standard value for boilers of
       standard locomotives of the Reichsbahn by the Locomotive Committee.

This then results in a value of 211 m². The realised value is significantly lower, namely 178 m².[64]

The reason for the large deviation lies in the choice of the factor 'b'. The value for 'b' was officially 57 kg/m² and was an important but arbitrary limit in the discussions of the Locomotive Committee. The choice of this value led to engines with relatively long the boilers. Because of their length, the boilers made a good use of the heat in the flue gases. On the other hand, at higher loads the firebox could not cope with the high fuel input and the resulting heat. In this case the flue gases got very hot, which led to an increased risk of leakage of the tubes.[85]

In Great Britain and the USA, various designs with extended fireboxes were already used in the mid-19th century. So-called 'combustion chambers' were fitted to many large locomotives in the USA from the beginning of the 20th century. This was a special design of the engine boiler in which the actual firebox jutted into the long boiler and resulted in a better combustion. In this case heating and evaporation of the water was much more effective due to the better use of the radiant heat of the fire box. The installation of a combustion chamber meant that, for a given boiler length, that some

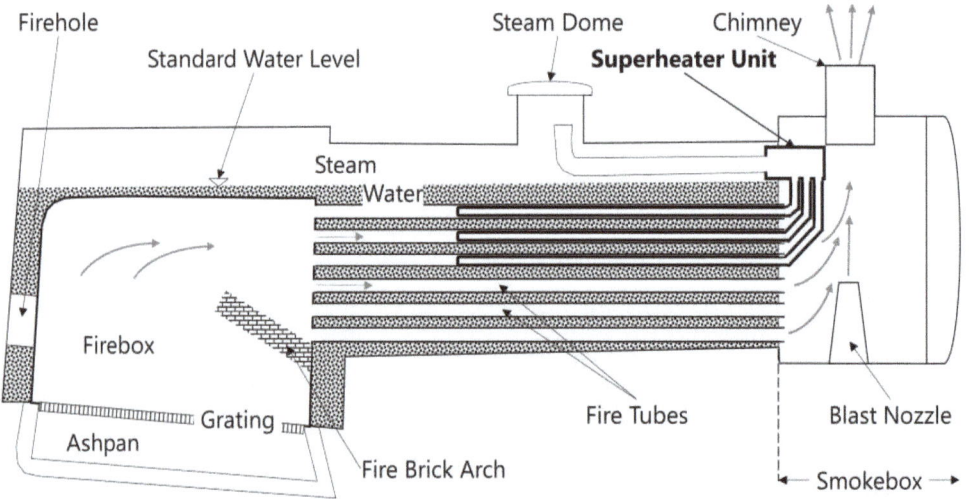

Fig. 1:   Main elements of a locomotive boiler with a superheating unit

---

[85] (Ebel, et al., 1988), page 12

length of the fire tubes was lost, but a much larger radiant heating surface was gained, allowing the boiler load to be increased.

In Germany the introduction of a combustion chamber was difficult as the heat transfer in the long boiler was considered to be more important than the radiation heat in the firebox. Some members of the Locomotive Committee had a strong belief that the factor 'b' should not exceed 57 kg/m²h for a well perfoming machines.

However, in 1935, leading representatives of the Reichsbahn and the Locomotive Committee had the opportunity to see the steam machine PO 240-701 of the French railway company 'Compagnie du Chemin de fer de Paris à Orléans' (P.O.). This steam engine was rebuilt by André Chapelon according to the latest standards. It followed continental European design principles.[86] Although the boiler was 'relatively small' (grate area only 3.76 m²)[87] with no combustion chamber, the enginee produced enough steam for an indicated power of 4,200 PS$_i$.[88] This made it one of the most powerful steam locomotives in Europe. Of course, its load of the heating surface was higher than 57 kg/m²h. The German visitors dismissed this construction as an 'overloaded' machine that should not be considered in detail.

Even the engineers of the German locomotive factories, who built engines for other countries, could not understand why this limit was defended by the some engineers

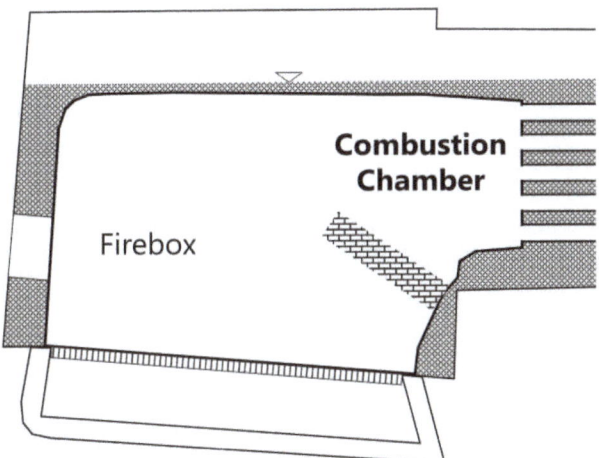

Fig. 2:   Firebox and combustion chamber

[86] On the different principles of designs of a steam locomotive in continental Europe, UK and the USA, cf. (Hartmann, 2011) and (Giesl-Gieslingen, 1986).
[87] (Lévi, 1935), pages 122f
[88] (Wikipedia002)

of the Reichsbahn so vehemently.[89] Already decades before when the Prussian Railways were building machines under the direction of Robert Grabe, he demanded a narrow and deep firebox.[90] This could be an indication that he already at least suspects the importance of transferring radiant heat more deeply into the boiler.

It was not until after the Second World War that boilers with combustion chambers became established in Germany, particularly on the railways in East Germany. The so-called 'Reko boilers'[91] for the classes 50 and 52, which were built as part of the boiler exchange programme. The new boilers, which were then installed, were equipped with a combustion chamber and had a heating surface load of 65-75 kg/m²h (see Chapter 10.10.6).[84] It was only on West-Germany's Bundesbahn that Witte was finally able to push through his ideas and raise the limit to the value of 75 kg/m²h, which roughly corresponded to the values of the 'Reko' boiler.

But back to the Locomotive Committee. By early 1938 there were now a number of conflicting demands on the boiler: on the one hand, the military requirement that the grate could not become smaller, and on the other, the practical impossibility of increasing the length of the boiler in order to increase the evaporation heating surface (the overall length and weight of the machine should not increase any further!). All this motivated the Chairman of the Committee, director of the Reichsbahn Max Gaedicke (head of the RBD[26] Essen), to reconsider to pragmatically raise the heating surface load limit from 57 to 64 kg/m²h. But the discussions did not stop and the Committee even considered to carry out appropriate experiments. Only when the Reich Ministry of Transport made clear after a meeting that it would not tolerate any more delaying experiments the discussions come to an end and the new design with a heating area of only 178 m² passed into the hands of the designing engineers.

Shortly after a contract with the locomotive factory Henschel & Sohn was signed for twelve units as pilot series, called 'Pr99'.[92]

Using the value of 64 kg/m²h into equation [13] results in an evaporation surface of $H_V = 188$ m², which was much closer to the actual value. In fact, the later realized value for the so much discussed value was about 67 kg/m²h, which was even higher than the limit considered by Gaedicke before.

The firebox heating surface (H_{VS})[93] can be estimated from the amount of fuel burned

[89] (Gottwaldt, 1978), pages 100f
[90] (Garbe, 1980/81), page 125, also pages 77f, 103, 128
[91] 'Reko' stands for '**reco**nstruction', see Chapter 10.10.5, 10.10.6
[92] (Ebel, et al., 1988), pages 21f
[93] I.e., the overall surface of the firebox.

(m_B) and the calorific value of the fuel (H_u):[94]

$$H_{vs} \geq \frac{m_B \cdot H_u}{600.000} \tag{14}$$

Using the values from equation [12], the radiant heating surface for the use of hard coal should be 19.5 m². In fact, an area of 15.9 m² was realised.[95]

The heating surfaces of the class 50 machine were equipped with a superheater. The total surface area of the superheater can be calculated using the following formula:[96]

$$H_{ü} = 0,3 \; to \; 0,45 \; H_V \tag{15}$$

If we now insert the value of H_V = 190 m² , we obtain values between 57 m² and 86 m² for the superheating area.

In fact, an area of 69 m² was realized.[64]

3.2.5 Tender

The locomotive was fitted with a new tender with an axle arrangement of 2'2'T26. This designation indicates that the tender ('T') rested on two bogies with two axles each (2'2') and had a water capacity of 26 m³. The tender should carry eight tons of coal.

It was fully welded, had an empty weight of around 26 tons. The full tender had a total weight of 60 tons and a maximum axle load of 15 tons.

Together the locomotive and the tender the whole unit had a length of 22.9 m over buffer. With an axle base (i.e. the length between the first and the last axle) of 18.89 m[64] it was possible to turn the unit on a 20 metre turntable.

3.2.6 Other elements

One essential element of the steam locomotive is the control of the steam entering the cylinders. There were many different control systems for steam locomotives, each with its own advantages and disadvantages. What they all have in common is that they consist of a complex system of rods, rockers, shafts and levers which, depending on the driver's settings, ensure that the cylinders receive the desired amount of steam at the right time.

---

[94] (Henschel-Werke GmbH, 1960), page 264
[95] The deviation between calculation and reality reflects the usage of a 'modern' formula in eq. [14] of engineers from East Germany after the Second World War, which already considered that a higher area for firebox is advantageous.
[96] (Schwarze, et al., 1998), pages 107, 162

On the standard machines of the Reichsbahn, the Heusinger or Walschaerts valve gear system[97] prevailed. The new engine used therefore this system.

The brake of the locomotive was the same as on other standard engines of the Reichsbahn: an air brake acted on the driving wheels[98], while the leading wheel remained unbraked. The tender was braked by a counterweight brake[99].

For the brake system two main air reservoirs were located across in the frame below the boiler. An auxiliary air tank was located directly in front of the cab under the running board.

Steam to heat the carriages in passenger trains was taken from a nozzle and then fed to the buffer beam of the tender.

---

[97] This form of control was developed by Egide Walschaerts in 1844. In parallel and independently of Walschaerts, Edmund Heusinger von Waldegg developed the same principle in 1849. This is why the valve gear is known as the 'Heusinger valve gear' in German-speaking countries, while elsewhere it is known as the 'Walschaerts valve gear'.

[98] In Germany the freight train brake (Kunze-Knorr Brake) was the first brake that could not only increase the braking force in stages, but also release it in stages. It was replaced in the 1930s by the improved Hildebrand-Knorr Brake (Hik).

[99] A counterweight brake is a manually operated brake that is independent of the train's air brake. It is applied by throwing a lever attached to a heavy weight. (Schwarze, et al., 1998), pages 664f.

4 At last the new freight locomotive

In mid-November 1938, the Reichsbahn signed a contract with Henschel & Sohn for the delivery of a preliminary series of twelve units based on their draft, called 'Pr99'.[92] It was decided that the locomotives would bear the numbers 50 001 to 50 012. The machines were delivered under steam to the station Kassel-Unterstadt: the first batch of six machines in December 1938, a further batch of six machines in January 1939.[100] Kassel-Unterstadt was chosen because it had a number of sidings, including one to Henschel's plant. In fact, No. 50 001 was delivered in March 1939, followed a month later by No. 50 002.[101]

As the engine was already behind schedule, it was not accepted by RAW[102] in Göttingen, but was sent directly to the 'Lokomotiv-Versuchsamt Berlin-Grunewald'[50] in Berlin for testing.

The test centre found it to be a *"simple ... reliable, but not overly economical type of locomotive"*[103]. The tractive power was determined to be around 27 tons. Starting with an 850 ton train on a 1:80 gradient it required *"a skilful driver ... and ... a sand ejector that must work perfectly"*. As the buffers at the end of the machine were too high, the locomotive was sent back to Henschel for reworking and was finally accepted in July 1939.[101]

The running characteristics were examined on the sister engine, as it was planned to use this unit on poor (eastern) railway lines. The machine performed very well and a maximum speed of 80 km/h could be set for both forward and reverse travel. The inspector even noted that it could tolerate higher speeds.[104] This is remarkable, as steam locomotives were usually approved for a lower speed in reverse than in forward. With this engine, the Reichsbahn got a machine that did not necessarily need a turntable.

During the initial testing of the locomotive, the issue of the discussion of the limit of the load of heating surface was not pursued further. However, after the start of continuous deliveries, there were repeated reports that the engine had a tendency for the

---

[100] (Ebel, et al., 1988), pages 98f
[101] (Ebel, et al., 1988), page 44
[102] RAW = **R**eichsbahn**a**usbesserungs**w**erk (Reichsbahn railroad workshop)
[103] (Ebel, et al., 1988), page 47
[104] (Ebel, et al., 1988), page 50

Fig. 3: Model of No. 50 007 (Märklin 37849), driver's (top) and fireman's side (bottom).[105]

The boiler carries four domes, from front to back: feedwater dome, sandbox, steam dome and another sandbox. Between the rear dome and the cab two safety valves are located. On each side of the steam dome is a nozzle for steam output to supply the pumps. The crossways placed feedwater heater[75] is mounted in front of the chimney. The air pump[106] is on the driver's side and the feedwater pump on the other. The main air reservoir is above axles #4 and #5. The auxiliary air tank is located under the running board on the right in front of the cab. The smoke deflectors have a removable recess at the height of the preheater to facilitate access.

The cylinders are marked with the name of the manufacturer and the production year. At the cab, the number '50 007' is written with 'pointed figures'[107], introduced in 1938. A red dot on the cab indicates that the locomotive was equipped with a steel firebox. The inscription is still without eagle and swastika. Unfortunately, the classification mark on the model is wrong, it should be G56.**15**. The tender shows the last brake inspection as of 9.8.40.

Information about the historic model:[108] Henschel 1939 → DRB 50 007 (RBD[26] Halle (Saale)) → 1945 DRw/DB 50 007 → 1968 DB 050 007-4 + 1968 Kassel

---

[105] In Germany, railway traffic is on the right. Therefore, the driver stood on the right side of the locomotive and the fireman on the left.

[106] The air pump generates the compressed air needed to operate the brakes on the engine and the attached train.

[107] (Diener, 2012), page 134. See also Footnote 114

[108] In the following figures: producer, year of delivery → first owner, first locomotive number, first use → position 1945 → further uses ... + removal from service, location (if known). For the abbreviation for the railway companies, cf. to Annex 'Railway companies'.

superheated steam to carry water.[109]

These reports prompted the 'Lokomotiv-Versuchsamt' to carry out an investigation. The result was that water could be observed in the superheated steam at high loads of the heating surface, i.e. loads of 83 kg/m²h and a speed of 60 km/h, but only when the standard water level was exceeded. This condition could only be achieved by special preparation of the locomotive and appropriate fire control by the fireman. However, these extreme conditions were provoked and far away from operational practice. In the end, the phenomenon could not be explained.[110]

A further 214 units of this engine were delivered in 1939. For 1940, the Reichsbahn intended to order 609 units as replacements and an additional 350 units (total 959 machines). For 1941, the plan was to order 637 engines and an additional 466 machines (a total of 1,103 units).[111] However, only 634 locomotives were delivered in 1940 (-325 pieces) and only 847 engines in 1941 (-256 units, a total deficit of 581 machines).

Fig. 4:   Model of No. 50 163 (Märklin 37816), driver's side.
This model of the peacetime version of the class 50 bears the newly introduced Nazi emblems. The inscription 'Deutsche Reichsbahn' has disappeared in favour of an eagle with a laurel wreath containing a swastika. The last brake inspection is given here as of 7.5.40.
Information on the historical model: Borsig 1940 → DRB 50 163 (RBD Dresden) → 1945 PKP Ty5-9 + 1976 Piła

---

[109] If liquid water containing steam enters the cylinder, a hydrolock can occur. A hydrolock occurs when the volume of water in the cylinder is greater than the volume at the end of the piston stroke. As water is incompressible, the piston cannot complete its stroke. If the engine hydrolocks while at speed, a mechanical failure is likely. The cover of the cylinder can be broken and also the piston rods, drive rods or the coupling rods can also be severely damaged. Steam engines are always fitted with cylinder cocks that may be opened to drain excess water from the cylinder.

[110] (Ebel, et al., 1988), pages 50f

[111] (Ebel, et al., 1988), page 100

In mid-1941 Germany attacked the Soviet Union (see Chapter 5.4) and with the logistic crisis that began shortly afterwards (see Chapter 5.5), the further procurement of class 50 engines changed drastically.

The locomotives were delivered in the standard colour scheme of the Reichsbahn from 1926 onwards, later coded with the RAL[112] colour scheme[113]: above the running board and the cylinder lining: jet black (RAL 9005), below the running board (except the cylinder lining): flame red (RAL 3000). The lettering was in DIN 1451[114] in grey white (RAL 9002).

---

[112] RAL is a colour management system used in Germany that was created by the German non-profit organization 'RAL' from 1927 on.

[113] (Diener, 2012), page 36f

[114] DIN 1451 is a sans serif font that was defined in 1931 and is widely used for transport, administrative, and technical applications in Germany. At the Reichsbahn the figures of the DIN were modified to be 'pointed' (cf. Figure 3)

5 From 1939 to 1941

5.1 The preparation of the war against the Soviet Union

With the further increase in traffic at the end of the 1930s, the Reichsbahn used up the capacity reserves it accumulated in the previous decade. This was due not only to a reduction in the number of freight locomotives (see Table 3), but also to a shortage of freight wagons. In addition, the wagons that were available were not unloaded quickly enough by the consignees. The result was that they could not be put back into service quickly enough. Especially at the beginning of the war there was a shortage of freight wagons to transport coal. The mining companies called the problem a 'transport disaster'. Hermann Göring complained to Kleinmann that Reichsbahn's failure to transport enough coal was jeopardising the German war effort. The operation management of the railways tried to persuade the Rheinisch-Westfälische Kohlen-Syndikat (RWKS)[115] to organise coal transport in so-called block trains.[116] The RWKS was unwilling to do this because it would have meant changing its own logistical processes.[117]

When Germany ignored the Munich Agreement and invaded Czechoslovakia, it was clear to everyone that the policy of appeasement had failed. As it became increasingly clear that Germany was threatening Poland. Britain and France issued guarantees for Poland's independence. The two powers began to explore the possibility of a pact with the Soviet Union against Hitler. The negotiations failed because Poland was unwilling to grant the Soviet Union a right of transit.[118] The Soviet Union then changed its position and entered into negotiations with Germany, resulting in a German-Soviet non-aggression pact in August 1939. This contained a secret additional protocol which, among other things, regulated the split of Poland. During the pact was negotiated, the German 'Oberkommando des Heeres' (OKH)[119] was working on a plan to

---

[115] The RWKS was a sales syndicate with central price fixing and quantity regulation for coal from the coalfield of the Ruhr. From 1934/35 the owners of the coalfields around Aachen and Saarland joined the syndicate.

[116] A block train is a freight train in which all wagons carry the same commodity and travel from the same origin to the same destination, without being split up or stored. It is faster and cheaper than a train made up of individual wagons.

[117] (Mierzejewski, 2000), pages 55, 92

[118] This was understood in the context of the Polish-Soviet War (1919 - 1921), in which Poland sought to re-establish the historic 1772 border with Russia. The Soviet Union, for its part, was seeking to extend its sphere of influence to the West.

[119] High Command of the Army. The OKH was together with the High Command of the Navy (OKM) and the High Command of the Air Force (OKL) subordinated to the **O**ber**k**ommando der **W**ehrmacht (OKW).

attack Poland, codenamed 'Fall Weiß', which was completed in mid-June 1939. After completing its plans, the army discussed the necessary railway services with the Reichsbahn.

This process alone showed that the Reichsbahn as a logistic element of warfare was not fully informed of the military's intentions. This didn't seem so critical because there was no overall strategic planning for the invasion of Poland. Neither the military nor the political leadership expected a long-lasting war. However, some high-ranking military felt that the railway had not been given sufficient consideration.[120]

In mid-August, the Reichsbahn began moving combat units to Germany's eastern borders. On 1 September 1939, fire was opened on the Weserplatte and the Second World War began.

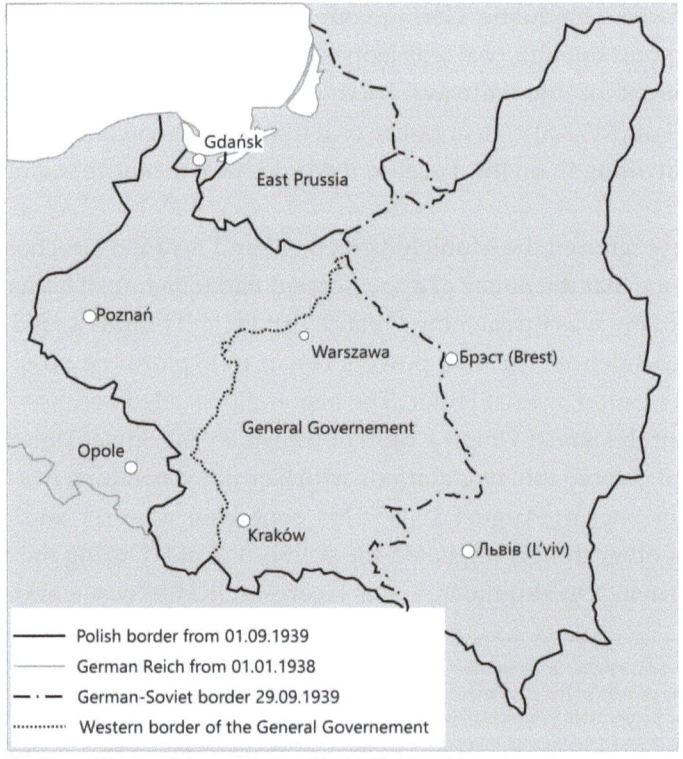

Fig. 5:   The partition of Poland in 1939 (sketch)

---

[120] (Kreidler, 2001), pages 46f

The supplies for the army were transported by trains to respective railheads[121]. There they were loaded onto lorries and transported to the front. This was not always a smooth process, as the lorries were badly worn and up to 50 % of them broke down.[122] Nevertheless, the railheads could be moved relatively easily as troops moved into invaded Poland. Although the rail network in Western Poland (west of the Wisła (river Vistula)) was destroyed, it had a dense structure with good connections. This could be restored relatively quickly with manageable effort. East of the Wisła the Germans found a less developed railway network. This was less important for the military advance in Poland as the demarcation line to the Soviet occupation zone in Poland was only 200 km away.

The Polish campaign was conducted in the classic manner of German military command at the time: Surround and encircle the enemy units by a rapid advance and then attack the enemy from the rear.[123] Poland had no chance, as it was simultaneously being attacked from the east by the Soviet Union.

The conquest of Poland was completed in just three weeks. Because of the brevity of the campaign, the Reichsbahn had no difficulty in meeting the Wehrmacht's needs.

However, the declarations of war by Great Britain and France did not fit into the plans of the German army leadership, as the invasion of Poland had been planned as a short, isolated campaign. Now it threatened to escalate into a war on two fronts. This danger was initially averted by the invasion and victory over France. There was no strategic planning (like in the First World War) on how to deal with the threat of a British entry into the war, which could potentially lead to a new 'world war' that the US and other countries could then enter.[124]

In German-occupied Poland, the Reichsbahn directorates (RBD) Danzig (Gdańsk) and Posen (Poznań) were set up and placed under the administration of the Reichsbahn. The RBD Oppeln (Opole) in was extended to include the Upper Silesian region.

In the rest of occupied Poland, the Reich-controlled General Government was established. The railways in the General Government were set up as a separate railway company, the Ostbahn, on the basis of a 'Führer Decree'.[125] The Ostbahn was managed

---

[121] The term 'railhead' refers to the terminus of the military logistical supply by rail in an enemy territory.

[122] (Kreidler, 2001), page 49

[123] (Groß, 2012), page 206

[124] (Groß, 2012), page 208. Hoping for a negotiated peace with Britain, Hitler made no preparations for an amphibious attack on Britain until after the fall of France. There were attempts to gain air supremacy ('Battle of Britain'). By mid-September 1940, Hitler was convinced that the operation was not viable as air supremacy had still not been achieved. He ordered the operation to be postponed.

[125] Announcement by the Governor General of 9.11.1939, see (Josten, 2013), page 13

Tab. 5: Some key figures of the Ostbahn [131]

	1940	1942	1943	End of 1943
Length of network [km][132]	4.598	7.461	7.482	7.482
Number of locomotives	1.592	1.435		
of which operational		941		
Locomotive density [number per 100 km network length]	35	19		
of which operational		13		

by the 'General Directorate of the Ostbahn', called 'Gedob', with its headquarters in Kraków. In November 1939 Emil Beck became its first president, who was succeeded by Adolf Gerteis in April 1940. The Ostbahn was divided into OBD[126] Kraków, OBD Lublin, OBD Radom and OBD Warsaw.

The status of the Ostbahn was never legally regulated.[127] As the Reichsbahn was responsible for transport in the Reich territory, the head of the General Government, Hans Frank, ensured that the Ostbahn was considered part of the General Government and could therefore operate independently of the Reichsbahn. Although the Reichsbahn provided staff at management level[128] and had to help out with rolling stock when Ostbahns' fleet was insufficient, the economic power of the railway stayed in Frank's hands. Although a 'Führer decree' of 17th January 1942 stipulated that the Reichsbahn and the Ostbahn should be run by the Reich Ministry of Transport,[129] Frank did not implement it. Another attempt in August 1942 also failed, so that in October 1942 Hitler gave up and transferred the Ostbahn to the General Government as a 'special asset'.[130] In day-to-day cooperation, this separation repeatedly led to friction and disputes over responsibilities. None of those involved were aware that it would have a decisive impact on the further course of the war.

---

[126] OBD = **O**st**b**ahn**d**irektion (Ostbahn Directorate)

[127] (Reimer, et al., 2004), page 32

[128] In accordance with the racial policy of the Nazis, Polish personnel was only allowed to occupy subordinate positions.

[129] Cf. 'Decree of the Führer on the Ostbahn' of 17.1.1942, (Moll, 1997), page 227

[130] (Reimer, et al., 2004), pages 34f

[131] Length of line including private railways according to (Reimer, et al., 2004), pages 29, 47, 55; locomotive numbers for 1940: as of 1.8.39, including railcars and electric locomotives

[132] After the invasion of the Soviet Union, the General Government was extended to include the 'District of Galicia'.

5.2 The bottleneck at the Ostbahn

It is worth to look at the situation of the Ostbahn in more detail in order to understand what later contributed to the so-called 'transport crisis' and ultimately to the start of the huge war locomotive construction programme.

When Poland was divided between the invaders, the best part of the Polish railway network became the responsibility of the Reichsbahn, the medium-quality part went to the Ostbahn, while the poor eastern part with its bad railway lines ended up in Soviet hands.

Interestingly, the reports of contemporary German witnesses reveal a certain 'surprise' that the victims of the invasion, as a defensive measure, had caused damage to their own railway infrastructure on an unprecedented scale *"with considerable thoroughness and much ingenuity"*.[133]

The German occupiers immediately started to rebuild and to extend the Polish railway network. This was in preparation for the Wehrmacht's advance on the border with the Soviet Union. For this purpose, the railway network was upgraded to German standards, with additional crossings, signalling and telephone systems, stations and depots being built and extended.

All the rebuilding work was done within the project called 'Otto Programm'; 60 % of which was financed by the Reich and 40 % by the Ostbahn. At the end of the programme, the success story was that the number of trains in the eastern direction increased from 84 trains per day in 1939 to 220 trains per day in mid-1941.[134] However, this 'success story' only referred to the incoming traffic over the Reich's eastern border[135] – nothing was announced about what would happen after the Reich's border was crossed. Moreover, the border of the Reich in these days meant the new border to the General Government, so the success report only referred to trains entering the General Government.

An overview over the concept of the 'Otto Programm' is given in Figure 6. It shows that it was planned to have 60 trains per day from Kutno, 72 and 36 from Koluszki, 72 from Rabsztyn and 72 from Kraków. This gives a total incoming capacity of 312 trains per day.

---

[133] (Pottgiesser, 1975), page 16
[134] (Reimer, et al., 2004), page 42
[135] (Pottgiesser, 1975), page 23

However, after the Wisła bridges in Warszawa, Dęblin and Sandomierz[136], only 180 trains could travel eastward. Adding the trains from Kraków, only 252 of the 312 incoming trains were able to continue east of the Wisła (Vistula). This resulted to backlog of 60 trains per day before crossing the Wisła and entering the General Government.

The situation was even worse at the eastern border from the General Government: Here, 60 trains a day could run from Siedlce to Brest, 36 from Lublin to Chełm or Hrubieszów, and a maximum of 72 trains a day from Przeworsk to Przemysl. In total, these train services amounted to a maximum of only 168 trains per day that could be brought to the German-Soviet border. Of the maximum 312 trains per day from the Reich, 60 trains per day jammed before the Wisła crossings and another 84 trains on the way from the crossings to the German-Soviet border. Overall, about 80% of

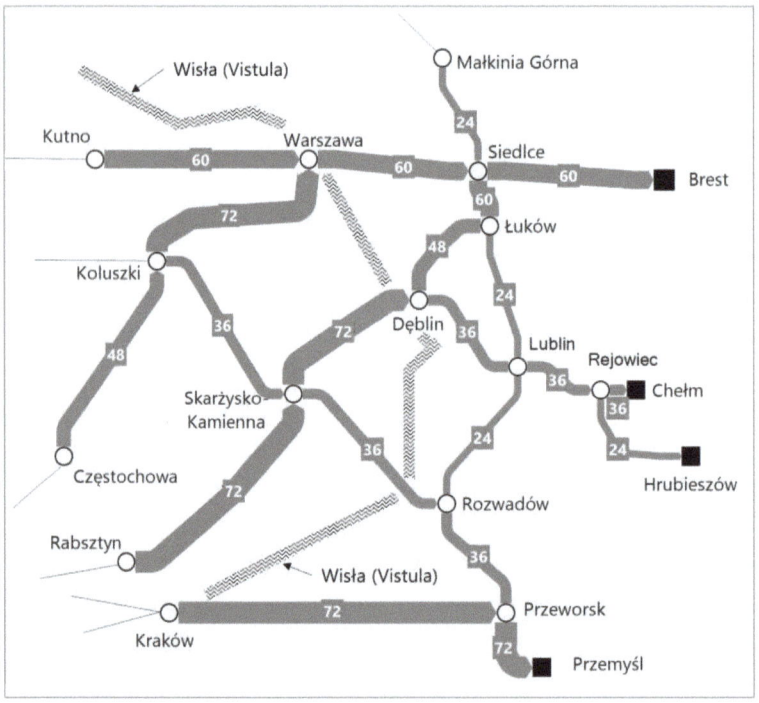

Fig. 6:   Required services (trains per day) according to the 'Otto Programm'[137]

[136] Skarżysko-Kamienna-Roswadów-Line
[137] Cf. (Pottgiesser, 1975), page 22

incoming trains from the Reich could be sent to the Wisła bridges and only 55% towards the Soviet border.

There was some relief by the line from the north-east of the Wisła via Małkinia Górna as this had only an additional capacity of 24 trains per day. In fact, these additional trains entering the area of the Ostbahn made the situation towards the demarcation line worse rather than relieving it.

The result of the work of the 'Otto-Programm' was that the capacity of the railway lines from west to east continued to decrease, creating a logistical bottleneck for the attack on the Soviet Union. The capacity of the tracks at the German-Soviet border determined the number of trains that could enter the Soviet Union. The 'Otto-Programm' increased the absolute capacity of the lines, it did not solve the problem of the decreasing capacity of the lines to the east. The decreasing capacity towards the east was not eliminated by the programme.

In the Soviet-held former eastern provinces of Poland, the density of railway lines decreased even further. Only in the southern area around Львів (L'viv) the number of lines was slightly higher. Since the Polish conquest of these areas and the signing of the Rīga Peace Treaty in 1921, the Poles had not made any major investments in these areas, only partly for strategic reasons: Some of the existing railway lines were converted from Russian broad gauge (1,520 mm) to standard gauge (1,435 mm), and in some cases the second main track was removed for material extraction. Overall, the railway network in this area was in poor condition.[138]

In contrast to the situation in western Poland, the Soviets took over railways with intact lines - albeit standard gauge - and undamaged rolling stock.[138] The only major investment was the conversion to broad gauge and to convert or replace the rolling stock. However, this was delayed for the entire network,[139] perhaps because the Soviet-Finnish War of 1939-1940 tied up many resources.[140]

In 1940 there was considerable trade between the Reich and the Soviet Union. For this purpose, the Ostbahn built transhipment stations on the eastern border, where bulk goods were transferred from Reichsbahn wagons to Soviet freight wagons. The main lines to the interior of the Soviet Union through former Polish territory had been converted to Russian broad gauge.

The bottleneck in Poland, however, remained and narrowed on the Soviet side of the

---

[138] (Ковалев (Kovalev), 1981), Chapter 1; (Taylor, 2007), page 53
[139] (Rees, 1995), page 208
[140] (Rees, 1995), page 206

demarcation line.

At the same time, the first major population exchange of the period began with the resettlement of Germans from the Soviet sphere to the Reich and from Poland to the General Government. The first Austrians and Czechs of Jewish faith were also deported to a planned 'Jewish reservation' at Nisko in the Lublin district.[141] This first attempt for deportation and possibly murder failed, but provided the Nazis with know-how for the later inhumane mass deportations (see Chapter 8).[142]

---

[141] (Gottwaldt, 2009), page 169
[142] (Wikipedia003)

5.3   The situation of the Soviet Railways in 1940

In order to better understand the railway situation during the invasion of the Soviet Union and the subsequent 'transport crisis', it is important to assess the pre-war state of the Soviet railways. It is often reported in German-language literature that the railways in the Soviet Union were in an ailing state, making it difficult to supply the advancing German troops by rail. In fact, there seems to have been little information or understanding of how the Soviet railway system worked that time.

This is shown by a simple look at the performance figures of the Soviet railways in comparison with the German and US railways, which do not fit the picture of an underperforming organisation at all (see Table 6). At the end of the 1930s, the Soviet railways carried more than four times as much freight on a network that was only about 1.5 times the size of that of the German Reich. Freight network utilisation in the 1930s exceeded that of the German Reich and even that of the USA by a factor of 3! These are contradictions that call for a closer look at the organisation of the Soviet railways.

After the end of the First World War, the Soviet Union's economic priorities were primarily to supply its own population. With the First Five Year Plan (1928 - 1932), the industrial development of the country began and all available resources were poured into further industrialisation, with the Soviets placing an emphasis on heavy industry. While this plan was somewhat successful and the Soviet Union's heavy industry grew significantly, it led to a famine in 1932/33, during which 3 - 7 million people lost their lives.

During these years, the existing railway network was heavily overloaded and worn out. With the Nazi seizure of power in Germany in 1933, the Soviet government's priorities changed and investment in the railways, which had been neglected for years, was seen as part of national defence. The second five-year plan from 1933 called for the construction of 23,000 km of new railway lines, much of which was earmarked for the industrial areas on or east of the Ural mountains. This prioritisation was also deliberate in the face of an attack from the west. However, till the mid-1930s only part of this plan was completed, and again there was a transport problem.

From 1936, great efforts were made to increase transport capacity. This was mainly

Tab. 6: Comparison of transported goods and network utilisation in different countries [147]

Country		1928	1932	1934	1937
Soviet Union	Network length [km]	76,887	81,569	83,200	86,500
	Freight traffic [m tkm]	93,400	169,300	317,100	354,800
	Network load with freight [1000 tkm/km]	1,215	*2,076 (!)*	*3,811 (!)*	*4,102 (!)*
German Reich	Network length [km]	56,359	58,208	58,232	59,126
	Freight traffic [m tkm]	73,822	44,822	57,553	80,564
	Network load with freight [1000 tkm/km]	1,310	770	988	1,363
USA	Network length [km]	401,223	398,465	392,449	383,890
	Freight traffic [m tkm]	636,544	343,474	394,537	529,591
	Network load with freight [1000 tkm/km]	1,587	862	1,005	1,380

achieved by the introduction of the Stahanov[143]-Krivonós[144]-campaign ('стахановско-кривоносовского движения') and the defamation of anybody who did not follow it enthusiastic enough as 'obstructionists'[145]. As a result, many workers felt insecure, as sanctions were often imposed for even minor mistakes or poor performance. As part of the campaign, successful 'Stahanovists' were promoted to management positions. Meanwhile, working standards were raised,[146] which again improved performance, but at the cost of accidents and increased wear and tear on tracks and equipment. The accompanying political pressure led to fearful and humble workers. At the same time, attempts were made to divert the flow of goods and raw materials for industry to other modes of transport. Although this led to a temporary easing of the problems, it was ultimately unsuccessful.

---

[143] The miner Aleksej Stahanov allegedly achieved a fantastic over-fulfilment of the plan on 30th August 1935, producing 102 tons of coal in one shift, which exceeded the working norm by more than 1,000%.

[144] Like Stahanov, the engine driver Pëtr Krivonós showed that trains can run with much higher loads, at higher speeds, with lower fuel consumption and fewer repairs, using the existing equipment.

[145] (Service, 2003), page 217

[146] (Вольфсон (Vol''fson), и др., 1939), pages 176f

[147] Soviet Union: 1928, 1932: (Grabe, 1942), 1934: (Центральное управление народнохозяйственного учёта (ЦУНХУ) Госплана СССР (Central'noe upravlenie narodnohozâjstvennogo učëta (CUNHU) Gosplana SSSR), 1936); 1937: (Центральное Статистическом Уравление (Central''noe Statističeskow Uravlenie), 1957), (Российский государственный архив экономики (Russian State Archive of Economics)); German Reich (Standard gauge lines: Reichsbahn and private): (Statistisches Reichsamt, 1930); (Statistisches Reichsamt, 1934); (Statistisches Reichsamt, 1936); (Statistisches Reichsamt, 1940); USA (only main land, network length only 1st track owned): (U.S. Department of Commerce, 1939), US units converted

In 1937, the political purge intensified again and was extended even to the 'political departments' of the railways. Many railway workers ended up in labour camps where they were forced to build new railway lines.

The Soviet network itself was similar to the French network, with star-shaped main lines leading to and from Москва́ (Moscow).[148] The density of the network was the greatest in the European part of the Soviet Union, for strategic reasons. The Moscow hub was such an important hub that the existing ring railway was even extended to include a freight train bypass. Other hubs were Ленингра́д (Leningrad), Харків (Kharkiv) and the Донецький вугільний басейн (Donets Coal Basin), as well as industrial centres in or east of the Ural mountains.

In addition, the Soviet railway system was not run like European railways, but rather like American railways. Trains in Europe were comparatively light and travelled at relatively high speeds, freight traffic in the USA, with its extra-long trains, was generally much slower than in Europe. The advantage of the slow speed was that you didn't have to worry so much about the track, which was understandable given the vastness of the country and the extreme climatic conditions. This kept track maintenance costs low and had an positive effect on freight costs. Unlike the US railways, Soviet trains were not as long and did not weigh as much.

The difference to the lines of the German Reich can also be seen in the railway track. The sleepers in the Soviet Union were made of untreated pine wood in a sand bedding (in Germany in 1939: treated beech, larch or pine[149] on a ballast bed). Only 2 % of the main lines had rails weighing 43 kg/m or more, and 16 % of all rails weighed 38 kg/m[150]. In Germany, on the other hand, almost all rails were already replaced in the 1920s and 1930s with rail weighing 49 kg/m. The rails in the Soviet Union were fastened only with nails, in some cases with bolted pads. The number of sleepers per kilometre of track was also much lower. Whereas in the USA there were usually 2,000 sleepers per kilometre of track, in Germany there were around 1,600[151] and in the Soviet Union only 1,440. There are a number of factors that influence the load-bearing capacity of the track[152], but the rail weight together with the sleeper spacing gives a quick insight into its low load-bearing capacity. The maximum axle load in the Soviet

---

[148] (Harris, et al., 1955)

[149] (Schramm, 1952)

[150] (Pottgiesser, 1975), Seite 27

[151] (Pottgiesser, 1975), page 27. Gustav Wulfert gives a standard sleeper spacing for Germany of between 65 cm and 72 cm, corresponding to between 1,030 and 1,111 sleepers per kilometre using 25 cm wide sleepers, (Wulfert, 1942), page 366.

[152] (Wulfert, 1942), page 363

Union was considered by the Germans to be 16 t.[150]

Thousands of class O (13-ton axle load) and series Э (16-ton axle load) locomotives operated on these lines. However, due to the track and the engines, speeds were much slower than in Germany. In 1937, for example, the fastest passenger trains had a scheduled speed of around 50 km/h, while the speed of freight trains had been increased to around 20 km/h by 1936[154] (for comparison: Reichsbahn's freight trains travelled at up to 65 km/h (from 1942: 75 km/h)).[155] However, the low speed had the advantage that the tractive power of a locomotive could be used to the maximum even for the heaviest trains (see Figure 7).

A significant difference to the German and US railways was the use of broad gauge. As a relatively flat country with few tunnels, it was possible to use a much more wider clearance gauge[156] than in Germany, allowing more loading space per wagon.[157]

The Soviet railways also had different rules for operating the line. In Germany, trains were allowed to run at different speeds on the same line, i.e. freight trains and passenger trains at different speeds. This meant that the capacity of the line was mainly

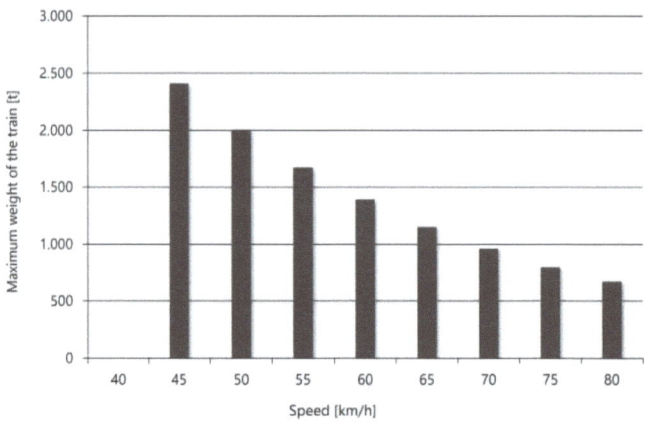

Fig. 7: Maximum weight of trains that could be hauled by a class 50 as a function of speed[153]

---

[153] (Deutsche Bundesbahn , 1953), page 173

[154] (Berkenkopf, 1942/1943)

[155] (Noßke, 2006)

[156] A clearance gauge sets minimum limits on the size of bridges, tunnels and other infrastructure, railway vehicles can pass without damage. The loading gauge defines the maximum height and width dimensions of railway vehicles and their loads and is defined differently in different countries.

[157] (Kuhlmann, 2002), page 8

determined by the number of passing tracks and the length of the sections of the signalling block system[158]. At the passing tracks a faster train on the line could overtake the slower train, which had to switch to the 'slower tracks'. The signalling block system determined the number of track sections and thus the maximum number of trains that could run. The difference in speed was responsible that the continuous flow of trains was constantly disrupted by the fast 'sprinters'.

The Soviet railway, on the other hand, ran the majority of its trains at the same (low) speed. The same speed created a continuous flow of trains on the line, which led to an increase in the maximum capacity. This allowed more trains to run on a track than, for example, in Germany. At the same time, the number of passing tracks could be kept significantly lower. As the operation was also handled by a dispatcher system (see Chapter 10.10.3), the capacity could be adjusted to the traffic volume.

There is no perfect way to organise train traffic on railway lines, but it should suit to local conditions. It is understandable that in Central Europe, with its dense population, high density of railway lines and close intervals of trains, an almost automated signalling block system increases safety on the line. On the other hand, it is difficult to imagine how such a technical solution could be implemented on a railway network like that in the Soviet Union (or the USA). After all, most of the lines ran through sparsely populated or unpopulated areas, and train frequencies were much lower than in Central Europe.

In the face of the imminent invasion of the Soviet Union, not only two opposite political systems clashed, but also two railway organisations that were managed in completely different ways. It was not just the presence of rolling stock or well-developed lines that mattered. The less than glamorous Soviet railway managed to transport huge quantities of goods over long distances – albeit at very low speed – with a large and military-run workforce. The Germans did not understand this at first, as it did not fit into their strategy of a 'blitzkrieg' or their ideas about being superior.

---

[158] The signalling block system is an important system for securing journeys on a railway line. Therefore the line is divided into sections ('blocks'). Only one train may occupy a particular block at a time. As soon as it leaves the section, the block may be used by the following train.

5.4   The attack on the Soviet Union

The Reichsbahn was now involved in the preparation for the attack on the Soviet Union. The military drew up detailed plans for the movement of hundreds of troop units to the border and cooperated with the Reichsbahn. Planning began in late 1940 and detailed plans were drawn up for the use of initially 15,000 and later 17,000 trains to transport the necessary military units and equipment by rail to the Soviet border. The infrastructure for this should be paid from the 'Otto Programm' (see Chapter 5.2).

However, the involvement of the Reichsbahn and the German railway authorities ended at this point of the planning. No preparation was done about the involvement of the Reichsbahn after crossing the Soviet border, as Hitler and the High Command of the Wehrmacht thought that based on the racial background of their ideas the campaign against the Soviet Union would take place as a 'blitzkrieg', similar those of the previous campaigns. They planned on the basis of maximum risk and assumed that the Soviet troops would be defeated relatively quickly, i.e. close to the border and not far from the existing railheads.[159]

The plan was to use motorised units (trucks) to supply the advancing army. In addition, it was expected that the Soviets, in view of their rapid withdrawal, would leave behind much of their broad-gauge railway equipment and related installations like in western campaign to continue the supply of the Wehrmacht. The Ostbahn, which was also under German control, did not play a major role in the planning, as it was considered that this part of the logistic chain 'only' would have to perform the transit of trains. No considerations were made about the logistic bottleneck there. Obviously they did not recognise this or did not consider it as critical. The planners saw no further need to include the Reichsbahn for the period after start of fighting, as it was supposed to be a 'blitzkrieg'.

Moreover, with their plan to advance by motorised means the strategists ignored reality in many respects. In 1939, only 16 of the German army's 157 divisions were fully motorised. The rest advanced on foot and/or horseback, as in the First World War. Overall, the army used twice as many horses in the Second World War than in the First World War.[160] The army was in fact a two-speed army: the small motorised force and a predominantly 'horse army' that fought its way through the Soviet expanses.[161]

---

[159] (Groß, 2012), page 273
[160] (Groß, 2012), page 209
[161] (Clement)

In addition, no account was taken of the fact that the future area of operations differed greatly in a number of respects (funnel-shaped widening towards the east, poor transport infrastructure, extremely cold temperatures) from the previous areas of operations in central and western Europe. In the previous campaigns, the Wehrmacht had operated in areas close to the borders of the Reich, areas the army was familiar with. Now they would be in an unfamiliar environment. Also in this respect, the whole undertaking was already highly risky from a planning point of view.

From the begin of the war it was clear to the army leadership that this would be a war of extermination, in which traditional military codes of honour and the norms of international law would no longer apply[162] – Hitler had made this very clear in a speech to the Wehrmacht generals.[163] It cost the lives of millions and brought suffering to all concerned.

It was not only the 'how' that had not been thought through to the end, but also the 'what'. While Hitler was aiming for gaining access to parts of the Soviet Union that were important for the war economy (raw materials, agricultural products, forced labourers), the OKH's[119] target was to take the important railway hub near Moscow and to achieve a military victory over the Red Army.[162] Hitler prevailed in the later course of planning and the hub near Moscow was not captured. The Germans were unable to block it. As a result, the Soviets were able to continue to supply their troops in defence and later during the advance westward.

During these events, the chief of transport in the OKH, Rudolf Gercke was not successful with several attempts to get the Reichsbahn under the control of the Wehrmacht. While the Reichsbahn employees in the previous French campaign were members of the Wehrmacht, he could not achieve this for the attack on the Soviet Union. So, in early 1941, a separate unit was formed, the 'Feldeisenbahn-Kommando' (FEKdo)[164], to put the railways back into operation behind the combat units. This was done by conscripted members of the Reichsbahn, led by Wehrmacht officers. These units were formed at very short notice and the commands were therefore not fully trained and equipped.[165] Because of their affiliation to the Wehrmacht, they were called 'grey railwaymen'.[166]

---

[162] (Groß, 2012), page 222

[163] (Groß, 2012), page 264

[164] Railway troops

[165] (Mierzejewski, 2005), page 111

[166] The name was derived from the colour of their uniform, which was grey like that of the army. Members of the Reichsbahn wore blue uniforms and were known as 'blue railwaymen'.

During the campaign the logistics of the advancing troops should be handled by three groups: first, the Reichsbahn in the Reich territory and the occupied Poland; second, the Ostbahn in the area of the General Government; and third, the Field Railway Commands in the area between the Soviet border and the front. It is easy to discover that in this system without central coordination, each sub-organisation would try to optimise itself without regard to the other organisations. In the end, this divided organisation meant that train operations at the interfaces were constantly disrupted. Five months after the establishment of the Field Railway Command, the 'Otto Programm' was terminated.

On 22 June 1941, the attack on the Soviet Union took place without a separate declaration of war. In the first few days, the Soviets were taken by surprise, despite previous warnings. They had to retreat without a fight, meaning that the attackers were

Tab. 7: The 'Feldeisenbahn-Kommandos' (FEKdo), established in 1941

Unit	established	First operation
Field Railway Command 1	15.01.1941	Southern USSR
Field Railway Command 2	20.03.1941	Middle USSR in the Smolensk area
Field Railway Command 3	23.03.1941	Southern USSR
Field Railway Command 4	10.05.1941	Northern USSR

able to capture rolling stock and intact infrastructure. This made the German leadership optimistic that the 'blitzkrieg' plan would work.

However, it soon became clear that a problem of supplying the troops had been overlooked at the interface from standard to broad gauge. Of course, the railway troops started immediately to convert the broad to standard gauge, the transfer point moved eastwards with the advancing troops, but did not disappear for the whole time of advance.

The interface was critical as all goods had to be reloaded. The Reichsbahn's standard freight wagons did not allow for the possibility of changing gauge (i.e. by changing axle sets). If the transhipment from standard to broad gauge did not take place quickly enough at the transfer stations, there would be a jam on the lines (on top of the backlog which was caused by the fault in the 'Otto-Programm').

In addition, after only a few days the attackers could see that the Soviets were moving wagons and locomotives eastwards with all their strength. This was done in a concentrated, all-out effort, with trains sometimes running within sight of each other, on double tracks, side by side, heading east.[167] This allowed the Soviets to make full use of the advantages of their railway system.

The many traffic hold-ups caused by the German trains on their way to the east created an additional problem: the circulation of freight wagons. In many places these were unloaded too late,[168] and in some cases field commanders 'confiscated' their own locomotives.[169] In this way they disregarded the requirements of a functioning logistics system, not least because they were not trained in it and had never before to operate so far away from the supply centres. For the officers in the field, the railways had to function no matter how. They did not care about the need of logistics, convinced that the railways would find a solution to the problems at hand. This may have worked well not far away from the Reich's borders (France, Belgium, the Netherlands, etc.), but the size of the Soviet Union caused massive problems.

Though the use of railways in a military campaign was not unknown to the German military: As far back as the American Civil War, Herman Haupt[170] had been concerned about the misuse of the railways and, among other things, had drawn up basic operating rules in 1862: *"No officer …, whatever his rank or position, shall have the right to detain a train or order it to run in advance of the scheduled time. If cars are not unloaded or trains made up when the hour of starting arrives, engines must proceed with parts of trains or without trains and all the facts in detail must be reported in writing by the conductor to be laid before the chief of transportation or the commanding general of the department."*[171]

Strict adherence to these rules ultimately led to a significant improvement of the Union Army's logistical problems in the US Civil War and contributed to its victory over the Confederates. These rules were well known in Germany, as Prussia's Army had sent observers to the US at that time to obtain detailed information on Haupt's successful reorganisation of the railways.[172] And Field Marshal Helmuth von Moltke[173] adopted this experience for the Prussian army. Cooperation between the military and the railways became an integral part of Prussian manoeuvres. This led to significant military advantages on the Prussian side during the deployment and at the beginning

---

[167] (Schüler, 1987), pages 250f

[168] (Pottgiesser, 1975), page 33

[169] (Hahn, 1954), page 55

[170] Herman Haupt was a Union Army General during the American Civil War. He revolutionized U.S. military railway transport system (Wikipedia004).

[171] (Davie, 2017)

[172] (Wolmar, 2010), pages 66f

[173] From 1870 'Count von Moltke'. He was Chief of the Prussian General Staff from 1857 to 1888.

of the Franco-Prussian War of 1870/1871.[174]

After orders were sent to the field commanders, the situation improved somewhat as trains were unloaded more quickly. In view of the widely represented basic attitude of the Wehrmacht, the change was not sustainable.[175] At the same time, the importance of effective logistics increased with the German Army moving eastward, especially as the Soviets managed to move more and more material away.

You have to consider, that a panzer division, the carrier of the planned 'blitzkrieg', had a daily supply requirement of at least 350 tons (possibly up to 1,000 tons in heavy fighting),[176] which meant that at least one supply train had to be unloaded and transported to the front line every day.[177] From the point of unloading (railway head) to the troops behind the lines, lorry columns were used, with a capacity of 720 tons of supplies and 300 tons of fuel.[178] Assuming that the average speed of a lorry-column on Soviet roads was 15-20 km/h, these columns could easily transport the daily requirements over a distance of about 200 km from the railway head to the division and return to the railway head the same day. If, for example, the distance from the railhead to the front increased to about 300 km, a lorry-column took two days to make a delivery, and if the distance was even greater, the transport took even longer.

The tactics of the German 'blitz' slowed down: after the armoured divisions broke through the enemy lines and surrounded the defenders, they had to wait for the horse-drawn infantry to open up and destroy the encircling.[179] This approach might have worked in Central Europe, but it failed over the long distances in the USSR.

It became clear that the previous 'blitzkrieg' concept could not work in the vast areas of the USSR, because if the advance was too fast – although it was easy to exploit for propaganda purposes – the fighting troops were increasingly in danger of losing their connection to the supply base.[180] How fast the 'blitz' really was becomes clear when one considers the speed of the initial advance of the (German) Army Group North: 13 days for about 250 km from Daugavpils to Псков (Pskov), which was an average speed of 19 km per day. The Army Group Centre, on the other hand, took 22 days to cover approximately the same distance from Vilnius to Полацк (Polotsk), an average

---

[174] (Epkenhans, 2020), pages 37ff

[175] (Mierzejewski, 2005), page 112

[176] (Davie, 2020)

[177] A German military train generally had 90 axles, a gross weight of 850 t and a payload of 450 t (Davie, 2017). This was also the order of magnitude for ammunition trains (Donat, 1964).

[178] (Davie, 2020)

[179] (Davie, 2018)

[180] (Kreidler, 2001), page 134

distance of about 11 km per day.[181]

When the German advance was not fast enough, the Soviet railwaymen, after removing the rolling stock, made much of their network unusable to the attackers. Apart from the destruction of tracks and the blowing up of bridges, perhaps the most sustainable measure was the destruction of operational facilities: the emptying of railway workshops, the destruction of depots and operation facilities for steam locomotives (coal, water, ash), as well as the turntables.[181] As a result, the German steam engines were only able to replenish coal and water using primitive means, and the operation of an approximately 100 km railway line was permanently disrupted.[182] The destroyed turntables prevented the machines from turning quickly and they had to travel to the nearest triangular junction to turn. The destruction of the depots meant that it was no longer possible to store the engines in a locomotive shed, which had serious consequences as winter set in.

While the railway troops repaired or re-gauged tracks relatively quickly, the restoration of depots and machine facilities was a much slower process – and usually not the focus of the troops, who were essentially fixated on being able to report the longest possible lengths of 'repaired' track. So, the troops' quick reports of completion had nothing to do with the operational capabilities of the field railway employees who needed these facilities.

Since the hoped for spoils of engines and wagons did not materialise during the advance, there was a shortage of rolling stock in the conquered areas. This can easily be seen from the figures for locomotive density after the eastern extension of the Ostbahn (see Table 5). Rolling stock had to be brought in from the Reich. Accordingly, the locations of the newly built class 50 units also shifted eastwards (cf. Figure 8).

Behind the front, field railway directorates were established in Псков (Pskov), Смоленск (Smolensk) and Полтава (Poltava). The employees of these directorates worked very pragmatically, i.e. without service instructions and regulations, in order to solve the respective transport tasks. With the advance of the front to the east, however, the staff was no longer sufficient enough, and Reichsbahn employees were transferred from the Reich to these directorates ('blue railwaymen')[166]. They lived in collective camps and were not well supplied.[183] As they did not wear Wehrmacht

---

[181] (Kreidler, 2001), page 126

[182] As steam locomotives could only carry supplies for about 200 - 300 kilometres, they were dependent on being able to take on fresh supplies at the destination station in order to return to their home depot (cf. Chapter 1).

[183] (Kreidler, 2001), pages 131f

uniforms, they were often regarded by the Soviets as 'armed non-combatants', not protected by the Geneva Convention, and were sometimes summarily executed during fighting.[184]

In September 1941, the so-called Haupteisenbahndirektion[185] (HBD) were established: HBD North in Rīga (Riga), HBD Central in Мінск (Minsk), HBD South in Львів (Lviv), later in Київ (Kyiv), and HBD East in Полтава (Poltava). Similarly, to the Ostbahn and unlike to the Reichsbahn, the railway workers had to take over parts of railway operation from the very beginning, as the local forces were considered 'inferior' for racial-ideological reasons and were not allowed to take on responsible tasks.

The HBDs proved less effective because their status was unclear. They were not part of the organisational structure of the Reichsbahn or the Ostbahn, nor were they integrated into military structures. Although there was a central coordinating office in Warsaw for transports across HBD borders, there were always coordination problems and disputes between HBD members and representatives of the Reichsbahn. In addition, it was difficult for the coordinating office to maintain contact with the HBDs due to poor communication links. In part, the HBDs also suffered from the fact that their Jewish specialists had been murdered by the SD[186].[187]

Then the распутица (mud period) began, and the supply of the troops by means of lorry transports literally sank in the ground. There were mass breakdowns of trucks, and the repair rate of the lorries rose from 24 % (August 1941) to 44 % (November 1941).[188]

This can be seen as the first victory over the German aggressor. There was no more talk of a 'blitz' within this war and the supposedly short field campaign became a long war for which no preparations had been made.

---

[184] (Pottgiesser, 1975), page 122

[185] Main Railway Directorates

[186] SD = **S**icherheits**d**ienst, Security Service of the Reichsführer SS, i.e. the secret service of the NSDAP and the SS.

[187] (Hahn, 1954), page 49

[188] (Kreidler, 2001), page 134

5.5   The transport crisis of 1941/42

With the onset of winter, temperatures in the eastern theatres of war dropped to as low as -40 °C. The severe frost lasted until March 1942. The crisis started slowly with the mud period and quickly worsened end of the year 1941 as the Reichsbahn locomotives – especially the classes 38^{10}, 55^{25}, 56^2, 57^{10} and 58^{10}, which had been hastily brought over from Germany to the east – began to break down.

None of these engines were prepared for such low temperatures. All exposed pipes on the machines froze, also the water in the tenders. In addition, the provisionally repaired water cranes and water tanks froze and the water sources dried up. Since there were only a few locomotive sheds left, engines parked outside cooled down severely and had to be defrosted in some cases over burning piles of wood. In some places, up to 90 % of the units went out of service.[189]

Traffic came to a virtual standstill. Even for short distances, individual trains had to be hauled by 4 - 5 spare locomotives.[190] The cold wind froze the engines' external units (air pump, preheater, etc.). In many cases, the machines did not even have enough power to heat the passenger coaches attached to them, so that the last coaches of a train were not heated at all, which e.g. led to deaths in hospital trains.[191] The Reichsbahn was forced to move more and more units from the Reich to the east, but this had a negative impact on the overall economy of the Reich and ultimately did not help much, as these locomotives also had no protection against the cold.

By the end of 1941, the High Command of the Wehrmacht had already demanded that the Reichsbahn and the locomotive factories had to increase their deliveries of engines and goods wagons significantly. This led to a heated discussion between the parties concerned. The locomotive company Henschel called for a simpler design, which would increase the production of freight units by up to 20 %.[192] Thus the idea of a simplified standard machines, a war locomotive, began to germinate.

Increasingly concerned about the situation in the east, Hitler took up the subject in late 1941, telling the head of transport that he needed *"a type of locomotive more suited to conditions in the east."* And *"no works of art should be built, but simple machines that would only last five years."*[193] This formulation was taken up by the Reich Ministry of

---

[189] (Pottgiesser, 1975), page 35
[190] (Hahn, 1954), page 53
[191] (Hahn, 1954), pages 54f
[192] (Gottwaldt, 2016). pages 14f
[193] (Schüler, 1987), pages 526f

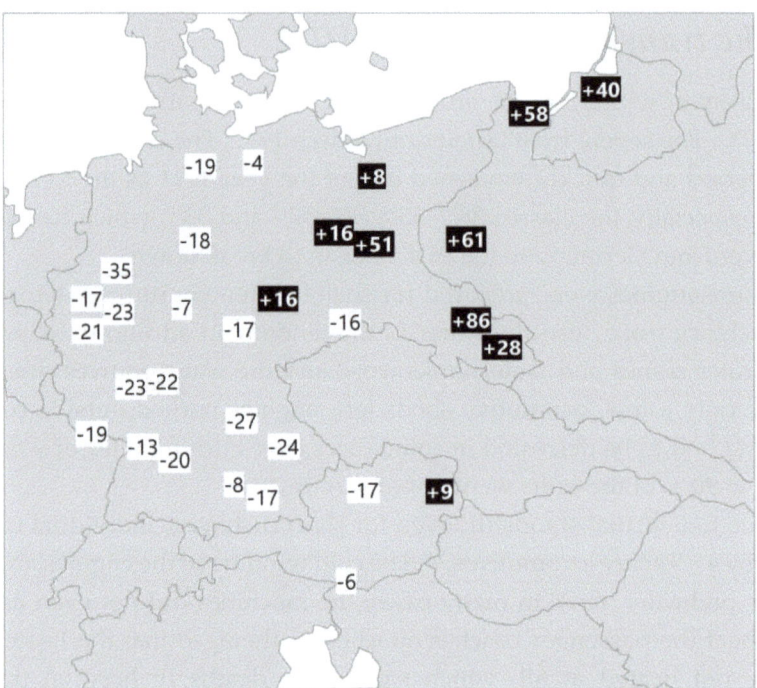

Fig. 8:   Transfers of class 50 units in 1941. Negative numbers indicate outflow, positive numbers inflow to the Directorates of the Reichsbahn[194]

Transport and later incorporated into a note on 'Conditions for the New Type of Lo-comotive to be Developed by the Locomotive Factories'. The requirement was that the engine should be built in such a way that they could be used without major repairs until the end of the war.

By this time, the Wehrmacht Chief of Transport, Gercke, had lost Hitler's confidence and in early 1942, on Hitler's orders, all the railways in the occupied territories of the USSR were transferred under the responsibility of the Reich Ministry of Transport. Apart from the Ostbahn, the railway troops were excluded and stayed with the Chief of Transport in Warsaw. Gercke's 'Management East', which coordinated operations in the occupied territories of the Soviet Union between the established HBDs, was incorporated into the Reich Ministry of Transport as the 'Zweigstelle Osten' (abbre-viation: Osteis) in January 1942 and later renamed in 'Generaldirektion Osten' (abbre-viation: GVD Osten) in December 1942. So, the Reichsbahn got the responsibility for

[194] (Ebel, et al., 1988), page 110

all traffic up the railway troops. However, the HBDs were not incorporated into the organisation of the Reichsbahn and remained as a special part of it.[195]

It was only now that senior officials from the Reich Ministry of Transport were allowed to enter the occupied Soviet territories to see for themselves the state of the transportion system. This was urgently needed, as Gercke worked almost exclusively at his desk in Warsaw and shunned visits to the occupied Soviet Union.[196]

There was also movement in the conflict area between the Reichsbahn and the locomotive industry. Sometime before, on Hitler's initiative, the 'Steering Committee for Tanks' was set up to promote tank production. It reported to Fritz Todt, the Reich Minister for Armaments and Ammunition. The Steering Committee forced all manufacturers to review their production processes and compare them with best practice to determine the most efficient and cost-effective method. Applications for investments in new machinery had to be submitted to the Committee. The Committee also had the power to send employees to other companies to exchange know-how or to relieve labour shortages. It could monitor production processes and provide any assistance needed to achieve the targets set.[197] Under the chairmanship of Ferdinand Porsche the industrial companies involved benefited in terms of knowledge of assembly line work and modern production processes. In the beginning Porsche was advised by Henry Ford, who admired Hitler. He also supported him by sending him some executives.[198]

Also, in late 1941, Hitler's decree to 'Simplify and increase the efficiency of our armaments industry' (the so-called Rationalisation Decree), which was primarily aimed at the production of tanks,[199] prompted the industry to optimise their work processes. Another decree[200] equated the production of locomotives with the production of weapons and ammunition used directly in combat – and allocated steel quotas accordingly. This laid the foundation for the production of a war locomotive.

Meanwhile the railway industry had become part of the German war economy. In order to avoid long discussions between industry and the Reichsbahn, it was obvious that this industry should be coordinated centrally. Also, in order to support the

---

[195] Cf. 'Decree of the Führer on Transport in the Occupied Eastern Territories' from 23.10.1942, cf. (Moll, 1997), pages 289f
[196] (Kreidler, 2001), page 137
[197] (Milward, 1966)
[198] (Creydt, et al., 1993), page 24
[199] (Michaels, 2020), pages 150f
[200] Cf. 'Decree of the Führer and Supreme Commander of the Wehrmacht concerning: production of weapons, ammunition and equipment' of 14.4.1942, cf. (Moll, 1997), page 245

fighting troops as quickly as possible. After Todt's death, Albert Speer took over as Minister of Armaments and Munitions. From the outset, Speer planned to reorganise the war economy by placing companies under tight central control. This was not a new idea and had already been pursued by his predecessor. It also served to shift responsibilities from the armed forces to his ministry in order to get this industry under his control.

The new minister was charged with implementing the 'Führer Programm', which called for the construction of '15,000 war locomotives within two years'. In order to achieve this goal, Speer reverted to the organisational form of a Steering Committee already introduced by Todt and founded the 'Steering Committee for Railway Vehicles' (HAS)[201] in March 1942. Now Oskar Henschel, the chairman of the German Locomotive Association (DLV)[202] reached his goal, whereof he had been working on since October 1941, sometimes using deliberately false arguments, namely to get rid of the Reichsbahn as a customer. His motivation was that the industry should make its own decisions in what was expected to be a big business with the war locomotive and to realise the full economic potential.[203] The Reichsbahn should not interfere. This led to the unusual situation that the supplier and not the customer decided what the product had to look like.

Gerhard Degenkolb was appointed chairman of the Steering Committee for Railway Vehicles. By ensuring the widespread introduction of assembly line work in locomotive and wagon construction, he paved the way for the use of foreign and forced labour.

Of course, the problems were not solved overnight. In February 1942, in a meeting with Dorpmüller's deputy, Kleinmann, and the Chief of Transport, Gercke, Hitler demanded that the problems with the railways should be *"solved in the shortest possible time."*[204] During the meeting, Gercke severely reproached the Reichsbahn and accused the head of HBD Kyiv, Erwin Landenberger, and the deputy head of HDB Minsk, Dr. Karl Eugen Hahn, as the root cause of the problems.[205] Shortly afterwards, the two were arrested and sent to Sachsenhausen concentration camp. The arrest can certainly be seen as a pawn sacrifice by the transport chief to divert attention from himself and

---

[201] HAS = **H**aupt**a**usschuss **S**chienenfahrzeuge
[202] The DLV (**De**utsche **L**okomotiv-**V**ereinigung) was a cartel of locomotive manufacturers in the German Reich. From 1923, the Reichsbahn divided its procurement equally between the factories of the DLV, thus excluding foreign competition.
[203] (Weisbrod, et al., 2012), pages 16f
[204] (Gottwaldt, 2009), page 189
[205] (Gall, et al., 1999), page 230

his mistakes. There were hints that at least Hahn's arrest had been prepared by the military.[206] Hahn might have been chosen for arrest because he refused to tolerate killings of Jewish people in his area of responsibility by the SD[186].[207]

Four months later they were released at the intervention of Dorpmüller and Speer. Both were psychologically demoralised and eschewed by many of their colleagues.[208] As a result of his experiences in the concentration camp, Hahn, who had joined the Nazi party in 1933, resigned from it in August 1942. The shunning by his colleagues was to continue until after the war and lead to a tragic end (see Chapter 10.9).

At the same time, at Speer's instigation, there was a change at the top management of the Reichsbahn, although its head, Dorpmüller, remained untouched. Instead, his deputy, Kleinmann, was replaced by Albert Ganzenmüller, who had made a name for himself at HBD Poltawa by clearing backlogs and rerouting lines. While Dorpmüller remained Reich Minister of Transport, the new man ran the day-to-day operations. It was Speer who succeeded in giving the Reichsbahn operational control over the railways of the occupied territories in the West (Benelux, France).[209] This meant that wagons and locomotives could be confiscated there to make up for losses in the Reich and in the eastern territories. Speer also assumed responsibility for the procurement of the Reichsbahn's rolling stock, especially since he was also in charge of controlling steel quotas. None of these measures were new, as they had already been discussed under his predecessor Todt. They were now being taken up and implemented. Compared to earlier times, the new personnel approached things with more dynamism, probably also motivated by the fact that failure could have serious personal consequences.

Hitler's interest in the railways with regard to warfare remained low. He preferred to occupy himself with his gigantomaniac broad-gauge railway[210], or to dream of 'autobahns' to the east, which he considered necessary for his 'opening' of the Soviet Union.[211] He failed to realise that even the USA at that time, which was much more

---

[206] (Hahn, 1954), pages 58ff

[207] (Hahn, 1954), pages 84f

[208] (Gottwaldt, 2009), page 190

[209] Cf. 'Decree of the Führer on the standardisation of the management of the wartime operations of the railways of the Protectorate, the occupied Dutch territories, Belgium and occupied France" of 23 January 1942, see (Moll, 1997), pages 229f.

[210] The broad-gauge railway was a railway with a gauge of four-metre (later three-metre). It was planned on Hitler's initiative to link the European territories conquered by the Nazis. It never got beyond the planning stage and should be seen in the context of Hitler's other plan of the 'World Capital City Germania' (Wikipedia005).

[211] (Picker, 1963), pages 299f, 418

advanced in terms of motorisation, considered the railways to be the backbone of its transport capacity: 90 % of the military equipment and 97 % of the military personnel of the USA were transported by rail during the Second World War.[212]

[212] (Wolmar, 2010), page 242

6 The great simplification or the transition to a war locomotive

The chairman of the Steering Committee for Railway Vehicles immediately got down to work. Degenkolb subdivided the Steering Committee into a number of working committees, which included representatives from industry, preferably with knowledge of assembly line production. A programme for the construction of 99,400 freight wagons, which was adopted shortly afterwards, got also part of the responsibilities of the Steering Committee.

His approach to the war locomotive was pragmatic: instead of spending time on new types of engine, whose success was by no means assured, he drew on the successful redesign of the new freight machine of the Reichsbahn, the class 50. His idea was to simplify it to the needs of wartime transport with lower material consumption and lower production times. All the 'unnecessary gadgets' of the existing (peacetime) design were removed or replaced by simpler and/or cheaper parts. The term 'de-refinement' was invented to describe this simplification of design and manufacture. Today it might be called the 'no-frills-edition'[213] of the peacetime class 50 unit.

As early as March 1942, the first decree for 'de-refinement' was issued to improve the current production of class 50 machines. It included minor simplifications to the boiler, frame, driving and running gear and, as a noticeable change, the omission of the smoke deflectors. Other changes were the omission of the dome for feedwater treatment, the combination of the two sandboxes into one welded box, the omission of the bell and the second cab window. The locomotive did not get any number plates anymore, as the engine numbers were only painted in white or applied as decals.[214] The loss of the smoke deflectors caused a lot of problems in the day-to-day operations and severely restricted the view on the track (see Figure 9).

In March 1942 it was stipulated that all new 'de-refinemed' and the war locomotives were painted completely in iron grey (RAL 7011), handles of the air pipes in red and the sockets and covers of the light cables in yellow.[215] This colour scheme was chosen to show that the engine was a war locomotive, which could maintained with lower quality criteria. The engine also carried a 50 mm wide ring on the each of its buffer

---

[213] (Wikipedia006)
[214] (Ebel, et al., 1988), pages 62
[215] (Ebel, et al., 1988), pages 62. The usage of red an yellow is not confirmed by Wolfgang Diener (Diener, 2012).

heads. This marking was required for all locomotives from 1940 on due to blackout regulations.[216] In June 1942, iron grey was replaced by black grey (RAL 7021), as iron grey was considered to be too light for camouflage. The initial instruction was to make the lettering in black, however this had to be subsequently cancelled as all pictures of new engines of this time showed a white lettering. For machines with the old colour scheme the flame red (RAL 3000) colour was replaced by carmine red (RAL 3002) during repair or maintenance.[217]

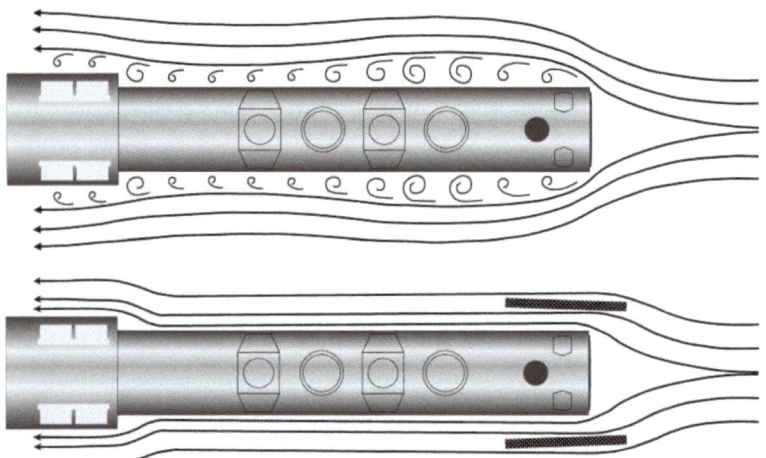

Fig. 9: Flow conditions in a steam locomotive without (top) and with (bottom) smoke deflectors: Without deflectors, the air swirls along the boiler and draws the smoke towards the unit. With smoke deflectors, the airflow is directed past the boiler without turbulence.[218]

In April 1942, Degenkolb signed an order that the locomotive factories instructed only to build the class 50 and a later class 42 from now on. Orders for other types of machines were cancelled immediately.[219]

In May 1942 the DLV[202] was liquidated and the 'Gemeinschaft Großdeutscher Lokomotivfabriken' (GGL)[220] was founded in order to get a better grip on the industry and to speed up negotiations. Hans Georg Krauss from Krauss-Maffei AG was appointed chairman in place of Henschel. Members of the companies which were part of the

---

[216] (Diener, 2012), page 44f
[217] (Diener, 2012), page 45
[218] cf. (Giesl-Gieslingen, 1986), page 157
[219] (Reimer, 1999), pages 88f
[220] Community of Great German Locomotive Companies

GGL are given in Table 8. Officially, they were supposed to act in 'industrial self-responsibility'. This was only propaganda and much of the entrepreneurial freedom was lost, as the Steering Committee could intervene into the production processes. Locomotive construction, like tank construction, had become an executive division of the Ministry of Armament and Ammunition.

The 'Zulieferungs-GmbH'[221], founded in April 1942, completed the picture. This unit took over the creation and the control of a much larger supplier base than before in order to relieve the locomotive factories of many tasks. In addition to pumps, brakes and air reser-

Tab. 8: Planned production numbers of the GGL companies for the war locomotive[219]

Producer[56]	Number
Henschel	2.500
Borsig	1.500
Krupp	1.500
Schwartzkopff	1.500
Floridsdorf	1.500
Krauss	1.400
Schichau	1.000
Orenstein&Koppel	750
Cegielski	500
Esslingen	500
Graffenstaden	500
Jung	500
Chrzanów	500
Škoda	500
Warszawa	250
ČKD	100
Total	15.000

voirs, which already had previously been manufactured externally, cabs, ash boxes and sand domes, as well as tenders, were now outsourced.[222] In addition, a work group 'boiler' considered the possibility of subcontracting the manufacture of engine boilers. The vertical range of manufacture of the locomotive factories was thus significantly reduced.

Initially, the head of the Committee 'Construction' had given the new war locomotive the designation 'class K 50' and stipulated that the class 50 units were numbered only up to No. 50 3044, and thereafter bear the designation 'K 50 3045', and so on. All simplified class 50 engines from the normal production (i.e. up to No. 50 3044) should receive the inscription 'ÜK'[223] after their number. In fact, No. 50 3164 ÜK was the last officially designated example of the class 50. In addition, a serial designation for each company was applied to the cylinder next to the company plate: K 1, K 2, K 3, … .

Only three weeks later, however, the decision was made that the new war locomotive would not be called the 'K 50', but the 'class 52'. So, the K 50 3045 etc. now had to be

---

[221] Subcontracting Ltd.
[222] (Gottwaldt, 2016), pages 36f
[223] **Ü**bergang zur **K**riegslokomotive (Transition to the war locomotive)

called 52 001 etc.[224] This change was not so much a result of technical reconsiderations, but rather an advertisement on his own behalf and was intended to show how effective the work of the Steering Committee headed by Degenkolb had been.[225]

To avoid confusion, the existing class 52[70] engines had to be renamed. They were renumbered to class 53[78] in August 1942.[226]

Meanwhile the final design of the war locomotive had been agreed by the Steering Committee. The only problem which existed was the axle load, which could not be reduced if the engine had the same tractive power as the class 50. Further simplifications and weakening of the material, such as reducing the thickness of the steel, were therefore limited. Material savings could only be achieved by optimising the cutting process and setting up the production chain in such a way as to minimise the need for machining. At the same time, attempts were made to replace non-ferrous metals with iron and steel, which meant that these quotas could be given to the defence industry.

At the end of the construction work, the Steering Committee listed the following successes:[227]

Class 52 compared to class 50:
- Reduction of components: from 6,000 to 5,000 (-17 %)
- 3,000 components were simplified
- Reduction of consumption of copper: from 2,358 kg to 127 kg (-95 %)
- Reduction of consumption of tin: from 480 kg to 24 kg (-95 %)
- Reduction of production time by 6,000 hours (-30 %)

This calculation is not entirely correct, as the savings for copper given refer to a class 50 unit with a firebox made of copper. However, class 50 was equipped with a firebox from steel already from start of production.[227]

The production quotas that the locomotive factories had to meet were set by Degenkolb himself (see Table 8). These were later changed several times. In the end, the first version was used again.[228]

In order to achieve the high level of production, not only the appropriate supply of steel was needed, but also the appropriate labour force. Many workers were needed for military service. To have enough workers, it was planned to release conscripted

---

[224] (Reimer, 1999), pages 95f
[225] (Weisbrod, et al., 2012), page 17
[226] (Hütter, 2012), page 447
[227] see (Griebl, et al., 1971), pages 10f; (Gottwaldt, 2016), pages 29f. Data for copper and tin based on gross weight.
[228] (Gottwaldt, 2016), page 36, footnote 72

Fig. 10:   Model of No. 50 1675ÜK (Roco 69250), driver's (top) and fireman's side (bottom).
This model shows a 'de-refined' class 50 machine. The recess for the former feedwater preheater can still be seen in front of the chimney. The wind deflectors have disappeared as well
as the feedwater pump on the fireman's side. Otherwise the boiler still appears to be the peace
version, as the cab and the inscriptions are still similar to the class 50. However, this machine
has the inscription 'ÜK'[223]. The tender shows the date 10.7.42 as the last brake inspection.
Information on the historical model: Krauss 1942 → DRB 50 1675ÜK (RBD Nürnberg) → 1945
DRw/DB 50 1675 + 1965 Oberhausen-Osterfeld Süd

workers from locomotive building factories from their service at the Wehrmacht. But
this solution was limited. Forced labourers (concentration camp inmates, prisoners of
war) and so-called 'foreign workers' (civilians who had originally come to Germany
voluntarily but later were not allowed to leave their jobs)[229] were used (see Chapter 8.2). The situation of the forced labourers and 'foreign workers' was very bad.
They worked under great pressure, were often maltreated, and lived under inhumane
conditions in barrack camps near the factories.

---

[229] (Pagenstecher)

In September 1942, the first war locomotive 52 001 was presented in a large propaganda event. A train consisting of No. 52 001 and No. 50 337 together with eight war freight wagons travelled to the factories of the GGL. In December 1942, the train went

Fig. 11:   Model of No. 50 3140 (Roco 62255), driver's (top) and fireman's side (bottom).
This model shows a stage of further 'de-refinement' of the class 50. It is one of the last engines from the official production of class 50. Displayed is a '50ÜK' in the DB version of the early 50s. The DB omitted the addition 'ÜK'. The machine is painted and lettered according to the DB colour scheme. With regard to the boiler and cab (type 'Norwegian', see Chapter 6.1) and the tender, the unit is almost indistinguishable from the later class 52. The chimney design and the cab inscription 'WM80'[230] still indicate that there are still relics from the class 50. The last brake test is dated 10.2.51.
Information on the historical model: Schwartzkopff 1943 → DRB 50 3140ÜK (RBD Essen) → 1945 DRw/DB 50 3140 + 1962 Mayen

---

[230] WM80 (**Wei**ß**m**etall 80, white metal 80) indicates the composition from the bearing metal (80 % tin, 12 % antimony, 6 % copper, 2 % lead) that was used in peacetime. For war locomotives, the metal was changed to WM10 (10 % tin, 15.5 % antimony, 1 % copper, 73.5 % lead) (cf. (Weisbrod, et al., 2012), page 22).

to Hitler's 'Wolfsschanze' for demonstration. After production had begun, 51 class 52 units were assembled for a propaganda movie in the marshalling yard at Seddin near Potsdam. The film was to show all starting to move at the same time. Photos and film documents taken there are still often seen today by using the keyword 'war locomotive'.[231]

All these activities did not go unnoticed by the British intelligence: as early as the end of January 1943, a report from the Ministry of Economic Warfare was handed over to the US military attaché in London, containing essential points about the engine and making assumptions about its manufacture and operation.[232]

---

[231] (Borel, 1943)
[232] (Clement, 2020), pages 177ff

6.1 A more detailed look at the war locomotive

The war locomotive was approved for an axle load of 15 tons due to the weight savings made. The maximum speed was set to 80 km/h in both directions, as with the peacetime version. This meant that it was not absolutely necessary to turn the engine.

The boiler

The feedwater dome, the feedwater heater and the feedwater pump were omitted. To feed the boiler with water, the machine had two steam injectors[233], each with a capacity of 180 l/min. Class 50 also had two independent pumps with a total capacity of 500 l/min. This meant that if one pump failed in the war locomotive, the engine's performance was adversely affected by the reduction in pumping capacity.

Instead of the usual two water level indicators (water gauge glass), there was only one water glass and two test valves (gage cocks).[234]

Although it was possible to check the boiler level with the test taps, their operation resulted in additional work for the fireman because the taps had to be operated separately to check the water level. This was an elimination of a safety feature as in case the water glass failed, the control of the water level with two test valves was much more inaccurate and faultier.

With the exception of the nozzle for the air pump, all steam extraction nozzles were mounted on the boiler in the cab. From there distribution pipes led to the steam heater, the generator, blower pipe[235] and injectors. The feedwater heater was omitted, which could be tolerated in view of the designed operating time and the war.

The frame

The frame was the basis on which the entire steam locomotive was built, and it ensured that the power of the steam engine was transmitted to the hauled train. The class 52 used either a plate or a bar frame. The plate frame consisted of plates of 25 to 40 mm thickness. The two sides of the frame were connected by longitudinal and transverse joints for stiffening. For the bar frame on the other hand, bet-

---

[233] The steam injector is a device which used steam to deliver water to steam locomotive boilers.

[234] Water gauge glasses are used to control the water level in the boiler. It is a vertical glass tube that is connected with the inside of the boiler. Test valves (gage cock) are water taps placed at different heights of the boiler. Opening these, you could find out whether there the water level reached the tap or not.

[235] The blower pipe is a device designed to increase the chimney draught in the boiler during firing up. It consists of a tube with openings that surrounds the blast pipe nozzle in a ring and from which steam emerges.

Fig. 12:   Model of No. 52 7535 (Liliput 105203), driver's (top) and fireman's side (bottom).
The class 52 with frost protection installations. This can be seen by the chimney hatch, the inlet pipes[236] (squared from insulation) and only few pipes above the boiler insulation. The two feed valves in front of the steam dome are clearly visible on the fireman's side.[237] The upper part of the air pump on the driver's side is covered. Above the steam chest there is the housing for the pressure-compensation valve, type 'Winterthur'.[238] The strut in front of the smokebox door has been omitted. The machine has a 'Norwegian' cab (see text) with a K 2'2'T30 tender. The last brake inspection date is indicated for 13.5.44 (for the tenders, cf. Chapter 6.2.1). The unit is painted iron grey and the tender in black grey.
Information on the historical model: Schichau 1944 → DRB 52 7535 (Gedob) → 1945 PKP Ty2-1141 + 1990 Chabówka

---

[236] The inlet pipes (right, left) connect the steam dome with the steam chests (above the cylinder). In the steam chests, the steam is distributed to the correct side of the cylinder via a piston valve.

[237] With the peace version (class 50), the valves were located on the feed dome.

[238] The pressure-compensation valves are part of the steam locomotive's control system, which is needed when the locomotive is idling. When running without steam, for example when going down a hill, the pistons in the cylinders act like an air pump. Smoke and particles could be sucked from the smokebox into the cylinders. This is prevented by the pressure compensator. With the Winterthur compensator, the two chambers are connected via an automatically operating valve. When idling, the valve opens to equalise the pressure. When live steam enters the cylinder, the steam closes the valve and separates the two cylinder chambers. Each of the two cylinders requires its own pressure compensator (cf. (Denzin, 2009), pages 44ff).

ween 70 and 100 mm thick steel plates were used. The low overall height gave very good access to all parts between the sole bars.

Both frame types were used for the war locomotive. Accordingly, two weights were given in the engine data sheet, one for the plate frame and one for the bar frame.

Class 50 was built on a bar frame, which consisted of 80 mm thick sole bars spaced 930 mm apart.

Frost protection

This was one of the most important features for operating on the lines in the occupied territories of the Soviet Union.

The cab was closed on all sides ('Norwegian cab') and had a round cut-out in the rear wall towards the tender. The cab floor was heated.

The cylinders of the steam engine and the inlet pipes[236] were insulated against frost. All lubrication pipes were laid under the boiler casing and insulated. They were heated by the hot boiler. The steam and water pipes were all laid at a gradient and insulated so that no water could accumulate and freeze during standstill. All steam outlets and exposed adapters were fitted with insulating protective boxes. The cylinders could be pre-heated by a special heating pipe.

On some of the later locomotives (in total 2,500 units), an extended frost protection was installed by special order.[239] This version included insulated boiler and tender side walls with thermal mats. The chimney had a hatch that could be opened and closed. To heat the water in the tender a steam heater was installed in the water tank of the tender.

Connecting and coupling rods

A particular simplification had been made in the production of the coupling and connecting rods, which were previously forged from a single piece and then machined on all sides. As part of the 'de-refinement', the rod heads have been dropped forged. This involved heating the blank to over 1,000 °C and pressing it into a specific shape using two forming tools. The rods themselves consisted of rolled sections to which the rod ends were electro-welded. Unlike the class 50, only the rod surfaces were machined. This made it possible to buy rods and rod ends from suppliers and only finish them at the locomotive factories.

---

[239] (Gottwaldt, 2016), page 46

Fig. 13:   Model of No. 52 241 (Gützold 32400), driver's (top) and fireman's side (bottom).
This second version of the class 52 is built in the same way as the one with the tub style tender, except that this version has a K 4T30 rigid-frame tender (for the tenders, see Chapter 6.2.1). This unit is equipped with a smokebox strut, so that the fireman can step on it for cleaning the smokebox. The model shows a photo finish that was used that time for pictures from locomotives.[240]
Information on the historical model: Floridsdorf 1942 → DRB 52 241 (RBD Posen) → 1945 SŽD TЭ-241 + ?

Smoke deflectors

The smoke deflectors were initially omitted from the ÜK-version of the engines. This was also intended for the war locomotives, as it was assumed that the visual obstruction caused by steam would not be very strong. In practice, however, this was not the case. The machine crews tried to reattach the smoke deflectors using their own designs. Witte tackled the problem and replaced the previously large deflectors with smaller pieces. Wind tunnel tests optimized the design and led to solution now often referred to as the 'Witte deflectors'.

---

[240] Since the black-and-white films of the time could not easily show the details of a dark painted locomotive, it was given a photographic finish for presentation or for company photos. This consisted of a washable white lime paint, which was washed off again after taking the photos.

The solution had two advantages: On the one hand, the staff's view of the track and signals was considerably improved, and on the other hand, the amount of material required was much less than with the original, large, so-called 'Wagner deflectors' [241] (for comparison: Wagner deflectors: approx. 1,000 kg per pair, whereas Witte deflectors: approx. 200 kg per pair). From July 1943 on, the small Witte deflectors were used for the war locomotive, according to the instructions of the Working Committee 'Construction'.[242]

Painting

As with the 50ÜK, the colour black grey (RAL 7021) was specified for the entire engine. Camouflage was ordered for machines and other rolling stock from end of 1944 on. The colours bottle green (RAL 6007), reseda green (RAL 6011), pale brown (RAL 8025), sand yellow (RAL 1002) and silver grey (RAL 7001) were used. Sometimes locomotives were lightened with lime or chalk to make them less conspicuous in winter. [243] It is not known to what extent the engines were actually camouflaged.

Fig. 14: Model of No. 52 369 (Liliput 5201), driver's side.
This model demonstrates how a possible camouflage paint scheme might have looked like. Whether this really existed is not known.
Information on the historical model: Borsig 1943 → DRB 52 369 (RBD Berlin) → 1945 SŽD T3-369 + 1945, afterwards industrial machine

---

[241] In fact, the Wagner deflectors were developed by Albert Betz, a German physicist and aerodynamicist. Thus, they should actually be called 'Betz deflectors', cf. (Hucho, 2002), pages 322f.

[242] (Gottwaldt, 2016), page 49. In addition, 2,000 pairs of wind deflectors were ordered for retrofitting in November 1943, cf. (Luckow, 2021), page 150.

[243] (Diener, 2012), pages 46ff; (Lange, 2005)

Fig. 15: Model of No. 52 3502 (Liliput 105213), driver's side.
A winter camouflage might have looked like this. The newer model (Liliput 131524) shows a different camouflage pattern.
Information on the historical model: Krauss 1943 → DRB 52 3502 (RBD Halle (Saale)) → 1945 DRo 52 3502 → 1947 SŽD TЭ-3502 → 1963 ČSD 5550257 + 1969 Veselí nad Lužnicí

Marking

The numbering was to conform to the standards of the Reichsbahn, using the 'Pointed digits' of 1938.[244] However, engines were also delivered with DIN 1460 medium and wide lettering. A national emblem (eagle) was no longer required. The machine's number, its type, the Directorate of the Reichsbahn and its home depot were painted in white on the side of the cab. From 1944 on, the short name of the home depot was written in large white letters on the smokebox door and tender.

Armouring

Although steam locomotives were easy targets for enemy low-flying aircraft during the war due to their plume, armouring was not considered. One of the reasons for this was the additional weight, as armour increased the axle load of the engine, making them unsuitable for their intended use (lines with low axle loads).

Entire armour-plated trains, which sometimes capture the imagination of the steampunk scene today, also existed during the Second World War. The Wehrmacht also had a number of armoured trains, which had evolved from former railway security trains of the Reichsbahn.[245] However, they were considered to be of little importance, first because they were tied to the railway lines, which could easily be interrupted,[246] and second because the armour made the trains very

---

[244] (Diener, 2012), page 134
[245] (Sawodny, 1996), pages 60f
[246] (Sawodny, 1996), page73

Fig. 16:   Model of No. 52 369 (Liliput 5201, modified).
To protect against low-flying attacks and shrapnel, attempts were made to protect the boiler and other vulnerable elements. This model shows a boiler protection as it was mounted on 52 1489 in 1945.[249] The existing cab armour is not reproduced. Information on the historical model: see Figure 14.

heavy, so that they could only be used on lines that had been approved for high axle loads. As a result, the Wehrmacht's armoured train force remained relatively small, with a crew of around 3,800 men.[247] The following class 52 units were used occasionally in armoured trains:[248]

- No. 52 1489 for the line protection train No. 350
- No. 52 1965 fully armoured for the armoured train No. 82 (uncertain).
- No. 52 5720 for the armoured train No. 24
- No. 52 6233 for the armoured train No. 21
- No. 52 7021 fully armoured for the tank train No. 80

Fig. 17:   Fantasy models of condensed units with regard to armour and camouflage paint..

Of all these engines, No. 52 1965 was a condensing locomotive with a 2'2'T13.5 condensation tender (see Chapter 6.2.2). No. 52 223 is also said to have had full armour, for a time, but there is no evidence of its use in front of an armoured train.

The armoured trains had special machines assigned and armoured

---

[247] (Sawodny, 1996), page 77
[248] (Sawodny, 1996), pages 179ff
[249] (Sawodny, 1996), page 189

for them. If one of these locomotives broke down or had to be serviced, an unarmoured replacement engine was requested by the Reichsbahn. Armoured replacement engines did not exist.

The engines for these trains were initially only leased from the Reichsbahn. From 1944 on, for some locomotive the note 'sold' can be traced.[250] On some units in the armoured trains, the 'Balkenkreuz' from the armoured troops was attached as a national emblem.

There were official guidelines for the armouring of armoured trains, but these were designed in such a way that there was much space for an individual design[248]. Also, as a result of the Führer's decree in early 1943 on the temporary armouring of engines,[251] armouring was mostly limited to the attachment of steel plates in front of the pumps (feedwater, air) and braking equipment (air reservoir, brake cylinder).[252]

In general, it can be said that deviations from the design of the war locomotive during production were the order of the day, especially at the start of production. This was certainly due to the rapidly changing external conditions and the availability of materials. In this situation, no one wanted to be blamed for delaying the production of the machines for whatever reason.

Due to lack of documentation it is impossible to list all details of modifications which were made during building of the machine.

---

[250] (Sawodny, 1996), page 187

[251] Cf. 'Decree of the Führer on rapid action for Flak and armour protection of railway trains', cf. (Moll, 1997), page 319. Flak = anti-aircraft gun(s).

[252] See photo report on the transfer of German railway material to the USA by the US 743rd Railroad Operating Battalion. (Cunningham, 2020), also (Clement, 2020), pages 11ff.

6.2   The new tenders

6.2.1   War tenders

As early as 1940, the Borsig company designed a lightweight tender with a tub-shaped water tank. The first four prototypes proved to be much cheaper to build than conventional box-shaped tenders. One of the reasons for this was the fact that the components were welded rather than riveted.

The idea for the construction was similar to a Vanderbilt tender, which was widespread on US- and Canadian railways. It had a cylindrical body like a tank wagon with a coal bunker set into the front end.

The company Westwaggon[253] followed up on this initial idea and delivered an experimental tender for No. 52 001, which had the bogies of a normal tank car but a tub-shaped water tank. However, it soon became apparent that although this principle worked well for a tank car, it could not easily be transferred to a tender that was closely coupled to the locomotive. So, the design had to be revised again, and the wartime engine had to be coupled to other tenders for so long, for example by fitting a standard class 50 tender with a corresponding class 52 coupler pocket and modifying the end wall of the tender accordingly.

Meanwhile, Westwaggon continued to develop and presented a tub-shaped tender with a capacity of 10 tons of coal and 34 m³ of water. However, it soon became

Tab. 9: Tender of the classes 50/50ÜK und 52[254]

Tender	Version	Water supply	Coal supply	Tare weight	Payload ratio[255]
2'2'T26	box shape	26 m³	8,0 t	25,5 t	1,3
K 2'2'T30(32)	tub shape	30 m³ (32 m³)	10,0 t	18,5 t	2,2 (2,4)
K 4T30	rigid-frame	30 m³	8,0 t	23,8 t	1,6
3'2'T16	condensing	16 m³	9,5 t	48,6 t	
2'2'T13,5	condensing	13,5 m³	9,0 t	41,6 t	

---

[253] The 'Vereinigte **West**deutschen **Waggon**fabriken' ('Westwaggon'), located in Cologne was a German manufacturer of wagons, railcars and trams.

[254] cf. (Weisbrod, 1991), pages 119ff; (Messerschmidt, 1987), page 56
Even though officially there has never been 'class 50ÜK', in the following the '50ÜK' will be referred to as class 50ÜK to distinguish it.

[255] Payload ratio is given by the sum of the amount of supplies related to the tare weight.

apparent that this tender, together with the war machines could not be turned on a 20-metre turntable.[256] It was also too heavy for a maximum axle load of 15 tons.[257] So the tender was shortened and a tub-shaped tender with 10 tons of coal and 32 m^3 of water (nominal) was obtained. With these modifications, and after a series of test runs, the tender was ready for full-scale production.[258]

The design of the tender was a technical and economic innovation, as it was both unrivalled in price and had an enormous payload capacity in relation to its tare weight. Whereas the regular class 50 tender, designated 2'2'T26 [259], could carry 1.3 times its own weight in supplies, the new tender, designated K 2'2'T30(32), tender could carry 2.2 to 2.4 times its own weight, and this despite the fact that the new tender had nearly the same weight than the regular tender when fully loaded.

It is often reported in the literature that after calibrating a tube-shaped tender, it was found that it could only hold 30 m^3 of water.[260] Whether this was really the case, or whether it was due to the fact that the filling marks had been lowered, so that the axle load stayed below 15 tons, cannot be clarified here. However, the designation K 2'2'T32 was retained for some time. With the end of the war it was changed to the correct designation K 2'2'T30. The letter 'K' stood for 'Kriegslokomotivtender' (war locomotive tender), but was dropped relatively quickly.

The innovative design of the tender did not go unnoticed by the US military. As a result, engine No. 52 3674, which was fitted with a tub-shaped tender, was taken to the USA after the war (see Chapter 10.24).

Another war tender that had been developed at the same time. It had been completed earlier and came from Henschel's company in Floridsdorf. This was a tender that had already been used on some Austrian machines – the so-called 'rigid-frame tender'. Initially it was only intended for class 50ÜK.

It had the advantage of being about two tons lighter than the box-shaped tender. This meant that it could carry more supplies (1.6 times its own weight). In addition, its manufacturing costs were 30 % lower than those of the box-shaped tender. After initial tests were satisfactory, production was transferred from Floridsdorf to Henschel's RAX-Werke[261]. The tender was given the designation K 4T30 and had an appropriate

---

[256] (Ziegler, 2012) according to a Russian source
[257] (Weisbrod, 1991), pages 47f, (Ziegler, 2009)
[258] (Stockklausner, 1950), pages 198ff
[259] Tender designation, cf. Chapter 3.2.5.
[260] (Weisbrod, et al., 2012), page 26
[261] located in Wiener Neustadt in Lower Austria

coal outlet for the 'Norwegian cab'. As the running characteristics with the tender in front were not satisfactory at higher speeds (up to 80 km/h), improvements were made, but the problem could not be solved permanently.

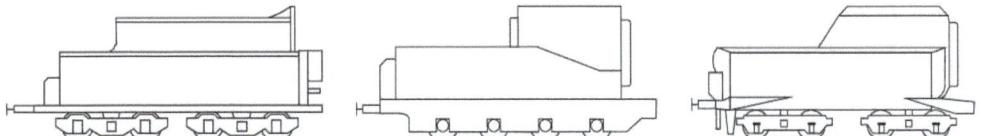

Fig. 18:   Sketches of the box-shaped (standard) tender, the rigid frame tender and the tub-shaped tender (left to right)

The class 50ÜK and 52 units were coupled to one of these three types of tender (standard, tub shape and rigid frame) as far as the connection between the cab and the front of the tender allowed it. Both during and after the war, tenders were changed if either the locomotive or the tender was broken, so it was not obvious for engine and tender to remain together for their entire service life.

6.2.2   Condensation tenders

As the German troops advanced into the southern part of the Soviet Union, they came across condensing locomotives of the Soviet series COк (SOк). These were units designed for the water-scarce lines there, and their exhaust steam was recovered. This was done in an air-cooled condensing unit in the tender, which allowed to recover up to 90 % of the water from the exhaust steam, significantly increasing the engine's range without water supply. The condensing unit was powered by the energy of the exhaust steam, so that the machine's tractive power was not altered. The condensate produced was returned to the boiler, where it significantly reduced the formation of boiler scale. In addition, the condensate had a temperature of almost 100 °C, which ensured optimum feedwater preheating and thus saving energy.

The system was developed at Henschel in the 1930s and was very successful.[262] It was supplied to South Africa, Argentina, Rhodesia and Iraq. In 1933, the Soviet Railways had the engine Эr 5224 (Ég 5224) converted to a condensing locomotive at the Henschel factory in Kassel. As Эrк 5224 (Égk 5224) it was brought back to service. It

---

[262] see also (Zander, 2012)

was the first powerful condensing engine in the USSR[263] and the blue-print for its USSR's own locomotive conversion program.[264]

The remarkable thing about this story is that condensing locomotives had been supplied by Henschel for almost a decade, and in 1939 Henschel had already offered a first design of a condensing locomotive based on class 50.[266] Until then little was known about these engines in Germany(!). The army administration quickly realised that these machines could play an important strategic role in the arid region of the

Fig. 19:   Model of No. 52 1911 (Märklin 34171), driver's (top) and fireman's side (bottom).
In addition to the boiler type class 52, an ID fan is installed in front of the chimney, which leads the exhaust steam through a pipe on the fireman's side via an oil separator to the condensation tender. The exhaust steam from the feedwater pump, the air pump, the generator and the safety valve also enter this pipe. The exhaust steam is condensed on both tender sides by six condensation elements each. The condensate is collected in a collection box in the tender. From there it is pumped directly back into the boiler by means of two pumps with a capacity of 290 l/min each.[265] In this version, the machine has Witte deflectors and a strut with two steps in front of the smokebox for easier maintenance of the smokebox and the ID fan. Information on the historical model: Henschel 1943 → DRB 52 1911 (RBD Berlin) → 1945 PKP Ty2-2 + 1987 Małaszewicze

[263] (Rakow, 1986), pages 196f
[264] (Gottwaldt, 2001)
[265] (Peters, 2005), also see (Henschel & Sohn GmbH, 1944)
[266] (Peters, 2005)

southern Soviet Union. Other alternatives discussed were the use of diesel units or the transport of additional water wagons.

In the end, the army command decided to order 240 condensing locomotives based on class 50ÜK. This initially met with resistance from the head of the Steering Committee, Degenkolb. He opposed any special design of war engines and feared that such a complex unit would jeopardise his mass production campaign. A few weeks later, however, a high representative of the Ministry of Transport met with the head of transport, Gercke, who demanded that the 240 condensing locomotives should be built as quickly as possible. A few days later, Henschel received the order. However, Henschel plans from 1939 could not simply be adopted, as they were primarily aimed at using condensing technology to avoid smoke plumes. With this order, however, the engines were used in the continental climate of the Soviet Union, which meant that not only the simplifications of the wartime design had to be considered, but also a pronounced frost protection. Accordingly, class 52 units with bar frames were therefore seen as the quickest option to realize the army orders.

With the decision to produce condensing locomotives, a new committee was set up, the working committee for 'Condensing Locomotives'. In addition to representatives of the company Henschel and the Reichsbahn, it included representatives of the main suppliers (Waggonfabrik Uerdingen (condensation tender), GEA-Luftkühlergesellschaft[267] (condensation unit)).

Work progressed rapidly and the first engine, No. 52 1850, was delivered to the Reichsbahn in February 1943. The water savings achieved were extraordinary, as the condensation device enabled the machine to travel up to 1,000 km without taking on water. This extraordinary performance led to the engine nicknam 'The Camel' by the US Railway troops after the war.[268]

As the locomotive factories were working at full capacity to build the class 52, the production of individual parts for the condensing locomotive were transferred to the Uerdingen and the Fuchs Wagonfabrik. Final assembly was carried out at the Henschel plant in Kassel. Due to the war, the turbines for the blowers could no longer being manufactured in Switzerland and the production was transferred to the French turbine company 'Société Rateau' in La Courneuve near Paris.[269]

As the weight of the tender should not to exceed 15 tons per axle, five axles were

---

[267] GEA = **G**esellschaft für **E**ntstaubungs-**A**nlagen (Company for dedusting systems)
[268] (Moroz, 1945)
[269] (Matthäus, 2004)

provided for the tender, which led to the condensation tender 5T16Ko.[270] This unofficial designation was soon changed to the official version 3'2'T16.

When going reverse with the engine the visibility was extremely poor due to the extra-long tender. So, the engines had to be turned on triangular junctions. Henschel later supplied special rear-view niches that could be fitted to the cab to improve visibility. These were designed to fit the wider Soviet loading gauge.[271]

Due to the later worsening shortage of materials (esp. copper for the radiators) and

Fig. 20:   Model of No. 52 2006 (Gützold G23), driver's (above) and fireman's side (bottom). A model of a condensing locomotive with a shortened tender. The number of condensers has been reduced to five elements each the same construction. The spoked leading wheels were not true to the original, as it carried disc wheels in front. The same applies to the three-light headlights, which were introduced to German railways after scrapping of the original.[272] Information on the historical model: Henschel 1944 → DRB 52 2006 (RBD Berlin) → 1945 USATC[273] L52 2006 + 1952 Fort Eustis/USA

---

[270] (Stockklausner, 1950), pages 199f

[271] (Luckow, 2021), page 155

[272] In Germany it was common that the vehicle at the head of the train had only two white lights. When traffic by car increased the three-light signal was introduced. This was done by the Reichsbahn of East-Germany in 1956 (Gesetzblatt der Deutschen Demokratischen Republik, 1956) and by the Deutsche Bundesbahn of West-Germany in 1957 (Bundesgesetzblatt, 1957), with corresponding transition periods in each case.

[273] USATC = **U**nited **S**tates **A**rmy **T**ransportation **C**orps

the extensive withdrawal from the USSR, one radiator panel was omitted and the four-axle condensation tender 4T13.5 (officially: 2'2'T13.5) was built. This was possible as the tenders were no longer used for water recovery but to prevent a smoke plume. The water capacity was reduced from 16 to 13.5 m³, the coal supply was slightly reduced by 0.5 tons. At the same time the material requirement was reduced by 9 tons.

The axle base was reduced to allow the engine to turn on 23 metre turntables, which was advantageous as the condensing locomotives could not run with the tender in front. However, the axle load of the tender increased to 16 tons when fully loaded, which was not a problem after their withdrawal from the Soviet Union and operation in Central and Western Europe.

The design of the condensing locomotives was fully developed, thanks to Henschel's many years of experience in this field. Nevertheless, changes were made during production as a result of the war.

Due to bomb damage, a supplier of blinds failed in February 1944 and the tender was fitted with a wide-meshed wire mesh (No. 52 1961-52 1970). This meant that it was no longer possible to close the tender with the blinds for frost protection, but this wasn't so bad as the original areas for use in the USSR had already been lost.[274]

In May 1944 there was a shortage of condensers at the company GEA, so some five-axle tenders were fitted with only ten condensers instead of twelve. The empty spaces were filled with metal sheets.

The condensing locomotives were built until the end of the war, even though the arid regions had long since been lost. This had to do with the fact that these engines had no smoke plume, which made them difficult to spot by enemy aircraft. To disrupt German supplies, Allied aircrafts in Western Europe favoured firing on steam machines, which were easy to spot. To maintain the supply, the Wehrmacht ordered a number of units to western Europe.

Like the normal class 52, the condensing locomotives were delivered in black grey (RAL 7021). Some also had white stripes on the running boards. The Wehrmacht also painted some engines in camouflage colours and patterns, and some were white-washed with chalk to make them more suitable for winter service.

---

[274] (Matthäus, 2004)

A total of 178 units were modified and fitted with a condensation tender:[275]

Tender 3'2'T16:	No. 52 1850-52 1986	137 engines
Tender 2'2'T13,5:	No. 52 1987-52 2027	41 engines

The last machines with condensation tenders (2'2'T13,5) were delivered in 1947 to the 'Oberbetriebsleitung United States Zone'[52] (UBL USZ) (No. 52 2026) and No. 52 2027 to the 'Hauptverwaltung der Eisenbahnen des amerikanischen und britischen Besatzungsgebiets'[52] (HVE), respectively.

---

[275] (Peters, 2005)

7 Mass production

7.1 Interrelations

Before we take a closer look at the mass production of class 52, a few things should be said about the involved locomotive companies of that time and their interrelations. After coming to power, and especially after the start of the war, the Nazis tried to gain influence over German industry or rather to expand its influence. In some cases, they found compliant supporters, in others there were managers with 'common interests'[276], in others they had to infiltrate existing structures to install managers loyal to the regime. The aim was to involve industry in rearmament and war preparations.

As a result of rearmament, government spending in armaments increased sharply. While in 1933 armaments accounted for 3 % of the national income, by 1939 it had risen to over 20 % of national income.[277] This had a particular impact on the Reich's currency reserves. The gold and foreign exchange reserves, which had already shrunk considerably due to the economic crisis, fell by more than 80 % between 1933 and 1935 (i.e. gold and foreign exchange reserves of the Reichsbank in 1928: 2,405 M RM, in 1933: 530 M RM, in 1937: about 7 M RM)[278]. Throughout the whole time of the Nazi regime, more money was spent than was earned. This permanent underfunding of the national budget and the Nazis' plans continued throughout their regime. Besides of their racial ideology, the financial situation was certainly a driver for the subsequent progroms and plundering of the Jewish population, as well as for the brutal policy of exploitation of the conquered future 'Lebensraum' in Poland and the Soviet Union.

In 1936, Hitler called for the creation of the capability of an economic and military war within four years. This should be achieved through economical autarchy (i.e. reducing foreign-exchange-consuming imports) and increased rearmament. A four-year plan was drawn up to achieve this goal.

One of the steps towards economical autarky was the exploitation of the iron ore deposits near Salzgitter, which were difficult to smelt due to the relatively low iron

---

[276] Rearmament was economically interesting and very profitable for large sections of the German industry. The 'Aryanization' of Jewish competitors (i.e. the total expropriation of Jewish property, which was usually staged as a proper 'sale') could be used to improve one's own market position.

[277] (Eichholtz, 1999), pages 14f

[278] (Forstmeier, et al., 1981), page 85

content and the chemical composition of the ore. In 1937, the 'Reichswerke Hermann Göring' (RHG) were set up as a state-owned company with the help of US specialists to start exploiting the deposits. Steel production soon proved to be unprofitable, but it allowed the Nazis to exert economic pressure on the business leaders of the Ruhr. As early as 1938, after the annexation of Austria, the Reichswerke were able to take over the ÖAMG[279], which in turn owned shares in the GKB company (see Ch 10.1.1). After the annexation of Czechoslovakia, Škoda and 'Československá zbrojovka Brno' (renamed to 'Erste Brünner Maschinen-Fabriks-Gesellschaft') were merged into the Reichswerke. The 'Československá zbrojovka' in turn held shares in the Reşiţa locomotive company in Romania (see Chapter 10.18).

After the Polish campaign, the Reichswerke got the control of the Upper Silesian heavy industry, which had previously been partly owned by the Polish state.[280] It took over shares from 'Wielkich Pieców i Zakładów Ostrowieckich', which brought the Warsaw locomotive company under the control of the Reichswerke.[281]

In Romania, the company 'Rogifer' was set up together with the pro-German industrialist Nicolae Malaxa, which temporarily brought the Malaxa locomotive company under RHG control (see Chapter 10.18).[282]

In 1942, the locomotive company SACM in Graffenstaden near Strasbourg became a branch of the 'Magdeburger Werkzeugmaschinenfabrik'[283], which in turn had been part of the 'Junkers Flugzeug- und Motorenwerke' since 1935. After the expropriation without compensation of its founder, aviation pioneer Hugo Junkers, in 1933 the company had been owned by the Reich Ministry for Aviation, again headed by Göring.

After the annexation of Austria, Henschel secured a majority of the financially unstable Austrian locomotive company 'Wiener Lokomotivfabrik in Floridsdorf'.[284] One of the Floridsdorf branches, the 'Aktiengesellschaft der Lokomotiv-Fabrik vormals G. Sigl', had been closed in 1930. This factory was reopened after the Henschel takeover and renamed them RAX-Werke GmbH. From 1942, Henschel started to produce tenders and armaments there. In order to make the RAX-Werke quickly profitable, the rigid-frame tender (K 4T30) developed in Floridsdorf was transferred to RAX and

---

[279] The ÖAMG (**Ö**sterreichisch-**A**lpine **M**ontangesellschaft (Austrian-Alpine Montan Company) was a public company, that combined ore mines, metallurgical plants and the steel industry in Austria.
[280] (Bähr, et al., 2008), page 406
[281] (Wysoki, 1992), pages 30f
[282] (Lacriţeanu, et al., 2007), page 482
[283] (Gieseler05)
[284] (Gieseler07)

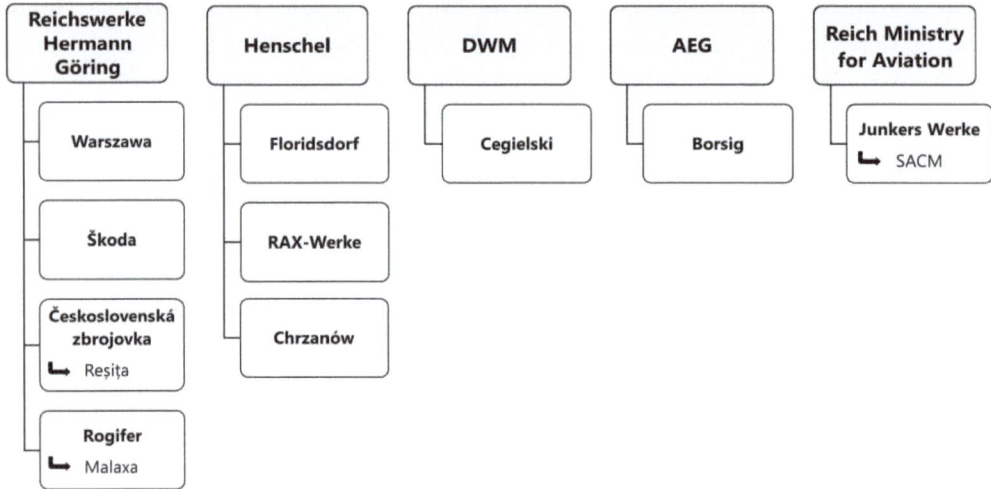

Fig. 21: Overview of direct, indirect, temporary or in trust holdings of companies[56] that were relevant for the production of class 50 and 52 before and during the Second World War.[286]

produced there.[285]

After the occupation of Poland, the Chrzanów locomotive works came under German administration. In 1941 it became the 'Oberschlesische Lokomotivwerke AG Kattowitz, Werk Krenau'. The main shareholder was the Henschel company and the minority shareholder was the Ferrum company, which belonged to the Ballestrem group (cf. Chapter 10.17.1).[287]

At the same time, the locomotive factory Cegielski was incorporated into the DWM group as 'DWM - Deutsche Waffen- und Munitionsfabriken A.G. – Werk Posen'. DWM was in turn owned by the Quandt family.[288]

The economic situation of Borsig in the late 1920s/early 1930s was difficult. In 1931, AEG bought the locomotive production from the struggling company and merged it with its own engine production to form the 'Borsig-Lokomotivwerke GmbH'. The remaining parts of the company were taken over by Rheinmetall.[289] Rheinmetall in turn was again part of the Reichswerke.[290]

---

[285] (Gieseler08)
[286] For sources see current text
[287] (Gieseler09), (Gieseler01)
[288] (Gieseler04)
[289] (Gieseler02)
[290] (Wikipedia007)

7.2   Subcontracting of components

Mass production was organised under the direction of the Steering Committee for Railway Vehicles. To support the production, steel quotas for the Reichsbahn were significantly increased from 1942 on.[291] With these increased quotas it was possible to implement the plans of building a war locomotive in large numbers. During 1943, however, the quotas were reduced as Hitler announced to double the production of tanks just one year after announcing to start a war engine production programme.[292] It soon became apparent that the locomotive factories did not have the capacity to produce the required quantities of machines at all, especially as some of them also produced other armaments. In order to achieve the high output numbers, individual components were outsourced to subcontractors, thus extending the factories' capacities and reducing the range of manufacture. The degree of outsourcing increased as the war progressed (cf. Figure 22). That is astonishing because, towards the end of the war, Allied air raids destroyed more and more German infrastructure and transport from the subcontractor to the locomotive factories became more and more difficult.

The use of subcontractors for the boiler production varied. Chrzanów in Poland, for example, was completely dependent on its supplier, Ferrum, as Chrzanów had no boiler production of its own (cf. Figures 23 and 24). Most of the boilers were bought

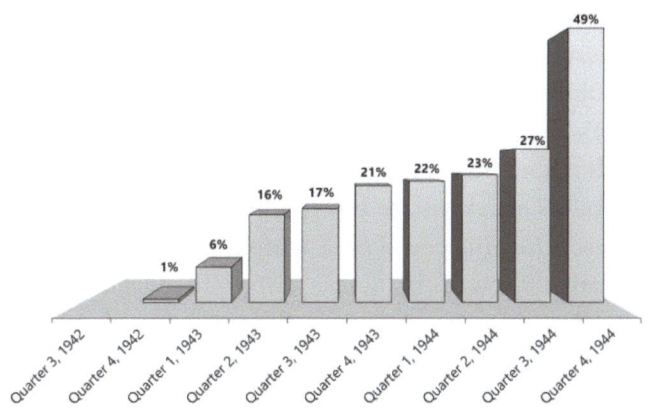

Fig. 22:   Share of boilers subcontracted for class 52 during the war[293]

---

[291] (Gottwaldt, 2016), page 65

[292] (Scheibinger, 2012), page 42

[293] (Hütter, 2012), pages 160ff, evaluation on basis of 4,829 boilers for class 52 engines.

from 'Dampfkessel- & Maschinenbau AG, W. Fitzner & C. Gamper' in Sosnowiec,[294] which was managed during the war by the Ferrum AG in Katowice.[295]

The company Jung, on the other hand, did not have the capacity to supply the required quantities of boilers due to its production portfolio and therefore purchased boilers from regional sources. Krauss and Cegielski also had to keep their capacities available for other armaments activities.

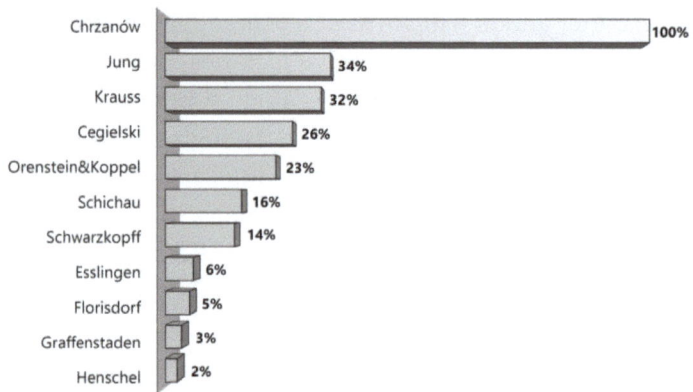

Fig. 23:   Subcontracting ratios of the individual factories for boilers[293]

Škoda and Borsig had sufficient capacity of their own and did not need subcontractors. In addition, Borsig was temporarily a shareholder of Fitzner & Gamper and therefore had the best contacts.[295]

For the supply of boilers there was no masterplan, as suppliers were allocated regionally to keep delivery distances short. Everyone tried to source from subcontractors they knew and with whom they had good contacts and relationships. It is also noticeable that some suppliers acted both as buyer and subcontractor of boilers (e.g. Kraus, Esslingen). The reason for this could be a temporary over or under capacity at the supplier's boiler plant.

Figure 24 gives an idea of the boiler supply flows for the production of the class 52. Pure suppliers are highlighted in white, locomotive plants in black. Delivery quantities are indicated by the thickness of the arrows. The flow of goods begins at the top or bottom of a box and ends at the sides of a box.

Although the Steering Committee for Railway Vehicles exercised strict control over

[294] (Wikipedia008)
[295] (Wikipedia009)

the industry and monitored the supply of raw materials, the company managers remained free to choose the means and routes within their area of responsibility. This allowed supply routes to develop that were individual to each of the suppliers involved.

In many cases, the tenders were also subcontracted. The suppliers were not always located near the delivery works, but often in the west of the Reich. The rigid-frame tender was only manufactured by the RAX-Werke.

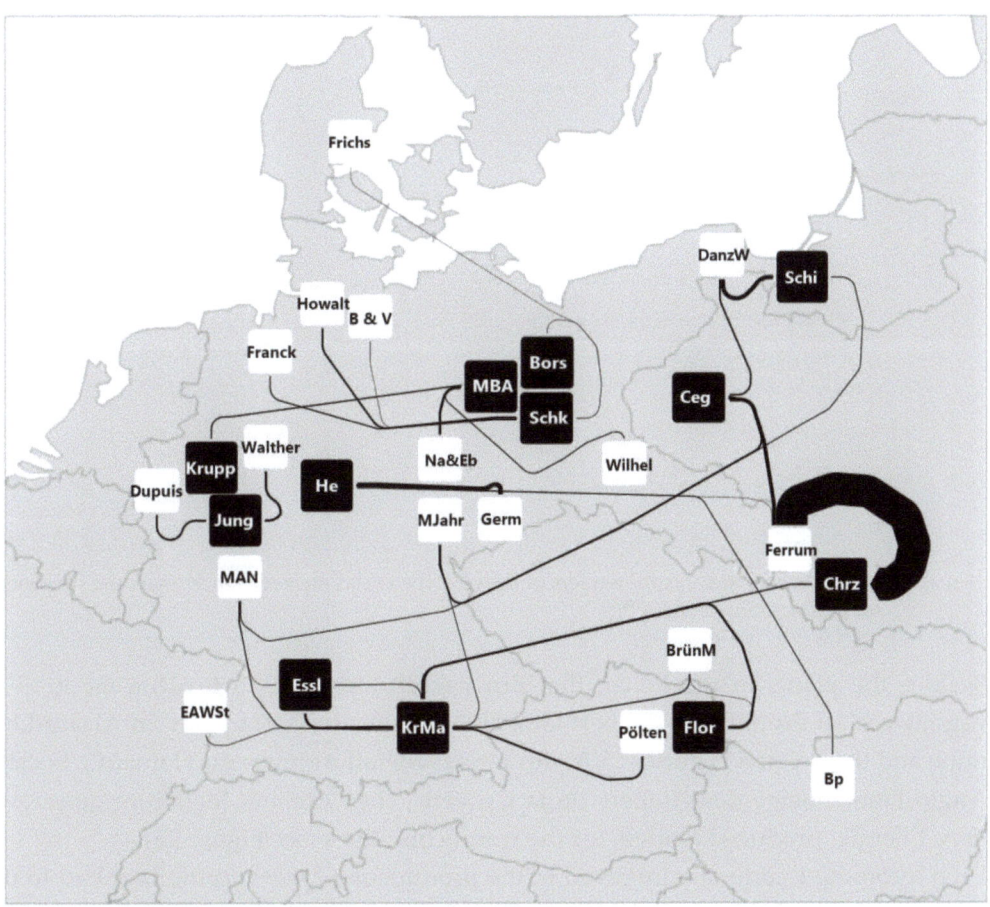

Fig. 24: Material flows for boiler subcontracting for class 52 until 1945 for quantities of more than four items.[293] For the suppliers' abbreviations, cf. Annexes 'Locomotive works', 'Boiler suppliers for war locomotive production'.

Fig. 25:   Verified subcontractors for tenders of class 52. The circles marked with 'K' mark the suppliers for condensation tenders.[296]

Besides the plants in the Reich, the 'Brněnsko-Královopolská továrna na stroje a vagony a.s.' in Brno, the 'B. Seibert GmbH, Maizières-lès-Metz plant' in Alsace-Lorraine and the Belgian factories 'S.A. des Usines Métallurgiques du Hainaut', 'Société Anglo-Franco-Belge des Ateliers de la Croyère', 'Les Ateliers Métallurgiques' and 'S.A. Énergie' produced tenders for the war locomotives (see Figure 25).

Each locomotive company involved in the production of war locomotives had to inspect and finally approve their engines by a Reichsbahn railway workshop. For this

[296] cf. (Weisbrod, et al., 2012), pages 52f; (Gieseler09); for Belgium: (Dambly, 1994), page 268

purpose, the locomotive factories were assigned to the appropriate workshops, which carried out the inspections (see Figure 26). After final inspection the machines were directly transferred to their first home depot. With the allocation of workshops to companies, care was taken to ensure that both were located close to each other.

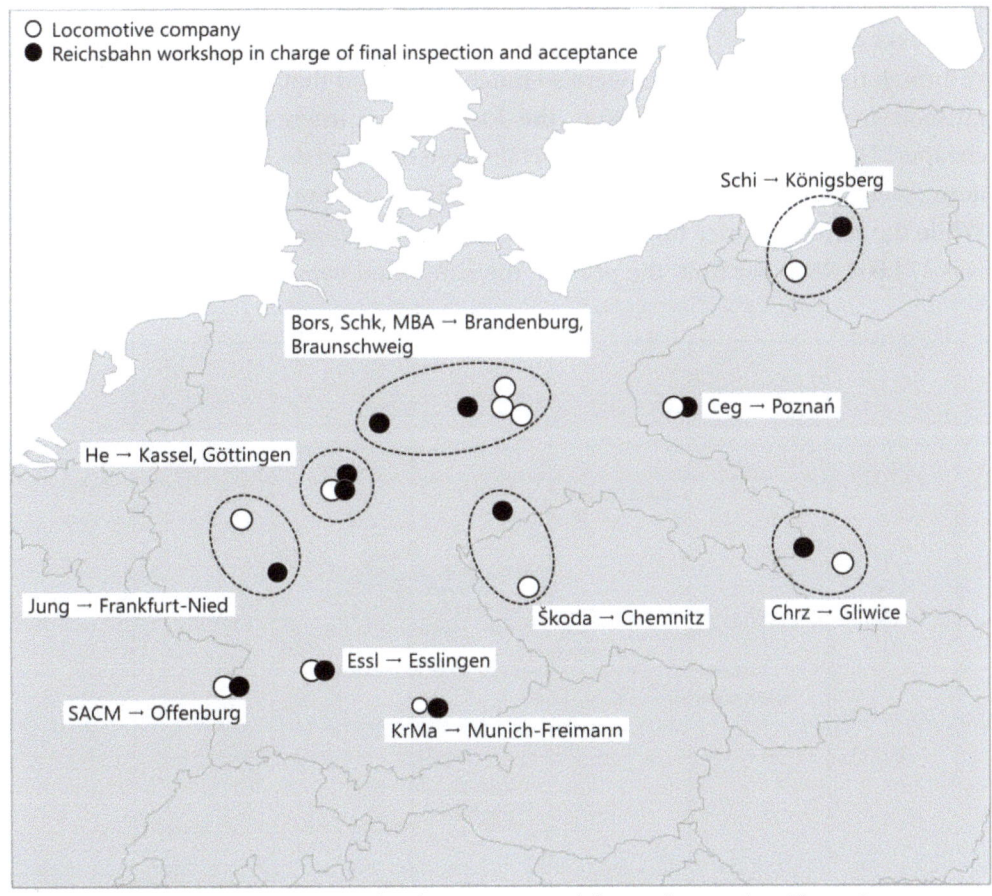

Fig. 26: Assigned railway workshops for the acceptance of the war locomotives. The assignment was sometimes temporarily changed.[297]

[297] (Weisbrod, et al., 2012), page 22

7.3   Settlement

For the procurement of the planned 15,000 units a system of fixed-prices was implemented, with three price ranges:[298]

- Group price I: No taxes should be paid on this lowest price.
- Group price II: Standard price
- Group price III: Higher price for special production. (However, this price was never applied.)

Although the class 50 engines were so much simplified that they could not be distinguished from a class 52 machine, the locomotives interestingly did not become cheaper. This even though valuable metals were replaced and the number of working hours were reduced also the labour costs fell due to the employment of forced labour. While the purchase price for the first batch of twelve Henschel locomotives (class 50) was 174,000 RM[11] per unit, the price of the simplified version (ÜK[223]-version) rose to

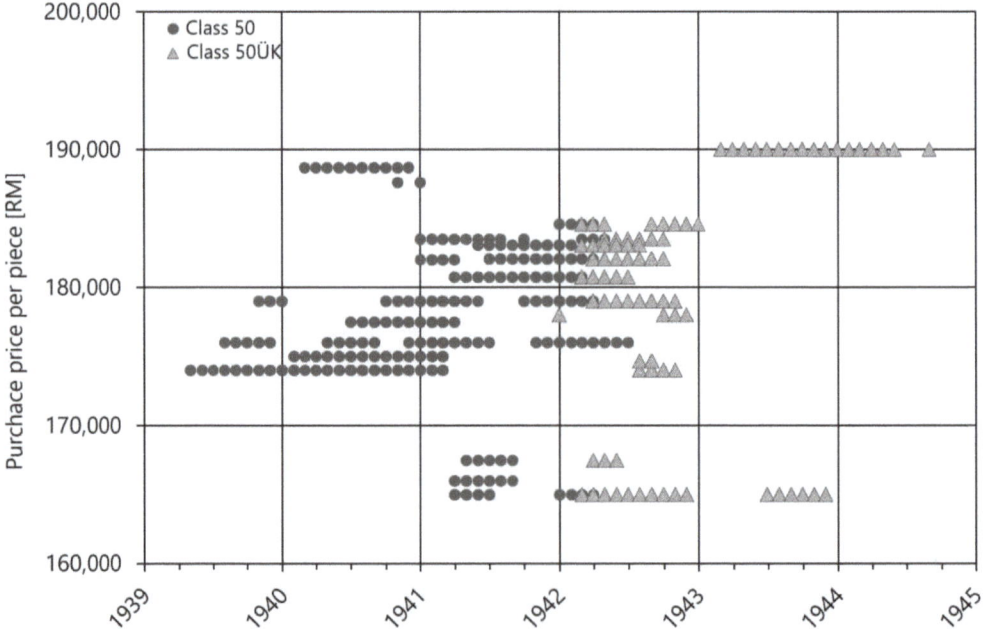

Fig. 27:   Purchase prices of individual locomotive lots of class class 50 and class 50ÜK[299]

[298] (Gottwaldt, 2016), page 66
[299] (Ebel, et al., 1988), pages 106f

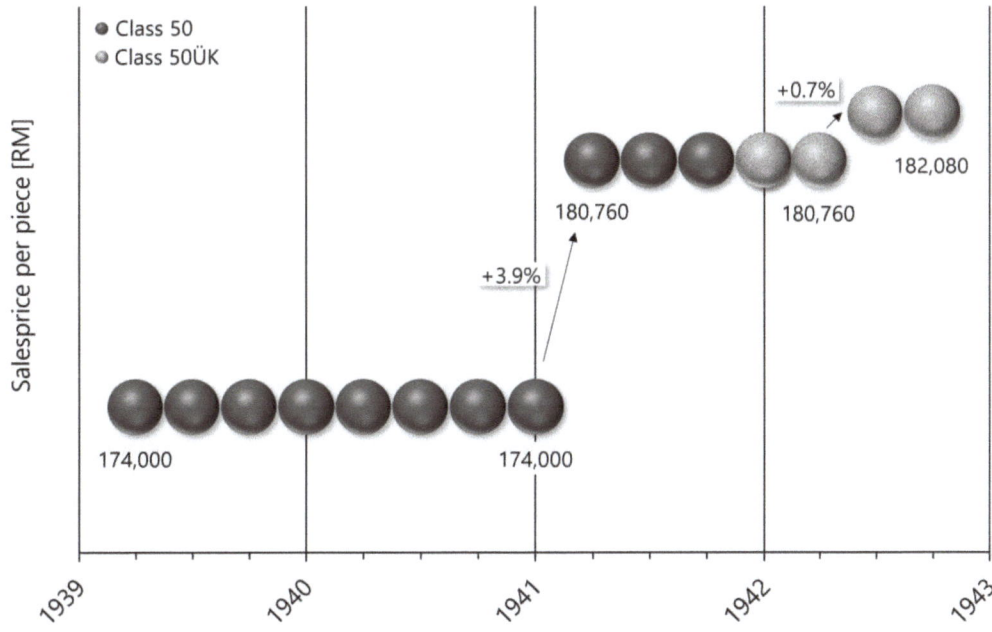

Fig. 28:   Average sales prices of Henschel & Sohn in Kassel for class 50 and class 50ÜK locomotives
(from 1943 on Henschel only manufactured class 52)[299]

190,000 RM per unit by the end of the war, despite the above mentioned factors that should reduce the price.[300] At today's spending power (2021), the amount of 190.000 RM corresponds to around 750,000 € per unit.[301] For class 52, on the other hand, the price was considerably lower, at around 90,000 RM per unit.[298]

As class 50/50ÜK were not subject to above price table, different prices could be set for them depending on the manufacturing company. However, it is unclear why a class 50ÜK, which after a number of simplifications was practically the same as a class 52, was priced differently. The Reichsbahn, which ultimately had no influence on the purchase prices of war locomotives, suspected that the manufacturers were acting in their own "*capitalist interests*"[298].

---

[300] This price seems also be valid for the company Hainaut (Gieseler06)
[301] (Deutsche Bundesbank)

7.4 The production numbers

As already mentioned, the transition from class 50 to 50ÜK and finally to class 52 was fluid, as the basic design of the locomotive had not changed over the years. Also, the assignment to the different classes (50, 52) was non-specific as there were class 50 engines (i.e. 50ÜK) that looked like class 52 engines. While production of the peacetime version (class 50) was discontinued in 1942 in favour of the class 50ÜK, it was already been replaced by the overwhelming production output of class 52. The production of class 52 continued even after the war. In the mid-1950s, class 50 was revived when it was copied in Romania.

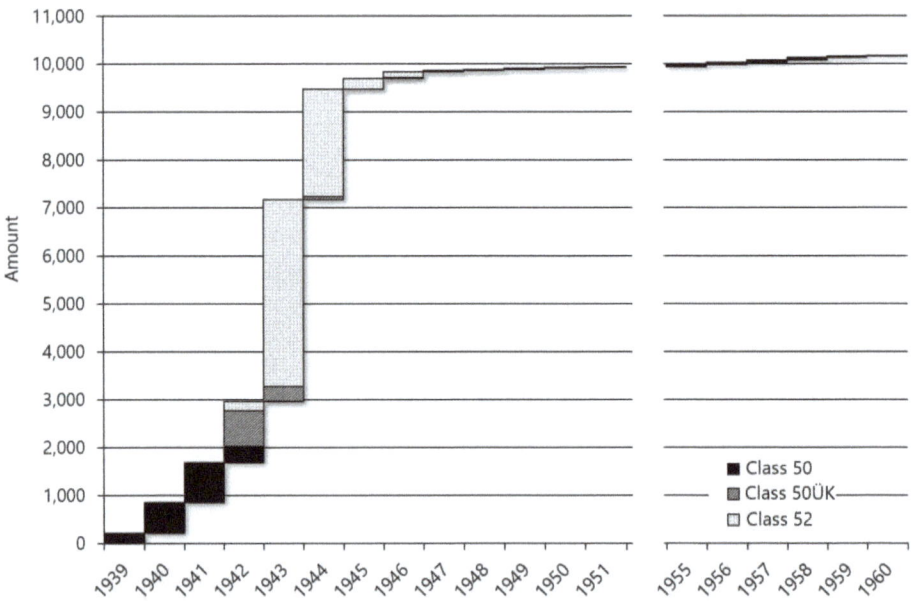

Fig. 29:   Produced units of classes 50/50ÜK and 52 over time.

For all classes combined, production reached 1,000 engines in 1941, over 5,000 by the end of 1943, and the 10,000 mark in the 1950s.

As far as production quotas were concerned, it was not possible to keep the planned output figures. On one hand, there were priorities in favour of tank production, and on the other, there were problems at Borsig and Krauss due to the destruction of their factories by Allied air raids. Krupp itself did not produce any war locomotives at all, as the destruction caused by the air raids were severe and the focus of the plants was on the producing tanks.

Table 10 gives an overview of all the units delivered. Of all the class 50/52 machines, Henschel had the largest production share with 1,990 units. Including the group's subsidiaries in Floridsdorf and Chrzanów, the Henschel group produced about 4,000 units.

By the end of 1944, 2,054 class 50 locomotives, 1,090 class 50ÜK engine, 6,163 class 52 units and 168 engines with condensation tender had been built. In total, 9,475 machines were built between 1939 and end of 1944. With the exception of about 2 % of the machines, the Reichsbahn put all of them into service. The rest went to countries that were considered to be friendly or were allied with Nazi-Germany. Some went to countries that Nazi-Germany wanted to bring into its sphere of influence.

The year of the highest production output was 1943. The majority of the class 50ÜK engines produced in that year were certainly very similar in design to the war locomotives, so that the differences were essentially only of a designation nature. The following year also saw very high production figures, although the Allied bombing had a noticeable effect. Even

Tab. 10: Actual production quantities by manufacturer

Manufacturer[56]	Class 50	Class 50ÜK	Class 52	Total
Henschel	470	175	1,345	1,990
Floridsdorf	305	63	1,192	1,560
Schwartzkopff	281	89	826	1,196
Schichau	135		595	730
Krauss	153	164	312	629
Orenstein&Koppel	55	115	423	593
Cegielski	30	42	448	520
Chrzanów			439	439
Borsig	154	25	177	356
Esslingen	13	56	281	350
Jung	62	43	243	348
Krupp	298	26		324
Škoda	77	63	169	309
Reşiţa	261			261
Graffenstaden			167	167
Cockerill		42	25	67
Tubize		38	25	63
Haine		28	25	53
Anglo-Franco-Belge		26	25	51
ČKD	17	18		35
Malaxa	31			31
Warszawa	4	26		30
Meuse		26		26
Hainaut		24		24
Énergie		16		16
Total	2,346	1,105	6,717	10,168

after liberation and the withdrawal of the German troops, the production of war locomotives continued in France, Belgium and Poland, mainly from parts of warehouses left behind.

In the 1950s, the Romanian locomotive factories Malaxa and Reşiţa started to rebuild class 50 locomotives. This production was based on a licence acquired by the Malaxa works in 1942.[302] By the 1960s, the company had built more than 200 units of class 50. For the total number of produced engines, here the calculation in detail:

Class 50/50ÜK:

Highest road number on the German railways: 50 3164, including	
4 machines directly commissioned by PKP and	
14 machines directly bought by SNCB/NMBS[52]	3,164 pieces
+ highest number assigned by the CFR for machines produced in Romania: 150.282	+282 pieces
+ engines delivered from Romania to China (CR)	+10 pieces
- minus the engines 50 2773-50 2777 which were re-designated to 52 002-52 006	-5 pieces
Subtotal class 50/50ÜK	3,451 pieces

Class 52:

Highest road number on the German railways: 52 7792	7.792 pieces
- minus 1,320 numbers, which were not used (893-1097, 1766-1795, 1819-1849, 2029-2089, 2894-3099, 3332-3349, 3624, 3638-3639, 3762-3763, 3768, 3888-3891, 3907-3912, 3926-3937, 3944-3949, 3962, 3964-3980, 4018-4044, 4050-4359, 4376, 4421-4499, 4646, 4651-4749, 4967-4975, 6440-6624, 7528-7534),	-1,320 pieces
including: 10 machines directly commissioned by CFL[52], 40 machines bought by CFR, 80 machines directly acquired by DB, 6 machines directly procured for EdS, 5 machines directly purchased by HDŽ, 149 machines directly bought by PKP and 17 machines directly procured by SNCF.	
In addition:	
+ engines directly delivered to CFR	+100 pieces
+ engines directly delivered to HDŽ	+19 pieces
+ engines directly delivered to PKP	+1 pieces
+ engines directly delivered to SDŽ	+15 pieces
+ engines directly delivered to SNCB/NMBS	+100 pieces
+ engines directly delivered to TCDD	+10 pieces
Subtotal class 52	6,717 pieces
Total classes 50/50ÜK + 52	10,168 pieces

Broken down by manufacturer over time, in descending order of delivery quantity (class 50: black, class 50ÜK: hatched, class 52: speckled):[56]

---

[302] (Lacriţeanu, et al., 2007), page 482

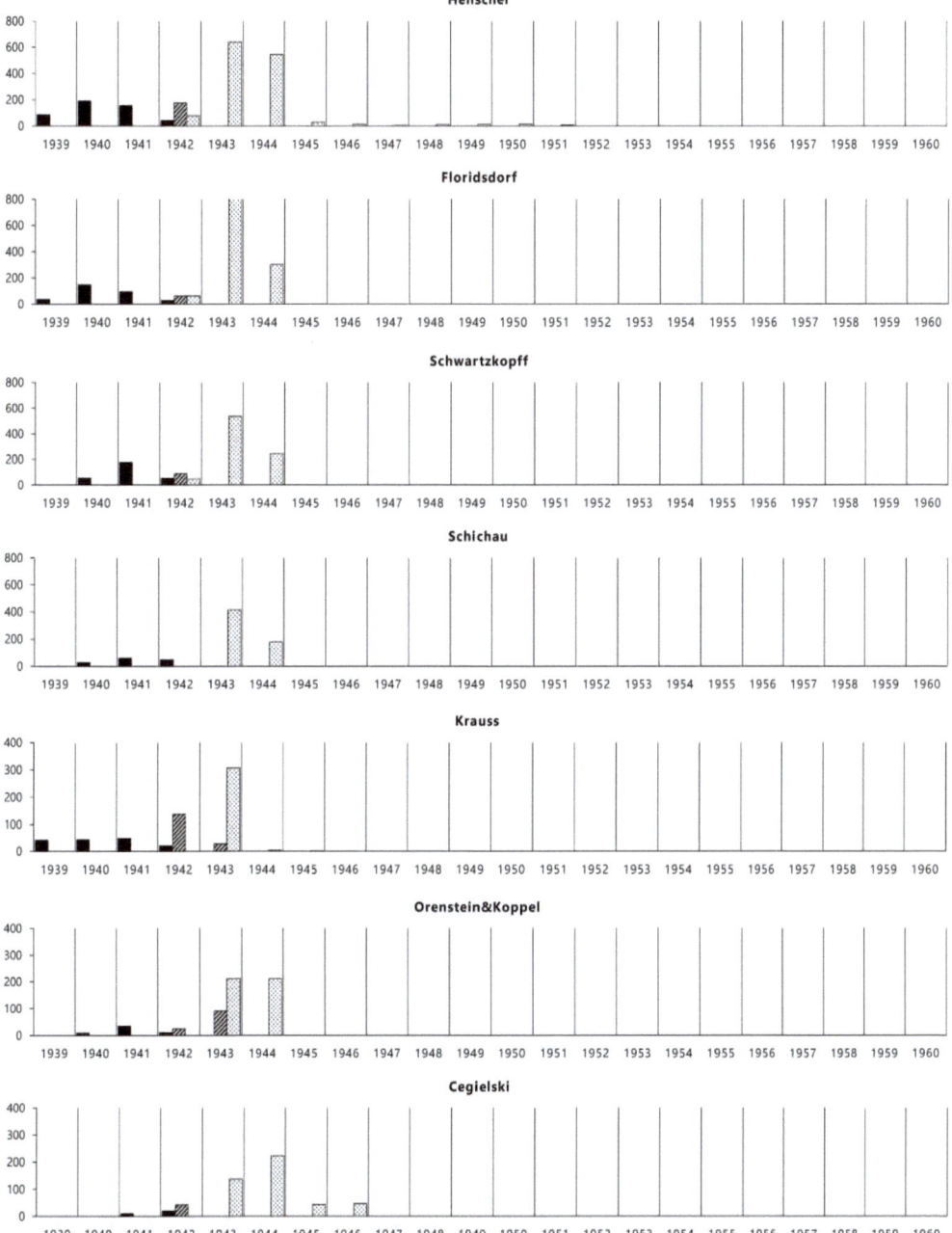

101

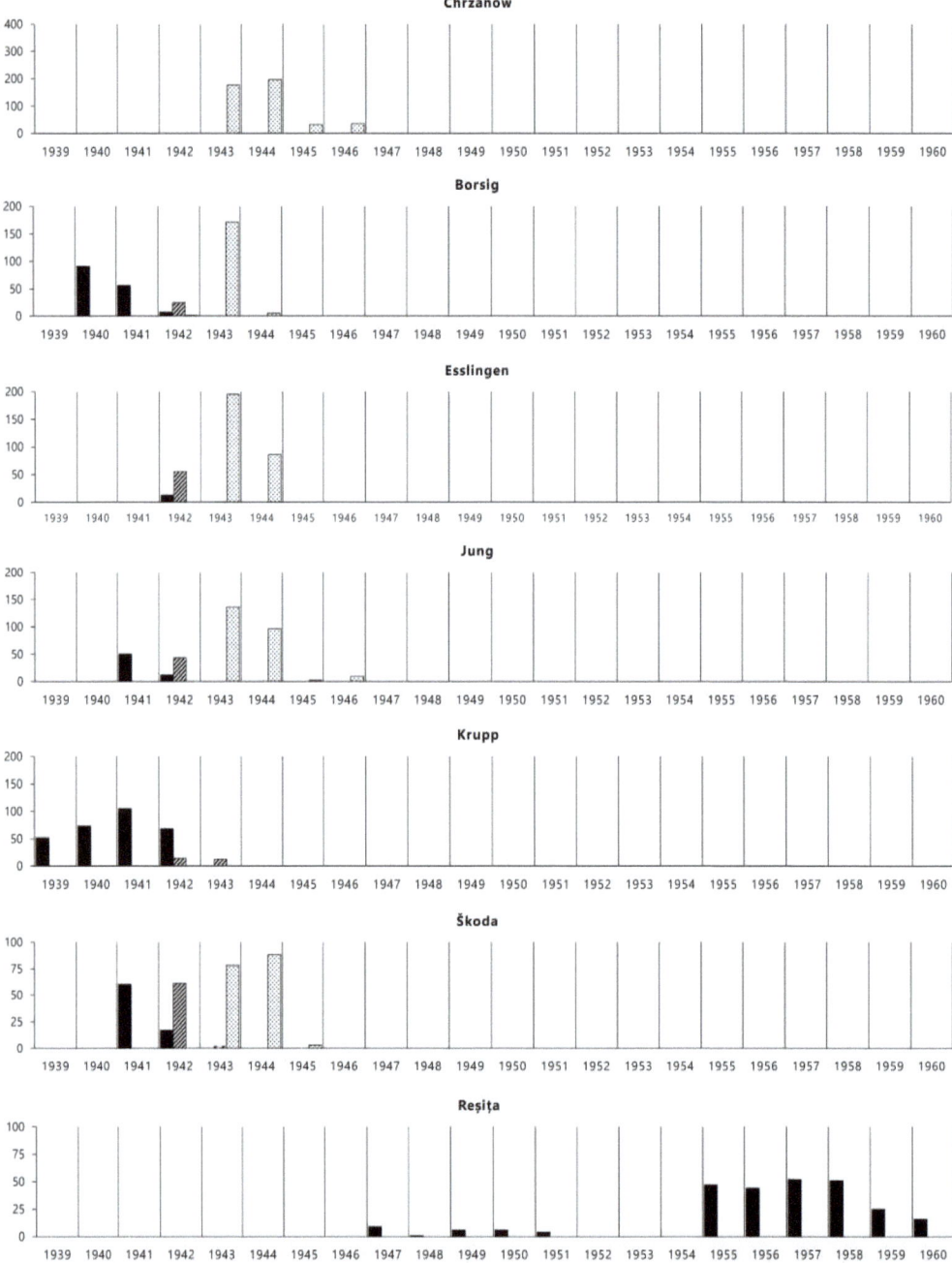

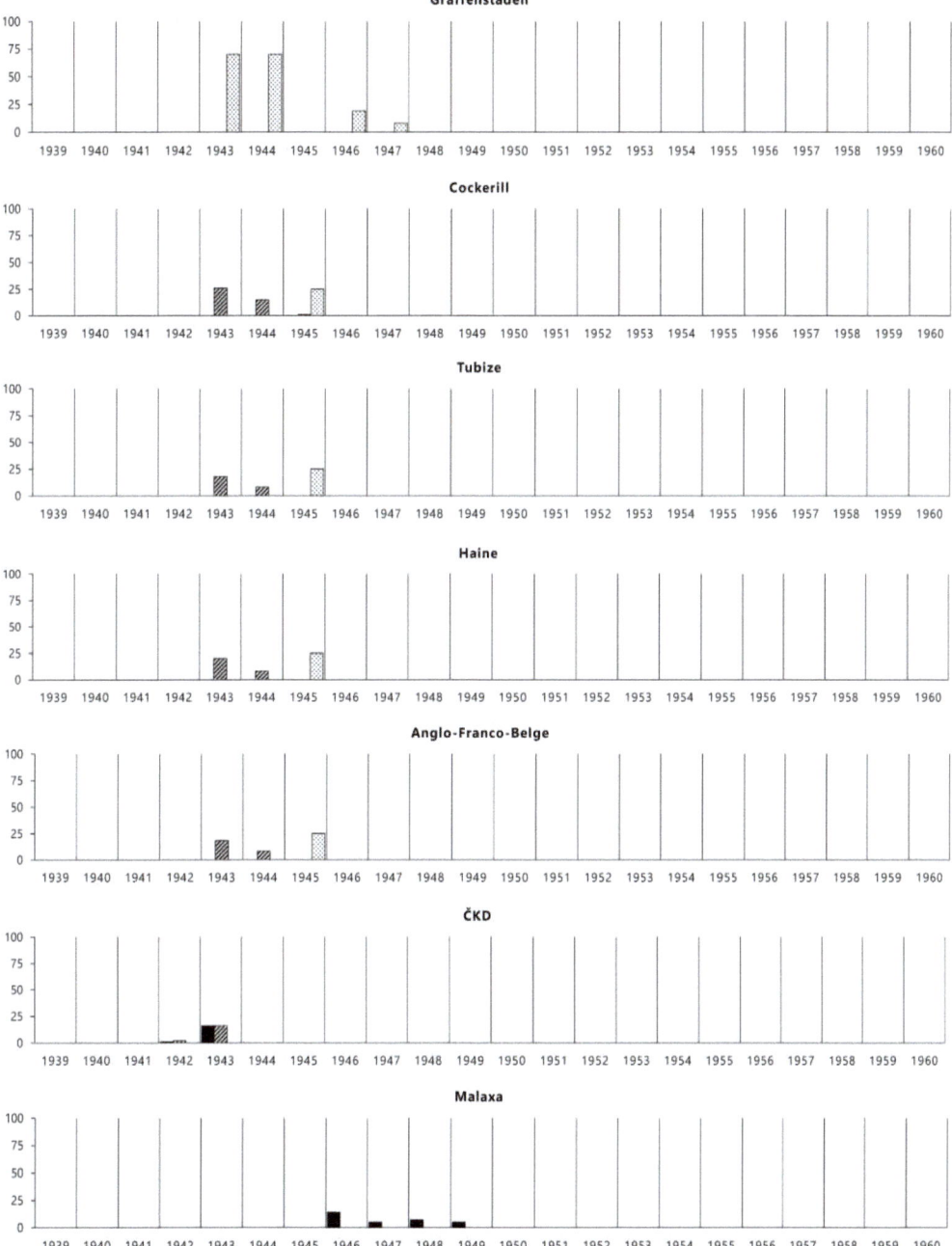

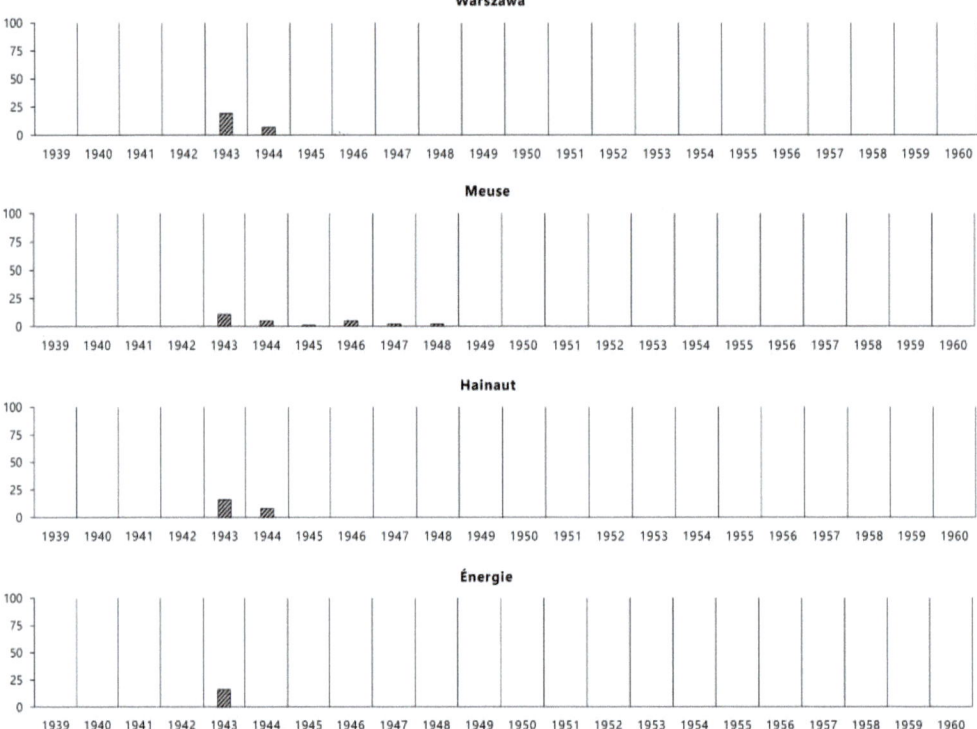

7.5   First deployment and end of the war

After acceptance by the railway workshops, the new locomotives were allocated to various Reichsbahn Directorates (RBD). However, this allocation can only be seen as a snapshot, as a number of initial allocations were immediately changed to other RBDs or to a field railway command. In particular, 'deployment in the east' was handled in such a way that the Directorates sent engines from the Reich to the east. The idea was that these would return to the sending RBD after the victorious campaign. Looking more closely at the distribution of the machines with regard to their initial

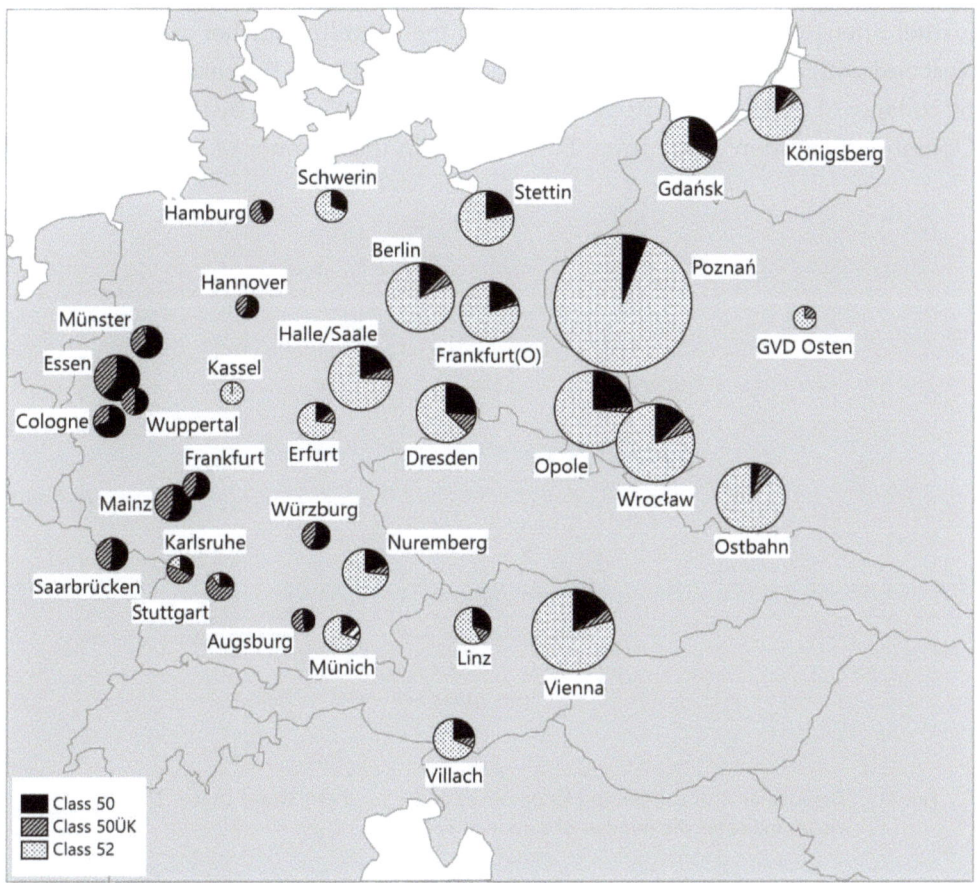

Fig. 30:   Distribution of the first deployments of class 50/50ÜK and 52. The size of the circles shows the number of deployed units in the individual RBD.

deployment, it is noticeable that the war locomotives were almost exclusively deployed east of 11° longitude, i.e. east of a line running roughly from Lübeck to Erfurt
and Munich.

All new condensing locomotives were gathered in Berlin-Schöneweide and then sent
directly to the theatres of war in the southern part of the Soviet Union.

After the Battle near the river Дніпро (Dnipro) in December 1943 [303], the four eastern
stations of the condensing engines (cf. Figure 31) had to be cleared. After a subsequent
Red Army offensive from December 1943 to April 1944, also the other stations were
abandoned. The use of the condensing machines, which had been intended for the
water-scarce areas of the southern Soviet Union, came to a relatively quick end.

Further offensives by the Red Army pushed the front line further and further to the
West and with it more and more locomotives flooded from the east to the west. After
the collapse of the 'Heeresgruppe Mitte' (Army Group Center) by the Soviet offensive
'Operation Bagration' (Оперция 'Багратион') in the summer of 1944, Soviet troops

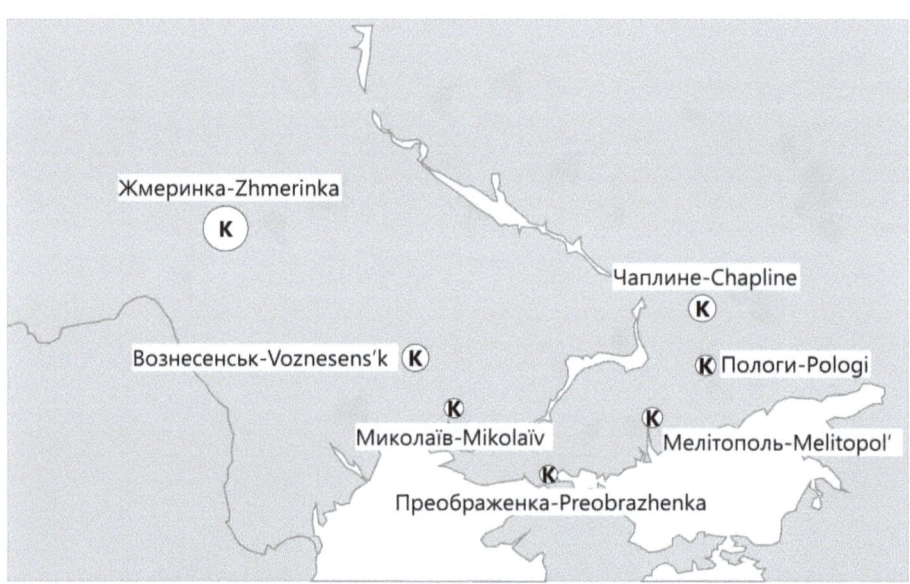

Fig. 31:   Deployments of condensing locomotives in the southern Soviet Union. The size of the
circles indicates the number of stationed engines.

---

[303] The 'Battle of the Dnieper' was a military campaign from August to December 1943 on the Eastern Front of the Second
World War. It was one of the largest operations of the war and it involved nearly four million troops and extended over
a distance of 1,400 km.

reached the Wisła (Vistula) and the eastern border of East Prussia.

In June 1944 the Western Allies landed in the Normandy (Operation 'Overloard'). Now, Germany was facing also a frontline on the western side and got under pressure from both sides. Already during the preparation of the invasion, US- and British-Allied logisticians drew up a detailed plan for supplying their troops on the continent. After D-Day the 'Red Ball Express' was set up to supply Allied forces moving quickly through Europe. When the port of Antwerp was captured in September 1944 and enough French rail lines were repaired the express was suspended as the supply routes changed considerably.[304]

The Western Allies made good progress and already in August 1944 Paris was liberated. In October 1944 the border to the Reich was crossed and the town Aachen surrendered.

At the end of January 1945, behind the eastern front a locomotive reception point was set up at Zbąszynek, a former border station on the railway line from Frankfurt (Oder) to Poznań, to collect and transport returning crews and engines in a controlled manner and sending them westward. Within six days, 242 units came in: 204 machines from RBD Poznań, 17 from OBD Warsaw, 14 from GVD Ost and seven others from various RBDs.[305] Among them were a large number of class 52 locomotives, but no class 50/50ÜK engines. The engines coming in were combined to loco trains[306] and sent to the West.

Shortly after it was set up, the reception point was closed again, as the Soviet troops reached the rivers Odra (Oder) and Nysa Łużycka (Lusatian Neisse) at the mid of April 1945 and were just 80 kilometres from Berlin. The Soviet railway troops followed the advance of the Soviet troops and converted the normal tracks to Soviet broad gauge. In Poland, broad-gauge lines were running from Vilnius via Черняховск (Chernyakhovsk) to Elbląg and from Львів (Lviv) via Kraków to Wrocław. Berlin-Köpenick was reached on 5th May 1945 via a converted line from Warsaw via Poznań.[307] The advance followed roughly the same routes that the Wehrmacht had taken on their way east a few years earlier. With moving westward the Soviets had to consider that their rolling stock might cause some problems when crossing the border to Poland. Even when the former Polish track gauge was changed

---

[304] An overview of the logistical operations after D-Day gives (USATC, 1945)

[305] (Scharf, 1981), pages 229ff

[306] These loco trains units consisted of a locomotive coupled together with other units which were hauled.

[307] (Kuhlmann, 2002), pages 14ff

to the Soviet broad gauge the clearance gauge of the Soviet rolling stock was larger than that of the Polish stock and that of the Reichsbahn.[157] A few days after the broad-gauge line reached Berlin.

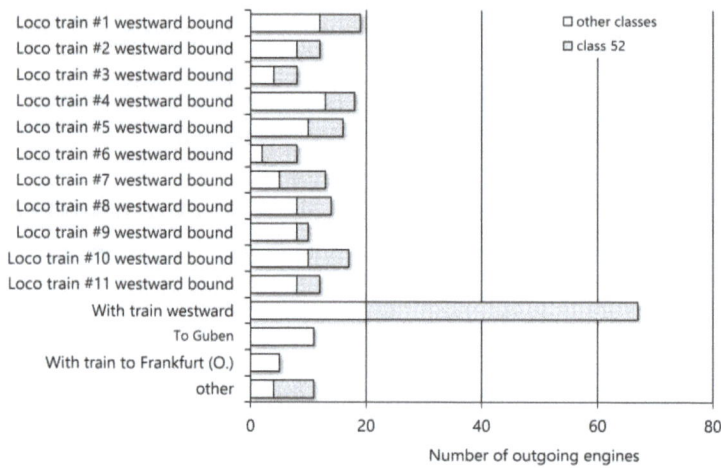

Fig. 32: Composition of outgoing loco trains from Zbąszynek between 22nd January 1945 and 28. January 1945[305]

Already in March 1945, before the end of the war, the Soviet Army handed over the network in Poland east of the Wisła (Vistula) to Polish staff, mainly in order to have its own personnel for operations in Western Europe.[308]

Also the Western Allies made go progress on their way into the Reich. End of March the river Rhine was crossed and only some weeks later (end of April 1945) Soviet and American troops met at the river Elbe, near Torgau in Germany ('Elbe Day').

Germany surrendered first to SHAEF[309] on 7th May 1945 and then to the Supreme Commander of the Red Army in Germany on 8th May 1945.

Finally, the war was over!

---

[308] (Kuhlmann, 2002), pages 32f
[309] SHAEF = **S**upreme **H**eadquarters, **A**llied **E**xpeditionary **F**orce

8 Mass deportations

8.1 Transports to concentration and extermination camps

Parallel to the events described above, the Reichsbahn, and with it the classes 50/50ÜK and 52, were involved in operations that represent the darkest chapter in German history.

In addition to fulfilling civilian tasks in the Reich, the occupied territories and orders for the Wehrmacht, the Reichsbahn was also involved in the Nazi 'racial reorganisation' of Europe. Throughout the war, the Reichsbahn and the railways it controlled in occupied Europe formed a transport system with almost unlimited capacity and was therefore predestined to carry out the transports to concentration and extermination camps.

In his speech in front of the Reichstag of 30th January 1939, Hitler made clear that the start of another world war would end with the annihilation of the 'Jewish race' in Europe.[310] From October 1939, about 5,000 Austrians and Czechs of Jewish faith from the 'Greater German Reich' were transported to Nisko (more precisely: Zarzecze, on the opposite bank of the river San) to set up a camp for more Jews to arrive later. Only a few of the deportees actually did the work required, the others were simply driven across the nearby demarcation line into Soviet-occupied Poland and left to their own devices. This initial action was quickly stopped by the RSHA.[311] In April 1940, only 501 people returned to their homes.[312]

Soon after, the Referat IV B4 ('Jewish Affairs and Evacuation') was set up in the RSHA, headed by Adolf Eichmann, who coordinated and organised the so-called 'Final Solution of the Jewish Question' from 1941 on. All the SS's transport requests were brought together here. This office met regularly with the Reichsbahn's department E II 21/1 ('Mass Transport, Segment Chartered Trains'), headed by Paul Schnell, to coordinate the departure and destination points and the timetables of the deportation trains. These two groups ensured that the results of the agreement were passed on to

---

[310] (Die Rede, in der er die Vernichtung der Juden ankündigte, 2019)
[311] RSHA = **R**eichs**s**icherheit**sh**aup**t**amt (Reich Security Main Office), established in 1939 and comprising of the SiPo (**Si**cherheit**spo**lizei, Security Police), divided into Gestapo[40] and Kripo (**Kri**minal**po**lizei, Criminal Investigation Department) and the SD[186]. It was headed by Reinhard Heydrich until June 1942, then by Ernst Kaltenbrunner.
[312] (Wikipedia003); (Goshen, 1981)

their subordinate offices.[313]

In order to get a 'systematic' approach to previous little coordinated actions to murder the Jews, it was agreed at the 'Wannsee Conference' in early 1942 to deport the Jews of Europe to the east and murder them there.[314] For this purpose, the construction of the extermination camps of Treblinka, Sobibor and Belzec began in November 1941. These were located on the outskirts of the General Government in isolated areas near railway lines.

The killings began in the spring of 1942 under the code name 'Aktion Reinhardt' and were aimed at the systematic murder of Polish citizens of Jewish faith as well as Romani.

However, of the approximately 6 million Jews murdered, only about half were transported in railway wagons to the death factories; the other half died in the immediate vicinity of their homes.[315] From mid-1941 on, in Poland and the Soviet Union, they were often shot at the edge of a pit dug near their homes.

Following Eichmann's promise in early 1941 that the RSHA would pay for the transports, the Reich Ministry of Transport developed a 'group price' for the deportations. For transports of 400 people this amounted half a 3rd class fare, but at least 200 RM.[316] If a transport contained fewer than 400 people, the SS was entitled to declare the number as 400 in order to obtain the cheaper fare.[317] One should not be blinded by the '3rd class' fare, the deportees were booked as humans indeed, but often were transported in worse conditions than cattle.[318]

The deportations took place in special trains. This was a common term for trains that did not run regularly but were added to the timetable at the request of a customer. Special trains were also used for the large-scale transport of members of the Reichsarbeitsdienst (Reich Labour Service), German resettlers, police and customs officers. Other transports carried out by the SD or the Gestapo on the special trains included the transport of prisoners to and from concentration camps, and transports by the 'Gemeinnützige Krankentransport GmbH' (Non-profit patient transport Ltd.),

---

[313] (Engwert, 2009)

[314] The purpose of the conference was to ensure the cooperation of the departments involved in the implementation of the Holocaust. This included the deportation and murder of the Jews of the territory occupied by Nazi Germany. In the course of the meeting, Heydrich outlined how the Jews should be rounded up and sent to extermination camps in the General Government.

[315] (Gottwaldt2, 2009); (Gottwaldt, 2013)

[316] (Hilberg, 1987), page 43; (Kuczynski, 2009)

[317] (Hilberg, 1987), page 45

[318] (Hilberg, 1987), page 41

which often transported patients to so-called 'euthanasia' actions, where they were murdered as part of 'Aktion T4'.[319]

Initially, 3rd class passenger wagons from the special train reserve were used for the deportations, as the Wehrmacht claimed almost all the freight wagons. The planning provided for 50 people in 20 wagons at a time. This was the traditional rule for special trains in the pre-war period. Later, up to 2,000 people were transported in the same number of carriages.[320] Single carriages carrying 50 people were also included in regular passenger trains ('smaller' transports) from Berlin or Munich to the transit camp at Theresienstadt.

The trains were hauled by any suitable locomotive available in the depots, including class 50/50ÜK and 52 engines. For example, the trains in the 1993 movie 'Schindler's List' were hauled by a class 52 machine.

Within the General Government, covered freight cars (standard type 'G') were used early on for the relatively short distances from the transit camps to the extermination camps, with up to 200 people crammed into them. The standard size of these trains, consisting of 50 to 58 cars, was 5,000 people.[321] Space was sometimes less than 0.2 m^2 per person.[322] From the beginning of 1942, freight wagons were also used for transports in the rest of the occupied Europe, and on their way back they were loaded with forced labourers to the Reich.

As the wagons had been taken from the special train reserve, they were in poor condition. In particular, the freight wagons used were in such a state that even cattle could not be transported any more.[323]

If one tries to determine the average speed of these trains, including all stops, the result was about 15 - 20 km/h, which was also the average speed of the Wehrmacht troop transports.[324] Since some journeys were over 1,000 km long, a deportation train could be on the track for up to a week. During the journey, the passengers received no food or drink and were exposed to the heat in summer and the cold in winter. There were no toilets in the freight wagons either, so they had to use the inside of the

---

[319] 'Aktion T4' was the name used after 1945 for the Nazi programme 'Aktion Gnadentod' (Project Mercy Killing) or 'Extermination of Life not Worth Living'. The name was derived from the address of the programme's head quarter (Berlin, **T**iergartenstraße **4**). More than 70,000 disabled people were murdered as part of 'Aktion T4'. This was only part of further killings on sick people, which totalled more than 200,000 persons (Wikipedia010).

[320] (Lichtenstein, 1985), page 96

[321] (Gottwaldt2, 2009)

[322] (Reimer, et al., 2004), page 77

[323] (Lichtenstein, 1985), pages 94f

[324] (Gottwaldt, 2013)

wagon or, at best, a bucket provided as a toilet. When deportation trains had to wait at stations, for example, the doomed would cry out for help. Civilian passengers noticed this, of course, which was unpleasant for the authorities, but it did not change the way things were done. The poor hygienic conditions led to the deaths of the sick, the infirm and children, many of whom died during transport.

It was clear to those responsible from the outset that the Reichsbahn's transport conditions not only contributed to the murder of the victims, but they were actively involved in the killing. From a legal perspective, this was not only aiding and abetting mass murder, it was condoning it.[325]

In general, the transport trains were marked with the sign 'Da'[326]. Transports of Polish Jews were marked 'Pj'[327] (within the Ostbahn 'P Kr'[328]). The timetables of the trains were not secret and were sometimes published together the official timetables.[329]

If the Reichsbahn could not comply with the wishes of Eichmann's department, the departure of the special trains was postponed for a few weeks, but never cancelled. In most cases, the condemned were not transported directly to the extermination camps, but to ghettos and transit camps, where they awaited their final transport.

After 'Aktion Reinhardt', the 'killing machine' covered all the territories occupied by Nazi Germany. It is estimated that up to six million Jews, 3.3 million Soviet prisoners of war, up to 250,000 Romani people, up to 250,000 mentally and physically disabled people, and tens of thousands of members of the Polish elite were murdered during the Nazi regime. Other victims included political opponents, Jehovah's Witnesses, men denounced as homosexuals, and people deemed to be 'anti-social'.[330]

We can only guess the number of trains that were used. Especially since a decree of the Reich Ministry of Transport from July 1941, the authorisation for those special trains (as long as there were no more than five of the same type) was transferred to the Reichsbahn directorates – as long as they *"obviously and undoubtedly served a war and vital purpose"* or were special trains ordered by the Inspector of the Security Police and the SD for the transport of prisoners to and from concentration camps respective orders by the Gestapo for the 'Gemeinnützige Krankentransport GmbH'.[325]

---

[325] (Kuczynski, 2009)

[326] 'Da', possibly derived from 'David' or 'Deutsche Aussiedler' (German emigrant).

[327] 'Pj', possibly derived from 'Polish Jews'. At the same time 'P' was the marking for surcharge-free passenger trains (Noßke, 2006), thus 'Passenger train Jewish' would also be possible.

[328] (Friedrich, 2013), page 371

[329] (Hilberg, 1987), page 92

[330] The term 'anti-social' was used by the Nazis for members of the Romanies, the unemployed and homeless, recipients of social benefits, prostitutes, beggars, alcoholics and drug addicts. (United States Holocaust Memorial Museum)

If we assume that about three million people were transported to ghettos and concentration and extermination camps, and that each train carried 1,000 people, then approximately about 3,000 trains were needed for this murder campaign, which essentially lasted for about three years. If we further assume that half of the victims were crammed into such a train a second time before being murdered, this means that in average about five to six trains per day were needed for this mass murder. Given the total number of about 20,000 trains per day (1942), the death transports did not have a significant impact on the capacity of the Reichsbahn.[325]

After the end of the 'Aktion Reinhardt's' killings the extermination camps of Belzec, Treblinka and Sobibor were closed in early 1943 and all traces were erased. To make sure that all traces were really covered up, the victims of the camps were exhumed and cremated as part of 'Sonderaktion 1005' (Special project 1005). At the same time, the murders continued, in Auschwitz and other camps.

One of the special features of the Holocaust, apart from the large number of people murdered, was the fact that it was a highly collaborative process, modelled on the standards of industrial assembly-line production. With the Reichsbahn, it were the employees who drew up the daily timetables to the extermination camps, checked the condition of the connecting tracks, fired up the locomotives, formed the trains and set the switches.[324] At their destination in the camp, the wagons carrying the deportees were uncoupled from the locomotives at the ramps. The railroad employees drove out of the camp, satisfied that the transport had been completed on time and as agreed. Ultimately, for them it was a matter of serving 'the deadly factories that received their raw materials by rail'.[324] In this machinery everyone involved was only a small piece of the puzzle of a great killing machine and could therefore easily shift his responsibility to the supposedly 'great manager' of the whole project. In this way, individual guilt could be quickly relativised.

There were attempts by some of Reichsbahn employees to resist against this system,[321] but only in isolated cases and always in fear for their own safety and that of their families.

The management of the Reichsbahn certainly knew about the transports, the manner of implementation and the purpose, although they – like many of those responsible at the time – seemed to have strange gaps in their memories. For example, for Ganzenmüller, the deputy head of the Reichsbahn, can clearly be shown to have known about the events.[331] It can be assumed that Dorpmüller was also aware of the events. The fact that Reichsbahn's transport capacities were a decisive factor in the genocide of the Holocaust was not, or only very rarely, considered after the war. The aura of the 'apolitical railway nerd' was used to evade responsibility. They saw themselves as part of an organisation that *"carried every paying individual, whether it travelled voluntarily or was forced to do so"*[325]. Even in Gerteis's 'memoirs'[332] there is no reference to the Holocaust, although Gerteis, as president of the Ostbahn, was deeply involved in the mass murder of millions of people and later made a career as a top manager of the West-German Deutsche Bundesbahn. For him, it was not a point worth mentioning nor did he feel the need to justify himself.

Whether the deportations were good business for the Reichsbahn is still disputed, but it can be assumed that they reduced costs for the Reichsbahn.[325] Whatsoever, in the end economic considerations did not play a major role for those responsible for the ideology or for the management of the Reichsbahn at that time.

---

[331] (Hilberg, 1987), page 14; (Kuczynski, 2009)
[332] (Gerteis, 1949), this also applies to Hans Pottgiesser (Pottgiesser, 1975)

8.2   Transport of forced labourers

Even before the war, there was a large shortage of labour due to the massive rearmament. A part of the missing labour could be relieved with the growing exodus from the countryside that started at the same time. These additional people were not sufficient to meet all needs of industry. As a result of this movement, there was a sudden shortage of agricultural labour, which the regime tried to compensate for by using schoolchildren and army units to harvest crops. Additionally it was decided to conscript foreign workers in the conquered territories.

Already with the invasion of Czechoslovakia, German industry demanded that the shortage of labour should be compensated for by the recruitment of foreign workers.[333] Czechoslovak workers were the first to be chosen to work in Nazi Germany.

A few weeks later, Göring gave the order to use prisoners of war, concentration camp inmates and ordinary prisoners in the German war economy.[334] After the occupation of Poland, Polish workers were brought into the Reich. With the proclamation of compulsory labour for all Poles between the ages of 18 and 60 in October 1939, mass deportations to the Reich increased. At the same time, the lives of Poles staying in the General Government had deteriorated to such an extent that they saw work in the Reich as the only alternative for survival.[335]

The situation of these 'foreign workers' was much worse than that of German workers. Their wages were 45-65 % of the German level, and from 1941 they were completely forbidden to go home.[335] From 1940 on, they had to wear a badge consisting of a diamond shape with a purple border and a purple letter 'P' on a yellow background.[336] They were forbidden to have any contact with the German population outside of the work. They were not allowed to have any money, had to be in their accommodation by nightfall and were not allowed to use bicycles or public transport, and so on. Violations were punished severely – up to and including death penalty.[337]

In early 1942, Göring ordered 'recruitment in the east' and forced labour for all inhabitants of the occupied eastern territories. 'Recruitment in the east' was to take place in all occupied Soviet territories. The recruitment methods were anything but voluntary;

---

[333] (Forstmeier, et al., 1981), page 167
[334] (Eichholtz, 1999), pages 92f
[335] (Eichholtz, 1999), pages 95f
[336] (Wikipedia011)
[337] (Eichholtz, 1999), page 99

there were forced recruitments and outright manhunts.[338] These 'eastern recruits' were even worse off than the Polish workers and were strictly separated from the German population, other foreign workers and prisoners of war. They also had to wear an 'Ostarbeiter'-badge (a blue badge with a white 'OST' inscription).[339]

When many of the workers 'recruited' in the occupied territories died during the harsh winter of 1941-42, the Nazis used surviving Soviet prisoners of war as forced labourers, some 750,000 Red Army prisoners by January 1945.[340]

There was a high turnover of forced labourers, many of whom were murdered, died of exhaustion, accidents or were unable to work. The total number of deported forced labourers, prisoners of war and concentration camp inmates is estimated at well over 20 million people. At the end of the war, 6 million civilian forced labourers, 2 million prisoners of war and more than half a million concentration camp inmates and prisoners of war were working in Germany. Of these, about 40 % were Soviet, 25 % French and 15 % Polish.[341]

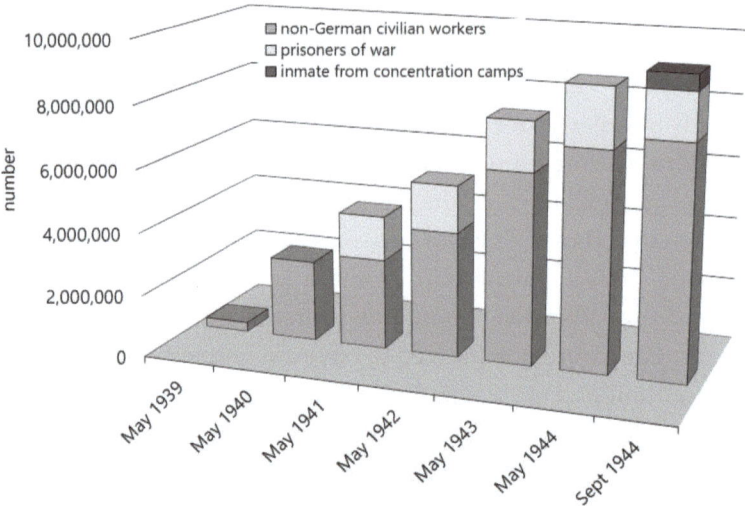

Fig. 33:   Forced labourers in Nazi Germany during the war without prisoners of justice[342]

---

[338] Cf. this with the so-called 'Heuaktion' (hay campaign) in early 1944 in Belarus and eastern Poland (Wikipedia012)

[339] (Bundesarchiv) Ostarbeiter = Worker from the east.

[340] (Wikipedia013)

[341] (Eichholtz2, 1999), page 530. Other estimates put the number of forced labourers at 12 million. (Kuczynski, 2009)

[342] (Buggeln, 2015)

The Reichsbahn had to cope with all this human transport. The cattle cars that had previously transported people to the death camps were used to transport forced labourers back into the Reich. However, there was a difference compared to the deportees to the death camps: these passengers were still provided with a minimum of care, as they had to arrive in the Reich in one piece.

It should not be forgotten that the Reichsbahn itself employed more than 270,000 forced labourers (August 1944),[343] making it the largest 'employer of forced labour' in the Reich.[325] Unfortunately, there has not yet been a comprehensive reappraisal of what happened, as it had been the case with other German companies (often only after the law establishing the Foundation 'Remembrance, Responsibility and Future').[344]

It should also be remembered that class 50 and 52 units were built by forced labourers. In Kassel, where Henschel was located, for example, up to 22,000 people were interned as forced labourers for various companies,[345] at the Henschel's plant in Floridsdorf worked up to 2,500 labourers,[346] in Schwartzkopff's factory in Berlin up to 6,000 people[347] and in Schichau's plant in Elbląg (near Gdańsk) up to 2,800 labourers[348] from the nearby Stutthof concentration camp. In the course of the war, more than a quarter, in some cases up to 60 %, of the workers in the factories under the control of the Steering Committee of Railway Vehicles were forced labourers and 'foreign workers'.

---

[343] Other sources give a figure of around 37,000 for spring 1943 (Wolf, 2015).
[344] Cf. also a report from RAW/HW Neuaubing: (Nerdinger, 2018)
[345] (Mosch-Wicke, 1985), page 21
[346] (erinnern, 2020)
[347] (Wikipedia014)
[348] (Wikipedia015)

9 What was the most produced locomotive of all?

9.1 Definition

Given the figures we saw in Chapter 7.4, one might be tempted to confirm that this is the most built steam locomotive in the world. Is this really the case? This chapter tries to answer that question by taking a closer look at other countries and their steam engine series.

The adjective 'most produced' is used relatively often, but the criteria for such a designation are not clearly defined. In the car industry, for example, the Toyota Corolla is considered to be the most produced car.[349] However, if you compare the first model of this car with the latest version, they differ significantly. Within aeroplanes, e.g. the Cessna 172 is called the most produced aeroplane.[350] If you compare the first machines from 1955 with the latest machines from recent times, you get the impression that, despite some improvements, the basic plan seemed to be unchanged.

The question is, what criteria should be used to award the title of 'most produced' to steam locomotives? The term 'class' cannot be used, as it is interpreted differently by different railway companies and we learnt from the previous chapter that the designation 'class 52' for the war version was only established for propaganda reasons.

In the USA, with its private railroads, groups of similarly built machines were initially grouped into 'classes' based on performance rather than construction. Later, the criteria for a class membership were based on the blueprints, usually using the axle arrangement as a starting point, to which an appropriate designation for each type was added. However, apart from the axle arrangement, each railway company had its own system for these designations, so that locomotives changed their designation when they were sold.[351]

In Germany, after the foundation of the Reichsbahn a uniform system of designating the engines was developed. A locomotive number consisted of a two-digit main number and a maximum four-digit sequential number. The main number indicated the class. More than 400 different machine designs inherited from the state railways were given their own main and sequential numbers. New builds and new purchases were

---

[349] (Hildebrandt, 2021)
[350] (Wikipedia016)
[351] (Wikipedia017)

given their own main numbers. Sub-series of these designs were marked with a corresponding exponent (e.g. class 03 and class 03^{10})[352]. This was later taken over from the later two German railway companies.

Tab. 11: Steam locomotive classes produced in large production numbers

Country	Designation/Class	Number	Remark
USA	2-8-0	33.400	'Consolidation'[353]
USA	4-4-0	25.600	'American'[353]
Russia/USSR	Э (É)	10.853	[354]
Russia/USSR	O (O)	9.129	[354]
Germany	52	6.717	War locomotive, simplified class 50
China	前进 (QJ)	4.715	Further development of a Soviet machine[355]
Germany	50	3.451	incl. 50ÜK
USA	USATC S160	2.119	War locomotive[356]
United Kingdom	WD Austerity 2-8-0	935	[357]

In Russia, from 1912, a uniform designation for steam locomotives was introduced for both state and (at that time) private railways. The letter 'Т' (Трехосные, three-axle) was introduced for all old freight engines with axle arrangements 0-3-0, 1-3-0, 0-3-1.[358] Machines with the axle arrangement 0-4-0 were given the name 'Ч' (Четырехосные, four-axle)[359] and passenger locomotives with the axle arrangements 1-2-0, 0-2-1, 2-2-0 and 2-2-1 were given the name 'Д' (Двухосные, two-axle).[360] Other types of steam engines were designated by other letters of the Cyrillic script, with an exponent in the form of a capital or lower case letter added to the letters to indicate the corresponding subtype. In addition, an appropriate lower-case letter was used to indicate the manufacturer, e.g. 'Б' for Брянский (Bryansk), 'х' for Харьковский (Kharkiv), 'л' for Луганский (Luhansk), 'А' for американские заводы (American factories), 'г' for

---

[352] (Wikipedia018)
[353] (Bruce, 1952), excerpt from table 20 (page 423)
[354] (Соколов (Sokolov))
[355] (Gibbons, 2017), page 16
[356] (Tourret, 1995), page 223. The USATC S200 is not mentioned, as only 200 units were produced. (Tourret, 1995), pages 200ff.
[357] (Tourret, 1995), page 81f; WD = **W**ar **D**epartment
[358] Soviet notation for axle arrangements; UIC notation would be: C, 1C, C1; 1'C, C1'.
[359] Soviet notation for axle arrangements; UIC notation: D
[360] Soviet notation for axle arrangements; UIC notation: 1B, B1, 2B2, 2B, 1'B, B1', 2'B2', 2'B

Геншель (Henschel) or Германия (Germany), etc.[361] A similar naming scheme was continued after the establishment of the USSR, but proved less practical. Then steam locomotives were often given series names after their main designers or famous personalities.[362]

Due to the significant differences in the definition and delimitation of a class, class designations can only be used to a limited extent to identify the most commonly built locomotive.

In order to come to a definition that is applicable to all railway undertakings in all countries, it is considered that a 'class' or 'series' is a group of engines that follow an 'end-to-end design'. An 'end-to-end design' means that this group of machines follow the same main dimensions from the first to the last item produced.

As not all values are available for the dimensions of all the units, a number of main dimensions have been selected that are characteristic of a steam locomotive in terms of steam generation, propulsion and running gear.

Weight has been included because a change in this parameter could be an indication that other things have changed that are not covered by the above selection of technical data. However, this parameter is only considered as an indicator and not as a strict criterion, especially since a change in weight can also be caused by changes that only slightly affect the 'end-to-end design' of the locomotive, e.g. spoked or solid wheels. These characteristics should only be applied to the machines, not to the tenders, as they can be changed. The main characteristic dimensions used are

Steam generator/boiler:
- Grate area
- Boiler pressure
- Total heating area (tubes and flues)
- Superheater area

Power unit:
- Number of cylinders
- Cylinder diameter, piston stroke

Running gear:
- Number/arrangement of running and driving axles
- Diameter of the driving wheels

---

[361] (Раков (Rakov), 1995), page 128
[362] (Wikipedia019)

Indicator: Weight:
- Weight (with supplies)
- Axle load

It can be argued that the selection of the main dimensions is arbitrary and that a different selection could lead to different results. However, at present there is no other pragmatic and effective way of fully describing and comparing individual locomotives. It could also be argued that the criteria are too strict, considering, for example, the German class 03 and 03[10], which, according to the above definition, would become two classes (two-cylinder engine versus three-cylinder engine). However, it should also be noted that in some cases Reichsbahn deviated from its own class definition.

Especially in the first half of the previous century, a number of locomotives and classes were built in large numbers (cf. Table 11). It is now the task to clarify the characteristics of these individual classes.

9.2   USA

In the 19th century, the 'American' (axle arrangement: 4-4-0 (2B or 2'B)) was the most widely built 'class' in the United States and represented the iconic engine of the Wild West that is firmly established in our imagination. At the time, there were a large number of small railroads in the USA with very different financial situations. Each company had its own ideas about how to design a locomotive and how it should be maintained. There was also a lot of experimentation going on at the time, mainly to reduce the cost of the operation of the machines. These experiments concerned all parts of the locomotive, starting with the boiler design, the firebox, the grate, the injectors, the safety valves and the design of the running wheels, etc. After the early successes with superheated steam became public (patents by A. de Quillacq and J. Moncheuil)[363], the first experiments were carried out at B&O[364] in 1857[365], but with no good results. Wilhelm Schmidt was the first to build a practical superheater in 1890,[366] as his design also adapted other elements of the engine to the technology. Tten years later a superheater was introduced as standard on US units.[365] The knowledge gained from the experiments led to further developments in engine design. As a result, the weight of the 'American' locomotive increased over time (see Figure 34).

Tab. 12: Produced classes in the USA[353]

Class	1831-1900	1901-1950	Total
2-8-0	9,400	24,000	33,400
4-4-0	24,700	900	25,600
4-6-0	10,200	6,900	17,100
2-8-2		14,100	14,100

However, engines were not standardised even within railway companies, as a list from the Pennsylvania Railroad (PRR)[367] shows (see Table 13). In the first 50 years of its existence, the PRR operated 29 different sub-classes of the 'American' machines out of 51 classes in total. The differences between the classes were in the main dimensionsions, such as driving wheel diameter, cylinder dimensions, boiler pressure and

---

[363] (Mallet, 1908), pages 430f; (King, 1907), pages 520ff

[364] B&O = Baltimore and Ohio Railroad, today part of CSX Transportation

[365] (White Jr., 1979), page 144

[366] (Meineke, et al., 1949), page 26; (The Babcock & Wilcox Co., 1914), pages 15ff

[367] The PRR is said to have been the largest railway company in the world in terms of traffic and revenue until 1882 (Wikipedia020). During her existence the PRR can be considered as a major innovator in locomotive design. Parts are now owned by Consolidated Rail Corporation, Norfolk Southern and CSX Transportation.

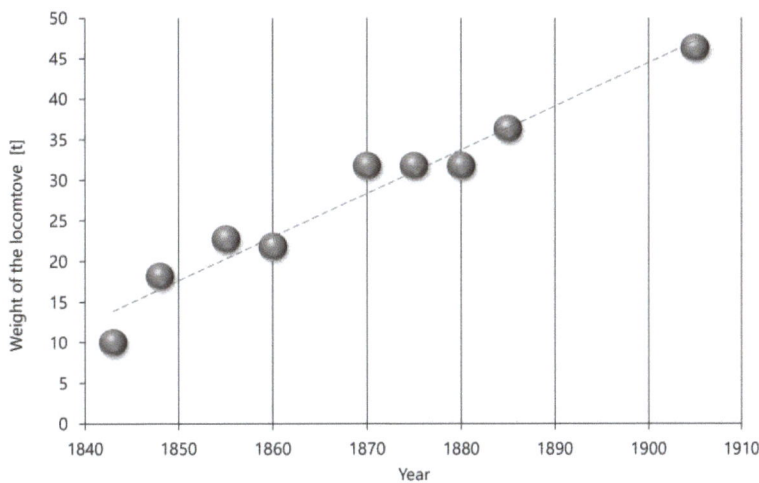

Fig. 34:   Development of the weight of steam locomotives of the type 'American' in the 19th century [368]

boiler characteristics (grate area, tube and flues). None of these units had a superheater, although boiler pressures of around 180 psi (approx. 12 bar) were achieved.

Tab. 13: List of a selection of 2'B ('American') PRR steam locomotives before 1900[369]

Class	Driving wheel dia.	Cylinder diameter x stroke	Boiler pressure [psi]	Grate area [sq.ft.]	Total heating area [sq.ft.][1]
O	62"	18" x 24"	*130*	18	*1,390*
O	62"	18" x 24"	160	18	1,285
O	*68"*	18" x 24"	160	18	1,285
O	62"	18" x 24"	160	*17*	*1,255*
O	*68"*	18" x 24"	160	*17*	*1,255*
P	62"	18½" x 24"	*140*	35	1,530
P	*68"*	18½" x 24"	*140*	*35*	1,530
P	62"	18½" x 24"	160	33	*1,380*
P	*68"*	18½" x 24"	160	33	*1,380*
P	62"	18½" x 24"	160	33	1,570
P	*68"*	18½" x 24"	*175*	33	1,570
P	*78"*	18½" x 24"	*175*	33	*1,585*
P	*80"*	*19" x 24"*	*175*	33	*1,585*

[368] (White Jr., 1979), pages 21f
[369] Tubes and flues

The situation did not change fundamentally with the appearance of the 'class' 2-8-0 ('consolidation'). In the beginning of the 20th century, some 24,000 units were built (cf. Table 12). Only about 13,700 engines are recorded as having been delivered to US railroads,[370] which means, considering misstatements or omissions by individual railroads, that a large proportion of these locomotives must have been exported.[370] Unluckily there are any data available for these machines.

The 13,700 examples of the Consolidation that are recorded were distributed among a total of 84 companies. Around 60 % of them were used by only ten railway companies (see Table 14).

The company with the most Consolidations (2-8-0) was the PRR. There about 1,900 units were divided into nine sub-series, two of which (H34a, H34b) had only four units each. Table 15 shows the main dimensions of these series. It can be seen that the changes in the main dimensions formed these sub-series.

The situation was similar for the NYC company. Here the about 1,720 units were again divided into 51 series, of which nine series accounted for 65 % of the stock. This massive number of sub-series at the NYC was due to the acquisition of smaller companies and repeated redesignations of engines (a total of four before the Second World War). As a result, the accuracy of the figures is very low.

Tab. 14: Distribution of the Consolidations on US railway companies (after 1900)[370]

Railway company	Number of 2-8-0
Pennsylvania Railroad (PRR)	1,901
New York Central (NYC)	1,724
Baltimore & Ohio (B&O)	996
Southern[371]	610
Chicago, Rock Island & Pacific (CRI&P)	562
Erie (ERIE)	557
Reading (P&R)	480
Louisville & Nashville (L&N)	461
Chesapeake & Ohio (C&O)	460
Southern Pacific Lines (SP)	418
others (74 companies)	6,627
Sales, rebuilds	-1,103
Total	13,693

---

[370] (Drury, 2015), evaluation over all specified tables
[371] incl. Alabama Great Southern; Cincinnati, New Orleans & Texas Pacific; Georgia Southern & Florida; New Orleans & North-eastern

Tab. 15: Main dimension of the 2-8-0 locomotives of the PRR which were operating in high numbers from 1906[372]

			H6b	H8	H8a	H8b	H8c	H9s	H10s
Running Gear									
Driving axles			4	4	4	4	4	4	4
Driving wheel diameter	D	mm	*1,422*	1,575	1,575	1,575	1,575	1,575	1,575
Leading wheel diameter	D_v	mm	*762*	838	838	838	838	838	838
Cylinders									
Number			2	2	2	2	2	2	2
Diameter	d	mm	*559*	610	610	610	610	*635*	*660,4*
Stroke	s	mm	711	711	711	711	711	711	711
Valve diameter	d_s	mm	305		356		356		356
Boiler									
Pressure	p_K	bar	14	14	14	14		14	14
Grating area	R	m²	*4.55*	5.12	5.12	5.11	5.12	5.11	5.11
Total heating area[369]	H_v	m²	*264*	357	357	357		390[a]/356[b] /342[c]	*342*
Number									
cf. (Drury, 2015)			146	25	117	352	192	586	473

[a]: Tracing#: none; [b]: Tracing#: 45442(A), 45442(B); [c]: Tracing#: E45442, E428887

The fragmentation of the US railways and the resulting large number of locomotives, in series and sub-series, and their negative impact on operating costs and rationalisation opportunities, was recognised by the Union Pacific Railroad (UP) at the beginning of the 20th century,[373] but ultimately not consistently applied by other companies. It would be speculative at this point to guess on the impact that US-wide standardisation and rationalisation would have had on the efficiency of the an US railways as a whole, and thus on the US economy.

For our discussion of the most produced locomotive, the US machines are probably not relevant. It is unlikely that there was another class in the USA from the above mentioned with more than 2,000 units with an 'end-to-end design.'

---

[372] Data from original drawings, cf. (Schoenberg)
[373] 'Harriman standardisation', cf. (Drury, 2015), page 302

9.3 Soviet Union

The railways in the Tsarist Empire were initially organised on a private basis. Some attemps for centralisation of the reailways started during the First World War. After the October Revolution, the all private railways were nationalised and incorporated into the 'People's Commissariat for Roads of the Russian Federation' (Narkomput)[52] (NKPS). From 1923, after the establishment of the USSR, the NKPS was renamed into the 'People's Commissariat for Road of the Soviet Union'[52]. Under the leadership of the NKPS, the railway network of the Soviet Union developed into one of the largest in the world. In 1922, the Soviet Railways[52] (SŽD), the State Railways of the Soviet Union, were established. It was organised as a federation of regional railway companies that operated largely independently. The SŽD was administered by the NKPS. In 1946, the NKPS was reorganized into the 'USSR Ministry of Railways'[52] (MPS), which in turn existed until 1992. Despite the more regional structure of the SŽD, the railways were centrally managed and the procurement of locomotives was highly centralised. This led to the development of only a few standardised engines, each of which was produced in large numbers (cf. Table 16).

Tab. 16: Important Soviet steam locomotives[354]

Class	Axle arrangement	Number	Built
Э (È)	E	10.853	1912 - 1955
O (O)	D	9.129	1890 - 1915, 1925 - 1928
CO (SO)	1'E	4.487	1934 - 1951
Л (L)	1'E	4.200	1945 - 1955
ФД (FD)	1'E1'	3.213	1931 - 1941

The class O was the first steam engine to become somewhat of a standard on the Soviet railways. It was designed and used in the Tsarist Empire and continued to be procured after the revolution in the 1920s.

The locomotives of the class CO were a further development of the series Э, whose development should result in building more powerful engines than the series Э without having to re-equip or reinforce the infrastructure (depots, turntables, tracks). The first machine of this class was unveiled in 1934. The class was named after an ally of Stalin 'Григо́рий (Серго) Орджоникидзе' (Grigórij (Sergo) Ordžonikidze).

The freight engine Л was built at the end of the Second World War. It was named after its chief designer Лев Лебедя́нский (Lev Lebedânskij).

The ФД class, named after the Soviet politician and founder of the ВЧК (Cheka)[374] Феликс Дзержинский (Feliks Dzeržinskij), was a freight machine built between 1931 and 1941. It was one of the most powerful and efficient engines of the Soviet Union. The class brought a number of innovations to Soviet locomotive design that were used in all subsequent Soviet steam engines.

The first ideas for building a machine with the axle arrangement 'E' came from the South-Eastern Railways[375] as early as 1905/06. The Tsarist Ministry of Transport rejected this axle arrangement, however, as they were not sure what the performance of the five axles in curves would be. They feared a large lateral displacement of the axles followed by a high wear of the tracks.[376]

A few years later, the problem of a missing five axle unit was raised again by the Vladikavkaz Railway[377]. The company faced the problem that their passing points were underutilised by the train lengths they had to use, as the tractive power of their four coupled locomotives was too low. Since the track allowed a maximum axle load of 16 tons, the only way to increase the engine's tractive power was to introduce a fifth driving axle, so that the machine could achieve a total adhesive weight[378] of 80 tons. The success of Gölsdorf's design[379] was then well known, so that there were no objections anymore to build such a locomotive. A first batch of these machines was built at Lugansk locomotive factory in 1911/12. Later these units were given the designation Э⁄¹¹ (Èᴸ¹).

It is remarkable that these were already oil fired, as the Vladikavkaz Railway operated lines close to oil fields and fuel was available at low cost. In 1913/14 more coal-fired

---

[374] Cheka is the acronym for the 'All-Russian Extraordinary Commission for Combating Counter-Revolution, Profiteering and Corruption', which took over state security in the Soviet Union after the revolution. From 1922 on, it became the GPU, whose activities were absorbed into the NKVD and then into the KGB. Dzerzhinsky was head of the Narkomput for a short time in the early 1920s.

[375] The 'Юго-Восточная железная дорога' (South-Eastern Railways) operated a railway network of about 4,000 km in the south of the European part of the Soviet Union. The headquarter of the company was Воронеж (Voronezh) (Wikipedia021).

[376] As the number of driving axles increases, it becomes more difficult to drive around curves. Therefore, ideas to improve the ability to drive around curves had been sought early on. A practicable solution was developed at the end of the 19ᵗʰ century by the Austrian engineer Karl Gölsdorf. He invented a radially-sliding driving axle by combination of locomotive axles with fixed bearings and their freedom to shift sideways ('Gölsdorf axle'), so that low-wear and low-noise curve running was possible (Wikipedia022).

[377] The 'Владикавказская железная дорога' (Vladikavkaz Railway) was a private railway operating a railway network north of the Caucasus in the area between the Black and Caspian Seas until 1918 (nationalisation). Headquarters of the company was Ростов-на-Дону (Rostov-on-Don) (Wikipedia023).

[378] The adhesive weight is the part of the total weight of a locomotive that rests on the driving axles. Since sufficiently high friction is the condition for effective power transmission, this number plays a decisive role in the tractive force. If the friction is too low for the tractive force, the engine may start to slide.

[379] Karl Gölsdorf was an Austrian locomotive designer and the inventor of the 'Gölsdorf axle', cf. footnote 376.

engines were built. At the request of the North Donetsk Railway[380], the cylinder diameter was increased. The machines of this batch were designated Э^{/12} (È^{L2}) or 'Type 1913'.[381] In 1914, this class was also purchased by the state railways, but with another increase of the cylinder diameter. Also the grate area and the heating surfaces were enlarged. This was done to give the locomotive more tractive power. With these changes, the class was given the designation Э (È).

During the First World War the copper parts were replaced by steel. This increased

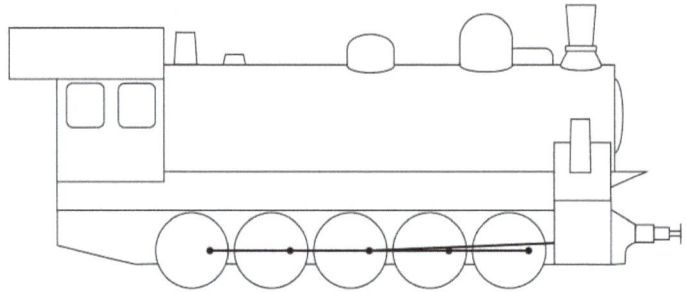

Fig. 35:   Profile sketch of series Э [382]

the service weight by about 600 kg. The axle load also increased slightly. After replacing the cylinders, the Э^{/11} and Э^{/12} locomotives were renamed to 'Э'. The series Э engines were built at the factories Lugansk, Bryansk, Kharkov, Kolomna and Sormovo[56] until 1926.

As a result of the First World War and the October Revolution, locomotive production fell sharply. As a result, a total of 1,200 units should be procured abroad in the 1920s. After some discussion, international suppliers were found:[383] 500 units were ordered from Nidqvist & Holm[384] in Sweden and 700 from DLV[202] under the direction of Henschel. While the first 15 units were built by Nidqvist & Holm exactly according to the plans of Lugansk ('Type 1917'), the following 100 units were built according to slightly modified plans by Henschel and the rest according to the plans of the Soviet Railway Mission in Berlin. Two of the units built in 1922 by Nidqvist & Holm were

---

[380] The 'Северо-Донецкая железная дорога' (North Donetsk Railway) was a private railway that operated a railway network in the Donbass before the Russian Revolution. Its headquarter was in Харків (Kharkiv) (Wikipedia024).

[381] (Rakow, 1986), pages 113ff

[382] cf. (Раков (Rakov), 1995), page 189

[383] Although the US companies Baldwin and ALCO were interested in supplying the equipment, the US government did not grant an export licence, and so these suppliers were cancelled (Chester (ed.), 2000), page 11.

[384] also, **N**ydqvist **o**ch **Ho**lm **AB** (NOHAB respectively NoHAB), located in Trollhättan, Sweden.

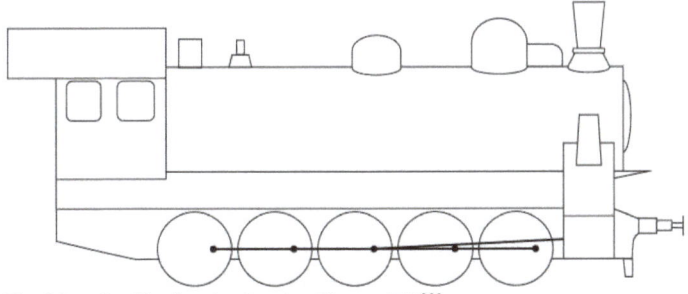

Fig. 36: Profile sketch of series Э^г resp. Э^{ш 389}

equipped with a uniflow steam engine[385]. The tenders for these engines were manufactured at their factory in Eskilstuna and then transported to Trollhättan. The engines
built in Sweden were designated Эш (Èš), while the two uniflow machines were designated Эмш (Èmš). The machines from Germany were given the designation Эг (Èg).[386]
The locomotives from Germany were not ordered directly in Germany, but the first
100 units were ordered via NOHAB, who appointed the DLV as subcontractor, and
the remaining 600 via the Victor Berg company.[387] Berg was the obvious choice because one of its directors was also Krupp's representative in Stockholm.[388] The business was done via Sweden because it allowed the Soviet Union to make payments in
gold to Germany without the risk of the Allies confiscating the Soviet gold as a result
of Germany's reparations after the First World War.

A price of around 260,000 SEK per unit was negotiated for the first 100 locomotives
and around 300,000 SEK for the remaining 600, giving an average price of 291,936 SEK
per unit. The first locomotives were cheaper because they had steel fireboxes instead
of the required copper ones. The NOHAB engines, on the other hand, cost only
218,225 SEK each.[390] It should be noted that the price of the machines from Germany
included fees for the parties involved in the bypass.[391] Converted to today's purchasing power (2021), the value of each locomotive was approximately 1.1 million €.[392]

---

[385] In a uniflow steam engine the steam flows only in one direction in the cylinders. After the expansion the steam does not
leave the cylinder through the inlet opening, but through outlet slots in the centre of the cylinder. This has some advantages as with this setup you get a stable temperature gradient along the cylinder. Steam always enters at the hot
ends of the cylinder and exhausts through ports at the cooler centre (Schwarze, et al., 1998), pages 317f.

[386] (Rakow, 1986), pages 173ff

[387] (Chester (ed.), 2000), page 11

[388] (Heywood, 1999), page 121

[389] cf. (Раков (Rakov), 1995), page 257

[390] The first 150 units of them also had only steel fireboxes because of copper shortage.

[391] (Heywood, 1999), page 211

[392] Due to the high inflation in Germany at the time, the SEK amount was converted into US dollars (exchange rate in 1923:

These prices were considerably higher than those later paid by the Reichsbahn for class 50/50ÜK (see Chapter 7.3).

In a first step, the locomotive Эг 5616 at Borsig was built entirely from supplied parts.[393] In order to ensure the greatest possible standardisation of locomotive parts in the individual German factories, special gauges were produced at the suggestion of the Soviet Railway Mission, which served as a quality standard in all factories. Ultimately, this can be seen as the first experience for the standardisation of supplied parts and division of labour for the production of a locomotive some 20 years later with class 50/52.

From 1925 onwards, attempts were made to increase the temperature of the superheated steam. These trials were successful and were achieved by increasing the superheater area at the expense of the surfaces for tubes and flues. However the axle load of the locomotive increased by about 0.5 tons. On the other hand there was a significant raise in economic efficiency. This new version was called the Эу (Èu). It was

Fig. 37:   Profile sketch of series Эу [395]

built at the factories Bryansk, Kharkov, Kolomna, Lugansk and Sormovo[56]. Externally, the series was easily distinguishable from the previous ones, as on the boiler of the Эу-machine was mounted with three domes (first and third high, second low).[394]

As the tractive power had not increased with the adhesive weight, from 1931 on efforts were made to increase the tractive power of the machine. This was achieved by further modifications of the boiler and, in particular, by increasing the boiler pressure from 12 to 14 bar. To achieve this, certain parts of the boiler were strengthened and the cylinders were upgraded accordingly. At the same time, the locomotive received

(Heywood, 1999), page 210) and extrapolated to today's value (Webster).

[393] (Chester (ed.), 2000), page 13

[394] Machine Эу 684-37 was selected for Krivonós famous train journey (cf. footnote 144)

[395] cf. (Раков (Rakov), 1995), page 259

an increased sand supply and improved sand ejectors. This again changed the appearance of the engine, as the boiler now had three domes of equal height.

This redesigned machine got the designation Эм (Èm) and was built in the above-mentioned factories between 1932 and 1935. During this period, welding technology was introduced into Soviet locomotive construction, reducing the weight of the unit by about 10 %.[396] This includes the usage of a steel firebox. The new Эм locomotives com-

Fig. 38: Profile sketch of series Эм [398]

pleted the Эу fleet and also replaced a number of older classes.

Together with the other engines, they formed the so-called 'Special Reserve Squad for Steam Locomotives' of the NKPS, which provided transport services to the western borders of the Soviet Union during the Second World War[397].

As early as 1933, new ideas came up to improve series Э. The ideas focussed on increasing the size of the firebox in order to improve the machine's performance and its load distribution. These engines, designated Эр (Èr), achieved a higher power of about 10 - 15 % and higher efficiency. However, their production was limited to a few hundred units before the Second World War.

As some 16,000 Soviet locomotives were damaged or destroyed during the Second World War, the NKPS decided to have machines and wagons built in the post-war

---

[396] (Rakow, 1986), page 179

[397] (Раков (Rakov), 1995), page 262. Each squad consisted of 15-30 units of one class (to make repairs easier) and had to work isolated from a depot. They consisted of the classes Э (È) and CO (SO), rarely ФД (FD) (Wikipedia026), see also Chapter 10.10.1..

[398] cf. (Раков (Rakov), 1995), page 261. The cabin was closed by a rear wall on the tender (Le Fleming, et al., 1969), Figure 30.

Tab. 17: Sub-classes of series Э

			Э^{л1} [399]	Э^{л2} [399]	Э [401]	Э^{ш} [400]	Э^{г}
Running gear							
Driving axles			5	5	5	5	5
Driving wheel diameter	D	mm	1,320	1,320	1,320	1,320 ?	1,320 ?
Cylinders							
Number			2	2	2	2	2
Diameter	d	mm	600	*630*	*650*	650 ?	650 ?
Stroke	s	mm	700	700	700	700	700 ?
Boiler							
Pressure	p$_к$	bar	12 [401]	12 [401]	12 [402]	12 [403]	12 ?
Grate area	R	m^2	4.2	4.2	*4.46*	4.46	4.46 ?
Total heating area[369]	H$_v$	m^2	194.4	194.4	*207.1*		
Superheater area	H$_ü$	m^2	52.6	52.6	*50.9*	*49.9* [406]	*49.9* [406]
Weight							
Engine only	G$_{Ld}$	t	80 [404]	80 [404]	80.6 (1915), *81.2* (1917)		80 [402 a]
Axle load		t			16.2 [405]	16.3 [406]	16.3 [406]
Number of units, cf.							
(Соколов (Sokolov))			30	28	>1,470	500	700
(Раков (Rakov), 1995)			30	90	1,408	500	700
(Wikipedia025)			← 1,528 →			500	700
(Le Fleming, et al., 1969)					1,150 - 1,600	500	700
(Chester (ed.), 2000)			← 1,528 →			← 1,200 →	

^{a}: (Knipping, et al., 2015), page 69 shows Э^г 5032 by Henschel with a weight (with supplies) of 80.5 t. The figure seems to be changed by hand afterwards.

[399] Unless otherwise stated, cf. (Раков (Rakov), 1995), page 184
[400] unless otherwise stated, cf. (Knipping, et al., 2015), page 69. Special features of class Э^М$_ш$ are not considered.
[401] (Rakow, 1986), page 116
[402] (Le Fleming, et al., 1969), pages 39f
[403] (Rakow, 1986), pages 173f
[404] (CIA, 1952), page 89
[405] (Le Fleming, et al., 1969), pages 40
[406] (Соколов2 (Sokolov))

Эу [407]	Эм [407]	Эр [407]	Эр [408]	Эр [409]	Эр [410]	Эсу [411]
5	5	5	5	5	5	5
1,320	1,320	1,320	1,320	1,320 [406]	1,320	1,320
2	2	2	2	2	2	2
650	650	650	650	650	650	650
700	700	700	700	700	700	700
12	*14* [411]	14 [411]	14	14	14	*13*
4.46	4.46	*5.09* [411]	5.09	5.09	5.09	*4.73*
195.2 [411]	*193.0 - 195.0* [g 404]	*200* [j 411]	*196.0*	*180.3*	*183.1*	*199.2*
66 [411]	66 [b 404]	66 [j 404]	*58.4*	*72.0*	*57.5*	*72.6*
85.6 [c 411]	85 (1931), *78 (1933)* [d 404]	*83.3* [h 411]	*85*	85	85 [f]	
16,7	*17* [e]	*17,5* [i]				
<2,166	>2,694	328	←	2,938	→	
	2,694	552	316	1,299	1,101	
2,535	2,325	<328	←	2,716	→	<22
3,450	2,700	←	>2,950	→		
←	8,119	→	224	1,345	1,258	

[b]: (Heywood, et al., 1995), page 30f shows a superheater surface of 64.6 m². [c]: (Chester (ed.), 2000), page 27 gives a weight (with supplies) of 81.5 t, (Le Fleming, et al., 1969) of 83.2 t. [d]: (Chester (ed.), 2000), page 27 indicates weights of 85 t (for 1932), 79 t (for 1933) and 82.9 t (for 1934). [e]: (Chester (ed.), 2000), page 27 shows an axle load of 18 t. [f]: only verified for Škoda. [g]: (Heywood, et al., 1995), pages 30f gives for 1931/32: H_v of 193 m², then 197.5 m². [h]: The CIA-report[404] indicates a weight of 81 t, (Le Fleming, et al., 1969): 87.2 t, (Chester (ed.), 2000): 85.8 t. [i]: (Соколов2 (Sokolov)) shows 16.7 t. [j]: (Heywood, et al., 1995), pages 30f gives: $H_v = 180.3$ m² and $H_ü = 72$ m²

---

[407] Built in USSR. Unless otherwise labelled, acc. (Le Fleming, et al., 1969), pages 47ff
[408] Built at Reșița and Malaxa (Perianu, 2000), page 101. Unless otherwise labelled, acc. (Perianu, 2000), page 121
[409] Built at MÁVAG, Data: (Rakow, 1986), page 224
[410] Built at Škoda, ČKD and Cegielski. Unless otherwise labelled, acc. (Chester (ed.), 2000), page 27
[411] (Rakow, 1986), pages 176ff

Soviet sphere of influence, probably as early as autumn 1944.[412] For their 'standard gauge'[413] engines, the choice fell on the series Эр.

As part of a compensation agreement with Romania from 1945, 224 units were built in Reșița and approximately 92 machines in Malaxa between 1946 and 1954.

The locomotives built by Reșița could be recognised by the semi-oval number plates on the cab, later the company logo was placed on the cylinders.[414] The boilers installed by Reșița differed from the original Soviet boilers by having a smaller superheater and a larger heating surface of tubes and flues.

In Hungary, MÁVAG built a total of 1,345 units of the Эр between 1947 and 1956.[414] These were initially classified as war reparations, but later deliveries were shifted to a commercial basis. During production, several modifications were made to the engines by MÁVAG. The most noticeable was the installation of a new type of superheater according to a Czech design. The locomotives could be identified by a cast plate

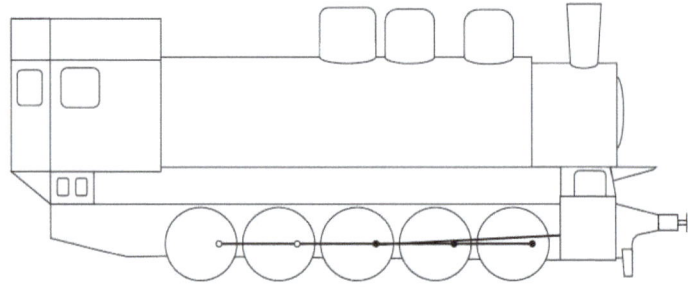

Fig. 39:   Profile sketch of series Эр [416]

attached to the underside of the cab, showing the inscription 'построен на заводе МАВАГ' ('built by MÁVAG') and the year of production.[414]

In Czechoslovakia, series Эр engines were built by Škoda and ČKD, with the majority of boilers and tenders supplied by 'Královopolská'[415]. Production at Škoda covered the years 1950 to 1952 (150 units) and at ČKD the years 1949 to 1952 (210 units)[414].

In Poland, Cegielski supplied a total of 898 units to the Soviet Union[414] on a commercial basis between 1949 and 1957. The wheelsets for these engines were supplied by

---

[412] At the Moscow Conference in October 1944, Stalin and Churchill agreed on a first draft of the division of spheres of influence in south-eastern Europe (Wikipedia027). At the Yalta Conference in February 1945, the foundation stone was laid for the Iron Curtain in Europe (Wikipedia028).

[413] In this case we are talking about locomotives with the Soviet 'standard gauge' of 1524 mm.

[414] (Chester (ed.), 2000), pages 24ff

[415] Today's name, successor of the former 'Československá zbrojovka Brno'

[416] (Раков (Rakov), 1995), page 264

Chrzanów and the tenders by PAFAWAG[417]. The machines supplied from there, like those from Czechoslovakia, differed in their boiler and the area of tubes and flues and superheater.

During the Second World War, Kolomna built about 20 units with boilers of the unfinished 1'C1'-locomotive of the class C^y (S^u), which differed significantly from the

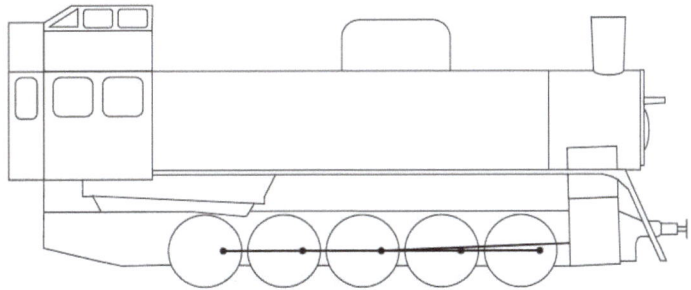

Fig. 40:   Profile sketch of series Э^{cy} [416]

main dimensions of the previous series Э. The name Э^{sy} (È^{su}) was chosen for engines of this design.

Looking at all variants (see also Table 17), the series Э was characterised by a number of changes of the boiler, which were in the end responses to changing requirements during its almost 50-year production period from 1910 to 1957.

As a result, the criteria of 'end-to-end design' cannot be applied to a large part of the series, as there were too many variations in the main dimensions. So, the total number of units built of series Э, which is officially stated to be over 10,000, cannot be confirmed for the most produced locomotive. In total, the criterion of 'end-to-end design' is only met by 3,000 - 3,500 units, depending on the information given. If this is interpreted generously, it may be possible to speak of around 6,000 units of series Э engines that follow an 'end-to-end design'.

The next most common class of the Soviet railways, the class O (see Table 16), follows the same trend. This class was also fragmented into a number of sub-classes, which will not be discussed in detail here. For this class the number of locomotives that followed an 'end-to-end design' is probably not more than 4,200.

---

[417] PAFAWAG = **Pa**ństwowa **Fa**bryka **Wag**onów (National Wagon Factory), former Linke-Hofmann-Busch (LHB), Wrocław

9.4   China

The 1950s were a decade of intensive cooperation between the People's Republic of China and the USSR. One result of this cooperation was the Chinese locomotive series 前进 (QJ)[418], a 1'E1' steam engine which was the most produced series in China with 4,715 units[419]. Originally the series was called 和平 (HP)[420], during the Cultural Revolution (1966-1976) it was renamed in 反帝 (FD)[421] and then later it received its final name 前进 (QJ).

The development of the engine took a relatively long time. While the first five prototypes were delivered from the Dalian factory in 1959 according to Soviet plans, over the next eight years a total of 41 further prototypes were built in batches of up to 18 units by various locomotive builders. It was not until 1964 that the decision was made to start series production at the Datong factory. These preliminary series of machines were called 老前进 (old QJ).[422]

Opinions vary widely about the Soviet series that was the model for the QJ-locomotive. One opinion is that it was the series ЛВ[423], of which a total of 522 units were built in the USSR.[354] Other sources suggest that although the ЛВ plans were initially the inspiration for the 和平 (HP), the series was later based on the plans for the ФД 21 (FD 21)[424], albeit with a new designed boiler.[425] A very detailed description of the locomotive design by Robin Gibbons[426] suggests that the 前进 (QJ) originated in the Soviet series OP 21 (OR 21),[427] which is considered to be the last steam locomotive design developed by the Soviet railways, but which was not built in series due to the switch from steam to diesel traction.

Regardless of the authorship, a comparison of the boiler dimensions of potential

---

[418] 前进 (QJ = **q**ián **j**ìn, go forward)

[419] (Gibbons, 2017), page 16

[420] 和平 (HP = **h**é **p**íng, peace)

[421] 反帝 (FD = **f**ǎn **d**ì, anti-imperialist)

[422] (Gibbons, 2017), pages 25f

[423] A 1'E1' - steam locomotive, named after the chief designer of factory Kolomna Лев С. **Л**ебедя́нский (Lev S. Lebedáńskij) and the factory **В**орошиловград (Voroshilovgrad, i.e. the name of the town Луга́нськ (Lugansk) in the period between 1935-1958 and 1970-1992.)

[424] The series ФД had two subseries ФД 20 and ФД 21, which differed in the superheater type used and the size of the totel heating area.

[425] (Schaefer)

[426] (Gibbons, 2017), pages 1, 23

[427] A 1'E2' - steam locomotive. OP stands for Локомотивный завод **О**ктябрьская **Р**еволюция (Locomotive factory 'October Revolution')[56]

Soviet engines shows that none of them match the Chinese machine, so it can be assumed that the Chinese locomotive is an original Chinese design.

How many units actually had the same main dimensions cannot be accurately estimated from the available sources. The available figures suggest that the main changes in the prototypes from the first engine, 和平 (HP) 0001, to the production series mainly concerned the boiler dimensions. Unfortunately, the main dimensions of the 老前进 (old QJ) are unknown.

Assuming, in the best case, that all locomotives produced except the first series of five had the same main dimensions, we can calculate a total of 4,710 examples for China that meet the criteria of an 'end-to-end design'.

Tab. 18: Main dimensions of series 前进 (QJ)[428]

			和平 (HP) 0001	Later 前进 (QJ)
Running gear				
Axle arrangement			1'E1'	1'E1'
Driving axles			5	5
Driving wheel diameter	D	mm	1,500	1,500
Leading wheel diameter	D_v	mm	920	920
Trailing wheel diameter	D_h	mm	1,120	1,120
Cylinders				
Number			2	2
Diameter	d	mm	650	650
Stroke	s	mm	800	800
Boiler				
Pressure	p_K	bar	14.7	14.7
Grate area	R	m²	6.8	6.8
Total heating area[369]	H_v	m²	*264*	255
Superheater area	$H_ü$	m²	*144*	149
Weight				
Operable	G_{Ld}	t	133	134-135
Axle load		t	20	20.1

---

[428] (Gibbons, 2017), page 23

9.5 Germany

Classes 50 and 52 were built in large numbers before and during the war. As mentioned above, class 52 was defined as a new class mainly for propaganda reasons (see Chapter 6). So, it seems that both classes meet the criteria of 'end-to-end design'.

The most important dimensions are summarised in Table 19. There was a high degree of agreement between the two classes. Only the service weight differs. This was probably due to the simplifications made, for example to the components of the class 52 (3,000 parts were simplified). As class 50 locomotives were also affected by the simplification measures (sub-class 50ÜK), it can be assumed that the value in the table only applies to the fully equipped 1939-peace-version, while the weight of the 50ÜK-engines tended to be in the direction of the class 52. The only difference in the class 52

Tab. 19: Comparison of the main dimensions of classes 50 and 52[429]

			class 50 1939	class 52 Bar frame	class 52 Plate frame
Running gear					
Driving axles			5	5	5
Driving wheel diameter	D	mm	1,400	1,400	1,400
Leading axles			1	1	1
Leading wheel diameter	D_v	mm	850	850	850
Cylinders					
Number			2	2	2
Diameter	d	mm	600	600	600
Stroke	s	mm	660	660	660
Boiler					
Pressure	p_K	bar	16	16	16
Grate area	R	m²	3.89	3.89	3.89
Total heating area[369]	H_v	m²	177.8[a]	177.8	177.8
Superheater area	$H_ü$	m²	68.9[b]	68.9	68.9
Weight					
Operable	G_{Ld}	t	86.9	*84.4*	*84*
Axle load		t	15.2	15.3	15.4
Total					
Cf. Chapter 7.4			3,451	6,717	
Condensing locomotives				-178	
			3,451	**6,539**	

[a]: (Ebel, et al., 1988) shows 177.6 m²; [b]: (Ebel, et al., 1988) shows 64.1 m²

---

[429] cf. (Deutsche Bundesbahn , 1953)

was the use of different frame designs.

For the other machines, no differences in frame type could be identified due to a lack of information. Although the frame type might be an important design feature, it is not considered in the 'end-to-end design' criteria.

Within the class 52 we have the variant of the condensing locomotives that have a significant change in smokebox and chimney. These engines consist of 178 units, which apparently do not meet the requirements of an 'end-to-end design' and therefore be have to be deducted.

It can therefore be assumed that the total number of machines of both classes (except the condensing engines) can be used to assess the most produced steam locomotive.

9.6   Summary

The definition of an 'end-to-end design' shows that it is necessary to look closely at the individual designations of the series, as these sometimes conceal different designs, or some of the designations were chosen for propaganda reasons.

In the USA, with its privately-owned railway system, it was not possible to develop a standardised locomotive and even large railway companies such as the PRR, had a fleet of units with many different designs.

In the Soviet Union, there were a number of high-volume classes. However, a closer look reveals that these were constantly evolving over the long period of their production, so that example from the early days of the class differed greatly from those from the final period. It can be assumed that perhaps some 3,000 - 3,500 units fulfil the definition of an 'end-to-end design'.

In China it was mainly the class 前进 (QJ) that was produced in large numbers. It can be assumed that around 4,700 examples were of an 'end-to-end design'.

In Germany, the events of the Second World War led to the development of an engine design that was standardised and produced in large numbers. Even if only class 52 is considered, more than 6,500 units were built according to an 'end-to-end design'. Together with the peacetime version of class 52 (i.e. class 50/50ÜK), which was identical to the class 52 in its main dimensions, 9,990 units with 'end-to-end design' were built. From the point of view of the definition of 'end-to-end design' the class 50/50ÜK and 52 can be regarded as one class – a twin-class – and considered as most produced steam locomotive in the world.

10 Helping hand for reconstruction

At the end of the Second World War, the railway network in the countries where the war had raged was in a catastrophic state. During their retreat, the Wehrmacht had tried to destroy the infrastructure (bridges, tracks, tunnels, etc.) of the cleared areas and, on Hitler's orders, extended this destruction to German territories, which should be passed over.[430] For post-war Germany, the destruction made the situation even worse, as the railway facilities had already been severely damaged by the Allied bombing raids.

Although attempts had been made to move as many locomotives as possible to the interior of the Reich before the surrender, a large number of German engines remained in the formerly occupied countries. There, in view of the enormous need for transport, the national companies tried to incorporated them immediately into the locomotive fleets of the respective railway companies. For the Soviet-occupied part of Europe, all German railway material found in the territory occupied or liberated by the Soviets were treated as Трофей (trophy, i.e. loot),[431] so it was often difficult to clarify the ownership of individual locomotives. This depended on whether the Soviets declared previously acquired material of German origin, also previously owned by the respective railway company, as 'German' or not. In some cases, this could only be clarified after difficult negotiations with the Soviet authorities/troops.

The distribution of twin-class engines (50/50ÜK and 52) at the end of the war, as shown in Figure 41, can only approximate the actual situation, especially as the 'end of the war' is officially marked by the German surrender on 7/8 May 1945, but in practice was a period that lasted from the liberation of the respective occupied territories until the official capitulation. Therefore, machine movements took place during this transitional period that cannot be recorded in detail. In addition, borders and state structures in the liberated territories did not yet exist in a peacetime sense, and individual railway companies, such as in Poland and Czechoslovakia, did not yet exist and had to be rebuilt in the coming months and years.

Of the 9,301 units delivered to the Reichsbahn, only 40 units can be definitively

---

[430] The Wehrmacht had special regulations to be carried out upon their withdrawal of occupied territories ('ARLZ'-measures: **A** for disaggregation (e.g. removal of goods); **R** for evacuation; **L** for paralysis (e.g. dismantling) and **Z** for destruction (e.g. production of 'desert zones', removal of the civilian population for forced labour) (Wikipedia029). Further actions were ordered by the 'Nero decree' (Wikipedia030) or the 'Scorched-Earth-Policy' (Wikipedia031).

[431] (Dejanow, 1990), page 76

classified as war losses: one each in 1940/1941, 14 units in 1943, 17 engines in 1944 and four machines in 1945. There is no trace of three locomotives.

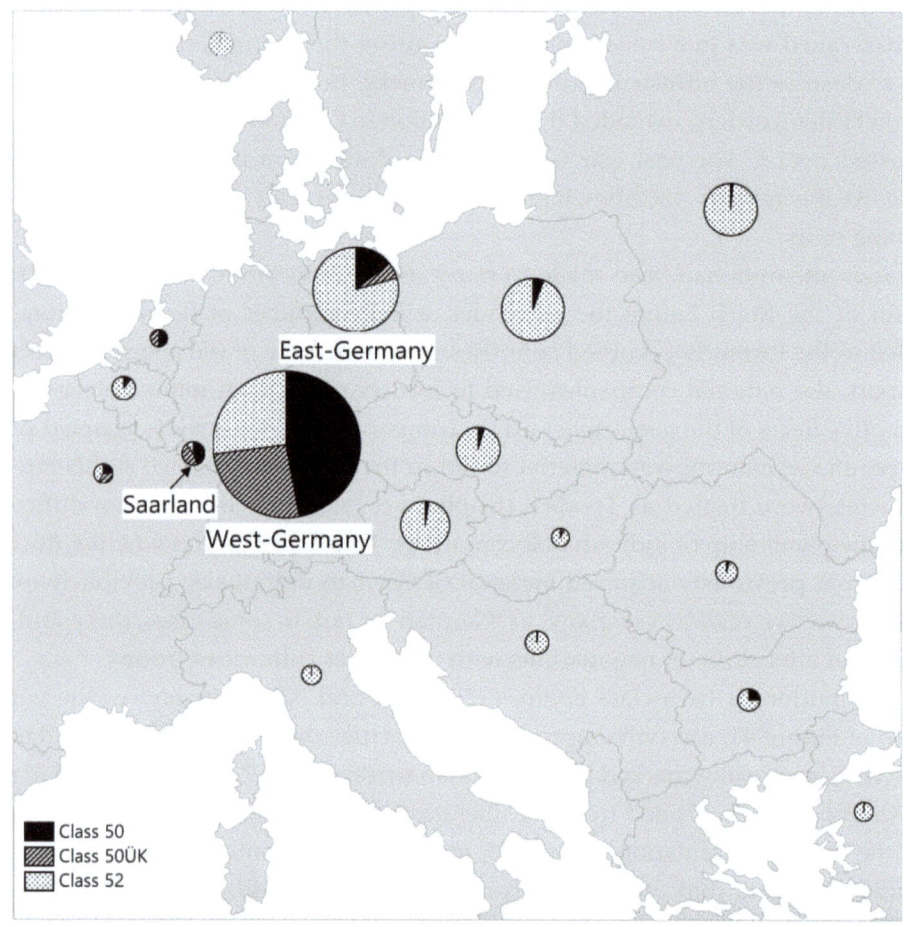

Fig. 41: Rough estimate of the location of class 50/50ÜK and 52 locomotives at the end of the war.[432] 9,301 units delivered to the Reichsbahn were recorded. (West-Germany: united British, US-American and French zones (without Saarland), East-Germany: Soviet zone).[433]

---

[432] The term 'end of the war' is here only vaguely defined. Although the Third Reich surrendered on 7/8 May 1945, by the end of 1944 France, Belgium, parts of the Netherlands, the Balkans, Hungary, Poland and parts of Slovakia had been liberated. For these areas, the war was over, although its effects would be felt for a long time to come.

[433] Due due to the sometimes confusing situation at the end of the war, the illustration can only be seen as an approach to the historical situation.

In the four German occupation zones that were set up after the war by the Allies, were a total of 5,170 units in any condition (including Saarland),[434] which still represented about 55 % of all the machines delivered to the Reichsbahn. The ratio of engines between the western and eastern zones was almost 3:1 (West-Germany (without Saarland) to East-Germany), which roughly corresponded to the ratio of the network lengths of the two emerging states (also about 3:1).[435] East-Germany on the other hand had a larger amount of war locomotives (class 52) in its fleet than West-Germany.

It is difficult to judge whether this was really an advantage, given the previous wartime conditions with their shortages of material and maintenance far away from peacetime requirements. However, it can be seen that the pattern that had already become apparent during the deployments to their first depots, namely that the war

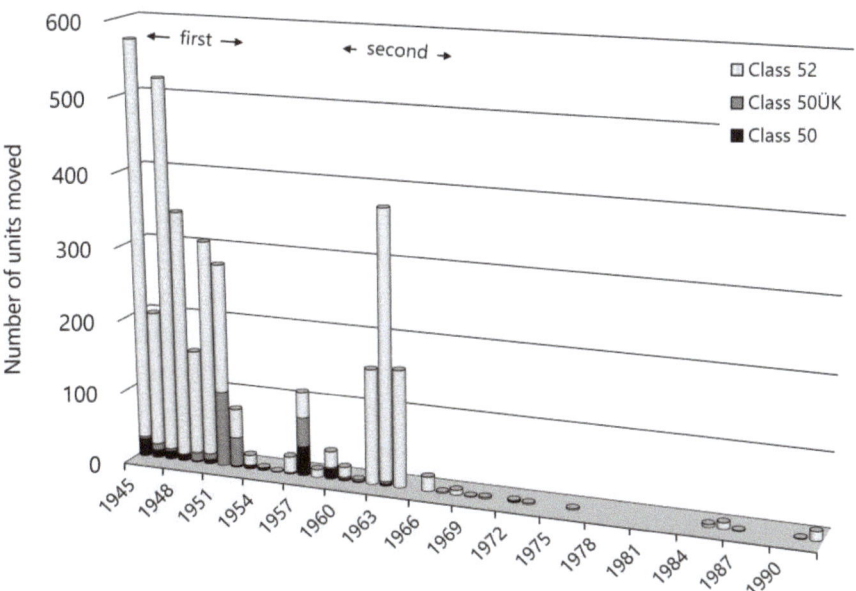

Fig. 42:   Movements of locomotives of the twin-class between the European railway companies over time

---

[434] It should be noted that in his book Hans-Jürgen Wenzel gives a significantly lower number of locomotives of the twin-class remaining in the western zones (Wenzel, 2014).

[435] Railway network: West-Germany (excl. Saarland): about 35.200 km, East-Germany: about 12.900 km (as of 1950) (Rahlf, 2015), pages 1185f

locomotives tended to be stationed more in the east (see Figure 30), while the class 50/50ÜK tended to remain in the west.

In the first eight years after the war, a number of locomotive movements took place (the first wave of movements) in order to consolidate, but also to meet restitutions and repairs, some of which were confiscations, imposed levies, but also purchases. This led to a clear redistribution of the available units after the war. In the part of Europe unter Soviet influence, some of the 'trophies' were given to the 'socialist brother countries' for use, but remained the property of the Soviet Union or the Red Army. The allocation of new locomotive numbers in the scheme of the countries concerned could be interpreted as an indication of the transfer of ownership, but it is not clear either, as it also happened that German machines ran for months/years with their old numbers, although they had already been transferred to new ownership.

At the beginning of the 1960s, a second wave of movements took place, which primarily affected the areas within the Soviet sphere of influence.

In order to get a quick and clear picture of the situation, the two movement waves have been displayed in so-called volume flow diagrams. The relevant railway com panies are shown as boxes in the diagram (cf. Figure 43, 44). Outflows from the companies are indicated by arrows starting at the top and bottom of the box, inflows to the companies by arrows ending at the vertical sides of the boxes.

The first wave of movements involved all railway companies in both East and West. The bulk of the movements were those of the railways east of the Iron Curtain, including Austria sending large numbers of units to the Soviet Union. Presumably these were 'repatriations' of looted machinery to the Soviet Union, some of which had been in service in the immediate post-war period for the local railway companies.

In 1951, the Belgian SNCB/NMBS received about 140 class 50ÜK locomotives, which had been built in Belgian factories in 1943/44. In 1946/47, the SNCB/NMBS sold a total of ten class 52 locomotives from Belgian manufacturers to the Luxembourgian CFL. In addition, in 1952 the Danish DSB bought 12 units of class 50ÜK locomotives from the SNCB/NMBS – also Belgian-built – to relieve its locomotive shortage. By 1951, the Italian FS had handed over all its remaining class 52 locomotives to the Deutsche Bundesbahn (DB) and the Österreichische Bundesbahnen (ÖBB). The transfer of locomotives from DB and ÖBB to the Yugoslavian railways (JDŽ) was the result of the beginning 'Cold War' and the attempt to draw the Federal People's Republic of Yugoslavia to the West or to reduce its anchorage in the Eastern Bloc. The exchange between the DB and the East-German Reichsbahn (DR), on the other hand, was small and limited

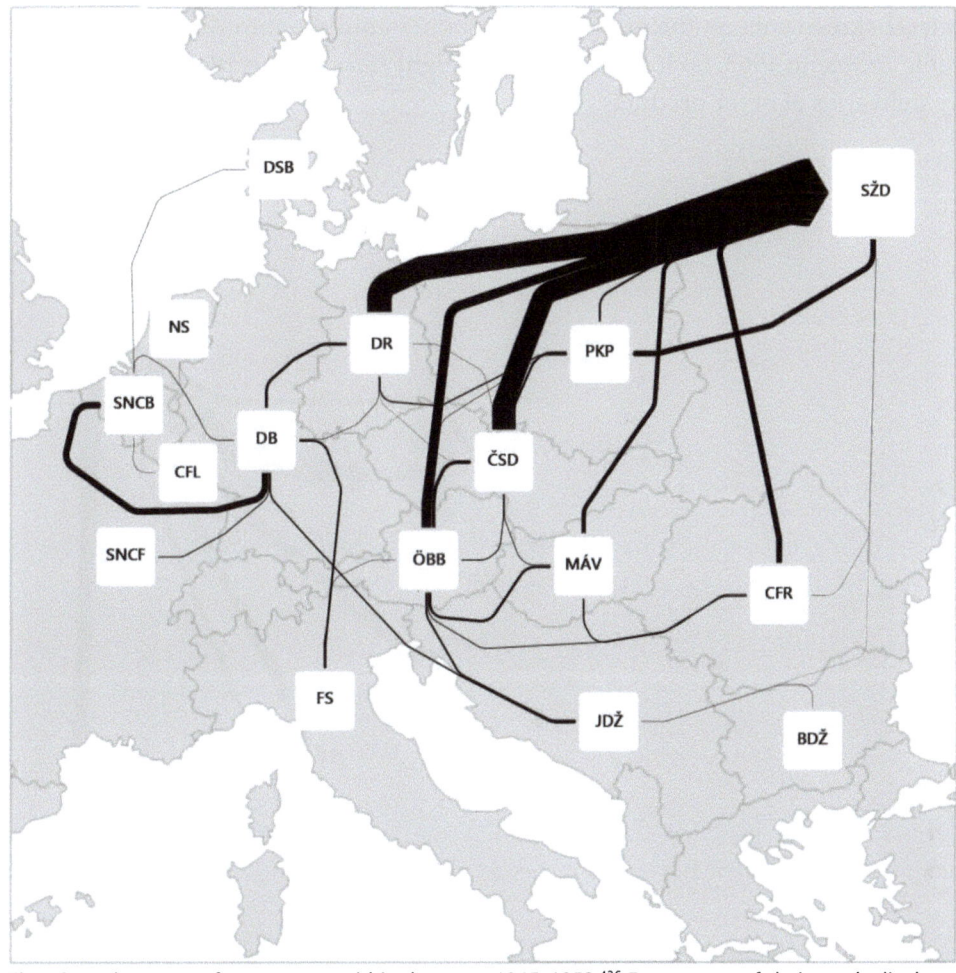

Fig. 43:   First wave of movements within the years 1945-1953.[436] For reasons of clarity, only displacements of more than four locomotives are shown.[52]

to a few units. Smaller returns from the USSR during this period went to the Polish PKP, which also received little contingents from the DR and the ÖBB.

At the beginning of the 1960s, the Soviet Union sold around 700 locomotives from its stocks to 'socialist brother states'. Not much is known about the price of the sales, or perhaps there was no price at all, as foreign trade in the Comecon was based on

---

[436] Status of the respective railway companies: 1953. DB and DR include predecessor companies between 1945 and 1949 and nationalised railway companies. DB includes the Saarland railway company EdS.

bilateral agreements on the exchange of goods[437] until the introduction of the transferable rouble in 1963. So locomotive sales might have been settled with compensatory deliveries of other products.

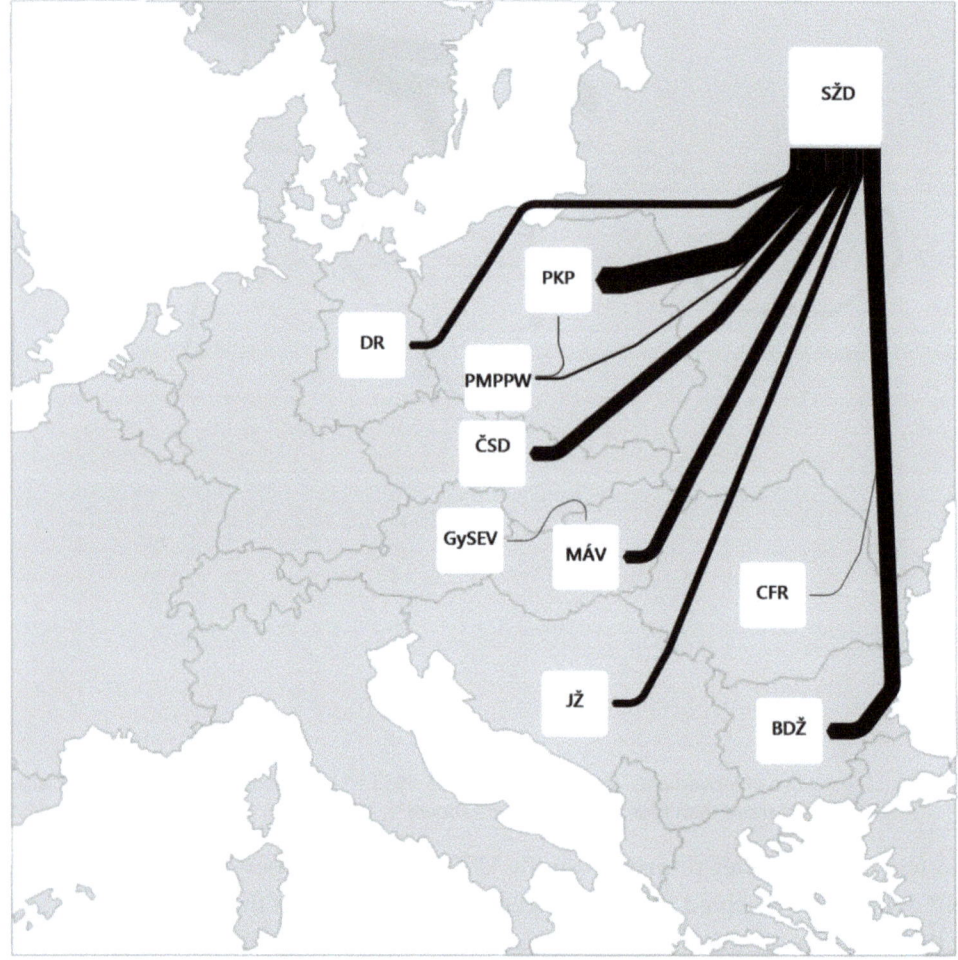

Fig. 44:   Second wave of movements within the years 1962-1964[52]

---

[437] (Kommunist, Moskau, 1964)

10.1 Austria

After the First World War, the state railways operated on the lines on the territory of the now smaller Austrian state, initially called 'Deutschösterreichische Staatsbahnen'. From 1919, they were called 'Österreichische Staatsbahnen'[52] and from 1921 'Österreichische Bundesbahnen'. However, the abbreviation 'BBÖ' was used for the company. After the incorporation of Austria into the German Reich, the BBÖ was taken over by the Reichsbahn and gradually merged with it. It thus became part of the wars of aggression and the deportations to the death camps or forced labour. The incorporation of Austria into the Reich was declared null and void with Austria's declaration of independence from the German Reich on 27th April 1945.

After the war, Austria was occupied by the Allies and divided into four occupation zones. The course of the occupation zones was roughly determined by the Allies in October 1943, but not definitively until July 1945. However, the division into zones seems to have been known to some extent earlier already in Nazi-Germany, as a number of Austrian Nazis fled to the Salzkammergut region, which was later occupied by the US, shortly before the end of the war, where they expected to be treated less harshly than in the Soviet zone.[438]

Initially, the British were still involved in fighting in their zone (Carinthia, East Tyrol, Styria), as troops of the Yugoslav People's Army tried to enforce territorial claims. However, the People's Army was then placed under Soviet command, as the USSR was interested in maintaining the negotiated occupation zones. This step led to a withdrawal of Yugoslav troops within a few days.

As early as June 1949, unlike in Germany, an understanding was reached among the Allies for a peace treaty settlement, with the participation of the foreign ministers of the USA, the United Kingdom, France and the Soviet Union. However, the negotiations lasted until 1955, when the treaty was signed and the Allied troops left the country. Part of this settlement was Austria's assurance of 'perpetual neutrality'. The idea behind this was to form a kind of neutral buffer between the communist East and the democratic West.

The war had caused great damage to the railway network, with about 40 % of the Austrian railway network destroyed.[439] In the summer of 1947, the Österreichische Bundesbahnen were re-established. 'ÖBB' was now used as the abbreviation for the

---

[438] (Wikipedia032)
[439] (Wikipedia033)

company. ÖBB was a state-owned until it was privatised in 1992.

At the end of the war, there were ten class 50 locomotives, eight class 50ÜK locomotives and 733 class 52 locomotives in the area covered by the future ÖBB. About half of these were withdrawn by 1949. Half of these engines were taken over by the Soviet Union, the other half to several other countries in Europe.

Fig. 45:　Model of No. 50.1022 (Roco 43289), driver's side.
The model represents the condition of the original of 1956 (last brake inspection 27.6.56). The coal box has been raised with boards, increasing the coal capacity. The locomotive number on the cab and smokebox door contains a '1' without an upstroke, which was unusual for German-speaking countries. Below the number is the inscription '15d', indicating the locomotive's axle load. The catenary warning signs on the sides of the cab are reversed. The locomotive is coupled with tender No. 9091.03 and based at the Linz depot.
Information on the historical model: Schwartzkopff 1940 → DRB 50 1022 (RBD Halle (Saale)) → 1945 ÖBB 50.1022 + 1968 Linz

Fig. 46:　Model of No. 152.301 (Gützold 32600), fireman's side.
Coupled with tender No. 9592.22 and based in Vienna, this model represents the state of 1956 of the former class 52 machine. The loco is kept in black, only the rod notches are painted red. Note the use of the '1' without upstroke for the locomotive number.
Information on the historical model: Floridsdorf 1942 → DRB 50 301 (RBD Posen) → 1945 ÖBB 52.301 → 1973 GKB 52.301 + 1976 Graz Köflacher Bhf.

In 1953 the ÖBB set a new numbering scheme into effect, and the twin-class locomotives remaining with the ÖBB were incorporated into the ÖBB fleet with their old sequential numbers. The bar frame 52's were given the series number '152', while the plate frame 52's retained the class number '52'. The series and sequential numbers were separated by a full stop.

In the early 1920s, a so-called DABEG feedwater[440] heater had been developed on behalf of the BBÖ. The BBÖ engineer Franz Heinl had also developed the Heinl feedwater heater, which was fitted to the BBÖ's series 729 express locomotive in 1931.[441] Convinced of the advantages of this technology, the ÖBB equipped a total of 40 locomotives of the 52/152 units with the Heinl feedwater heaters.[442] The systems were installed in the mid to late 1950s. They were installed in the smokebox in front of the chimney, similar to the East-German Reichsbahn feedwater heaters, and could be recognised by the hump in front of the chimney. The heaters were removed at the end of the 1960s as the maintenance costs outweighed the savings. The last 52 with a preheater was 52.4364, which was based in Linz as a fuel test locomotive and lost its preheater only in 1974.

In the mid-1950s, tests were also carried out with the Giesl-Ejector[443] developed in Austria. 52.1340 was used as a test locomotive. The results showed a coal saving of 5-10 %, which prompted ÖBB to order a total of 136 Giesl-Ejectors for installation in the 52/152 series.[444]

This meant that ÖBB had four different combinations in use for the 52/152 series: with Heinl-Preheater, with Giesl-Ejector, with Heinl-Preheater + Giesl-Ejector and unmodified machines.

Based on similar considerations of the German railways (West and East), the ÖBB developed a caboose tender at an early stage, so that the conductor of freight trains could travel in a separate room without having to carry an extra caboose. The design of the tender was similar to that later adopted by the German railways (cf. Chapter 10.9.3).

Due to the shortage of coal during the occupation, some engines were converted to oil main and oil auxiliary firing. When supplies of coal improved after the withdrawal of the Allies, these firing systems were removed and the locomotives were converted

---

[440] DABEG = **Da**mpfappara**teb**au-**G**esellschaft, Wien (Steam Equipment Construction Company, Vienna)
[441] (Giesl-Gieslingen, 1986), pages 179
[442] (Unknown, 1998)
[443] More detailled information on the Giesl-Ejector, see Chapter 10.9.2.4.
[444] (Slezak, 1967), pages 25ff; (Unknown, 1998).

Fig. 47: Model of No. 52.7088 (Märklin 3416), driver's side
The class 52 locomotive is fitted with an ÖBB type caboose tender (slightly larger than DB). The tender number is: 9793.51. The machines carry red handrails and the boards on the coal box to increase the coal capacity. The locomotive is stationed in Wien Ost.
Information on the historical model: Floridsdorf 1943 → DRB 52 7088 (RBD Wien) → 1945 ÖBB 52.7088 + 1972 Wien Ost

Fig. 48: Model of No. 52.3540 (Roco 72228), fireman's side.
This loco is equipped with a Giesl-Ejector[443]. The handrails are painted red. The locomotive is coupled with tender number 9593.109. According to the label on the model, it is based in Attnang-Puchheim. The last brake inspection is scheduled for 22.6.61.
Information on the historical model: Krauss 1943 → DRB 52 3540 (RBD München) → 1945 ÖBB 52.3540 + 1973 Linz

back to coal firing.[445] As a result of contact with the Soviet occupying forces, Trofimoff pressure compensating piston valves[446] were installed on some locomotives as a trial. From 1938, the Austrian railways had to follow Reichsbahn's colour scheme, which was retained by the ÖBB until the end of steam locomotive service. Sometimes the

---

[445] (Slaughter, et al., 1996), page 27
[446] This pressure-compensation piston valve[238] was invented in 1908 by the foreman of the Московско-Казанская железная дорога (Moscow-Kazan Railway), И.О. Трофимов (I.O. Trofimov) and, after initial difficulties and improvements, adopted for SŽD in 1925 (Wikipedia045).

coupling rods and rod notches were painted flame red (RAL 3000), sometimes also the handrails. The wheels and rims were either black or red.[447] The Reichsbahn standard lettering (DIN 1451) with pointed figures was also used for the inscriptions,[448] although some of the lettering on the class 52 was done in a corporate font (cf. digit '1' without upstroke).

The class 52 engines were the backbone of the fleet until the 1960s, when increasing electrification and conversion to diesel led to their retirement. As with other railways, they were used to pull freight trains and even international express trains.

The last machines were taken out of service in the late 70s. Some of them were sold to the railway company GKB (see Chapter 10.1.1.), which used them to replace even older locomotives, and others were placed in the army's strategic reserve. Some engine frames (35 units) were used to build snow ploughs of the type Klima[449] (series 9760).[450]

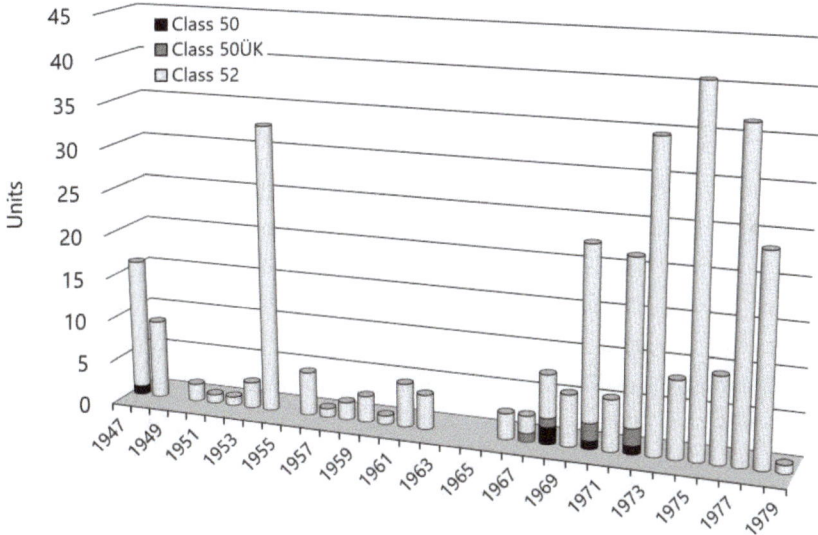

Fig. 49:   Retirements of the locomotives of the twin-class at ÖBB

---

[447] (Mehrl)

[448] (Rollo, 2017)

[449] Until after the First World War, locomotives were fitted with snow ploughs that could clear snow up to a maximum height of 40 mm. The Austrian engineer Rudolf Klima designed a snow plough using a tender running in front of the pushing locomotive with snow plough blades (Wikipedia034).

[450] (Slaughter, et al., 1996), page 27.

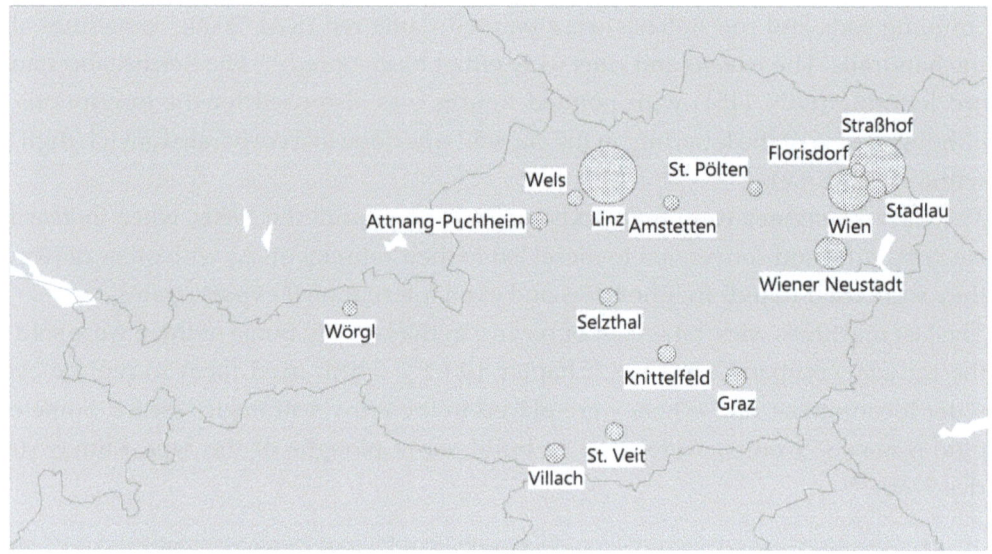

Fig. 50:   Last depots of class 52/152 locomotives at ÖBB

10.1.1   *Graz-Köflacher Eisenbahn- und Bergbau Gesellschaft*

The 'Graz-Köflacher Eisenbahn- und Bergbau Gesellschaft'[52] (GKB) was an Austrian private railway founded in the mid-19th century by seven mining companies in western Styria to transport the produced brown coal. To bring the coal to market, a railway line was built between Graz and Köflach, the 'Graz-Köflacher Eisenbahn'. After the later merger with the mine companies the railways operated under the name 'Graz-Köflacher Eisenbahn- und Bergbau-Gesellschaft'. During the Second World War, the GKB was part of the 'Reichswerke'[451]. After the war, the company was placed under public administration. All shares in the company were transferred to the Republic of Austria. In the mid-1960s, the Austrian railways (ÖBB) refused to take over the company. In 1998 it was split into a mining and a railway division again. Although both ÖBB and GKB were state-owned, GKB continued to be run as a private railway.

After the war, the GKB steam locomotives continued to haul freight trains with their steam engines. To replace the worn-out machines, class 52 units were bought from

---

[450] cf. also Chapter 7.1

the ÖBB. These were ten series 152s and two class 50s, plus two more series 152s for spare parts.

In the mid-1970s, the steam locomotives were gradually replaced by diesel engines until steam traction was discontinued in 1978. The last steam machines of the GKB were sought after by museum railways and collectors.

Fig. 51:   Model of No. 152.3110 (Roco 62266), driver's side.
A model of the locomotive shortly after its transfer from ÖBB to GKB (last brake inspection: 4.7.68). It is equipped with a Giesl-Ejector[443] and plate wheels in the front. The livery corresponds to the ÖBB colour scheme.
Information on the historical model: Jung 1943 → DRB 52 3110 (RBD Osten in Frankfurt (O)) → 1945 ÖBB 52.3110 → 1968 GKB 52.3110 + 1977 Graz Köflacher Bhf.

Fig. 52:   Model of No. 50.1171 (Roco 43303), fireman's side.
A model of an engine from 1987, after the end of regular steam service of the GKB. The locomotive is used today for tourist excursions. Note that the boiler has only three domes, which differs from the original class 50. The livery corresponds to that of the ÖBB.
Information on the historical model: Škoda 1942 → DRB 52 1171 (RBD Linz) → 1945 ÖBB 52.1171 → 1972 GKB 52.1171 + 1994

10.2 Belgium

Just five years after the foundation of the Kingdom of Belgium, the first railway line was opened in 1835. It was the first railway in continental Europe. The operating company was the state-owned 'Chemins de fer de l'État belge'[52] or simply 'L'État belge' (EB). In order to develop the network, the state sold concessions to private companies which, after a few years, operated most of the lines of the new Belgian railway network.

In 1926, the 'Société Nationale des Chemins de fer Belges/Nationale Maatschappij der Belgische Spoorwegen'[52] (SNCB/NMBS) was founded as the state-owned company of the Belgian railways. Even before the First World War, the EB had started to gradually take over and integrate loss-making private railway companies. The creation of SNCB/NMBS was an attempt to reform the state railways, which had previously been characterised by political interference and cumbersome structures.

A new company was set up and had structures similar to those of the 'Deutsche Reichsbahngesellschaft' in Germany at that time. The state retained control of the new company through a system of shares, but private investors could also participate in the company. The logo of the SNCB/NMBS, representing a 'B' in an oval, was designed by Henry van der Velde in 1936 and was deliberately chosen as a language-neutral trademark in multilingual Belgium.

During the Second World War, Belgium was occupied by German troops in 1940. On behalf of the occupying power, the Belgian railways got also part of the logistics of the deportation system. For this purpose, a concentration camp was set up in Mechelen in the Dossin barracks (1942-1944). It served as a transit camp for deportations from Belgium to the German extermination camps in the east. Special mention should be made on the attack on the 20th deportation train on 19th April 1943, when Belgian resistance fighters stopped the train carrying 1,618 Jews to Auschwitz-Birkenau on open track and helped 231 people to escape.

In Belgium, a total of 200 units of class 50ÜK and 100 units of class 52 were built as part of the German locomotive construction programme.

Originally, the Germans had planned to have a large number of class 52 units built in Belgium (around 200). However, Belgian workers delayed deliveries to such an extent that by the time the Germans withdrew from Belgium, only some of the ordered machines had been completed, and the half-finished locomotives were not finished until after the war.

Fig. 53:   Model of No. 25.002 (Roco 62252), right side.
The model shows a typical representative of a class 50ÜK of the Belgian railways. The boiler is missing a dome, the preheater has been removed. The pressure compensator valve[238] above the steam chest is also different from the peacetime version. The engine has a ÜK-style cab (i.e. one window missing, no roof ventilation), which bears the locos number, the manufacturer's mark (SAFB)[56], the abbreviation of the Latour depot (MUT)[452] and a yellow circle. It is coupled to tender 26.002. The machine has three lanterns at the front.[453]
The boiler except the smokebox is painted green, as well as the sides of the cylinders, the cab and the sides of the tender. The side of the running board, the headstock and the notches of the rods are painted in red.
Information on the historical model: Anglo-Franco-Belge 1944 → SNCB/NMBS 2502 (Schaer-beek) → 1946 SNCB/NMBS 25.002 + 1959

The production in Begium was distributed as follows:[56]

Anglo-Franco-Belge

26 machines of class 50ÜK: 25 units (numbers: 50 2130-50 2154) were delivered directly to the Reichsbahn. Another machine (intended number: 50 2155) was delivered directly to the SNCB/NMBS at the end of 1944, which put it into service under the number 2502.

- 25 units of class 52: None of these were delivered to the Reichsbahn as they were not completed until 1945. The SNCB/NMBS put them into service as 2675-2699 after the liberation.

- In addition, 50 tenders were delivered to the Reichsbahn.[454]

Cockerill

- 42 units of class 50ÜK (planned numbers: 50 2034-50 2075): These were delivered to the Reichsbahn, except for the last two of this class. The last two were ordered

---

[452] The abbreviations for the home depots correspond to the abbreviations for the Belgian railway stations, cf. (Kevers).
[453] Locomotives of the Belgian class 25 and 26 often had only one central lantern at the front, sometimes an additional one on the smokebox door, cf. (Dambly, 1994), pages 277ff.
[454] (Dambly, 1994), page 268

directly by SNCB/NMBS as 2500 and 2501.

- 25 machines of class 52: All these were delivered directly to SNCB/NMBS, who took them over as 2625-2649.

Énergie

- 16 machines of class 50ÜK (numbers: 50 2156-50 2171): These were all delivered to the Reichsbahn in 1943.
- 32 tenders were delivered with the locomotives.[454]

Hainaut

- A total of 24 units of class 50ÜK: These were delivered to the Reichsbahn (numbers: 50 1972-50 1994) with the exception of the last locomotive. The last one was directly put into service by SNCB/NMBS as 2503.

Haine

- 28 units of class 50ÜK (numbers: 50 2102-50 2129): These were delivered to the Reichsbahn in 1943/1944.
- 25 machines of class 52: These machines were delivered directly to the SNCB/NMBS, who took them over as 2650-2674.
- In addition, 38 tenders were delivered to the Reichsbahn.[454]

Meuse

- 26 machines of class 50ÜK (intended numbers: 50 2076-50 2101): Of these, only the units with the numbers 50 2076-50 2091 were delivered to the Reichsbahn, the rest went directly to SNCB/NMBS as 2504, in 1946-1948 as 25.005-25.012 and 25.023.

Tubize

- 38 units of class 50ÜK (numbers: 50 1996-50 2033): These were all delivered to the Reichsbahn.
- 25 of class 52 machines: All went directly to the SNCB/NMBS, who put them into service as 2600-2624.
- The steam locomotives were built at the Tubize main plant, while the Nivelles plant of Tubize supplied the tenders. Some tenders also went to Cockerill.[454]

At the end of 1945, three class 50 units (50 1458, 50 1098, 50 1729) were taken by the USATC[273] to Salzinnes near Namur for overhaul by the 755th Railway Shop Battalion. After the overhaul, the SNCB/NMBS took them over and added them to their locomotive fleet as 2521-2523. In early 1946, however, the Americans reclaimed the engines and took them back to Germany, where they remained.[454]

Seven other locomotives, numbered 2513-2519, were added to the SNCB/NMBS fleet after being left behind during the German withdrawal. In 1946, 50 2700 ÜK (renumbered to 25.022) was added after being released from the blocked line at Losheimergraben in East-Belgium.[454]

Not all series 25 machines of the SNCB/NMBS hat their origin in the former German twin-class. One of the series 25 engines was in fact a former German class 44ÜK (No. 44 1804), which had fallen into the hands of the USATC in 1944 and was overhauled at Salzinnes. At the beginning of 1946, the Americans handed it over to the SNCB/NMBS, which then misclassified it as series 25 (No. 2520, later 25 021). In 1950, the engine was given to the DB, which gave it to the SNCF a few months later. There it was immediately written off and scrapped.

It should also be noted that the series 26 (ex-class 52) from the Belgian factories were delivered without a chimney cap[455]. Instead, they were often fitted with small smoke deflectors (type 'Witte'). In many cases, at the request of the SNCB/NMBS, they did not have a closed cab, but the open cab like those of series 25 (ex-class 50).[456]

The driver in the cab of the Belgian locomotives was located on the right-hand side, like in the German version of the engine. This caused a additional work for driver and fireman[457], as railways in Belgium drive on the left-hand side.

In 1946, the SNCB/NMBS introduced a new numbering system for locomotives. Since 1931, all units had been given four-digit numbers, with the first two digits indicating the series and the last two the sequential number. However, this had the disadvantage that when the number of engines of a series exceeded 100 units, there was an overflow and not all machines could be summarized under one series number. Therefore, the series number had to be increased by one. This meant that machines of one kind could have several series numbers.

In 1946 the system was changed so that the locomotive designation consisted of two parts, a two-digit series designation followed by a three-digit sequential number. The series and sequential number numbers were separated by a full stop.[458]

Accordingly, the designation for the twin-class engines changed as follows:

class 50 and 50 ÜK: old: 25xy → new: 25.xyz

---

[455] The chimney cap extended the chimney beyond the boiler and contributed to improve visibility by reducing smoke drawing down to the locomotive (Niederstraßer, 1939) page 117. If no smoke deflectors were fitted, this device was all the more important.

[456] (Dambly, 1994), page 281

[457] As the fireman had a good view of the signalling in this case, he had to take over the observation of the track as well, similar to the situation in Germany when the locomotive ran backwards, i.e. with tender ahead.

[458] (Dambly)

Fig. 54: Model of No. 25.016 (Märklin 3314), left side.
The model of the locomotive corresponds to the peacetime version of the class 50. The chimney cap is shortened. The cab carries a label of the Latour depot (MUT) and a yellow circle next to the engine's number. The manufacturer's logo is printed on the cylinder. The engine is coupled with tender No. 26.036. Its frame was later installed by the German DB to loco 50 2755, in exchange it got the frame of No. 50 382 ('Schwerter Rahmentausch').[459].
Information on the historical model: Schwartzkopff 1941 → DRB 50 1314 (RBD Breslau) → 1945 SNCB/NMBS 2515 → 1946 SNCB/NMBS 25.016 → 1950 DB 50 1314 → DB 051 314-3 + 1970 Wuppertal-Vohwinkel

Fig. 55: Model of No. 26.033 (Märklin 37157), right side.
This model represents a class 52 from Cockerill, but equipped with a cab from a class 50ÜK. It is marked with the manufacturer 'Cockerill', the Bertrix depot (MBX) and the last brake inspection (28.7.53). It is coupled to tender 26.028, a 2'2'T26 box tender of the standard Reichsbahn construction. Note that the leading wheels have only seven spokes, while class 50 had leading wheels with 8 spokes. It is possible that a set of leading wheels from another series was fitted at a later date. The front lamps have not yet been converted to SNCB/NMB specifications.
Information on the historical model: Cockerill 1945 → 1945 SNCB/NMBS 2633 → 1946 SNCB/NMBS 26.033 + 1960 Belgium

---

[459] (Wenzel3, 2019), for 'Schwerter Rahmentausch', cf. Chapter 10.9.1

class 52:   old: 26xy → new: 26.xyz
class 52 with condensation tender: old: 27xy → new: 27.xyz

Of class 50ÜK engines produced in Belgium, a total of 14 remained in Belgium, while 186 were delivered to the Reichsbahn. Of those delivered to the Reichsbahn, 140 units were returned from West Germany to Belgium by the ORE[460] between 1949 and 1952, cold (73), hot (under steam) (33) or without tender (34). They were initially parked around Liège, Namur and Brussels.

Before the work of ORE came into effect, the SNCB/NMBS had ordered 300 units of a 1'D h2 machine (later Belgian series 29) in the USA and Canada, partly to compensate the heavy losses of engines due to the war. These were delivered in 1945/1946. The SNCB/NMBS was therefore reserved about the ORE's action, especially as the returned locomotives were not in good condition and had to be overhauled in their own workshops.

For this reason, twelve of the ORE's parked engines were sold to the Danish State Railways (see Chapter 10.6) and a further 16 machines were returned to Germany in 1955, where they were directly sold to a scrap yard. The remaining 112 units of the ORE action were scrapped in Belgium between 1952 and 1956.

After the German withdrawal, three condensation machines (52 1973, 52 1977, 52 1992) remained in Belgium. No. 52 1973 and no. 52 1977 were equipped with a 3'2'T16 condenser tender, the third unit with a 2'2'T13.5 tender (for tender types, see also Chapter 6.2.2). They were first incorporated into the SNCB/NMBS fleet under the numbers 2800 to 2802 and assigned to the Schaerbeek depot. In 1946 they received the numbers 27.001 to 27.003 and were returned to the German Bundesbahn in 1950. There they were taken out of service in 1951.

The locomotives on the Belgian railways were painted in the colour scheme of the SNCB/NMBS for both types 25 and 26: black chassis, the boiler except the smokebox in green (approx. RAL 6029 or RAL 6005).[461] Occasionally, a red stripe was applied to the running board and tender. The rest of the locomotive was painted black (e.g. RAL 9005).

---

[460] ORE = **O**ffice de **R**écupération **é**conomique. (Office for Economic Recovery). A Belgian authority set up in November 1944 to recover and restitute Belgian property, either private or public, at home or abroad.

[461] Steam locomotives were painted in shades of green without RAL markings. Today for renovations, the shade of green is determined by an analysis. (Train World Heritage) The RAL shades mentioned are approximations to the colours of the time and are used in today Belgian railway modelling. (Le forum de N belge)

Fig. 56: Model of No. 25.004 (Märklin 3316), left side.
The model is a class 50ÜK with a closed cab and a tub-shaped tender (No. 25 004). The whistle and bell are still attached at the 'peacetime' position on the boiler. The cab bears the Latour depot's initials (MUT), where the locomotive was transferred in early 1948.[462]
Information on the historical model: Meuse 1945 → SNCB/NMBS 2504 (Schaerbeek) → 1946 SNCB/NMBS 25.004 + 1959

Fig. 57: Model of No. 26.005 (Märklin 34156), right side.
The model of the locomotive is coupled to the tender 32.045, which carries several protective railings. The cab has the inscription of its depot Montzen (GMN), the sign of the manufacturer Tubize, a yellow circle and the inscription GR FAZ 28-7-53, which indicates that a 'Grande Réparation'[463] is carried out on 28.07.1953 at the Salzinnes depot (FAZ).
Information on the historical model: Tubize 1945 → SNCB/NMBS 2605 → 1946 SNCB/NMBS 26.005 + 1957

---

[462] (Dambly, 1994), page 280

[463] The 'Grande Réparation' corresponded more or less to the 'main inspection' of the Reichsbahn, Bundesbahn or East-German Reichsbahn, cf. (Vandenberghen, 1991).

The type 27 (ex-class 52 with condensation tender) had red frame and wheels (e.g. RAL 3000), the rest grey (e.g. RAL 7021).[464] For the lettering, the SNCB/NMBS used a corporate typeface.[465] The colour of the lettering was ochre (e.g. RAL 1024).[466]

Like the condensing locomotives, all series 25 units were initially based in Schaerbeek. At the end of the 1940s, some of them were transferred to south-eastern Belgium, where they were used in heavy freight service. At the end of the 1950s, the engines were taken out of service.

Fig. 58:   Model of No. 27.003 (Märklin 37172), left side.
It is coupled to the 40.002 tender. The cab has the Schaerbeek depot abbreviation (FSR) and a yellow circle. Externally, the engine is the same as the Reichsbahn version, with the grey livery of the wartime machines.
Information on the historical model: Henschel 1944 → DRB 50 1973 (RBD Berlin) → 1945 SNCB/NMBS 2800 → 1946 SNCB/NMBS 27.003 → 1950 DB 50 1973 + 1951 Bochum-Dahlhausen

The series 26 locomotives were not only stationed in Schaerbeek (twelve units), but also in Liège and south-east Belgium. In the course of the following years, a number of re-stations and tender changes took place. Like the series 25 engines, the machines were taken out of service at the end of the 1950s/beginning of the 1960s.

The rapid demise of the twin-class units in Belgium can be explained by the fact that the SNCB/NMBS had been pushing hard for the conversion to diesel and the electrification of its network since the mid-1950s, which meant that steam traction in Belgium ended quickly.

---

[464] (Traintamarre)
[465] (Grenier Ferroviaire - Spoorse Zolder) offers this for download under the name 'Santa Fe Regular'.
[466] (Train World Heritage)

10.3 Bulgaria

After start of the Second World War Bulgaria had declared itself neutral and signed a non-aggression pact with Germany and the USSR. Later, in early 1941, a meeting took place between the German military and representatives of the Bulgarian government, during which the representatives were persuaded to place itself under the protection of Nazi Germany. As a result, Bulgaria declared its accession to the Axis powers[467] at the beginning of March 1941. At the same time, German troops invaded Bulgaria. At the end of 1941, Bulgaria declared war on the USA and Great Britain, but not on the Soviet Union, with which it continued to maintain diplomatic relations. As a result, no Bulgarian troops were sent to the Eastern Front until the end of the war.

In 1943, more than 50,000 Bulgarians of Jewish faith were living within Bulgaria's borders. Although anti-Jewish laws had been in force in Bulgaria since early 1941, the Bulgarian authorities did not participate in the deportations, and many Bulgarian Jews were saved. Similarly, passports and transit visas were issued to thousands of Jews who had fled to Bulgaria from many countries.[468] Later, in September 1944, the country was occupied by Soviet troops and came under Soviet influence.

The railway system had already been nationalised before the First World War and placed under the Ministry of Railways, Posts and Telegraphs. There were close contacts with Germany in the railway sector, which was reflected in the fact that Bulgarian locomotives followed the basic principles of German standard steam machines and were further developed for local needs.[469]

As early as 1940/1941, it became apparent that the existing engines of the 'Български държавни железници'[52] (BDŽ) could not cope with the increased transport requirements of the war. As a result, a total of 50 class $58^{10\text{-}21}$ (G 12) units were leased from the Reichsbahn after the country joined the Axis powers. As the transport requirements could still not be met, more locomotives were hired during the war.

At first, the Bulgarian railways (BDŽ) did not want to use the class 52 engines, fearing that this type would interfere with the standardisation programme of the Bulgarian railways. In addition, the management of the BDŽ was irritated by the change of the German locomotive industry towards the construction of war machines. Initially, there was no clear idea how to develop one's own fleet. Finally, the management

---

[467] Axis Powers in the Second World War: German Reich, Kingdom of Italy, Empire of Japan
[468] (Wikipedia035)
[469] (Schnell, 2017)

requested a class 50 as a test engine. The test runs were completed in mid-1942 and led to the purchase of a total of 29 used class 50 machines in the peacetime version from the Reichsbahn.[470] Together with the test locomotive, these got the numbers 14.01-14.30.[471]

As there was still a need for engines and a huge backlog of defective machines to be

Fig. 59: Model of No. 15.215 (EuroforceCZ 105200.18), driver's (above) and fireman's (below) side. The model shows the original design of a class 52 with the typical large headlight on the smokebox door, the distinctive cowcatcher and the whistle near the chimney. Behind the coal box on the tender you can see the small extension, the oil tank.
Information on the historical model: Schwartzkopff 1943 → DRB 52 5915 (RBD Poznan) → 1945 ÖBB 52 5915 → 1945 ČSD 52 5915 → 1945 SŽD ТЭ-5915 → 1964 BDŽ 15.215 + 1982, now in museum Pyce (Ruse)

repaired, the BDŽ decided, for lack of alternatives, to rent 70 and later possibly 100 units of class 52 units. The increase was linked to a positive test of a 'test locomotive' of this class. As a result, 52 6801 was transferred to BDŽ. As the tests results were positive, more war locomotives were leased. The maximum number of hired class 52

---

[470] (Dejanow, 1990), pages 71ff

[471] In the BDŽ, the class number and the sequential number were separated by a full stop.

machines was reached in mid-1944 with 133 units. In September 1944, Bulgaria was occupied by Soviet troops. At that time, 125 class 52 engines were still on Bulgarian territory.[472] All hired machines were immediately declared 'war trophies' by the Soviets and placed under Soviet command, as they were considered German property. From the end of 1944, the Soviets leased the same units to the BDŽ, but rent was only charged for the machines that were used on Bulgarian territory. Locomotives that had previously been in service with the BDŽ and were taken out of the country by the Soviets did not return to Bulgaria.

Of the hired engines, a total of 85 units remained in Bulgaria[473], which were purchased by the BDŽ from the Soviets and added to the BDŽ inventory in December 1946 as 15.01-15.85.

Due to the confusion during and after the Second World War, the BDŽ had moved away from its guide line to operate its own fleet only with a few standardised types. Before the war there were 21 different series, after the war there were 41 series.[474] This resulted in considerable additional maintenance and repair costs.

In order to come somewhat closer to the pre-war status of the vehicle fleet and to satisfy the increased demand for locomotives, the BDŽ focussed on the twin-class machines. Accordingly, class 52 units were purchased from:

1956	20	units from the East-German Reichsbahn (DR),
1958/59	17	engines from Czechoslovak (ČSD),
1959-1961	10	units from the DR,
1960-1964	190	machines from Soviet (SŽD) and
1967	2	machines from ČSD.

In total, the BDŽ had 324 class 52 units. In addition to the existing class 50/50ÜK, in

| 1958-1960 | 21 | units were bought from ČSD. |

This brought the total number of class 50/50ÜK units to 51.

On the Bulgarian railways, steam locomotives for passenger trains were given the series numbers 10 to 19. Although the twin-class 50/52 was built as a freight engine, it was given the series numbers 14 (for ex-50/50ÜK) and 15 (for ex-52) for passenger service.

The machines were largely fitted with small smoke deflectors (similar to the 'Witte' type) and painted to BDŽ color scheme of the 1950s, e.g. moss green (RAL 6005) for

---

[472] More information of the leased class 52 units (reporting date 09.09.1944), cf. (Dejanow, 1990), page 77
[473] (Dejanow, 1990)
[474] (Dejanow, 1990), page 81

the wind deflectors on the outside, the cylinder cover, the upper part of the air pump, the side walls of the cab and the side walls of the tender's water tank.[475] The running gear, head stock and cowcatcher were painted carmine red (RAL 3002). The wheels rims were white and the buffer heads carried a white frame.

In addition to the locomotive's number, a board was mounted on the cab showing its use, its axle formula in Russian notation[358-360] and the average axle pressure. For a twin-class locomotive this meant : П 1-5₁₅. ('П' : 'P' for passenger engine; '1-5' : Axle arrangement 1'E; '15' : for 15 t axle load).

The BDŽ made attempts to increase the economic efficiency of the steam locomotives. In 1952, machine 14.01 was transferred to Stendal/East Germany for the installation of a pulverized-coal fired boiler. The installation was successful, but trials showed that the softening temperature of the slag from the Bulgarian coal was too low, so the inside of the tubes and flues were clogged by cooled slag. This reduced the boiler's

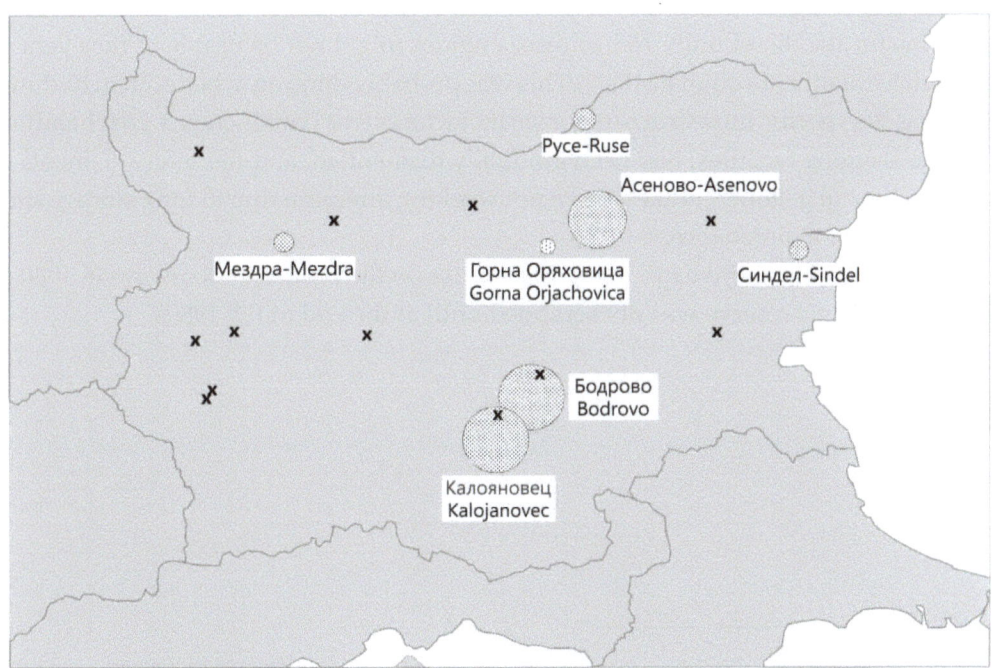

Fig. 60: Last depots of series 15 (ex-class 52) locomotives in Bulgaria (locations of less than three units are marked with 'x')

[475] (Dejanow2), (Holding BDZ EAD, 2021)

evaporation capacity, resulting in a shortage of steam.[476] As the company did not want to give up its local coal source, no further tests were carried out.

From the 1950s onwards, a further measure to improve efficiency was the installation of a mazut main or auxiliary oil burning system[477]. This involved either converting the tender to an oil tender or carrying a separate oil tank. The additional oil burning had the advantage of making the engines more resilient to load fluctuations and allowing more economical use of the boiler.[478] At the same time, the cost of retrofitting was much lower than for a main oil firing system.

It is reported that two engines were fitted with a Giesl-Ejector[443], one with an auxiliary oil burner and one with main oil burning.[479]

From the early 1960s, the BDŽ network began an accelerated transition to diesel and electric traction, resulting in the withdrawal of more and more steam locomotives. Some were sold to industrial companies and many were placed into the 'strategic reserve'. The background for this was that in the event of war there might be not enough gasoline for the diesel units and/or these engines might not be usable in the event of nuclear escalation through EMPs[480]. This was probably done on a 'better than nothing' basis, as the specific infrastructure for steam locomotives (water cranes, coal handling and de-slagging facilities) had been gradually dismantled, and the safety elements of the machine (e.g. boiler, brakes) were not working anymore due to long storage time and/or lack of maintenance.[481]

The last steam locomotive ran in regular service on the Bulgarian Railways in 1980,[482] and the strategic reserve was not scrapped until at the end of the 1980s.

---

[476] (Pierson, 1967), pages 9f
[477] Mazut is a low-quality heavy fuel oil, that is produced according Soviet specifications (GOST) (cf. also Chapter 10.10.7).
[478] (Henschel-Werke GmbH, 1960), page 306
[479] (Slezak, 1967), page 28
[480] EMP = **E**lectromagnetic **p**ulse, short-term broadband electromagnetic radiation emitted during a nuclear weapon explosion that can damage or destroy any electrical or electronic equipment and also the control of Diesel engines.
[481] (Wikipedia036)
[482] (Dejanow, 1990), page 84

10.4 China

In 1958, 毛泽东 (Máo Zé Dōng) announced the second Five-Year Plan. This took place on the background of deteriorating relations between the USSR and the People's Republic of China, which had already become apparent during the XXth Congress of the Communist Party of the Soviet Union in Moscow in 1956. The reasons for this were fundamentally different ideological views on the further development of communism and different ideas on geopolitical issues. In 1960 the relationship between the two countries worsened to such an extent that about 5,000 Soviet scientists and engineers staying in China for supporting technical projects had to leave. Also, any further supplies of steam locomotives from the USSR could be expected nor even support for the further development of China's own vehicle industry.

Possibly having heard of the large amount of class 50/52 engines in Europe, the People's Republic of China ordered ten engines of class 50 from the Reșița Locomotive Works in Romania, which were built on/copied there after the war (see Chapter 10.18.1). The engines were used for transporting coal trains in Manchuria and were adapted to the customer's specific requirements at the factory.[483]

The machines were delivered in 1958 (Reșița production numbers: 1266-1275) and were classified in China into series 迪克 (DK) as sub-series DK5 with sequential numbers 240-250. Some sources indicate that 40 units were built and delivered, but this cannot be confirmed on the basis of the Reșița delivery lists.[484]

As the locomotives quickly proved to be too weak for the coal trains, they were used for track construction and shunting in the non-electrified areas.[485]

The machines DK5 241, 244, 249 and 250 were known to have been used in the western part of the 抚顺 (Fǔshùn) open-pit coal mine. DK5 241 was sighted in 1986, but has probably been scrapped. DK5 244 was scrapped at the 长春 (Chángchūn) locomotive factory[486] in 1984. DK5 249 was seen as a wreck in 1987. DK5 250 was probably still in service until 1985, when it was transferred to the Railway Museum in 沈阳 (Shěnyáng) for display.[487]

The following changes to the original class 50 replica can be discovered at the exhibit

---

[483] (Perianu, 2000), page 102
[484] (Perianu, 2000), Annex No. 2, pages 150ff
[485] The mine's railway network covered some 500 km and was constantly adapted as mining progressed.
[486] today 中车长春轨道客车股份有限公司 (China Railway Changchun Railway Bus Company)
[487] (Pritchard, 1996), pages 63, 68

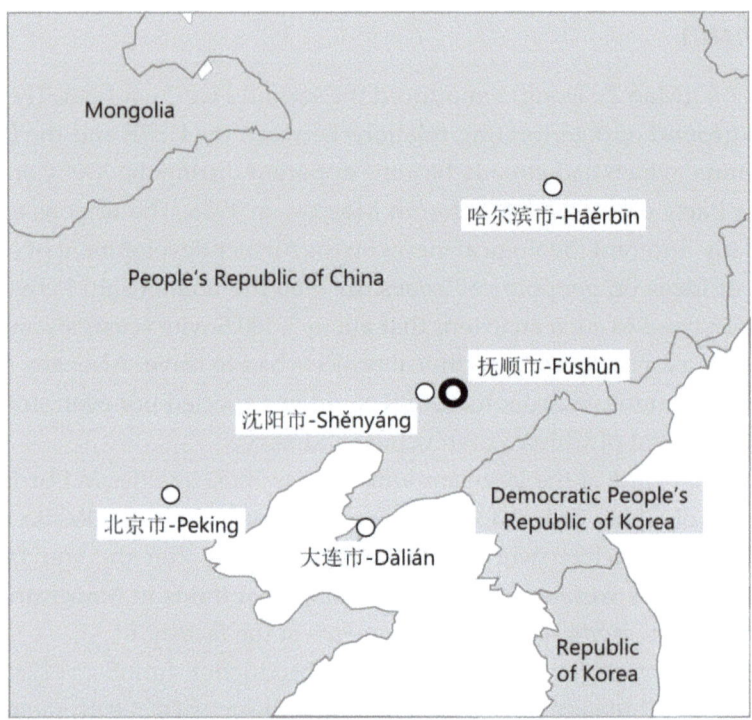

Fig. 61:   Location of the town and the Fǔshùn open-pit coal mine

of the railroad museum:[488]

- Larger and closed cab adapted to Chinese clearance gauge, with seats for driver and stoker. There are two air horns on the cab.
- Three domes are located on top of the boiler: two sand domes of Chinese design and one steam dome. The steam dome, which is clearly elevated, lies approximately above the third axle. A feedwater heater like in the 'peace' version of class 50 is missing. The boiler water is fed by injectors[233] of the Chinese X10 design, both on the right and on the left side of the boiler.

    The boiler has a small Soviet-style firebox door. Whether the smokebox was completely rebuilt according to the Soviet version like with the TЭ (ex-class 52 in the USSR) is unknown.[489]
- On the right side of the boiler, there are three air pumps of Chinese design. Behind

---

[488] see also (Forschner, 2017), pages 237f
[489] cf. Chapter 10.21

them, two lubrication reservoirs can be seen, one of which was used for the running gear and the other for the air pumps.

- At the front, the locomotive only carries one headlamp. The handles on the German-style headstock are still present. The engine is equipped with an automatic coupling, presumably of the Janney type[490], which was common in China, with two air hoses. Underneath there is a footboard for the engine crew.
- The tender corresponds to the version of the 2'2'T24 box tender with oil tank[491], but the tank has been removed. The water inlet is in the middle of the tender end. On the side of the tender are the inscriptions: 'Water 13 m^3, coal 6 t', which is a much smaller capacity than the tenders used in Romania (cf. Chapter 10.18). This indicates that they did not operate far from any supply infrastructure (water, coal).

---

490 (Wikipedia037)
491 cf. Chapter 10.3, 10.10.7, 10.17 and 10.18

Fig. 62:　Class DK5 250 in the museum in 沈阳 (Shěnyáng) in 2021.
The pictures from the previous page: ① list of exhibits in area 'A' of the museum (the DK5 250 is the 6th exhibit from the bottom of the list); ② the locomotive on the fireman's side; ③ inscription on the cab.
The pictures on this page: ④ rear view of the exhibit (The sign on the water inlet indicates a wrong year built); ⑤ additional air pumps; ⑥ view into the cab from the driver's side.

10.5 Czechoslovakia

The 'Československé státní dráhy'[52] (ČSD) was established shortly after Czechoslovakia declared its independence in October 1918. The new company took over the railway network of the Austro-Hungarian State Railways and parts of the Hungarian State Railways. Some private railways that existed before independence remained independent, but were nationalised in the 1920s. During this period, stations were given Czech or Slovak names. Bilingual names were introduced in the so-called Sudetenland. The first decades of the company's existence were marked by the adaptation of the network to the needs of the new state and a reduction of its former focus on Vienna and Budapest.

After the signing of the Munich Agreement in September 1938, the lines in the Sudetenland had to be handed over to the Reichsbahn, including the rolling stock. After the occupation of the rest of Czechoslovakia by German troops, the 'Protectorate of Bohemia and Moravia' and the 'First Slovak Republic' (German vassal state) were established. The ČSD was divided into the 'Protektoratsbahnen Böhmen und Mähren – Českomoravské dráhy'[52] (BMB-ČMD) and the 'Slovenské Železnice'[52] (SŽ). The BMB-ČMD remained organisationally independent, but was subordinated to the Reichsbahn.

In 1943-1944, the BMB-ČMD leased a total of 17 units (twelve class 52, five class 50/50ÜK) from the Reichsbahn. At the beginning of 1945, the Slovak Railways leased a total of 29 units of class 52,[492] some of which had been built in Czech factories a few months earlier.

The ČSD was re-established on the day of the German capitulation. As the railway network suffered only minor damage, rail traffic was resumed relatively quickly. All German station names used during the German occupation and the Sudetenland were replaced by Czech or Slovak names by 1948.

In 1948, a bilateral agreement was signed between the USSR and the Czechoslovak Republic[493], in which the Czechoslovak Republic committed itself to renovate or rebuild 600 engines and 600 two-axle standard and broad-gauge passenger carriages at its own expense as part of its reparations to the USSR. In return, the USSR promised

---

[492] (Bek, et al., 2000), pages 159f

[493] In February 1948, the Czechoslovak Communist Party seized power in a coup d'état (the 'Third Defenestration of Prague'). The 'Československá Republika' (ČSR) thus became communist. It was not until 1960 that the name of the state was changed to 'Československá Socialistická Republika' (ČSSR).

to hand over 98 engines and carriages from its spoils of war to the Czechoslovak Republic that were located on the territory of the Czechoslovak Republic and were no longer needed by the Soviets. They needed to be overhauled in accordance with the standards and regulations of the Soviet railways.[494]

As part of this agreement, 445 class 52 units were overhauled and rebuilt. 100 machines of these should come from the Soviet Zone in Germany and Austria. The remaining units were selected from the booty on the territory of the Czechoslovak Republic. The schedule for the delivery of the overhauled class 52 machines was 150 units in 1949, 250 machines in 1950 and the remaining 45 locomotives in 1951. The delivery point was the border station of Чоп (Čop)[495] on broad-gauge tracks. In fact, the work only began during 1949 and lasted until 1952.[494]

This meant that by the beginning of the 1950s, only 180 units of the 710 twin-class engines originally available on Czechoslovak territory remained, and these were incorporated into the ČSD fleet.

When taken over, the machines were fitted with red enamel plates with white frames and numbers. A house typeface was used for the lettering.[496]

The numbering scheme was based on a 1921 design by ČSD chief designer Vojtěch Kryšpín. Accordingly, the twin-class was marked as follows:[497]

1st digit	Number of driving axles, i.e. for the axle arrangement E: five driving axles	→ **5**
2nd digit	Maximum speed divided by 10 and then subtract 3, i.e. for the maximum speed 80 km/h: 80 divided by 10 equals 8; 8 minus 3 equals 5	→ **5**
3rd digit	Axle load in tons reduced by 10, i.e. for the axle load 15 t: 15 minus 10 equals 5	→ **5**

This results in the coding '555' for the twin-class. The following locomotive number was written in smaller letters and usually follows without a space: [498]

0xyz	ex-class 52
1xyz	ex-class 50/50ÜK
3xyz	oil fired engines

---

[494] (Motyčka, 2001), page 7

[495] The Slovak border station opposite, Čierna nad Tisou, became famous for a meeting between Alexander Dubček and Leonid Brezhnev in August 1968. During this meeting, Dubček was pressured by Breznev to abandon the Czech reform process ('Prague Spring').

[496] (Meszároš); (Banko, 1986)

[497] (Wikipedia038)

[498] In the literature, however, a dot is often used to separate the two.

05xy	'trophy' locomotives for the USSR or from the USSR to remain in Czechoslovakia (uncertain)
06xy	broad-gauge units
07xyz	engines in the stock of the USSR army (uncertain)
09xy	machines bought from the Soviet Union in 1963 and used as works locomotives for 'Nová huť Klementa Gottwalda'[499].

The tenders were numbered separately. The numbering was as follows:[500]

1st digit	For coal boxes >12 m³ capacity: digit 9	→ **9**
2nd digit	water capacity, e.g. 30 m³	→ **30**

This gives, for example, the code '930' for a tub-shaped tender:

930dxx   d was the type, xx was the sequential number

Accordingly, the coding for the tube-shaped and rigid frame tenders was 9302xx and for the box tenders 926xxx.

In 1976 it was decided that sequential numbers should be four digits and that the class code should be separated by a space. Accordingly, a leading '0' was added to the previous three-digit sequential numbers. For example, 555030 became 555 0030, which meant that a number of locomotive plates had to be recast and enamelled. From 1988 the UIC[501] numbering scheme[502] was introduced, i.e. a three-digit class code, a three-digit sequential number and the check digit, so the engine in the example above no longer had the number 555 0030 but the new number 555 030-6.[503]

From May 1951, as part of the Czechoslovak workers' state, machines had to carry a large red star with a yellow edge. Later, stars without edge were also used. From 1968, the star was often removed by staff in protest against the invasion of Warsaw Pact troops and the suppression of the Prague Spring. After the government of Alexander Dubček was replaced by a new leadership, the stars returned, albeit in a smaller form.[504]

The organisation of the ČSD underwent a number of changes during the period of the twin-class in the fleet of the Czechoslovak Railways. In 1952, six regional directorates were established (Košice, Bratislava, Ostrava, Praha, Ústí nad Labem and Plzeň). This

---

[499] 'Nová huť Klementa Gottwalda' was a metallurgical complex in Ostrava, integrated along the entire value chain with coke, pig iron and steel production. A rolling mill and other processing plants were also part of the combine.
[500] The rigid frame tender only carried this designation until 1950 (Bek, et al., 2000), page 158.
[501] (UIC, 2017)
[502] See also Chapter 10.9.4
[503] (KPZS)
[504] (Rubeš, 2018)

Fig. 63: Model of No. 555064 (EuroforceCZ 105200.13), fireman's side
The modifications of the ČSD can be seen on the outside of this model: additional window in the cab, modified boiler safety valves and a plate under the smoke chamber. The tender number is 930246.
In addition to the owner's mark, the engine number and the brake weight, the inscription 'SEVEROZÁPADNÍ DRÁHA DEPOT ČESKÁ LÍPA' (North-Western Railway, Česká Lípa Depot) is attached.
Information on the historical model: Henschel 1943 → DRB 52 2530 (RBD Regensburg) → 1945 ČSD 555064 + 1971

organisation was changed in 1963 so that only four regional sections remained: 'Východní dráha' (Eastern Railway) in Bratislava, 'Střední dráha' (Central Railway) in Olomouc, 'Severozápadní dráha' (North-Western Railway) in Prague and 'Jihozápadní dráha' (South-Western Railway) in Plzeň. This organisation lasted until 1988, when the railways were merged into an independent economic entity and separated from the state administration. The intention was to create seven regional directorates by 1990. However, this change did not take place due to the events of the 'Velvet Revolution' in 1989/1990. When Czechoslovakia split into the Czech and Slovak Republics in 1993, two railway companies were created: 'České dráhy'[52] (ČD) and 'Železnice Slovenskej republiky'[52] (ŽSR).[505]

10.5.1   Series 5550

Only 172 engines of the class 52 (including one condensation tender locomotive) that operated on Czech lines after the war were taken over by the ČSD. The engines were given the designation 5550 ('Němka', the German). The water overflows (and filling marks) on the tank tenders were modified to increase the volume of the water tank by 2 m^3. The designation of these tenders was changed accordingly to '9321'.

---

[505] (Ambros, et al.)

The condenser tender locomotive (ex-52 1965), which was fully armour-plated during the war, was first used by the Czechoslovak Army and had the number 559 0701. In 1958 it was sold to the ČSD and taken to the Kralupy nad Vltavou depot, where its condensation tender was replaced by a 'normal' tender, but the ID fan was initially retained. It was then incorporated into the ČSD fleet under the number 555 0177.

The other engines were gradually converted to ČSD standards. From 1947, nine units were converted to broad gauge at the Čierná nad Tisou depot for border traffic with the Soviet Union. They were renumbered 555 0601 to 555 0609. Engine 555 0604 remained in the Soviet Union (as TƏ-3780)[506], all others were later converted back to standard gauge and given new numbers within the 5550 series.

At the end of the 1950s, 36 units were sold to BDŽ and two (ex-class 52) to JŽ for use in the Kreka coal mine near Tuzla.

Similar to other Eastern Bloc countries, the ČSD bought a total of 111 class 52 from the Soviet Union between 1961 and 1963. They got the numbers 555 0201-555 0300 and were added to the fleet. One of the engines purchased was a former condensing locomotive

Fig. 64: Model of No. 555008 (EuroforceCZ 105200.1), fireman's side
The model still has the original cab of a class 52. It carries new boiler valves, the whistle in front of the cab and a plate in front of the smokebox. The large headlamp on the smokebox was not often observed, but not atypical for Czech steam locomotives.
On the cab wears the coat-of-arms of the Czechoslovak Socialist Republic (from 1960 the coat-of-arms also had a star). Next to it is the inscription 'ÚSTEKÉ DRÁHA, DEPOT KRAPULY n. V.'. (Railway of Ústí nad Labem, Depot Kralupy nad Vltavou), which indicates that the model shows a state before the railway reform in 1963. The tender has the number 930208 and the red star on the smokebox door is missing.
Information on the historical model: Škoda 1943 → DRB 52 7447 (RBD München) → 1945 ČSD 52 7447 → 1945 ÖBB 52 7447 → 1951 ČSD 5550554 → 1952 ČSD 555008 → 1964 ČSD 5553008 + 1972 Bratislava

---

[506] The locomotive was sold by the Soviet Union to BDŽ in 1962.

(52 1875) whose condensing unit had been removed by SŽD. The remaining engines were given the new number range of 555 0901 to 555 0912. These twelve units were taken over directly by the 'Nová huť Klementa Gottwalda' combine[499], where they functioned as works locomotives. It is interesting to note that these bought engines from the USSR had a standard gauge (1425 mm). There they might have been used in the western part of the former USSR on 1435 mm tracks, or parked there as a strategic reserve. They differed from the ČSD machines by the small smokebox door and missing spark arrestor mesh and baffle plate[507]. They also had no smoke deflectors.

Some machines had two generators, one for lighting and one for an electric adjustment of the valve gears. Parts of the 5550's design were used and further developed for the later Czechoslovakian Series 5650 series ('Štokr'), which gradually replaced the 5550.[509]

Fig. 65: Model of No. 5550266 (EuroforceCZ 105200.7), fireman's side. Small picture: driver's side of the cap.
A model of a newly acquired locomotive, bought back from the Soviet Union. A steam outlet can be seen between the chimney and the sandbox. The cab still bears the original Soviet inscriptions (MPS emblem, number ТЭ-5837 and БЕЛ ЖД[508]). An allocation to a ČSD depot has not yet given. However, the tender already has the number 9302266.
Information on the historical model: Schichau 1944 → DRB 52 5837 (RBD Königsberg) → 1945 DRo 52 5837 → 1947 SŽD ТЭ-5837 → 1963 ČSD 5550266 → 1965 ČSD 5553266 + 1968 Kladno

---

[507] Between the rear wall of the smokebox and the spark arrester there is a plate (baffle plate) which is designed to break up the coal particles carried along by the flue gases.
[508] **Бел**орусская **ж**елезная **д**орога = Belarusian railway, in this case a subsidiary of the SŽD
[509] (Bek, et al., 2000), pages 160f

Fig. 66:   Model of No. 5550259 (EuroforceCZ 105200.2), driver's side.

Another buyback locomotive. Here, the transfer to the conversion to the ČSD standard is more advanced. However, its past can still be seen in the steam outlet on the boiler. The engine has a large smokebox door and a large red star. In front of the cab, above the running board, you can see the motor for adjusting the valve gear, which was installed during the time in the Soviet Union.

The inscription is 'ČSD', the number of the machine and 'ČESKÁ LÍPA' (Česká Lípa depot). The tender is numbered 9302259.

Information on the historical model: Floridsdorf 1944 → DRB 52 7625 (RBD Oppeln) → 1945 ÖBB 52 7625 → 1948 SŽD TЭ-7625 → 1963 ČSD 5550259 + 1973 Česká Lípa

Fig. 67:   Model of No. 5550204 (EuroforceCZ 105200.4), driver's side

This model shows a repurchase from the Soviet Union with a small smokebox door and on it a small red star. At the same time, the large Soviet headlamp has been retained. The colour scheme is all black with white stripes on the running board.

The cab has the ČSD ownership mark and the inscription 'BRATISLAVSKÁ DRÁHA, DEPOT BRA-TISLAVA VÝCHOD' (Bratislava Railway, Bratislava East Depot) on the bottom right. The inscription indicates the condition of the model just before the railway reform of 1963. The number of the tender is 9302204. The locomotive and tender numbers were only inscribed, not yet applied with enamel plates.

Information on the historical model: Esslingen 1943 → DRB 52 3670 (RBD Oppeln) → 1945 ČSD 52 3670 → 1945 MÁV 52 3670 → 1948 CFR → 1951 SŽD TЭ-3670 → 1962 ČSD 5550204 → 1965 ČSD 5553204 + 1968 Břeclav

10.5.2   Series 5551

Among the all foreign machines that remained with the ČSR after the war we can find 29 units of class 50/50ÜK. All of these machines came from the German Reich (in this case Silesia) or the Ostbahn of the General Government, with the exception of two units, which originally were leased by BMB-ČMD from the Reichsbahn.[510]

After the spoils issue was settled with the Soviet Union, these remaining locomotives were transferred to the ČSD fleet under the numbers 555101 to 555128. One of the machines was used as a spare parts donor. The class 50ÜK machines received the numbers 555120, 555125 and 555126.[511]

During their service with the ČSD they were adapted to Czechoslovakian standards. The feedwater heater was removed and the German lubricators were replaced by a Czechoslovakian design. The German safety valves were replaced by Pop-Coale valves.[512] Also Trofimoff valves[446] were also installed. All 5551 engines were fitted with a 9261 tender.[511]

Kylchap blowpipe systems[513] were fitted to 555105, 555108, 555118 and possibly also to 555102.[514] Engine 555108 was also fitted with a Giesl-Ejector[443] in 1958.[515] Tests showed that the Giesl-Ejector was economically superior to the Kylchap system. For this reason, Giesl-Ejectors were temporarily used in a number of ČSD locomotives to save fuel[516] – until the shortage of foreign currency for paying the licence fees put an end to their use.[517] In 1959/1960, the 21 units of series 5551 were sold to BDŽ, where they became series 14 (cf. Chapter 10.3).

10.5.3   Series 5553

The low price of oil and the positive experience with oil firing in steam locomotives operated by other railway companies prompted ČSD to convert a number of its 5550 series engines to oil main firing. The first 30 units were converted in 1963 with the

---

[510] Zdeněk Bek refers to 28 engines (Bek, et al., 2000), page 165.

[511] (Bek, et al., 2000), page 165. Unit 555125 is not regarded as an ÜK variant there.

[512] These were safety valves made by the US company 'Coale Muffler and Safety Valve Co.' in Baltimore. These were also used on some Reichsbahn engines, as well as with the ÖBB.

[513] Cf. Chapter 10.18.1

[514] This is only a single exhaust system, i.e. with only one chimney.

[515] (Slezak, 1967), pages 25ff

[516] Josef Slezak reports a total of 856 units delivered (Slezak, 1967), pages 25ff.

[517] (Bek, et al., 2000), pages 165f

help of experts from Slovnaft in Bratislava.[518] They were given the class code 5553, retaining their original sequential numbers. Another 14 locomotives were rebuilt at PLB[519] Most and Nymburk.[520] The various conversions had different designs depending on where they were rebuilt.

This changed when the total of 100 units of ТЭ series locomotives were purchased from the Soviet Union between 1961 and 1963 were converted to main oil-main firing at the Soviet depots in Ковель (Kovel) and in Івано-Франківськ (Ivano-Frankivsk).

Fig. 68: Model of No. 5550274 (EuroforceCZ 105200.7), driver's side
The model shows the locomotive shortly after it was purchased from the Soviet Union and converted to oil-firing. The coal box on the tender has been lengthened and a flat oil tank has been fitted at the top. The side walls of the original coal box have been reinforced with additional gusset plates. The length of the tender remained unchanged. In addition to the original Soviet markings (MPS emblem, ТЭ-2471 and former ownership mark БЕЛ ЖД (BEL ŽD[508]), the ČSD mark and the new number have been added. The tender has no number.
Information on the historical model: Henschel 1943 → DRB 52 2471 (RBD Osten in Frankfurt (O)) → 1945 SŽD ТЭ-2471 → 1963 ČSD 5550274, 5553274 + 1968 Bratislava

Another group of 99 locomotives of the 5550 series were sent to the USSR by the ČSD and also rebuilt there, so that 199 units were converted to oil main firing. All these machines got the series designation 5553.

During the conversion, the firebox was lined with firebricks up to the top, increasing the operating weight of the engine from 84.3 tons to 86.6 tons and the axle load to 16 tons. However, the conversion was accompanied by a 20 - 25% increase of power of the machine.

---

[518] Slovnaft operated and still operates the largest oil refinery in the Slovak Republic, succeeding the former Apollo refinery, founded in 1895 and nationalised in 1949. During the Second World War, the refinery was run by the German I.G. Farben.

[519] PLB = Pobočné lokomotivní depo (Branch locomotive depot)

[520] (Bek, et al., 2000), Seite 167

Fig. 69:   Model of No. 5553278 (EuroforceCZ 105200.8), fireman's side
This model shows an oil-fired locomotive bought from the Soviet Union after complete take-over into the ČSD stock: The Soviet lettering has been removed and the large front lantern has disappeared. The steam outlet behind the chimney, the modified safety valves on the boiler and, of course, the flat oil tank from the conversion were reminiscent of the Soviet time and conversion. The locomotive has a white stripe around the running boards and under the cab. The tender number is 9303278.
Information on the historical model: Cegielski 1944 → DRB 52 1336 (RBD Wien) → 1945 ČSD 52 1336 → 1945 SŽD TЭ-1336 → 1963 ČSD 5550278 → 1964 ČSD 5553278 + 1972 Bratislava

Fig. 70:   Model of the 5553029 (EuroforceCZ 105200.x), driver's side
In this model the engine was probably modified by a Czech workshop to oil firing. The cylin-drical oil tank is placed in the coal box. The water supply (30 m³) seems not having changed, according to the inscription. As the clearance on ČSD tracks is larger than for example in Ger-many, running with such a tank on domestic lines should be no problem. Inscriptions on the cab: 'DEPO BRATISLAVA VÝCHOD' (Bratislava East Depot). The tender number is 9303288.
Information on the historical model: Škoda 1944 → DRB 52 7470 (RBD Regensburg) → 1945 ČSD 5550290 → 1964 ČSD 5553039 + 1970 Bratislava

A heavy oil tank for Mazut[477] was installed in the tender's coal box. Various capacities of oil tanks between 10 and 13 m³ were used. Locomotives rebuilt in the Soviet Union can be identified by the 14 m³ tank, which was flattened at the top. As with the other heavy oil machines, the mazut had to be liquefied by an external steam source before the burners of the locomotive were started.

The water capacity was reduced to 26 m³ and the tender designation was changed to '9303'.[521] It is reported that one of these machines was also fitted with a Giesl-Ejector[443].[522]

After their return from the Soviet Union, the machines were distributed to four locations: Bratislava-Východ, Brno-Maloměřice, Kralupy nad Vltavou and Zdice. The staff called them 'Mazutka' or 'Mazutova' (from the fuel mazut).

The ČSR received its oil from Slofnaft, which in turn was supplied by a branch of the 'Pipeline of Friendship'. At the end of the 1970's, there was a significant rise in oil prices, which accelerated the decline and retirement of this series, especially as the electrification of the lines was pushed forward.

Fig. 71:   Model of No. 5553289 (EuroforceCZ 105200.9), fireman's side
This model shows an engine from a Soviet conversion and a Giesl-Ejector.
Inscriptions on the cab: 'BRATISLAVSKÁ ŽELEZNICE-DEPO BRATISLAVA VÝCHOD' (Bratislava East Railway Depot). The tender number is 9303289.
Information on the historical model: Chrzanów 1943 → DRB 52 5230 (RBD Osten in Frankfurt (O)) → 1945 DRo 52 5230 → 1947 SŽD ТЭ-5230 → 1963 ČSD 5550289 → 1964 ČSD 5553289 + 1971 Bratislava

Unfortunately, there have been three boiler explosions of these machines (Bratislava's 5553277, Zdické's 5553280 and Maloměřice's 5553231) that can be directly attributed to the conversion. In all cases, the cause was too low a water level in the boiler. This was due to the installed boiler fittings (one water gauge glass and two test valves), which differed from the ČSD standard (two water glasses). In addition, the staff was inexperienced in heating these units, which were very different from coal-fired locomotives.[523]

---

[521] (Bek, et al., 2000), pages 166ff
[522] (Slezak, 1967), page 28. More detailled information on the Giesl-Ejector, cf. Chapter 10.9.2.4.
[523] (Bek, et al., 2000), page 167. See also the experience of the staff with the oil-fired units in Poland (cf. Chapter 10.17)

In Czechoslovakia, as in other countries, class 5550, 5551 and 5553 engines were used for all types of rail transport. A number of them were used as heating units after they were taken out of service.

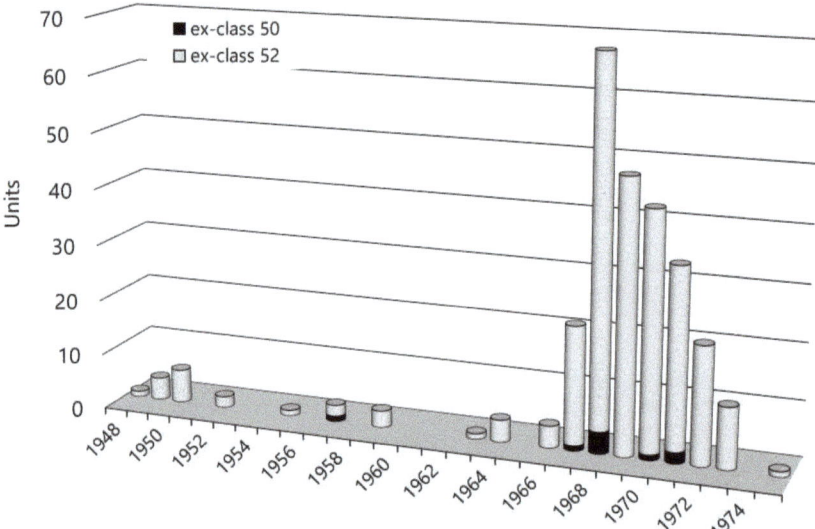

Fig. 72:   Retirements of locomotives of the former twin-class at ČSD

Fig. 73:   Last depots of the 555 series at the ČSD

10.6 Denmark

Denmark also had a great need for locomotives after the war. As it was known that there were a number of engines in Belgium that the SNCB/NMBS wanted to sell, the 'Danske Statsbaner'[52] (DSB) contacted the SNCB/NMBS in 1951 and ordered twelve class 50ÜK machines. It was planned that ten units would be put into service, while two would be used as spare part source.

The contract was signed at the end of 1951. The total purchase price was 996,000 DKK[524]. The transaction was formally handled by the companies Sanico in København (Copenhagen) and M. - G. Herbillion & Co. in Liège.[524]

For technical supervision of the purchase, in early 1952 a delegation from DSB travelled to Schaerbeek in Belgium to inspect the purchased machines and prepare them for transport to Denmark. The transfer took place in two trains of six units each. The first train transferred the machines 50 2113 (later N 201), 50 2119 (later N 202), 50 1989 (later N 203), 50 2114 (later N 205), 50 2017 (later N 207) and 50 2141 (later N 208). The second train started six days later with the engines 50 2088 (later N 204), 50 2122 (later N 206), 50 2133 (later N 209), 50 2009 (later N 210) and the spare parts donors 50 2019 and 50 2139.[524]

The route was from Schaerbeek via Antwerp, Arnhem, Oldenzaal, Osnabrück, Bremen, Hamburg to Padborg on the Danish border. The driving and coupling rods of the locomotives were removed for transport. The journey to Padborg took three days in each case.[524]

On arrival in Denmark, it became apparent that extensive repairs and adaptations to Danish standards were necessary. As part of this, some boilers were replaced: N 208 received the boiler of 50 2139, N 209 received the boiler of N 208 and N 210 received the boiler of N 209. N 210's boiler thus remained as a the spare boiler. The chimney was replaced by a lower chimney, a running board was fitted in front of the smokebox and the smokebox door was replaced. All machines were also fitted with wheel flange lubrication[525].

The engines were fitted with fixed large cowcatchers and an access ladder behind the

---

[524] (LC). With the historical exchange rate (1953) DKK/DM = 0.604 (FXTOP) and the historical development of spending power (Deutsche Bundesbank), this results in a value of approx. 130,000 € per unit according to today's values (2021).

[525] Wheel flange lubrication reduces abrasion on wheel flanges and rails. In the simplest case, grease is applied to the front wheelset. As the grease is distributed along the sides of the rail, this automatically results in lubrication of the following wheelsets.

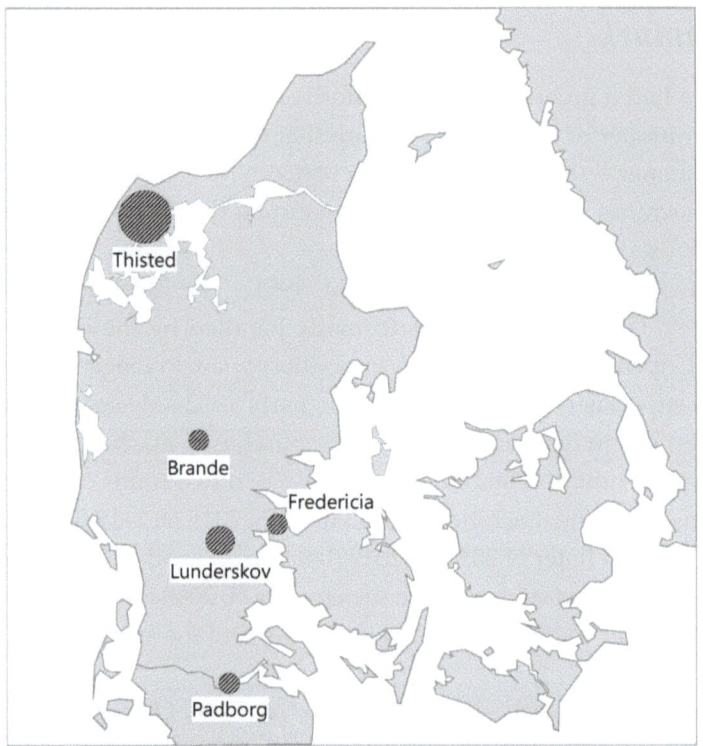

Fig. 74: Last depots of the locomotives of series N in Denmark

right cylinder.[526] The overhaul of the machines to the desired standard took until early 1954.

The locomotives did not wear the brass plates of their numbers that was usual for the DSB. Instead, the order numbers were applied by means of rub-off letters, later these were applied to plates so that from a distance it looked as if they had brass plates. For the lettering the DSB did not use a special font. Stencils were used to apply the individual letters to the engines. The lettering on the cab side was 18 cm high, others, such as on the smokebox door, were 11 cm high.[527]

The units were painted with RAL 9005 (jet black), some of them had a roof painted with basalt grey (RAL 7012).[528] A red-white-red banderol in the national colours was placed around the chimney.

---

[526] (Ebel, et al., 1988), pages 326ff
[527] (Danmarks Jernbanemuseum, 2021)
[528] (Wikipedia039)

Fig. 75:   Model of No. N 201 (Roco 62261), driver's side.
The model shows the machine without feedwater heater and feedwater dome. The running board is open with a simple access to the smokebox. The boiler has no smoke deflectors. The unit has an ÜK-style cab (i.e. no roof ventilation) with two windows. Note the Danish headlights consisting of only two lanterns. The revision date is given as 26.12.52, i.e. the condition shortly after arrival in Denmark is shown.
Information on the historical model: Haine 1943 → DRB 50 2113 (RBD Mainz) → 1945 DRw 50 2113 → 1949 SNCB/NMBS 50 2113 → 1952 DSB N 201 + 1970 Fredericia

Fig. 76:   Model of No. N 202 (Roco 63252), fireman's side.
This model shows the version of the engine from 1959/60 (brake inspection: 26.11.59). Also, without water heater and smoke deflectors, but with four domes. The running board is open with simple access to the smokebox. The cab is of peacetime design. Snow plough and ladder at the front of the cylinder were not (yet?) fitted.
Information on the historical model: Haine 1943 → DRB 50 2119 (RBD Mainz) → 1945 DRw 50 2119 → 1949 SNCB/NMBS 50 2119 → 1952 DSB N 202 + 1966 Thisted

The machines were valued as powerful machines, but their axle load meant that they could not be used on all lines. They were mainly used to haul freight trains and occasionally helped out with passenger trains. For transport to Germany, the tender of the N 205 was fitted with three headlights according to West-German standards. The unit then ran from Padborg to Flensburg with the tender in front.[529]

With the increasing procurement and use of diesel engines of the series MX and MY[532], the class N was increasingly replaced. The last active locomotives were N 207, N 209 and N 210, with N 207 making its last run in 1970.

Fig. 77: Model of No. N 205 (Märklin 37831), driver's side.
This model shows the engine as it was in late 1961. The machine has a four-domed boiler with a feedwater heater and a frost protection on the steam pipes[530]. The boiler carries small smoke deflectors. The cab has a 'de-refinement' (front window ist missing). The ladder at the cylinder is not shown in the model.
Information on the historical model: Haine 1943 → DRB 50 2114 (RBD Mainz) → 1945 DRw 50 2114 → 1949 SNCB/NMBS 50 2114 → 1952 DSB N 205 + 1966 Lunderskov

Fig. 78: Model of No. N 206 (Roco 43307), fireman's side.
This model looks like a class 50 without a feedwater heater. However, generally it is considered that this unit was part of the 50ÜK series, i.e. with 'de-refinements'.[531] The last brake test is dated 22.4.58.
Information on the historical model: Haine 1943 → DRB 50 2114 (RBD Mainz) → 1945 DRw 50 2114 → 1949 SNCB/NMBS 50 2114 → 1952 DSB N 205 + 1968 Thisted

---

[529] (LC)

[530] Jürgen Ebel thinks assumes a boiler exchange with 50 091 (Ebel, et al., 1988), page 330.

[531] On original photos of the locomotive, the engine has an ÜK–style cab (Jernbanen.dk).

[532] The MX and MY engines are diesel-electric locomotives built by the Swedish company Nydqist & Holm for the DSB.

10.7 France

When Alsace-Lorraine became French again after the First World War, the railway network had essentially been developed according to German standards due to 45 years of belonging to the Reich. This meant that all the signalling on the lines was designed for right-hand traffic. For switching over to left hand traffic as usual for the French railways, a lot of investments were necessary. The private French railway company 'Chemin de fer de l'Est'[52] (EST), which had owned the network before the German era, did not want to cover these costs and therefore refused to take it back.

To maintain the traffic on the network, the French state set up the state-owned railway company 'Administration des chemins de fer d'Alsace et de Lorraine'[52] (AL) to ensure the operation of the railways, including the network in Luxembourg.[533] With this new company, the signalling was reverted to the French standard but, interestingly, right-hand traffic was retained.

The creation of the 'Société Nationale des Chemins de Fer Français'[52] (SNCF) in 1938 brought together six major railway companies: EST, the 'Compagnie des Chemins de fer du Nord'[52], the 'Compagnie des Chemins de fer de Paris à Lyon et à la Méditerranée'[52], the 'Chemin de fer de Paris à Orléans et du Midi'[52], the 'Chemins de fer de l'État'[52] (ETAT) and the AL. The ETAT was already formed before to collect ten smaller railway companies which were threatened with bankruptcy in 1878. The former EST and the AL formed the eastern region of the new state railway.

As also the SNCF maintained right-hand traffic on the former routes of the AL, this area was, of course, ideal for the remaining and newly arrived twin-class locomotives. They were stationed in this region and did not leave it until they were retired.

At the end of the war, 13 units of class 50, 19 class 50ÜKs, 22 class 52 engines and one class 52 with a condensation tender remained in France. One of these (50 3134) was so badly damaged in the war that it was dismantled by the SNCF in 1945. This group was joined by a further 17 class 52s units from the Graffenstaden factory, which were under construction there during the time of liberation and were completed after the war in 1946. In 1945, two more class 50s were taken over from West Germany and another 14 class 52s in the years from 1946 to 1952.

A condenser tender locomotive (52 1993) was handed over to the DB in 1951 and scrapped there a few months later.[534]

---

[533] For the special regulation for Luxembourg, cf. Chapter 10.14.
[534] (Gillot, 1985), page 280; Peter Slaughter, Michael Reimer and Mario Fliege indicate the engine retired in 1952 (Slaughter,

The main locations for the stationing of the class 52 were Hausbergen, Sarrebourg and Île Napoléon, whereby Île Napoléon was replaced by Mulhouse Nord in 1951. Only a single machine was stationed at Sarreguimes and Thionville by the mid-1950s.

The arriving machines were for the most part classified according to the French numbering plan. This meant that the locomotive number was preceded by a number indicating the region in which it was based. For the eastern region this was '1'.[535] This is followed by the axle arrangement in French notation. For an engine of the twin-class with the axle arrangement 1'E this is: '150'. Then follows the code for the class: the 'Y' for the class 52 and the 'Z' for class 50.

Those delivered directly from Graffenstaden were numbered 1-150 Y 1 to 1-150 Y 17, while the remaining class 52 units were given the class code 150 Y, but kept the old Reichsbahn sequential numbers. For example, Reichsbahn's 52 6178 became SNCF's 1-150 Y 6178.

In France, the tenders had their own designation. Here the same letters were used, but the water capacity was prefixed. For example, the 1-150 Z 011's box-shaped tender (former German tender 2'2'T26) was designated 26 Z 011.

The SNCF had two different types of tender for the class 50:[536]

- Tender '26 Z', with a supply of 26 m³ of water and 8 tons of coal (former 2'2'T26) for all the 150 Z series locomotives, and the
- Tender '25 Z', which was only coupled to the 1-150 Z 1264 and had 25 m³ of water and 8 tons of coal. The origin of the tender type is not clear, as either it was not a tender of the twin-class or a misnomer.[537]

The class 52 carried the following tenders:[538]

- Tender '32 Y', which corresponded to the German K 2'2'T30 tub-shaped tender. The 150 Y supplied by Graffenstaden were coupled to this tender. The specified supplies were: 32 m³ of water and 9.4 tons ofcoal.
- Tender '30 Y', which corresponded to the German rigid frame tender K 4T30. The supplies listed were: 30 m³ of water and 8 tons of coal.

No livery is known to have been specified for these engines. Most likely no further major investment was made, as they were only a small series in the fleet of the SNCF and 'nothing special' in the country of the almost legendary creator of steam

---

et al., 1996); (Reimer, 1996). (Fliege), Patrick Paulsen and Ingo Hütter think that it was 1959 (Paulsen, et al.), (Hütter).

[535] It is not certain that all the units operation showed the leading '1'.

[536] (Gillot, 1985), page 285

[537] As the tare of the tender is the same as that of the 2'2'T26 tender, the latter is considered more likely.

[538] (Gillot, 1985), page 281

locomotives, André Chapelon.

Normally SNCF's steam machines were painted black for the boiler, tender and frame, with a red headstock. A special colour scheme was the green painting of the boiler (without smokebox), the sides of the cab, the sides of the tender and the outside of the cylinders in SNCF 306 ('vert extérieur foncé', until 1961) and SNCF 301 ('vert celtique', from 1961).[540] The green surfaces were contrasted with red stripes. The SNCF used its own colour chart. The colour SNCF 306 is similar to RAL 6007.

For the lettering, the SNCF used the typeface 'Univers' (from 1957), which had

Fig. 79:   Depots of class 150 Y (ex-52) in the east of France[539]

---

[539] (Gillot, 1985), page 280
[540] (Dufrenoy)

probably not yet been used for the twin-classes as most of then they were already retired before the introduction.

SNCF's use of these engines did not last long: By 1953, all of the 150 Z class machines had been withdrawn from service, followed by all of the 150 Y engines in 1959. Four of them were sold to the HBNPC[541], where they remained in service for some time with the designation Y 1 to Y 4.

Fig. 80: Model of No. 150 Y 1993 (Gützold 23200), right side.
The locomotive bears SNCF's first logo from the merger period on the smokebox door. It is represented by the interweaving of the letters S, N, C and F. It was in use from 1937 to 1947. The number of the engine is inscribed on the buffer beam (not visible in the photo). The tender is numbered 13 Y 1993.
Information on the historical model: Henschel 1944 → DRB 52 1993 (RBD Berlin) → 1945 DRo 52 1993 → 1945 SNCF 150 Y 1993 → 1951 DB 52 1993? + 1951

Fig. 81: Model of No. 150 Y 17 (Märklin 34157), left side.
The historical engine was one of the machines delivered by Graffenstaden directly to the SNCF after the war. The intended Reichsbahn number was: 52 1755. The tender number is 32 Y 17.
Information on the historical model: Graffenstaden 1946 → SNCF 150 Y 17 + 1959

---

[541] HBNPC = **H**ouillères du **b**assin du **N**ord et du **P**as-de-**C**alais, the nationalised coalfields in northern France

Fig. 82:   Model of No. 150 Z 095 (Roco 43290), left side.
The engine looks like a class 50 without war modifications, therefore it carries big smoke de-
flectors. The tender (still?) without number, but with inscription: 'Dépôt d'attaché Haguenau'
(associated to depot Haguenau).
Information on the historical model: Henschel 1940 → DRB 50 095 (RBD Halle (Saale)) → 1945
DRw 50 095 → 1945 SNCF 150 Z 095 + 1953

Fig. 83:   Model of No. 150 Z 2217 (Märklin3414), right side.
The model shows a former class 50ÜK locomotive, which stayed in France after the war. However the 'de-refinement' seemed not far advanced, as it seems that only the smoke deflector
were missing. After entering in SNCF's fleet it carries it new numbers, however the tender is
(still?) without number, but shows the last brake inspection on 26.4.46.
Information on the historical model: Borsig 1942 → DRB 50 2217 (RBD Berlin) → 1945 SNCF
150 Z 2217 + 1953

10.8 Post-war Germany

As early as 1944, the representatives of the EAC[542] had signed the so-called 'Zone Protocol', which proposed the establishment of occupation zones after the war. The Protocol was amended twice. In its final version it planned the establishment of four occupation zones on the territory of the German Reich.[543] Later at the Potsdam Conference, it was decided that the areas east of the Oder and Lusatian Neisse would be placed under Polish administration for the time being, rather than being part of the Soviet Zone as stipulated in the Zone Protocol.[544] East Prussia was divided between the Soviet Union and Poland, subject to a final peace settlement[545]: The northern part should be under Soviet control, the southern under Polish. The city of Berlin, divided into four sectors, got a special position. From mid-1945, the Allied Control Council exercised governmental power in Germany.

Concerning the German railways, the Americans wanted to administer the Reichsbahn as a whole. In this respect they agreed with the senior management of the Reichsbahn. However, this failed due to the opposition of France, who insisted on an independent administration for each of the occupied zones. The discussions ended with the formation of a 'Railway Committee' in which all four occupying powers were represented. The Committee was responsible for implementing the directives of the Control Council concerning the railways, traffic to and from Berlin and the setting of the tariffs.

As the reconstruction of the destroyed railway infrastructure progressed, it became clear that traffic flows had changed completely after the end of the war. Whereas until May 1945 traffic in Germany had been dominated by the west-east direction, now the north-south direction now became more important.

In their zones, the Allies began to set up their own railway administrations:

British Zone:

In the British zone, the 'Reichsbahn-Generaldirektion in der Britischen Besatzungszone'[52] (RGBD) was established in Bielefeld in August 1945 as the highest

---

[542] EAC = **E**uropean **A**dvisory **C**ommission. A committee set up by the Great Powers (Great Britain, Soviet Union, USA) to discuss the Allied conditions for the surrender of the German Reich and the further course of action after its occupation.

[543] (Wikipedia040)

[544] The Oder-Neisse border was acknowledged as Poland's western border by East-Germany in June 1950 and by West-Germany in 1971. Poland's western border was reaffirmed in 1990 by the 'Treaty on the Final Settlement with Respect to Germany' of the Four Powers and the two Germanies and confirmed by another German-Polish border treaty in 1992.

[545] This final arrangement was made with the signing of the 'Treaty on the Final Settlement with Respect to Germany' in 1990.

administrative authority. It was responsible for the former railway divisions of the Reichsbahn in Hamburg, Hanover, Münster, Essen, Wuppertal and Cologne.

American Zone:

In the American zone, the 'Oberbetriebsleitung der US-Zone'[52] (OBL USZ) was set up in Frankfurt/Main in July 1945, comprising the Reichsbahn divisions of Kassel, Frankfurt, Stuttgart, Augsburg, Munich and Regensburg.

Although there was a ban on building new locomotives, the High Command ordered the completion of the engines already started at the Henschel factory. These first machines built after the surrender carried both the company's factory plate and that of the 757th Railway Shop Battalion's factory.[546] A total of 36 class 52 machines were built at Henschel between 1945 and 1948 (1945: 12, 1946: 13, 1947: 1, 1948: 10). Some of the units were coupled to existing tub-shaped tenders. In addition, nine condensation tender locomotives were built (1945: seven, 1947: two), making a total of 45 units. The Reichsbahn was charged with 147,885 RM per unit (excluding rolling bearings[547] and wheelsets)[548] and 127,585 RM per unit (excluding rolling bearings and wheelsets)[549] for engines delivered without tenders.[550] It is unclear whether all these machines were built by the US Battalion.

In addition, in 1945/46, on the instruction of the Göttingen Central Office, the Jung factory assembled class 52 machines from available parts. This resulted in eleven locomotives with tub-shaped tenders, each costing 139,110 RM (excluding roller bearings and wheelsets)[551]. Five of these units were delivered directly to the French Zone in Mainz and six to the railways of the 'Saarländische Eisenbahn'[52] (SEB) in Saarbrücken to relief the shortage of machines there.

The machines with condensation tenders were stationed in the Reichsbahn division in Frankfurt/Main, Essen, Hanover and Münster.[552]

French Zone:

In the French zone, there was initially only one supervisory authority, the 'Détachement d'Occupation des Chemins de fer Français'[52] (DOCF) in Speyer, which

---

[546] 'BUILT BY 757TH RWY SHOP BN AT HENSCHEL LOCO. WORKS', (Weisbrod, et al., 2012), page 59. More information about this battalion, cf. (Unknown, 1945)

[547] Rolling bearings consist of two components (inner and outer ring) that can move relative to each other and are separated by rolling elements (e.g. balls, rollers). They are characterised by low friction.

[548] According today's (2021) spending capacity: about 385,000 € (cf. (Deutsche Bundesbank))

[549] According today's (2021) spending capacity: about 332,000 € (cf. (Deutsche Bundesbank))

[550] Prices according (Weisbrod, et al., 2012), page 59

[551] According to today's (2021) spending capacity: about 362,000 € (cf. (Deutsche Bundesbank))

[552] (Wenzel, 2014)

oversaw operations in the former divisions of the Reichsbahn in Mainz, Karlsruhe and Saarbrücken. As this did not work well, the 'Oberdirektion der Deutschen Eisenbahnen der französisch besetzten Zone'[52] (ODE) was also set up in Speyer at the end of 1945. This was the first attempt to organise the railways in the French Zone in a centralised and uniform manner. However, this attempt failed only a few months later, and the ODE was liquidated and management returned to the DOCF. In order to secure German expertise, the 'Verbindungsamt der deutschen Eisenbahnen der französisch besetzten Zone'[553] (VADE) was set up to advise the DOCF.

After the separation of the Saarland in April 1947, a separate railway company was founded there, the 'Saarländische Eisenbahn'[52] (SEB), which was merged into the 'Eisenbahnen des Saarlandes'[52] (EdS) in 1951. As a result of the separation of the Saarland, the lines of the former RBD Saarbrücken that were not in the

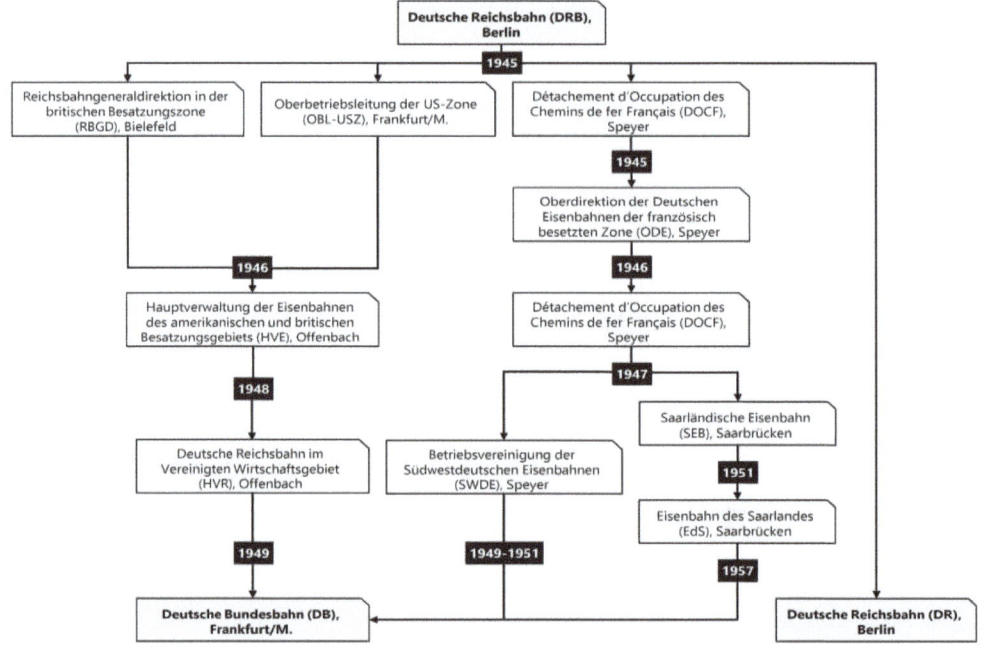

Fig. 84:   Development of the state railway companies in post-war Germany[52]

---

[553] Liaison Office of the German Railways in the French Occupied Zone

separated area were divided between the RBD Mainz and the newly established railway directorate Trier.

After the failure of the ODE, the French military government set up a committee to draw up proposals for the organisation of the railways in the French zone. The German states of Rhineland-Palatinate, Baden, Württemberg-Hohenzollern[554] and the VADE were represented in this group. Since the Reich no longer existed as the owner of the railway, the German states saw themselves as the 'heirs' of the Reichsbahn and its assets. However, as the legal situation was unclear and subject to Allied reservations, the committee concentrated on organising the operation of the railways. At the beginning of July 1947, the 'Betriebsvereinigung der Südwestdeutschen Eisenbahnen'[52] (SWDE) was founded, based in Speyer.

The stock of locomotives in the Zone was very limited shortly after the war, as at the end of the war some 250 units had been taken across the river Rhine into the Reich ahead of the advancing Allies. These could not be returned as the Allies had decided that all equipment had to stay where it was at the end of the war. In addition, the engines built in Belgium and France during the war had to be returned in 1949/1950 as so-called restitution locomotives.[555] Between 1947 and 1949, machines were leased from France, including 28 units of the series 150 Z (ex-class 50).

Soviet Zone:

In the Soviet zone, the 'Советская военная администрация в Германии' (СВАГ)[556] was established in Berlin-Karlshorst in June 1945. In July 1945, with Order No. 17, the SMAD ordered to establish so-called 'Deutsche Zentralverwaltungen'[557] within its zone and, as a consequence, the transfer of railway traffic in the Soviet Zone and Greater Berlin to the German railways present there on 1st September 1945.

For post-war Germany, the stocks for locomotives of the twin-class are shown in Table 20. It should be noted that in the Soviet Zone a number of twin-class engines were used for so-called convoy service (see Chapter 10.10.1). These are not shown separately in the figures. It is therefore not clear whether they are included.

---

[554] Baden, Württemberg-Hohenzollern and the state of Württemberg-Baden in the US Zone formed in 1952 today's German federal state 'Baden-Württemberg'.

[555] (Wenzel2, 2014)

[556] Soviet Military Administration in Germany (SMAD)

[557] German Central Administrations

Tab. 20: Stock figures of the twin-class in post-war Germany[558]

Zone	Date	Class 50	Class 52	Cl. 52 condens.
US-, British	31.12.1948	2,180	67	55
French				
incl. Saarland	12.1945	357	89	
, without Saarland	1.7.1950	253	86	
Soviet[a]	28.12.1946	111 (150)	223 (404)	not stated
	1.1.1949	217 (12)	437 (68)	10 (10)

[a]: Numbers in parentheses: damaged locomotives

The former Reichsbahn was one of the economic enterprises in Germany that suffered the greatest material losses during the war. On the one hand, the railway infrastructure (lines, bridges, tunnels, stations, etc.) destroyed by the war and the Scorched-Earth-Policyof the Wehrmacht[430] had to be repaired. On the other hand, railway operations had to be resumed with rolling stock that had been destroyed or damaged in the war.

It might have been first priority to concentrate on supplying the population with food and coal. That was difficult, as millions of people had lost their homes, were sheltering with family and friends or were homeless. Many – especially the forced labourers and prisoners in the camps – were on their way home or looking for a new home.

As a result of the decisions of the Potsdam Conference, some 14 million Germans[559] fled or were expelled from those parts of the former 'Greater German Reich' that were not within the four occupation zones. In addition, there were more than 10 million German war returnees[560] who had been released from war captivity by the mid-1950s and wanted to join their families. And then there were up to 11 million so-called 'displaced persons'.[561] According to the SHAEF's[309] definition, these were *"civilians who were outside the borders of their home states"*, mostly forced labourers (but also inmates of concentration camps, etc.), who had been deported by the Nazi regime and were in the former territory of Nazi Germany at the end of the war. For example, in 1946, more than 6,000 special trains alone were used in the Soviet Zone to transport more than six million people from these groups.[562]

The Reichsbahn faced financial difficulties in all zones of occupation because its

[558] (Wenzel, 2014), (Wenzel2, 2014), (Wenzel3, 2014), (Frister, 2014), pages 20, 34ff, 62
[559] (mdr)
[560] (Wikipedia041)
[561] (Wikipedia042)
[562] (Gall, et al., 1999), page 252

central treasury at the Deutsche Verkehrs-Kredit-Bank[563] in Berlin had been confiscated by the Soviets. In consequence the railways were partly dependent on municipal loans to cover their running costs. However, in a joint approach of the Allies and the Reichsbahn, individual branches of the bank were soon able to create the financial basis for operations.[564]

All Allies had the idea that the German railways should give top priority to military transport and the removal of the increasing amount of dismantling, in addition to their own transport needs. It is true that the Three-Power Conference in Potsdam had agreed to treat defeated Germany as one economic unit.[565] However, it was agreed that each power should satisfy its claims from its own zone,[566] which, as it turned out later, led to significantly different treatment in the different zones. In the Soviet zone, for example, much of what was needed to keep the railway running was confiscated. About 80 % of all double-track lines were converted back to single track.[567] The confiscated items were then transported to the Soviet Union by 'special trains' (see Chapter 10.10.1).

In the British and American zones, the Allies used some of their own war locomotives (WD 2-8-0, USATC S160), but there were not enough to meet the transport requirements. Therefore, Reichsbahn engines were confiscated and used for Allied transports. The confiscated machines were marked with 'Allied Forces' and 'BRITISH' or 'USA'[568] and then used for Allied purposes. In the French zone, the situation was initially much worse than in the Soviet zone, because the destruction caused by the war was greater here and the rolling stock had been withdrawn before the end of the war. Here, too, the second track of some double-track lines was removed by the French authorities after the war. The situation was complicated as France kept its zone strictly separate from the British and American zone[567] and treated them like foreign countries. As a result, the French Zone accepted relatively few German displaced persons from the areas of the former Reich, which were now under Soviet or Polish administration.[569]

Although Potsdam still spoke of an economic unity of Germany, France and the Soviet

---

[563] The 'Deutsche Verkehrs-Kredit-Bank' was Reichsbahn's principal bank.
[564] (Gall, et al., 1999), page 247
[565] (Potsdam Agreement - Protocol of the Proceedings, August 1, 1945), section II.B.14
[566] (Potsdam Agreement - Protocol of the Proceedings, August 1, 1945), section III.1., III.3. and III.4.
[567] (Gall, et al., 1999), pages 256f
[568] (Diener, 2012), page 141
[569] (Frister, 2014), page 25

Union rejected the economic unification of their zones at the Paris Conference of the Foreign Ministers in 1946. It was clear, therefore, that the intention of the Potsdam Conference to treat Germany as an economic unit would have to be abandoned.

Shortly afterwards, a merger of the British and American occupation zones was discussed, as this promised a number of economic advantages. The British Zone contained the Ruhr and its basic industries, while the American Zone had a substantial manufacturing sector. A merger promised a win-win situation for both Allies in their efforts to achieve a long-term economic independence for their zones. Accordingly, it was decided to merge the railway administrations by setting up a joint administration in Offenbach. In early 1947, the British and American zones were economically united under the name 'Bizone'. The railways of the Bizone were now operated and was administered by the 'Deutsche Reichsbahn im Vereinigten Wirtschaftsgebiet'[52] (HVR).

Fig. 85:   Model of No. 50 2501 (Roco 43145), driver's side and front.
The model represents the class 50ÜK of 1947,[570] which is said to have been used at the end of the Berlin Blockade.
The lettering of the engine is the simplified Reichsbahn lettering from 1941.[571] The smokebox carries a plate with British and US flags, which was recognized there during Berlin Blockade. The meaning for the letters 'D' and 'Д' is historical correct, but unclear.[572]

Information on the historical model: Krupp 1942 → DRB 50 2501 (RBD Essen) → 1945 DRw/DB 50 2501 → 1968 DB 052 501-4 + 1976 Lehrte

---

[570] last brake inspection according to inscription: 16.3.47. The Berlin Blockade was from 24.06.1948-12.05.1949

[571] (Diener, 2012), pages 140f

[572] Jürgen Ebel states that the letters refer to '**D**eutschland/**Д**еутсцхланд' ((Ebel2, et al., 1988), page 210). However, this is questionable, as the designation 'Deutschland' did not exist for the Bizone that time (where the locomotive was apparently stationed), and the word 'Деутсцхланд' does not exist in the Russian language either. The use of 'G' (English: Germany) or 'Г' (Russian: Германия, Germániâ) by the occupying forces would be more plausible here. One guess is that the plate was unofficial.

The railroaders hoped that the creation of the Bizone would also improve relations to the French zone. By March 1948, the BISEC[573] had discovered that about 8,000 wagons from the French Zone had not been returned. The British and Americans were suspicious that the French had renamed the freight wagons to be in owenership of their zone and had placed them on the railway of their zone. The Bizone management imposed an embargo on the French zone, i.e. no more freight wagons were allowed to cross the zone border. This was lifted six days later, after the start of the Berlin blockade.[574]

Fig. 86:   Model of No. 52 1953 (Gützold 23500), fireman's side.
The model represents the condensing locomotive of 1948 (last brake inspection: 11.2.48). The engine is equipped with smoke deflectors, although these machines were characterised by their low steam and smoke plumes. It bears the simplified markings of war locomotives, without national insignia. The ownership mark already reads 'Deutsche Bundesbahn', although this was only founded on 24.5.49. The inscription 'WM10' indicates that the tin content of the metal of the bearing of the rod is 10 %[230].
Information on the historical model: Henschel 1944 → DRB 52 1953 (RBD Berlin) → 1945 DRw/DB 52 1953 + 1951 Kirchweyhe

In the spring of 1948, the USATC made 25,000 freight wagons available to the HVR free of charge in order to deal with the transport problems. In addition, an application was made by the Bizonal Board of Economic Affairs for the construction of 30,000 new goods wagons. The request was, of course, rejected due to a lack of materials, but the construction of 3,000 new freight wagons was approved. More optimism came with the announcement of the 'European Recovery Programme' ('Marshall Plan'), which was a great benefit for the war-torn Europe west of the 'Iron Curtain'[575]

---

[573] BISEC = The **Bi**partite **Sec**retariat was a British-US agency that was part of the Bipartite Board (BIB) to promote the economic cooperation in the Bizone (Military Government, 1947), pages 22f; (Bundeszentrale für politische Bildung).

[574] (Gall, et al., 1999), pages 267f

[575] The 'Iron Curtain' was a term used to describe the division of Europe into two separate areas from the end of the Second World War until the end of the Cold War in 1991. During this time, the Soviet Union tried to isolate itself and the states

between 1948 and 1952. It included aid totalling $14 billion[576] (about $172 billion in today's money (2022))[577]. The Programme was also offered to the countries of Central and East Europe that had become communist – but they were forbidden by the Soviet Union to accept it.

The currency reform in all three western zones of occupation brought a further noticeable improvement, which also removed a number of obstacles in the factories and workshops of the western railways. It also reduced the demand for passenger trains, as 'hoarding' disappeared once money had a real economic value again.

The division of Germany, which had already begun, was consolidated in May 1949 with the creation of the 'Federal Republic of Germany' (FRG) and the 'German Democratic Republic' (GDR) in October 1949. With the creation of the FRG, the railways there were established as the 'Deutsche Bundesbahn'[52] (DB). This new name was based on a French request, that they could not imagine to incorporate their SWDE into a new West German railway that included 'Reich' as part of its name.

In the east, the old name 'Deutsche Reichsbahn'[52] (DR) was retained.

under its influence from the West.

[576] (Wikipedia043)

[577] (Coinnews Media Group LLC), (Deutsche Bundesbank)

10.9 Federal Republic of Germany

After the war, new federal states were created in the Allied territories to replace the former German states, which had emerged from earlier independent German kingdoms and principalities.

The American and British Powers gave the German states some participation in the running of the railways. With the formation of new federal states in the French Zone in 1946, the pressure to give them a participation grew, especially as the states were forced to cover the railways' deficits with loans. The SWDE, for example, was considered to be the property of the three states (Rhineland-Palatinate, Baden and Württemberg-Hohenzollern[554]).

The Western Powers favoured a state-run railway: France's SNCF had been state-owned since 1938, and Britain's railways had been nationalised shortly before in 1948[578]. The Americans were sceptical about a state-owned railway, but did not interfere as long as the financial figures were in order.[579]

Finally, the Deutsche Bundesbahn (DB), the railways of West-Germany, was set up as a state agency and was directly subordinate to the federal government. The rights of participation the federal states to control the railway were regulated by cooperation duties of the federal government with the Bundesrat[580] and respective representatives on the board of the DB.[581] This meant that the efforts, together with the state's new start, to establish a new railway company as a market-based company had failed.[579]

With the transformation of the Reichsbahn into the Bundesbahn, all departments were renamed accordingly: The Reichsbahn divisions became 'Eisenbahndirektionen'[582], the 'Reichsbahnausbesserungswerke' became 'Eisenbahnbesserungswerke'[583] and the 'Reichsbahnzentralämter' became 'Eisenbahnzentralämter'[584]. In 1952, the railway divisions were again renamed in 'Bundesbahndirektionen'[585]. Despite the clearly different name, the esprit de corps and corporate culture of the old Reichsbahn were 'saved' for the young Bundesbahn.

At the beginning of the 1950s, for example, the management of the Deutsche

---

[578] Transport Act 1947, foundation of British Rail

[579] (Gall, et al., 1999), page 278

[580] Bundesrat (Federal Council) is a legislative body that represents the federal states of Germany at the federal level.

[581] cf. §73 Nr. 6a, §80(2) and §87e of the Constitution of the Federal Republic of Germany, (Sarter, et al., 1953), pages 13f

[582] Railway Divisions

[583] Railway Workshops

[584] Railway Central Offices

[585] Federal Railway Divisions

Bundesbahn ordered a documentation that was to honour the achievements of the Reichsbahn in the Second World War by means of 'reports of experience'.[586] In many statements, apart from a few isolated instances[587], there were only success stories of exemplary actions by the railways, but no reference to the crimes committed during the Nazi era or any reflection on the company's own actions. In particular, there has been no corresponding reappraisal of the activities of the Ostbahn, the important instrument for the Holocaust, from which some leading figures had risen to the highest levels of DB management.[588] One can only speculate about the reasons for this 'defence of remembrance'[589]. Perhaps the image of the 'apolitical railwayman doing only his duty' continues to have an effect till today.

Whether it was the result of the bullying by his colleagues in the young Bundesbahn that drove an independent mind like Dr. Hahn[590] to suicide after the war is anyone's guess. He took his own life on 8th February 1957 in the offices of the Federal Railway Division in Stuttgart.[591] The fact that harassment by old party members and sympathisers of the old regime was no exception is shown by other fates of railway men, that were against the Nazis.[592]

When the constitution for West-Germany came into force, the SWDE was placed under federal law. The SWDE was thus a 'federal railway' and formally formed the new Deutsche Bundesbahn together with the railways of the Bizone. Accordingly, the SWDE was renamed 'Deutsche Bundesbahn – Betriebsvereinigung der Südwestdeutschen Eisenbahnen'. De facto, the two railways remained separate. It was not until 1951 that the financial and economic union was established through a series of agreements, and it was not until mid-1952 that SWDE was fully merged into the DB.

In 1951, a Federal Railways Act was passed to regulate DB's position in the Federal Republic of Germany. It regulated that the DB was a special asset with no legal capacity of the Federal Government with its own economic and accounting management.

---

[586] (Sammlung Sarter)

[587] (Ruyters, 1953)

[588] for example: Adolf Gerteis: former President of the 'Ostbahn' (1940-1945) → now Deputy President of the DB (1949-1952); Fritz Schelp: former Member of the Board of the Reichsbahn (responsible, among other things, for the tariffs for transports to the extermination camps) → now Member of the Board of the DB (1952-1963), etc. However, it should also be noted that Johann Hartje (DB board member 1952-1957) and Werner Hilpert (DB board member 1952-1957) were victims of persecution by the Nazi regime. It is difficult to imagine perpetrators/sympathizers and victims of persecution were member of the same board at the same time.

[589] (Zug der Erinnerung)

[590] cf. Chapter 5.5

[591] (Gottwaldt3, 2009), pages 248f

[592] E.g. Leopold Prinz zu Schaumburg-Lippe, cf. (Gottwaldt3, 2009), pages 256f

However, the administrative board – comparable to the supervisory board of a joint stock company – was not committed to the success of the company, but to its benefit for the state, while the Management Board was committed to the company's success. Conflicting objectives were thus built into the system: The state benefit opened the door to political influence by politicians and trade unions. However, the political influencers did not take economic responsibility for the company's actions, but instead passed the buck to the Board of the railways. This conflict has not changed over the years, and even today's German railways, the DB AG, is still caught up in it. As long as this is not sustainably solved, it will stay one of the main root causes of the todays railway problems in Germany.

In 1957, the young Bundesbahn experienced another political change. A solution to the Saar question was found in the Bonn-Paris-Conventions. The French government renounced the final separation of the Saar region from West-Germany, but the region should receive an 'European statute'. This statute should be confirmed in a referendum. In this referendum, however, the people of Saarland rejected by a clear majority the 'European statute' for the Saarland, which was seen as an expression of their will to join the Federal Republic of Germany. As a result, in 1957 the Saarland became the tenth federal state to join the Federal Republic of Germany, and the railways of the Saarland were incorporated into the DB.

The business of the DB was difficult in the early years, especially as the company had a large surplus of staff due to the employment of expellees and refugees. In addition, there were pension payments to surviving dependants and refugees. As there had been no significant investment in the infrastructure since the 1930s, the railway had a massive investment backlog. The rail network and operations had to be financed from the company's own budget, which meant that there was a great risk of the company quickly becoming loss-making and accumulating debt.

In addition, West-Germany became and stayed fascinated by the automobile. The motor vehicle (car and truck) remained the symbol of economic upswing, social progress and the guardian of prosperity and personal freedom.[593] The current debates about a changing transport policy in Germany against the background of global warming show how deeply this symbol is still anchored in the population. The railways did not and do not have enough to counter this new, old symbol of progress; they were

---

[593] (Rinn, 2008), pages 107ff. In February 1974, Germany's largest automobile club launched a campaign entitled 'Free citizens demand free travel', which was primarily directed against the attempt to introduce a speed limit on German motorways. To this day, Germany is the only country in the world without a speed limit.

and are too busy to solve their own problems.

Since the end of the war, the twin-class locomotives were stationed in large numbers in the network of the later DB and formed the backbone of their traffic. As early as the beginning of the DB, there were discussions about a successor of this class. The discussions from the time of class 50's construction were reopened, but it was decided that rebuilding or a new construction would be far too expensive, and it was better to concentrate on the development on a new passenger train locomotive (class 23).[594]

Fig. 87:   Model of No. 52 5956 (Gützold 32700), driver's side.
The model represents the 1949 war locomotive with Witte smoke deflectors and a rigid-frame tender. It's lettering is done in the simplified form of the war engines with the inscription 'Deutsche Bundesbahn', but without logo, which was not introduced until 1955.
Information on the historical model: Schwartzkopff 1943 → DRB 52 5956 (RBD Posen) → 1945 DRw/SWDE/DB 52 5956 + 1954 Betzdorf

Fig. 88:   Model of No. 52 2158 (Roco 62282), fireman's side.
The model represents the machine from 1953 (last brake inspection 19.2.1953) with a tub-shaped tender. It still bears the lettering in the simplified style of the war locomotives, but with the 'Deutsche Bundesbahn' markings and still without the DB logo.
Information on the historical model: Henschel 1943 → DRB 52 2158 (RBD Berlin) → 1945 DRw/DB 52 2158 + 1954 Hof

---

[594] (Ebel2, et al., 1988), pages 9f

Fig. 89:   Model of No. 52 3329 (Märklin 3415), driver's side.
Another model of a class 52 with a tub-shaped tender from the DB in the state of the year 1961. The historical model was one of the engines built for the French Zone after the war in Germany. Unlike the war locomotives, the generator is now mounted in front of the cab. The cab is decorated with the DB logo[595]. The lightning symbols on various parts of the machine indicate that the unit was used on electrified lines.
Information on the historical model: Jung 1946 → EdS 52 3329 (ED Saarbrücken) → 1957 DB 52 3329 + 1962 Homburg (Saar)

Fig. 90:   Model of No. 50 622 (Fleischmann 1105), fireman's side.
The model shows a locomotive with an ÜK boiler (three domes) and an open cab. As the frame originally comes from No. 50 133, the correct number of the locomotive should be 50 133.[596] Its original frame was installed in 50 2847[597] ('Schwerter Rahmentausch' (see Chapter 10.9.1)). Note the angular shape of the two sand boxes in front of and behind the steam dome.
Information on the historical model: Borsig 1940 → DRB 50 133 (RBD Oppeln) → 1945 SNCB/NMBS 2513 → 1946 SNCB/NMBS 25.014 → 1950 DB 50 622 → 1968 DB 050 622-0 + 1976 Duisburg Wedau (today in the DB Museum in Nuremberg)

---

[595] Nickname of the logo: 'DB Keks' (DB biscuit)

[596] In Germany, the locomotive's number is associated with its frame. If e.g. axles or the boiler are replaced, the machine number is retained. If the frame is changed, the engine should receive a new number.

[597] (Wenzel3, 2019)

10.9.1　Exchange campaigns

In order to reduce weight and save material, from about 1941, the twin-class boiler was made of 'St 47K' steel[598], which replaced the 'St 34' steel previously used. The 'St 34K' steel could be easily processed in riveted boilers, but it was not resistant to ageing. As the war locomotives had a planned lifetime of only five years, the use of this material was acceptable. It soon became clear, however, that the maintenance department had problems with this type of steel, the Reichsbahn reverted to the more reliable 'St 34' steel in 1942.

Given the need for replacement class 50 boilers, the Bundesbahn came back to well-preserved class 52 boilers. They were not only replaced, but in many cases completely overhauled. In addition to normal replacement, a number of additional works were carried out to bring the wartime boilers up to peacetime standards. Most of the boiler replacements and modifications were carried out in the repair workshops at

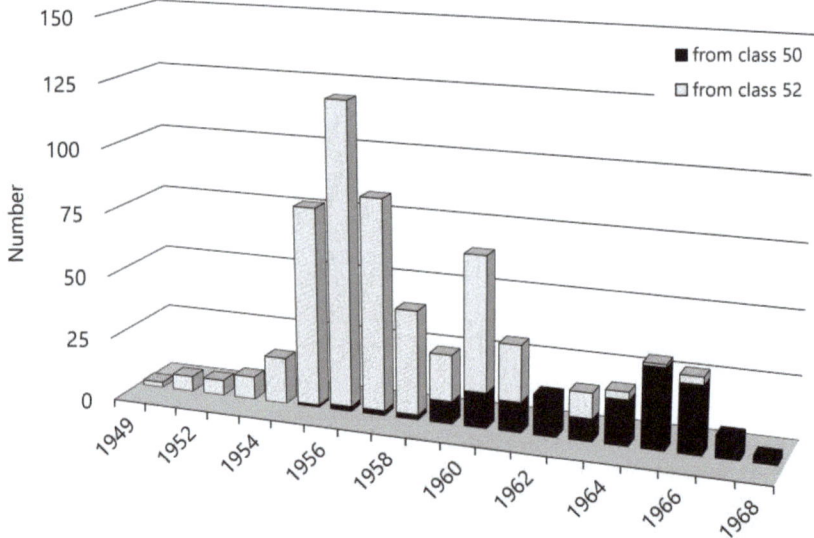

Fig. 91:　Number of boiler replacements on class 50 machines shown by donor class boiler. Due to the loss of operating records, this is not a complete picture.[599]

---

[598] For unalloyed structural steels of the formerly common 'St grade', the most important characteristic was the minimum tensile strength (originally expressed in kg/mm² or later in kp/mm²). The designation e.g. 'St 47' was a kind of steel with a minimum tensile strength of 47 kp/mm². The suffix 'K' indicated that the steel could only be processed cold ('kalt'). It was therefore not suitable for welding which increasingly replaced the use of rivets during the war.

[599] (Ebel2, et al., 1988), pages 14ff

206

Schwerte, Bremen and Esslingen.

However, there were no central specifications for this work, especially as there was not enough material available. As a result, the replacements and conversions resulted in a colourful variety of boiler types, which could be roughly distinguished by the arrangement of their domes. If the steam and feedwater dome are designated with a 'D', the sand dome of the peacetime design with a 'S' and that of the ÜK design 'ÜK', it is possible to classify the various boilers. The combinations D-S-D-S then represent the arrangement of the domes of the peacetime version of class 50 and S-D the class 52. However, the combinations D-S-D-S (angled)[600], S-D-S, S-D-S (angled), ÜK-D, D-ÜK-D, ÜK-D-ÜK and D-ÜK-D-ÜK were also found. The D-S-D-S, S-D-S and ÜK-D arrangement was the most common.[601]

The class 52 boilers naturally led to the rapid withdrawal of class 52 engines from Bundesbahn service, so that by 1963 these machines had been completely withdrawn from Bundesbahn's operation. However, some units were kept for many years as spare part donors for the still operating class 50 engines.

As a result of boiler replacement, the number of locomotives with boilers made of 'St 47K' steel had fallen to a total of 409, and by 1960 to less than 200 units.[604] These

Fig. 92:   Model of No. 50 1356 (Roco 62246), fireman's side.
This locomotive got the boiler from 52 6157 in 1955 and the boiler from 50 2419 in 1962. Engine 50 2419 again got its boiler in 1953 from 52 5833.[602] However, the boiler from 52 5833 did originally belong to 52 5772.[603]
Information on the historical model: Borsig 1941 → DRB 50 1356 (RBD Berlin) → 1945 DRw/DB 50 1013 → 1968 DB 051 356-4 + 1975 Bayreuth

---

[600] Here the sandboxes were designed like the peacetime version, but not round, but angular, cf. also Figure 90.
[601] cf. (Budde)
[602] (Ebel2, et al., 1988), pages 16ff
[603] (Griebl, et al., 1971), pages 224f
[604] (Ebel2, et al., 1988), Seite 21

remaining units were closely monitored, with samples of boiler steel examined and welds inspected using ultrasonic methods. In some cases, the boilers of the class 50 locomotives were replaced repeatedly by those of the class 52 locomotives (54 incidents[599]), but as time went on they were increasingly replaced by boilers from other class 50s, mainly to keep the locomotives in service until the 1960s.

At the same time as this rebuilding campaign, and even before it, the Schwerte workshop did not only replace and rebuild boilers, but also changed the frames of a number of locomotives without any order and without much documentation. In the course of time, these 'wild' rebuilds took such a dimension that got completely out of hand for those responsible and could no longer be traced.

In total, it is estimated that more than 100 locomotives were likely to be affected by this action, which means that the 'frame' criterion for locomotive numbering of the twin-class can no longer be used at the Bundesbahn. This action has gone into DB's history as the 'Schwerter Rahmentausch'.[605]

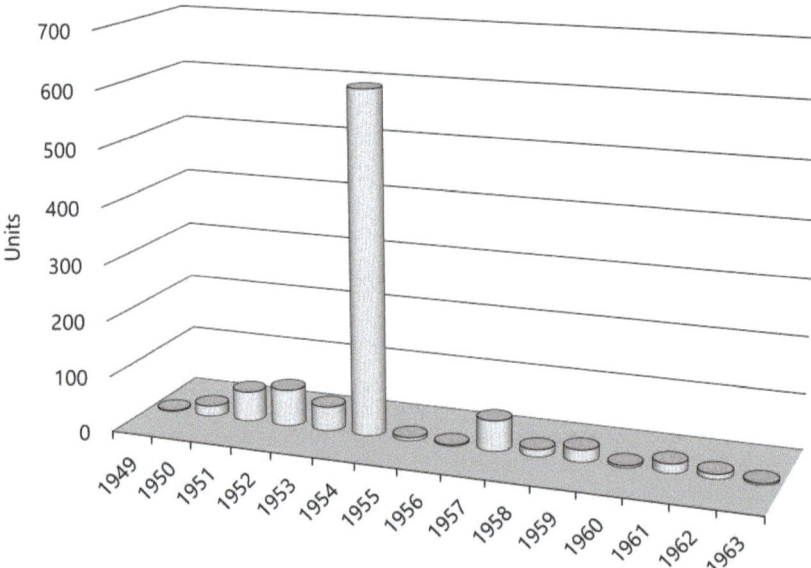

Fig. 93:   Removal from service of class 52 units at DB

[605] Frame exchange of Schwerte, cf. (Ebel2, et al., 1988), page 85

10.9.2   Optimization experiments

The class 50 engine had already s feedwater heater. The principle of it was to heat the cold feedwater from the tender with the exhaust steam from the cylinders before it left the chimney. This had several advantages:

- By using the waste steam from the cylinders, the feedwater entering the boiler was already preheated and relieved the boiler. This led to coal savings.[606]
- By preheating the water, the formation of limescale in the boiler was reduced.[607] As a result, the heat transfer in the boiler was increased, which also led to a reduction of coal consumption.

As a rough estimate, it was assumed that a locomotive equipped with a feedwater heater would be about 10 % more efficient.[608]

Since a relatively large number of newly built class 52 locomotives remained with the Bundesnbahn after the war, these locomotives offered themselves for a thorough investigation and targeted optimisation of the mixing preheater technology. DB officials also hoped to gain insights for other steam locomotives.

10.9.2.1   Closed feedwater heater

At the beginning of the 20th century, a development by 'Knorr-Bremse GmbH' brought a breakthrough in feedwater preheating in Germany.[609] A bundle of water pipes was installed in a cylindrical drum almost 2 m long, around which the exhaust steam flowed. Cold feedwater from the tender flowed into the pipes, where it was preheated to 90 - 100 °C.[610] The Knorr preheating drum could be conveniently mounted anywhere on the side of the boiler, on the running board, under the boiler or, as with the standard locomotives, above the smokebox in a hutch in front of the chimney.

A similar principle was used in the USA at the same time with the Elesco heater[611].

---

[606] It should be noted that at a boiler pressure of 16 bar, water only boils at about 200 °C.

[607] Hard water contains dissolved calcium and magnesium compounds. When heated above 60 °C, a chemical reaction takes place to form limestone ($CaCO_3$), which has a much lower thermal conductivity than steel and copper and might form an insulating layer in the boiler. This leads to an increase in temperature on the walls of the heating surfaces, causing them to overheat and to expand more than expected. The result are cracks and stresses in the boiler, particularly at the joints.

[608] Value from calculation, cf. (Niederstraßer, 1939), page 51

[609] (Giesl-Gieslingen, 1986), pages 174f

[610] (Schwarze, et al., 1998), page 248

[611] 'Elesco' is the phonetic transcription of the abbreviation 'LSCo' (=**L**ocomotive **S**uperheater **Co**mpany).

This unit was usually mounted on the smokebox in front of the chimney, which usually made the locomotive look a bit unsightly.

The advantage of such a closed feedwater heater was its relatively simple design, which made it cheap and promised low maintenance costs. As there was no contact between the exhaust steam and the feedwater, there was no risk of lubricating oil leaking from the exhaust steam into the feedwater. The disadvantage was that efficiency was only high if the preheater was kept clean, i.e. the water pipes were kept clear and limescale was removed. In practice, therefore, the efficiency was assumed to be only about 60 % of the theoretical value.[613]

10.9.2.2   Open feedwater heater

Another type of feedwater heater was the open feedwater heater. In this unit, the exhaust steam and feedwater were mixed in a mixing chamber. The advantage of this design was that there was virtually no loss of efficiency due to limescale. Furthermore it recovered some the water from the exhaust steam as new feedwater. The ability to store the heated feedwater in the mixing tank meant that hot water could be pumped to the boiler even when the throttle was closed at standstill.

The disadvantage was that the lubricating oil from the cylinder mixed with the feedwater. This had to be removed by an additional oil separator.

Franz Heinl patented such a heater in 1932, in which the feedwater from the tender was sprayed into a low-pressure chamber into which the exhaust steam was injected.

Tab. 21: Tests on class 52 from West German railways with feedwater heating system[612]

Operation number	Delivery date	Feedwater device
52 128	08.1948	temporarily with heater from Krupp
52 129-52 133	08.1948-12.1948	Open heater from Henschel (OHH) with additional structure
52 134	01.1949	OHH without additional structure
52 135-52 137	03.1949-05.1949	OHH with additional structure
52 138	05.1949	Three-drum-heater from Henschel
52 139-52 141	07.1949-09.1949	OHH with additional structure
52 142-52 143	10.1949-11.1949	OHH without additional structure
52 875-52 890	01.1950-03.1951	OHH without additional structure
52 891-52 892	04.1951	Open heater from Heinl

---

[612] (Ebel, et al., 2002), page 21
[613] (Henschel-Werke GmbH, 1960), page 292

The hot feedwater was then pumped into a second chamber, the high-pressure chamber, where it was injected under pressure into the exhaust steam from the feedwater pump. Further heating under pressure rose feedwater temperatures to 110 - 120 °C.[614] The Reichsbahn had already gained some experience in 1944 with the installation of the Heinl-Preheater in a class 42 war locomotive.[615] This proved to be complicated and prone to failure, and was later used in a simplified form by the West German railways. Among a number of other types of mixing preheater, the Henschel preheater is worth mentioning. This was of simple construction. The cold water from the tender was also pumped into a mixing tank and mixed with the exhaust steam. The hot feedwater

Fig. 94: Model of No. 52 138 (CN 5103009030), driver's (above) and fireman's (below) side.
The model shows 52 138 equipped with a Henschel three-drum preheater. Two drums can be seen on either side of the chimney. The third drum is not clearly visible located between the two visible drums. The overflow nozzle is located in front of the chimney.
Information on the historical model: Henschel 1949 → DB 52 138 (BD Hannover) + 1963 Duisburg-Wedau

---

[614] (Ebel, et al., 2002), page 8
[615] Lokomotive No. 42 2687, (Ebel, et al., 1988), page 87

(about 100 °C) was then fed directly into the boiler. Henschel stated that the lubricating oil in the exhaust steam hardly interfered with the operation of the boiler, as it should be bound and removed by the limescale in the mixing preheater.[613]

As part of an intensive programme, a number of class 52 units were fitted with various preheaters (see Table 21). Different designs were tested. They can be separated in those where the smoke chamber had to be raised in front of the chimney ('with additional structure') and those where the device was completely built into the smoke chamber ('without additional structure'). The locomotives equipped with a Henschel open preheater without additional structure could be identified from the outside by a nozzle for the overflow of the mixing box in front of the chimney.

In addition to the class 52 locomotives, a further 62 units of class 50 were fitted with open preheaters, mainly of the Henschel type. [616]

10.9.2.3   The Franco-Crosti-Heater (50⁴⁰)

An even more consistent use of waste heat was the utilization of the excess heat from the exhaust steam and the flue gases. These left the chimney at a temperature of 300 - 400 °C. This made them a valuable source of unused energy that could be used to preheat the feedwater and thus increase the efficiency of the steam locomotive.

This source was unlocked by the principle of Italian engineers Attilio Franco and Piero Crosti, who developed an exhaust gas heater. The Franco-Crosti heater used the high temperature of the flue gases to heat the feedwater that was then fed into the boiler.

The concept split the existing boiler into a heater and a main boiler. The heater boiler, installed below the main boiler, was completely filled with feedwater. There the exhaust gas from the main boiler and the exhaust steam flowed back in direction of the cab through pipes and transferred their heat to the feedwater. After passing through the heater boiler, the flue gases and exhaust steam were discharged to atmosphere through two side chimneys. The original chimney at the front of the main boiler was closed.

The size of the main boiler was reduced, as it was no longer required to heat the water but only to evaporate it. Both boilers were under full pressure, which meant that the water in the preheating boiler could get well over 100 °C.[606] However, care had to be taken that the feedwater in the heater boiler did not start to boil, as it could not absorb

---

[616] (Ebel, et al., 2002), page 8

the steam generated.

The first test vehicle of this system was put into service by the Belgian and Italian railways in the early 1930s. The Italian locomotives had flue gas temperatures of 200 °C at the side chimneys and feedwater temperatures of 160 °C, corresponding to coal savings of 15 - 18 %.

As early as the end of 1948, the management of the future Bundesbahn was considering a plan to test the Franco-Crosti concept. It was decided to have two class 52 units converted in Italy. Initially, the two engines 52 1817 and 52 2893 were earmarked for conversion. After problems with the contract with the Franco-Crosti-Company, Henschel was commissioned to convert and build the machines.

Henschel's design called for two pre-heating boilers, one on each side of the main boiler. After some back and forth, the two units were completed at the turn of the year 1950/1951. However, it was not the two engines originally intended for the conversion that were used, but the new units 52 893 and 52 894. The cost of the rebuild was much higher than planned, partly because two new machines were used instead of the existing ones and the costs for the redevelopment.

As a result, the new locomotives using Franco-Crosti concept were considerably heavier than the original class 52. The axle load rose to over 18 tons, which was more in line with the wartime class 42. For this reason, the original numbers were not used anymore and the units were reclassified as sub-class 42[90].

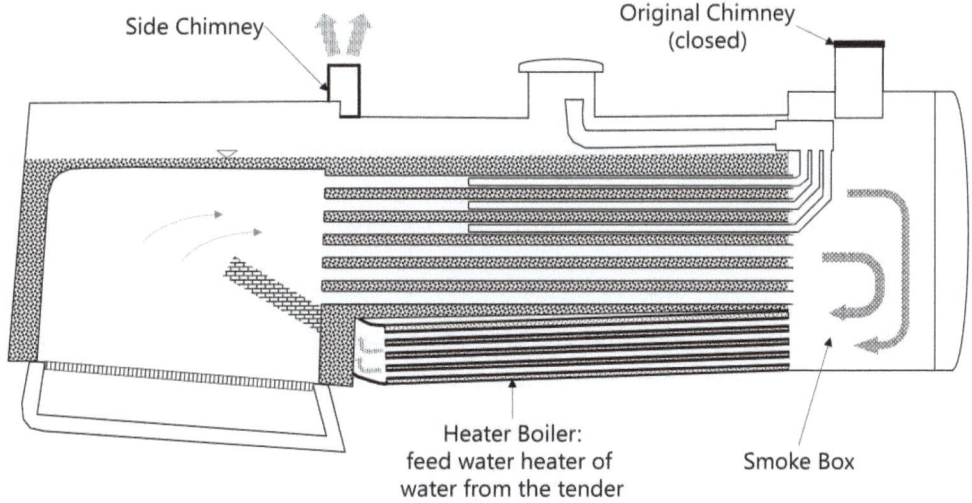

Fig. 95:   Additional elements of a Franco-Crosti boiler

If we compare the main dimensions of the 42^{90} with those of a class 50 (see Table 22), we can see that the evaporation heating surface is about 30 % smaller. This is the result of the Franco-Crosti concept, in which the main boiler had to work much less on its evaporation work.

The operational tests showed significantly higher efficiency in water evaporation and traction. Feedwater temperatures averaged 125 °C and fuel savings of 10 - 15 % were achieved during the test runs. The operational use confirmed the results of the test runs. However, the idea of having Henschel redevelop the concept had resulted in many errors and teething problems, which ultimately led to greatly increased maintenance costs.[617]

As the coal savings were clearly visible, the concept was also tested on a class 50 unit. As the DB already had a number of class 50 machines with boilers made from a problematic steel type (see Chapter 10.6.1), one of these units could was used. The choice fell on engine No. 50 1412.

This time only one heating boiler was used, which was located centrally under the smaller main boiler. As a result, this engine had only one side chimney on the fireman's side instead of the two used on class 42^{90}. Further improvements were made to Henschel's initial concept. This first unit was completed in December 1954 and was designated as class 50^{40} and given the number 50 4001 (cf. Table 22).

Like the first experimental locomotives, it showed good results, but not as good as the class 42^{90}. Above all, the 50 4001 showed that the basic problem of the German Franco-Crosti-locomotives had not been solved, namely the corrosion in the heating boiler. This had already become apparent on the class 42^{90}. It was considered that additional measures would bring it under control. A good remedy against the corrosion was to fit chrome steel tubes[618] to the heater boiler. Although this solved the corrosion problem, it added considerably more costs to building of the boiler, threatening the economic viability of the concept. All further trials gave an ambivalent picture of the conversion.

It is not known whether DB sought advice or support from the Franco-Crosti-Company. However, the decision to do it themselves instead of buying a 'turnkey'-solution was probably not so fortunate for the project's chances of success.

---

[617] (Ebel, et al., 2002), pages 33ff
[618] (Ebel, et al., 2002), pages 85f. In all cases, chromium steels are stainless or at least corrosion-resistant.

Tab. 22: Comparison of the main dimensions of the class 50, class 42[90] and class 50[40] [429]

			Class 50 (1939)	Class 42[90]	Class 50[40]
Running gear					
Driving axles			5	5	5
Driving wheel diameter	D	mm	1,400	1,400	1,400
Number of leading axles			1	1	1
Leading wheel diameter	D_v	mm	850	850	850
Cylinders					
Number			2	2	2
Diameter	d	mm	600	600	600
Stroke	s	mm	660	660	660
Main Boiler					
Grate area	R	m²	3.89	3.90	3.05
Pressure	p_K	bar	16	16	16
Total heating area[369]	H_v	m²	177.8	*121.2*[a]	*99.25*[a]
Superheater area	$H_ü$	m²	68.9	*63.5*	*48.8*
Weight					
With supplies	G_{Ld}	t	86.9	*98.7*	*90.6*
Axle load		t	15.2	*18.5*	15.7

[a]: Without consideration of the feedwater heater

Despite the ambivalent picture the German concept, the managers of the Bundesbahn ordered new Franco-Crosti-boilers and stipulated that all new boilers for the class 50 were to follow the Franco-Crosti-concept. A further 30 units of class 50 were converted to the Franco-Crosti-principle by the railway workshop in Schwerte and given the numbers 50 4002 to 50 4031. Locomotive 50 4011 was also converted to oil firing (see also 10.10.7). For this purpose, an oil tank with a capacity of 10 m³ was installed in a 2'2'T26 tender. Engine 50 4011, on the other hand, proved to be a good performer, showing exceptional efficiency and consumption values. It could have been used as a model for the conversion of other class 50 units. However, no further action was taken as the corrosion problem had not been solved yet. In addition, in view of the looming structural change to diesel and electric units, the company did not want to invest too much in the further development of its own steam locomotive fleet.

Fig. 96:   Model of No. 42 9000 (Märklin 39160), fireman's side (in photographic grey).
           All that remains of the former war locomotive were the running gear, the power unit, the cab
           and the tender. The smoke box was closed as it was no longer used. Below the small main
           boiler, there were the heater boilers on both sides, each with a side chimney. Last brake in-
           spection: 3.2.51
           Information on the historical model: Henschel 1950 → DB 42 9000 (BD Mainz) + 1959 Ober-
           lahnstein

Fig. 97:   Model of No. 42 9001 (Märklin 39161), driver's side.
           Similar in construction than No. 42 9000, but this time fitted with large smoke deflectors, which
           both locomotives received after the test runs were completed. Last brake inspection: 29.9.52.
           Information on the historical model: Henschel 1950 → DB 42 9001 (BD Mainz) + 1959 Ober-
           lahnstein

Fig. 98:   Model of No. 50 4005 (Märklin 37040), driver's (above) and fireman's (below) side.

In front of the chimney an additional Knorr feedwater heater is mounted to degas the feed-water. The feedwater valves were mounted on the left side behind it. On the steam dome there were two steam outlets for auxiliary equipment. The hatch on the original chimney can be opened by compressed air to start up the locomotive. The feedwater and air pumps were mounted at the front next to the smokebox.

The boiler has only one chimney on the fireman's side. Above the cab there is an additional smoke deflector to improve the view of the driver on the track. The tender has two lateral hinged coal box covers, which were closed when the engine was running to reduce the soiling of the train and to prevent fumes being sucked into the cab. These additional deflectors were necessary because the flow conditions had changed due to the side chimney.

This machine was also a victim of the 'Schwerter Rahmentausch', as it's frame came from 50 1509.[619] Last brake inspection: 13.7.63.

Information on the historical model: Krauss 1942 → DRB 52 2828 (RBD Linz) → 1945 DRw/DB 52 2828 → 1958 DB 50 4005 + 1967 Kirchweyhe

---

[619] (Wenzel2, 2019)

10.9.2.4 Giesl-Ejector

In a conventional steam locomotive, the exhaust steam from the cylinders is blown through a blast pipe into the smokebox, from where it escapes through the chimney. This design acts like a jet pump, using the momentum of the escaping steam to create a low-pressure environment. This ensures that the flue gases escaping from the boiler tubes were drawn towards the chimney and expelled. The design of the blast pipe nozzle, the geometry of the smokebox and the position and size of the chimney all have a major influence on the performance of the machine. Any pressure built up in the smokebox would not only reduce the ignition of the fire, but would also reduce the performance of the steam engine itself – in a similar way as the design of the exhaust system affects the performance of a car engine.

This basic design of the steam locomotive, to fan the fire in the firebox by the exhausting steam of the cylinders, created a self-acting control circuit that controlled the firing, and thus the generation of steam, as a function of the current output of the steam engine.

The designer's task was to coordinate the blast pipe nozzle, the firebox and the chimney in such a way that they produced a maximum fanning of the fire with a minimum of counter-pressure, thus achieving maximum efficiency.

It had been known for some time that blast pipe systems had an influence on the performance of a steam engine, and accordingly there were a large number of blast pipe systems. Among these, the standard Giesl-Ejector is probably the best known.

At the beginning of the 19th century, David Lewis in the USA and Karl Gölsdorf had already published first drafts. The Austrian railway company kkStB[52] even fitted it to a locomotive (kkStB 80), but these first attempts were not followed up. This was probably due to the fact that a flat chimney was fitted transverse to the direction of travel.[620] In 1921, Henry Oatley of the Superheater Co.[621] had a patent for a flat chimney installed in the direction of travel, but the nozzle head was of a different design.[622] The inventor of the Giesl-Ejector, Adolph Giesl-Gieslingen, based his design on the existing Gölsdorf development and developed his design from it.[623] Based on experimental results which showed that most of the momentum of the flue steam was lost

---

[620] (Slezak, 1967), page 6
[621] The Superheater Co., London, was a company founded in 1911 that offered superheaters for locomotive and ship boilers. (Grace's Guide).
[622] (Oatley, 1921)
[623] (Giesl-Gieslingen, 1986), page 153

in the collision with the slow flue gases, Giesl-Gieslingen tried to accelerate the flue gases before they came into contact with the main steam line. To do this, he spread the exhaust steam with seven optimally dimensioned nozzles arranged in a fan shape. This increased the suction on the combustion chamber without increasing the counter-pressure on the cylinders. A new feature was that the blowpipes and the stack were firmly connected to each other and represented the optimised geometry, so that the entire system could be installed as a ready-made module. There was no need to adjust the system and no inadvertent adjustments could occur during operation.

In 1955, the Bundesbahn decided to carry out trials to improve the blast pipe nozzle system, especially as reports from Austria, where several locomotives had already been fitted with Giesl's new design, were quite positive. At the same time, the installation promised to be relatively inexpensive. Test engine No. 50 1503 was fitted with such an ejector.

Broad tests initially produced very optimistic results. However, the later detailed report found no measurable coal savings. [624] The experts explained this by stating

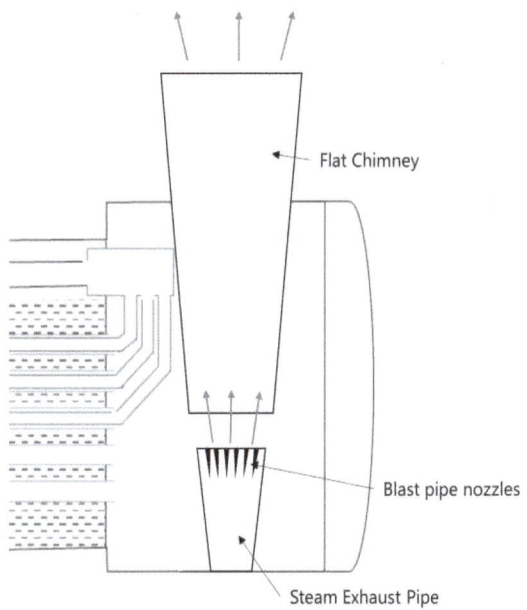

Fig. 99:   Sketch of a Giesl-Ejector unit

that locomotives with a Giesl-Ejector were operated with in a different way in Austria. They argued that the Bundesbahn had already achieved the coal savings with its own exhaust gas optimisation (cf. Chapter 10.9.2.5). However, this does not explain why, only a few hundred kilometres away, in East-Germany the Giesl-Ejector achieved good results with the same engines on similar routes (cf. Chapter 10.10.11).

It is to the credit of those responsible that they proposed additional tests, in view of the limited data available. This was done on the background that the test vehicle was

---

[624] (Knipping, 2012)

not fitted with additional ash pan dampers (as required by Giesl), but only with temporary slits.[625]

After the Bundesbahn rejected the technology, the Giesl-Ejector was removed from the test engine in 1958.[626] The company did not make any further trials and this stayed the only device used by the Bundesbahn.[627]

Looking back, you get the impression that there was a certain lack of interest in bringing the project to a successful end, which is difficult to understand as steam locomotives were still in service with the DB for about 20 years after these trials.

10.9.2.5 Other approaches for improvement

Over the years, further trials have been carried out with the class 50/50ÜK engines, but similar to the above projects, they have not (with one exception) led to or been used to further develop the class 50/50ÜK fleet.[628]

Additional oil burning

From the Reichsbahn period there were still components available from trials of an additional oil burning system. These were adapted to the class 50 after the war and installed in two locomotives (50 2458, 50 2764) at the end of 1945. As the conversion took place so soon after the end of the war, it can be assumed that the conversion was ordered by the British occupying forces. The system was removed from 50 2458 in mid-1947. The other engine suffered a boiler explosion and was scrapped in late 1946. Nothing is known about the outcome of the tests.[629] The subject was never taken up again by the DB.

Oil burners were later used by the DB on other classes (class 01[10], class 41, class 44 and one unit of class 50[40]), but it was never again used on standard class 50/50ÜK.

Shaking grate

The coal was burnt on a grate in the firebox. This consisted of individual bars lying side by side and supported by a beam across the firebox. Each bar had a gap between it and its neighbour to allow ash and slag to fall into the ash box. Since the length of the bars were limited, the whole grate was made up of several fields. Such a field was formed by a row of grate bars lying side by side. To make it easier

---

[625] (Ebel2, et al., 1988), page 45. Possibly the only provisionally attached slits were too small to provide for effective fire kindling, so that the principle of the ejector could not function properly at all.

[626] (Paulsen, et al.); (Fliege); (Wenzel, 2019) state: 1959

[627] (Slezak, 1967), pages 25ff

[628] The following list, cf. (Wenzel, 2019)

[629] (Ebel2, et al., 1988), page 46

to dump the ash, the fireman in the cab could swing one of the panels away, opening the grate downwards. Such a 'dumping grate' was fitted to class 50 engines.[630] To further facilitate cleaning and control of the fire on the grate, some machines had several of these panels arranged in a way that they could move up and down to each other to shake the ashes from the fire through the ash pan below. These 'shaking grates' allowed the fire being cleaned at any time without affecting it.

During the Allied occupation, the railways in the Bizone (HVE) already installed shaking grates in ten class 50 units in 1948 and followed the orders of the US supervisory authority. The grates were removed the following year as they were not considered to be of any use.

Poppet valve gear

In order to direct the live steam to the correct cylinder chamber, a control system was needed, such as a Walschaerts valve gear[97]. The control drove a piston valve which distributed the live steam to the two-cylinder chambers. The movement of the valve opened and closed the inlet and outlet channels so that the steam found its right way. Among other things, this type of steam distribution created throttling effects that reduced the performance of the steam engine.

By using poppet valves to control the live steam, similar to those used in internal combustion engines, these throttling effects could be avoided. A number of different designs have been developed for this purpose.

To test the potential of valve control, the Reichsbahn had already carried out trials with various designs, but without much success. Among them was a trial with No. 52 4915, which was equipped with a 'Lentz valve control system'. This locomotive was withdrawn from service in 1954 by the 'Lokversuchsanstalt Göttingen'[631]. Nevertheless, a 'Tolkien-type valve gear' was fitted to 50 819 in 1955. These tests also showed no improvement, so the control was removed again in 1956. No further trials were known.

Exhaust optimisation

After a series of tests with a class 50, a class 52 and a class 42 in the years 1952-1955, it was found that a certain geometry of the blast pipe nozzle and the chimney had a favourable effect on the fanning of the fire and thus on the evaporation rate of the boiler. Accordingly, it was decided that all class 50 machines should be

---

[630] (Ebel, et al., 1988), Seite 26
[631] Locomotive Research Institute in Göttingen

converted to this optimised geometry. This was done between 1955 and 1961. It was difficult to distinguish this change from the outside as it could be only detected by a slightly smaller diameter of the chimney.

Grate reduction

With a number of smaller locomotives being taken out of service, the DB also wanted to use class 50 engines for shunting and branch line work. Of course, the locomotive was far too powerful for this and it was foreseeable that it would be uneconomical for the machine to operate. The boilers of ten units were therefore modified.

In addition to reducing the size of the grate, a water pocket[632] was installed in front of the firebox rear wall to increase the proportion of radiant heat for steam generation. At the same time, the superheater surface was increased by extending the superheater elements towards the firebox (cf. Table 23). As a result, the superheated steam became so hot that it had to be cooled in the superheated steam chamber by injecting water.

The locomotives showed significant coal savings compared to the branch line engines used previously and paid for the conversion costs within a year.

There are no reports, whether these results were used to optimiuze the standard 50/50ÜK machines.

Tab. 23: Comparison of the boiler dimensions[429]

			Class 50 1939	Class 50 Small grate
Boiler				
Grate area	R	m^2	3.89	*2.68*
Total heating area[369]	H_v	m^2	177.8	*153.78*
Superheater area	$H_ü$	m^2	68.9	*82.25*

10.9.3   Caboose tenders

Until the 1970s, freight trains had to be accompanied by staff. This was usually a conductor, sometimes accompanied by a loadmaster and a shunter. To allow the staff to travel with the train, a caboose was added to the freight train. The Reichsbahn usually

---

[632] A water pocket or thermic siphon is a heat exchange element in the firebox or combustion chamber. It is directly exposed to the radiant heat from the combustion, so that high evaporation rates are achieved. These elements have been used in locomotive design in many countries.

used a caboose called 'Pwg Pr 14'[633] for this purpose. This was equipped with a work-place, a viewing dome and a loading space for general cargo. The workstation was for the conductor, who had to process his papers (e.g. waybills) during the journey. The dome was used to monitor the proper running of the freight train.

If it was not possible to include a Pwg-car in the train, this was not a problem for trains hauled by diesel or electric engines, as there was place for the conductor in the rear cab of the machine. On steam locomotives he had to ride in the cab together with the fireman and the driver, which was not ideal for the engine crew (interference) and the conductor (dirt) either.

As early as 1942, the Reichsbahn had a tub-shaped tender with a conductor's cab. This was all that remained of the project, which was abandoned due to the war and the post-war period. In 1952, the Austrian Railways (ÖBB) revived the idea and intro-duced a tub-shaped tender with a cabin for their class 52 locomotives. Although the tender lost some of its water supply due to the installation of the cabin, it was possible to omit the baggage car and replace it with a goods car, whose additional freight space earned extra money. At the same time, the conductor had a place where he could do his work, which was sheltered, with heating and lighting. This initiative was well received by the staff.

In 1955, the DB also became interested in this innovation and built a conductor's cabin as a 'backpack' onto a box tender. They chose this method, which differed from the Austrian model, because they

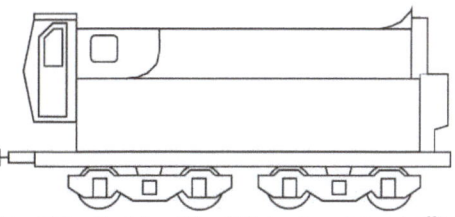

Fig. 100: Sketch of the DB's backpack tender[634]

did not want to accept a reduction of the water supply in their tenders. A total of ten such backpacks were built.[635] Unfortunately, the design of the 'backpack' was so poor that it was not possible to keep the vibrations of the tender away from the cabin, mak-ing the journey an adventure and making it impossible to do any paperwork. When such a backpack was badly damaged in an accident, the concept was abandoned. The result was the dismantling of these tenders.

The ÖBB lent out their caboose tenders and test runs were carried out. It soon became

---

[633] Pwg Pr 14 = Gep**ä**ck**w**agen für **G**üterzüge, **preuß**ische Bauart 19**14** (Baggage car for freight trains, Prussian design from 1914)

[634] cf. (Messerschmidt, 1987), page 61

[635] (Weisbrod, 1991), pages 72f

clear that their design with the cabin positioned behind the coal box and between the bogies, was clearly the better solution. A total of four prototypes were built and optimised according to the wishes of the staff.

Fig. 101: Model of No. 50 2733 (Roco 62248), fireman's side.
The model of the ÜK-version of the class 50 is supposed to show the condition at the end of 1964. The model is coupled to a caboose tender, version 2, built by the workshop in Lingen (Ems).
Information on the historical model: Henschel 1942 → DRB 50 2733 (RBD Augsburg) → 1945 DRw/DB 50 2733 → 1968 DB 052 2733-3 + 1974 Rottweil

Fig. 102: Model of No. 50 493 (Fleischmann 4177), driver's side.
The model represents the locomotive presumably with original boiler with a conductor's cabin (version 2) in the tender.
Information on the historical model: Borsig 1940 → DRB 50 493 (RBD Osten in Frankfurt (O)) → 1945 DRw/DB 50 493 + 1967 Flensburg

The Lingen (Ems) workshop began series production of the cabin tenders in 1959.[636] The entire cabin was mounted on the tender as a module and could be removed without affecting the function of the tender. The cabin was covered (with wood?) on the

---

[636] (Messerschmidt, 1987), pages 60f

inside and included a table, two folding seats, lighting, heating and a food warmer. Compared to the ÖBB cab, the interior of the DB version was slightly smaller. To compensate for the loss of space for the water supply, the water tank was slightly enlarged at the rear, so that it again had a water capacity of 26 m³. A total of 491 conversions were made, so that together with the prototypes, 495 caboose tenders were put into service[636].

Possibly more tenders could have been converted, but due to the decline in freight traffic in favour of lorries and the replacement of steam locomotives by diesel and electric units, the need for these tenders steadily decreased.

10.9.4 New numbers and end of operation

Over the years, the class 50 engines were gradually withdrawn from service. The remaining machines were given new numbers in accordance with the new UIC[501] identification system in 1968.

These new numbers consist of seven digits. The first three digits represent the class number, the next three the sequential number and the seventh digit is a check digit. The check digit is calculated using the so-called Luhn algorithm[637]:

You multiply the digits of the locomotive number alternately by '1' or '2' (i.e. the first digit by 1, the second by 2, the third by 1, etc.). If the result of the multiplication is greater than 9, subtract 9 from the two-digit number. Then the cross sum is formed and the number that gives the nearest ten is searched for. This is the check digit. Table 24 shows how the check digit is determined using the engine number 50 058. The result of the example calculation is the digit '7'. The correct UIC coding of the machine

Tab. 24: Example for the calculation of a check digit according to the Luhn algorithm

Loco-number	0	5	0	0	5	8	
	×	×	×	×	×	×	
Multiplication	1	2	1	2	1	2	
Interim result	0	10	0	0	5	16	
Reduction of numbers greater 9		-9				-9	
Horizontal sum	0	1	0	0	5	7	= 13
Number up to the next ten = check digit							7
Next ten							20

---

[637] (Luhn, 1960). The system is now in place for all UIC members for both traction units and wagons.

number is therefore: 050 058-7. The algorithm has also used in other areas besides railways, e.g. for debit cards.

As the new numbers allowed only 100 units for one class and there were still more than 100 machines in operation, the class 50 was now divided into the following classes 050, 051, 052 and 053.

All Bundesbahn locomotives of the twin-class retained their Reichsbahn livery, i.e. they were painted jet black (RAL 9005) above the running board and flame red (RAL 3000) below the running board. Cylinders, ash boxes, air and feedwater pumps and steps were also painted black (RAL 9005).

Initially, the engines still bore the plates of the former Reichsbahn. In the beginning,

Fig. 103:   Model of No. 53 045-1 (Roco 62253), fireman's side
The model of class 50ÜK has a closed cab and a tub-shaped tender. After being renumbered according to the UIC code, it became class 053.
Information on the historical model: Krupp 1943 → DRB 50 3045 (RBD Essen) → 1945 DRw/DB 50 3045 → 1958 DB 053 045-1 + 1975 Duisburg-Wedau

the Bundesbahn marked its machines with the inscription 'Deutsche Bundesbahn' in the centre above the number, usually in white. As this quickly became illegible, in 1953 it was decided that the locomotives should once again be given cast aluminium number plates. Additionally separate plates were fixed to the front lower corner of the cab side wall to indicate, if the clearance gauge[638] was exceeded (▲ resp. ⵒ)[639]. In the back corner the name of the Bundesbahn Directorate and the home depot was located. Welded boilers were indicated by a red dot. In some cases, the kind of bearing metal ('WM')[230] was also indicated. The lettering was in DIN 1451 font.[640]

---

[638] Exceeding the clearance gauge[156] was marked by a triangle above the axle load on the locomotive type plate. If, for example, a removable chimney top exceeded the gauge, an additional bar was placed above the apex of the triangle.
[639] Actually, the triangle and dash were two separate signs.
[640] (Diener, 2012), pages 148ff

After the majority of class 52 units had been withdrawn from service in the mid-1950s (see Figure 92), the withdrawal of the class 50/50ÜK began on a larger scale about ten years later. In the second half of the 1960s, an average of around 200 units were retired each year. From 1970 onwards, the number of retired machines fell to an average of about 150 per year. The last six machines were taken out of service in 1977, the year of the 'Steam Locomotive Ban'[641].

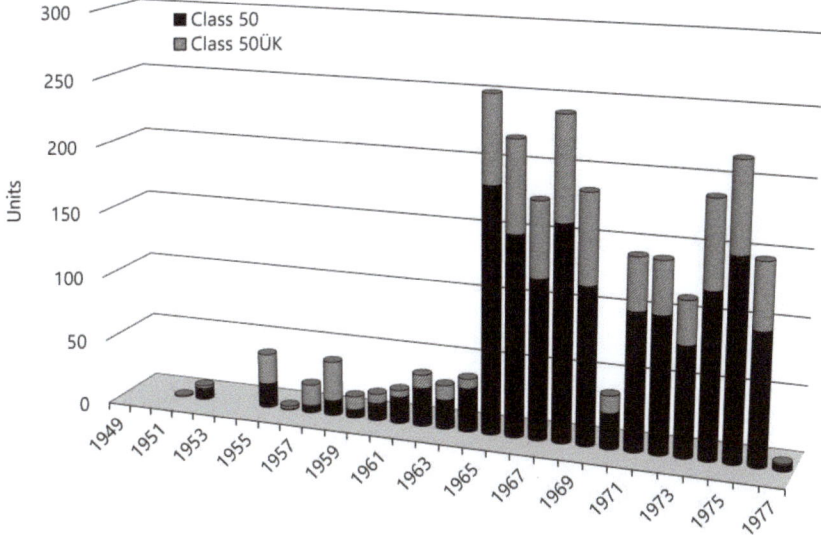

Fig. 104: Retirement of class 50 and 50 ÜK from the DB operation

[641] The 'Steam Locomotive Ban' prohibited the use of steam engines on DB lines between 1977 and 1985. The Bundesbahn could not impose such a ban on private railways, so they could continue to be used there. Operators of private sidings were also allowed to continue using their steam machines to deliver and collect goods wagons on DB lines.

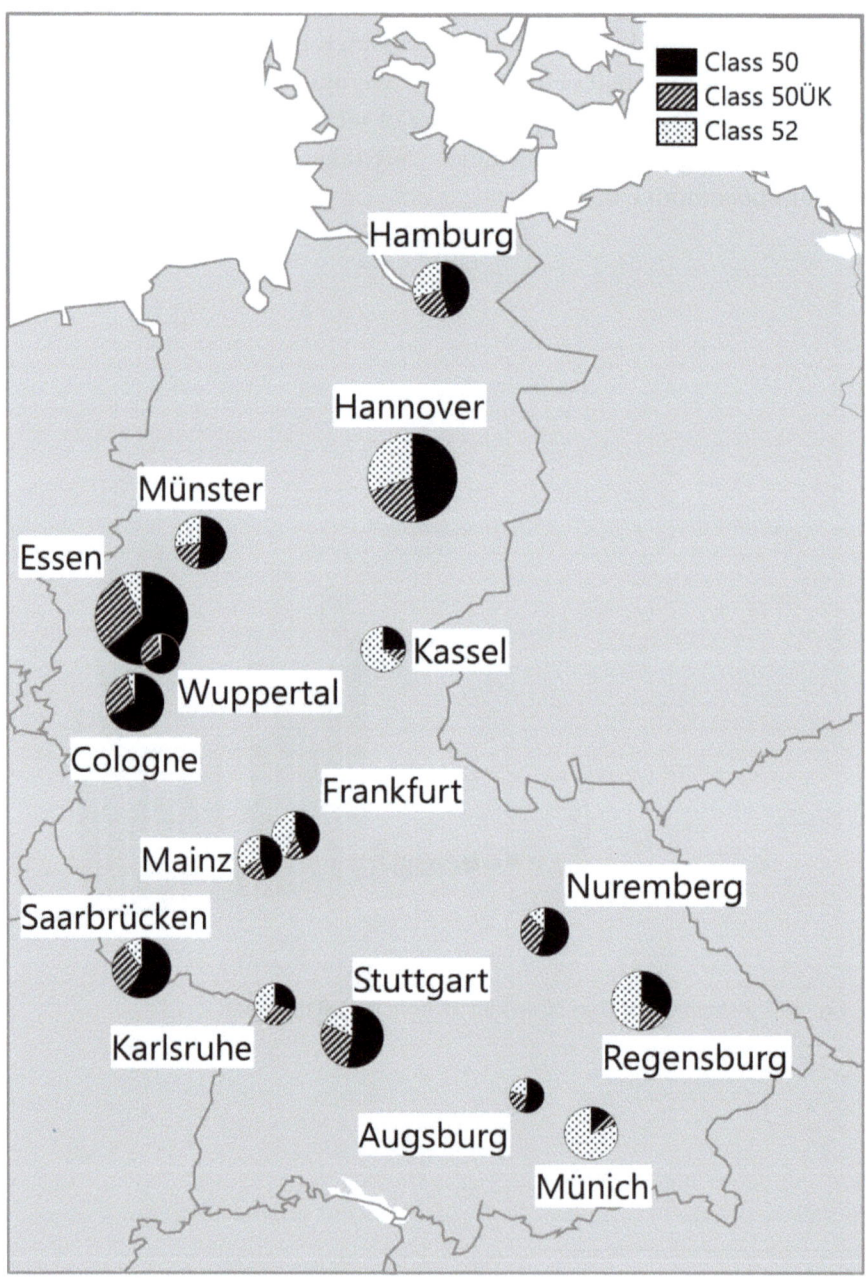

Fig. 105: Last depots of the twin-class in West-Germany

10.10 German Democratic Republic

10.10.1   Transport of war reparations

The Soviet Union suffered by far the greatest losses of life and material damage during the Second World War. More than 2 million Soviet citizens were forced labourers in the Reich at the end of the war. Taking into account fluctuation (death, escape, arrest, accident, illness or expiry of contract), there were as many as 5 million Soviet citizens.[642] A further 750,000 prisoners of war toiled for the German war machine.[643] Whole areas were plundered by the German occupation policy, the infrastructure was severely damaged or destroyed by the 'Scorched-Earth-Policy'[430]. These assets should be replaced by the Germans after the war. Since the Allies had decided that each Power should meet its reparations claims from its own zone[566], the Soviet Union took all its claims from the their zone or what became later the German Democratic Republic.

Determining the exact amount of reparations actually paid is complicated, especially when comparing the two parts of Germany. It is also not always easy to assess the value of a reparation service in its final consequence. For example, the value of dismantling a machine that is in continuous use is different from the value of the same machine that is only in temporary use. The value of war reparations must also be assessed differently if the machine remains in operation for the reparations service, but its products have to be ceded, so that the company incurs costs but no income.

The reparations paid by the Soviet Zone or the German Democratic Republic must therefore be divided into one-off losses of assets and permanent withdrawals.[644]

Loss of assets:

It is estimated that East-German assets worth 7.1 billion Reichsmarks (compared with 2.9 billion Reichsmarks in the later West-Germany) were lost to looting and dismantling. Considering the material damage caused by the war, e.g. by bombing, this amounted to some 40.5 billion Reichsmarks in West-Germany (compared with 12.7 billion Reichsmarks in East-Germany). In terms of national assets of the year 1939, the damage in East-Germany was about 18.5 % (compared with 16 %

---

[642] (Eichholtz2, 1999), page 530
[643] (Meyer, 1999), page 196
[644] (Karlsch, 1993), pages 84ff

in West-Germany).[645]

Although the loss of assets was roughly the same in both parts of Germany, it is the reduction in industrial capacity that reveals the true extent of the differences between the two German states. While the dismantling in East-Germany affected about 30 % of its industrial capacity, West-Germany lost only about 3 % of its industrial capacity.[645] The critical point was the high proportion of small and medium-sized enterprises in East-Germany that were affected, so that they often had no substance left to begin reconstruction.[646] Since the communists in East-Germany had no great interest in allowing small and medium-sized structures to exist and especially not in private hands, the dismantling in many parts supported the transformation of the economy into the socialist economic structure. It was precisely this double burden of dismantling and change in the economic system that drastically hampered the recovery of the economy of East-Germany.

Permanent withdrawals:

This point is perhaps more important in assessing the burden of reparations, because it shows what resources were ultimately available to East-Germany to cope with the war damages and its consequences. In the initial period of reparations by permanent withdrawals, the share of value taken out of the production amounted to up to 50 % of the gross national product of East-Germany, and then fell to 13 % by 1953. On the other hand, the later West-Germany started with 13 % after the war and never exceeded 7 % of West-Germany's GNP (cf. Figure 106). Due to the comparatively high loss of industrial substance through dismantling, the economy of East-Germany was to a large extent fastened to the production of goods for permanent withdrawal. In West-Germany, on the other hand, the burden of dismantling was much less, and since the loss of industrial substance due to dismantling was comparatively small, West-Germany was able to cope with it well and also had sufficient capacity to push its own reconstruction. In addition, West-Germany received good financial resources from private and public foreign aids,[647] so that reconstruction quickly gained momentum.

Among others, the withdrawals in East-Germany were carried out by the so-called 'Sowjetische Aktiengesellschaften'[648]. These were trading companies set up

---

[645] (Karlsch, 1993), pages 232f; all data: in price from 1944
[646] (Karlsch, 1993), pages 86f
[647] E.g. Marshall Plan (Wikipedia043), CARE Packages (Wikipedia044),
[648] Soviet public limited companies

by the Soviet Military Administration (SMAD) to cover the USSR's war reparation claims. These companies were gradually bought back by the former German states in the Soviet Zone or by the East-Germany government itself and often were re-established as VEBs[649]. The last of these companies were taken over by East-Germany at the end of 1953, with the exception of SDAG Wismut.[650]

Most of the transports of the war reparations to the USSR were done by rail. In the beginning, Soviet locomotives, including the classes Э^{Л2}, Э^{ш}, Э^r and their condensed tender versions Э^{тк}, as well as the classes Э^y, Э^м and Э^р, were used mainly on the broad-gauge lines in Germany.[651] In the long term, the Soviet Army did not want to handle the slowly growing flow

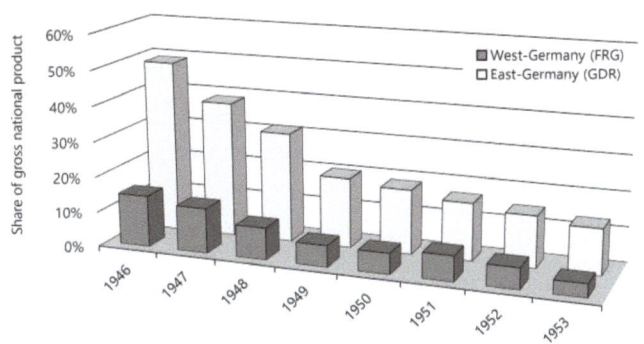

Fig. 106: Ongoing war reparations as a percentage of gross national product (in billions of Reichsmarks, 1944 prices)[653]

of goods on its own, especially as so much manpower and material could not be permanently withdrawn from the Soviet Union. As a result, the broad-gauge lines were converted to standard gauge so that East-German Reichsbahn could take over a re-gauged network when the operating rights were reassigned.[652]

In order to continue the transport of reparation goods to the Soviet Union, the Soviets ordered to set up so-called locomotive squads to shuttle the goods to the Soviet border. For this purpose freight engines of different classes were combined. Additional locomotives of the Soviet Army were transferred from Poland, Romania and Hungary and had to be repaired by the East-German Reichsbahn workshops.

For each machine provided, two driver brigades (first driver, second driver, fireman) and two conductor brigades (train manager, conductor, wagon technician) had to be

---

[649] VEB = **V**olkseigener **B**etrieb (Publicly Owned Enterprise) was the main legal form of the industrial enterprises in East-Germany.
[650] SDAG Wismut = **S**owjetisch-**D**eutsche **A**ktiengesellschaft **W**ismut (Soviet-German Joint Stock Company Bismuth). Formerly the fourth largest producer of uranium with sites in Saxony and Thuringia (until 1990).
[651] (Kuhlmann, 2002), page 51; for Soviet locomotive classes cf. also Chapter 9.3.
[652] (Kuhlmann, 2002), page 53
[653] (Karlsch, 1993), pages 234f

provided, so that each engine was manned by twelve people and could thus run round the clock. About 30 units were then grouped together in a squad. The machines were taken to their workplaces in locomotive trains, with only the first engine heated. There should be no more than two classes of machines in one squad. Each unit should have a caboose (two-axle passenger or freight car), which could be heated and in which the brigades could spend the night.[654]

The number of squad units varied from month to month according to the needs of transport. For March 1947, 945 units were mentioned in up to 34 squads – with over 11,000 personnel as train crews.[655] According to a rough estimate, more than 75 % of the twin-class locomotives remaining in the Soviet Zone were used for this purpose during the period of peak activity.

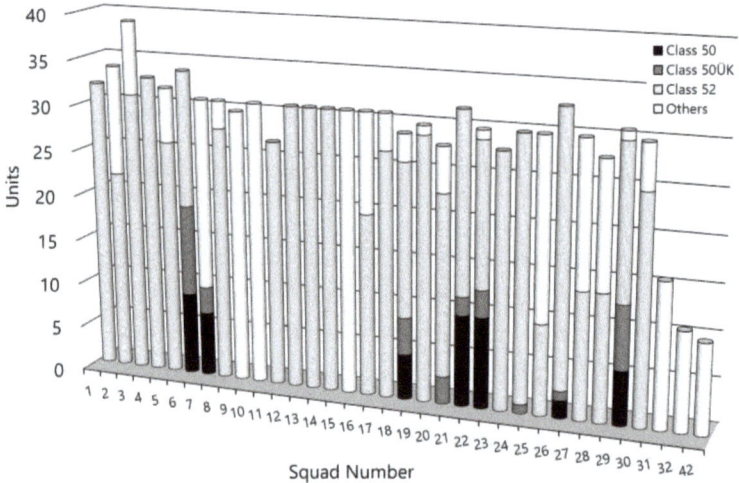

Fig. 107: Share of class 50/50ÜK and 52 within the individual squads (as of 1946)[656]

For journeys through Poland, the Reichsbahn had to pay the Polish railways for coal and water that was bunkered. This also applied to the removal of slag. The coal was loaded by local Polish staff, while the water was taken by the machine crew.[657] On the way back, some trains were taking Soviet-made agricultural machinery to Germany.

---

[654] (Reimer, et al., 1998), page 24
[655] (Werner, 2017)
[656] (Reimer, et al., 1998), Seite 126f
[657] (Kuhlmann, 2002), Seite 65f

The journeys through Poland were delicate, as the memory of the German occupation was still fresh in the minds of the Polish people. On Polish territory, the engine was accompanied by a German speaking Pole acting as a pilot, who was mainly responsible for communicating with station and signal box personnel.

The Soviets were keen to keep the convoy locomotives looking good, so they were regularly cleaned. Some of them were also fitted with white ornaments in the Soviet style.

Fig. 108: Model of No. 52 4916, driver's side
The unit was member of squad No. 22 in Wittenberge (20.6.46) with SMAD sovereign marking and white decorative paint on the wheel rims, cylinders and tyres. After the special train service the machine was transferred to the USSR.
Information on the historical model: Orenstein&Koppel 1943 → DRB 52 4916 (Gedob) → 1945 SMAD 52 4916 → 1947 SŽD TЭ-4916 → 1984 SŽD 1042 3242-6 + 1988

After negotiations with the Soviet Union, it was agreed that East-Germany would no longer have to pay reparations to the Soviet Union anymore from the beginning of 1954 on. Accordingly, the locomotive squads were gradually disbanded and integrated into the Reichsbahn's normal operations. However, many of the former squad engines were shipped to the USSR. The machine crews, most recently more than 1,500, returned to their home stations.

10.10.2 Allied transports through East-Germany

In addition to the convoy service, the East-German Reichsbahn (DR) also had to meet the transport needs of the Western Allies. These were journeys to and from West Berlin, but also within Berlin itself.

The timetables for the Western Allies' trains were agreed at timetable conferences of the Bundesbahn and the Reichsbahn. Requests for changes by the Western-Allies were brought to the conferences by the Bundesbahn. Special Reichsbahn dispatchers (see Chapter 10.10.3), who had been trained to deal with deviations from the agreed timetable, were used to run the trains.

The trains ran from the border station Berlin-Griebnitzsee to the border station Helmstedt and vice versa. From Helmstedt, the Bundesbahn was responsible for transporting the trains to the destinations in West-Germany. The Reichsbahn was responsible for transporting the trains to the destination stations in Berlin. At the border stations, the trains were controlled by Soviet armed forces, who were not allowed to board the trains. The driver was an employee of the Reichsbahn. He had no information about the people on the train and/or the documents for the goods being transported.

The Reichsbahn also had to run trains for the Soviet army to the east. This included the demobilisation of combat troops, the return transport of prisoners of war, the so-called 'EVR-Pendel'[658] and the passenger train transports of other military personnel to and from the USSR. The Frankfurt (Oder) station played a central role, as a Soviet train control centre was set up there in 1945 to coordinate traffic to and from the Soviet Union. They and all other command posts of the soviet forces in the RBDs of the Reichsbahn were known by the abbreviation 'Wo so' for 'Военное сообщение'(**Vo**en- noe **so**obŝenie, Military Communication). It supervised the work of the Reichsbahn and, from 1963 on, the marshalling yard in Frankfurt (Oder). The 'Woso' ended its activity after the withdrawal of the Soviet troops from Germany in 1994.[659]

10.10.3   Socialist development of the railways

In addition to the requirements arising from its previous tasks, the Reichsbahn had to cope with a profound change in its internal organisation, which was justified by the transformation of East Germany into a socialist society. After the SED[660] was founded in 1946, it tried to gain influence in all areas of the railway. The Soviets had set up a special committee to control the East-German Reichsbahn, made up of high-ranking SED-functionaries. As a result, the railway management was slowly but steadily infiltrated by SED officials, with political orientation taking precedence over

---

[658] EVR-Pendel = Transporte für die **E**inberufung und **V**ersetzung in die **R**eserve der sowjetischen Truppen (Transports for conscription and transfer to the reserve of the Soviet troops). These trains transported the change of personnel of the Soviet army in East-Germany. (Bossig, 2017)

[659] (Kuhlmann, 2002), page 72

[660] SED = **S**ozialistische **E**inheitspartei **D**eutschlands (The Socialist Unity Party of Germany), informally the East German Communist Party, ruled East-Germany.

professional qualifications.

Another point of influence was the appointment of SED loyalists to important posts in the DWK[661]. The DWK was subordinate to the central administrations set up by the Soviet Military Administration (SMAD) and formed the first post-war administrative structures after the capitulation. After the establishment of the Bizone, the DWK's powers were extended to include economic planning and management.

The many changes in the railway organization were reflected in the rapid rotation in the senior management of the East-German Reichsbahn: only between 1945 and 1950 there were three CEOs, one of whom was presumably murdered.[662]

In order to improve the miserable situation of the railways in the Soviet zone, the Stahanov measures[143] were first used to try to increase transport services. Although this had some success, the Soviets' demand that the railway should be run according to their dispatcher system stood in the way of smooth traffic. This meant a significant change in the way how the railway was operated.

In Germany, trains have been and still are mainly operated in train announcement mode. Here the line is divided into block sections and a train only runs if the block section is free and the following or oncoming train cannot enter the section. A train is announced to a traffic controller either verbally or automatically and enters the block section after the controller has accepted it. After leaving the section, the train must sign off again and the complete clearance of the track is confirmed verbally or automatically. The control rooms were decentralised.[663]

In the dispatcher[664] system, on the other hand, a central train manager (dispatcher) gives each train permission to proceed to the next control point. The dispatcher and the train crew were in constant contact.[665] This makes it possible to go without with signals or track block, resulting in significant savings in track infrastructure. This system was and is used in various forms in the Soviet Union and the USA, and is particularly effective on lines with low train traffic.

After many teething troubles and acceptance problems, the dispatcher system was introduced universally in 1954/55. This was supported by the political leadership, which was thus able to implement a 'unified command' in the railways in the sense of a socialist economy. The tight organisation made it possible to issue instructions

---

[661] DWK = **D**eutsche **W**irtschafts**k**ommission (German Economic Commission)

[662] Willi Kreikemeyer (Wenzel3, 2014)

[663] Thanks to modern interlocking block technology, various positions of the controllers are now centralized.

[664] The word 'Диспетчер' (Dispetčer) was phonetically transferred from English to Russian.

[665] Nowadays, this is usually done by radio. In the past, orders were given at stations or even while the train was moving.

from the central dispatcher to a local dispatcher. By constantly monitoring the trains and the traffic situation, the central dispatcher had an overview of the current traffic situation. In the event of traffic disruptions, he had the right to issue appropriate orders to the railway's operational units.

The system was an important management tool in the company's operations, especially after the war. It made the best possible use of the low reserves in the network

Fig. 109: Model of No. 52 006 (Gützold 32100), fireman's side.
The model represents the condition in 1964. Largely still in wartime design (though with retrofitted smoke deflectors) with a rigid frame tender. The historical model was also fitted with a Giesl-Ejector in 1969.[666]
Information on the historical model: Henschel 1942 → DRB 52 006 (RBD Halle (Saale)) → 1945 DRo/DR 52 006 → 1970 DR 52 1006-7 + 1977 Kamenz

Fig. 110: Model of No. 52 2523 (Liliput 105202), driver's side.
Same as above, but from 1954 still without smoke deflectors. It carries a tub-sheped tender. Note that the generator moved from the chimney to the cab.
Information on the historical model: Henschel 1943 → DRB 52 2523 (RBD Stettin) → 1945 DRo/DR 52 2523 → 1970 DR 52 2523-0 + 1976 Frankfurt (Oder)

---

[666] (Weisbrod, et al., 2012), page 82

and the fleet. It was not so much the result of pragmatic rationalisation but the consequence of adopting the socialist system of the USSR. Nevertheless, the system remained with the Reichsbahn until the end of the German Democratic Republic.[667]

10.10.4 *Pulverised coal boilers (52⁹⁰)*

After the Allied zones had been defined, East-Germany was cut off from the important coal fields of the Ruhr and Upper Silesia. Although it was possible to import coal from the Ruhr and Poland, the quantities were insufficient for the needs of the railways and the local industry. During the currency reform and the Berlin Blockade, supplies from the West were also interrupted.

Although Saxony had its own coal deposits around Zwickau, Lugau-Oelsnitz and in the Döhlen basin, these were by far able to fulfil the demand at the time. However, there were large deposits of brown coal in Lusatia and central Germany, which could be mined by open-cast mining.

In principle, brown coal can be used to heat steam locomotives. However, its heat value is much lower than that of hard coal (see 3.2.3), so the use of brown coal in steam engines significantly reduced their performance and required adjustments to the grate and blast pipe nozzle. The use of brown coal also meant hard work for the fireman, who had to shovel more coal into the firebox to compensate for the lower heat value. Assuming that brown coal had only half the heat value of hard coal, twice as much brown coal was needed to supply the unit with the same amount of primary energy. Also, the coal box of the tender was designed to hold a given volume of hard coal, so the machine's range was drastically reduced as coal had to be refilled much more frequently.

As the brown coal had a smaller grain size than the hard coal used, it fell through the gaps of the grate into the ash pan without burning. Initially, the Reichsbahn made attempts to reduce the width of the grate, which meant that not enough combustion air reached the fire.[668] This was followed by the use of a 'dead fire bed', where non-combustible material (e.g. stones) was placed on top of the grate, significantly reducing the amount of brown coal falling through.[669] Later, most of the brown coal was

---

[667] (Gall, et al., 1999), pages 295f
[668] Reduction of the gaps of the grate from 14 mm to 7 mm (Hengst, 2021).
[669] (Hengst, 2021)

pressed into coal briquettes,[670] which reduced the combustion problems, but increased the cost of the coal.

Already decades ago railway engineers thought about to power engines with pulverised coal. As early as 1904, the first locomotive on the Manhattan Elevated Railroad ran on pulverised coal, but this first attempt failed. A few years later, in 1912, the Swedish State Railways resumed the trials, but with peat dust firing. This second attempt was successful and a further 23 units were converted. A further five were fitted with pulverised coal firing.[671] At the beginning of the First World War, the New York Central Railroad and other railroads in the USA began to equip their units with the Lopulco[672] equipment. However, the results were inconsistent. Similar attempts in other countries with home-grown developments were also unsuccessful.

While these countries did not pursue pulverised coal firing for the time being, the pre-war Reichsbahn began to consider making this type of heating available in Germany. Therefore the 'Studiengesellschaft für Kohlenstaubfeuerung auf Lokomotiven'[673] (STUG) was founded in 1923. It brought together leading members of the German locomotive industry and the brown and hard coal industries. The most important result of their work was a special coal dust burner that could be installed in the rear firebox wall at the level of the ash pan. It was designed to be equally suitable for hard and brown coal (from 1926). The coal dust was conveyed to a nozzle by means of a screw, and swirled into the combustion chamber by blown air. The development was designed in such a way that the pulverised coal firing system could be replaced by a conventional firing system at any time.[674]

At the same time, AEG, which was not member of STUG, began to develop its own pulverised coal firing system for steam locomotives. They had already put in operation pulverised coal firing systems for stationary power stations at their Hennigsdorf plant[675]. This system also used screw conveyors to remove the dust from the tender. The dust/air mixture was then blown into the combustion chamber from the side of the furnace via slit burners.[676]

Both systems showed promising results and the test units No. 58 1353 and

---

[670] (Schwarze, et al., 1998), pages 887ff

[671] (Pierson, 1967), pages 11ff

[672] Lopulco = **Lo**comotive **Pul**verized Fuel **Co**mpany

[673] Society for Studying Pulverised Coal Firing on Locomotives

[674] (Pierson, 1967), pages 20f

[675] AEG founded the Hennigsdorf factory in 1914 to build and market locomotives.

[676] (Pierson, 1967), pages 23ff

No. 58 1677 (both with the STUG system) were ordered, followed a year later by two more machines. Units No. 56 2906 and No. 56 2907 were fitted with the AEG system and, following the positive experience, four more were ordered.[677] The most spectacular appearance of the AEG pulverised coal firing system was in the express locomotive No. 05 003, which was streamlined cab forward. A tender was attached to the rear of the machine, from which pulverised coal was fed through a 14-metre pipe to the boiler at the top of the machine. The engine was built by Borsig in 1937, but unfortunately the technological leap was too great for this design, as the machine already showed major problems during test runs.[678] In 1939, the Reichsbahn returned the unit to the factory and in 1944, it was rebuilt with standard grate firing and boiler and cab arrangement.

A total of ten units from the earlier trials were parked on the premises of RBD Halle (Saale), but parts of the associated infrastructure (grinding plant, compressors) had been dismantled by the Soviets.[679] It was therefore decided to pursue a two-step approach:

- Resumption of operations with the existing test units
- Optimisation of the weak points of the existing machines, particularly with regard to the transport of the coal from the tender to the firebox.

Hans Wendler, who had been involved in the conversion of No. 05 003 and had subsequently converted industrial boiler plants to pulverised fuel firing, was recruited for this last task. Under his direction, the grate was removed from the firebox and lined with fireclay. The firebox was hermetically sealed and its door was locked. This meant that all the combustion air had to enter the firebox through the burners.

Shock and collection nozzles were fitted to the coal dust tender and, once filled, the tender was placed under slight overpressure. Compressed air from the main air reservoir was fed through a shock nozzle, which then propelled the coal dust into a collector nozzle. From there the coal dust fell into the suction pipe for the combustion air, which immediately created a combustible mixture. This mixture then entered the combustion chamber where it ignited.[680]

Wendler had thus reversed the original principle. Instead of the dust being pushed by a screw to the nozzle to be swirled by compressed air, the combustion air flow took

[677] (Pierson, 1967), pages 35ff
[678] (Pierson, 1967), pages 42ff
[679] (Winkler, 2003), page 47
[680] (Pierson, 1967), pages 57ff

Fig. 111:   Model of No. 52 5762, driver's (above) and fireman's (below) side.
The locomotive was fitted with a single chamber coal dust tender in 1954. The two air pumps on the left side can be seen and also an additional air reservoir on the right hand's side at the front of the running board just behind smoke deflector and cylinder.
Information on the historical model: Schichau 1943 → DRB 52 5762 (RBD Stettin) → 1945 DRo/DR 52 5762 → 1970 DR 52 9762-7 + 1978 Senftenberg

the dust with it, swirled it and both entered the firebox. As a result, the gas flow in the furnace had to be redirected. For this purpose, an additional brick arch was installed in the firebox. To ensure good ignition, the geometry of the blast pipe nozzle was changed to create more draught in the firebox.

As the temperatures in the firebox became very high, the superheater tubes had to be shortened to prevent material damage. A second air pump was installed on the fireman's side to provide sufficient compressed air for the coal dust intake.

The first trials were carried out with class 58 engines. As these proved successful and the shortage of coal continued, a total of 13 class 52 units were converted to pulverised coal firing in 1953/54.[681]

All the locomotives in this first conversion campaign were fitted with a single-

---

[681] (Winkler, 2003), page 112; Manfred Weisbrod indicates eleven machines and two others with unclear conversion date (Weisbrod, et al., 2012), page 77

chamber pulverised coal tender rebuilt from old tenders. The water supply of the coal tender was slightly smaller than that of the earlier tender, as the pulverised coal container with its conveyors was built right down to the bottom of the water tank, which meant that the corresponding water space was lost.

During operation, it became apparent that only part of the coal dust in the bunker could be used, as the remainder in the tender could not be discharged. This problem was solved by dividing the coal dust bunker into three individual chambers, which were isolated from each other when full, but connected when empty. As each chamber could be emptied individually by using compressed air, it was possible to empty one chamber after the other.[682] Unfortunately, again some water supply was lost, but

Fig. 112: Model of No. 52 9426-9 (MMC 529001), driver's (above) and fireman's (below) side.
The historical model was fitted with a coal dust firing system and a three-chamber tub-shaped tender in 1957. The additional air tank on the right side and the double air pumps on the left side were clearly visible.
Information on the historical model: Esslingen 1943 → DRB 52 1426 (RBD Halle (Saale)) → 1945 DRo/DR 52 1426 → 1970 DR 52 9426-9 + 1976 Senftenberg

[682] (Winkler, 2003), pages 142ff

operational safety increased. From the end of the 1960s, the single chamber tenders, which were built from old rigid frame tenders and whose water tanks had become leaky, were replaced by the new three-chamber coal dust tenders.[683]

In 1957/58 a further 13 class 52 units were converted to pulverised coal boilers.[684] The machines of this second conversion series were immediately fitted with the more modern three-chamber tenders.[682]

It was characteristic of the pulverised coal engines that the coal filling pipe was present at the end of the tender also during operational service. From time to time, coal dust wagons[685] were also hauled behind the tender to replenish the coal dust during the journey.

The pulverised coal boilers initially retained their operating numbers. This made it difficult to identify the type of firing. It was only when the numbers were changed to UIC coded numbers[686] that '9' was chosen as the first digit in the four-digit sequential number. In the case of four-digit sequential numbers, the first digit was omitted (e.g. 52 3250 became 52 9250). This created a sub-class of the class 52, the 52[90]s.

The units were stationed at the Senftenberg depot, sometimes at Finsterwalde or Ruhland, i.e. in the heart of the Lusatian open-cast brown coal district. They were reliable and popular with the workforce. In the mid-1970s, however, they were increasingly replaced by diesel engines, and by 1979 they had all been taken out of service. Engine 52 9900-3 has been preserved under its old number (52 4900) in the Bundesbahn Museum Halle (Saale) (from 2021).

10.10.5   *The General Repair*

Many of the locomotives in the squads had been taken as 'war trophies' to the Soviet Union or had never returned from a journey to the border of the the USSR. After the end of the convoy service in 1955, the DR had about 1,100 twin-class machines (class 50: 230 units, class 50ÜK: 105 units, class 52: 806 units) in its fleet. This figure included engines that had been out of service for several years and/or used as spare parts donors.

As early as the 1950s, problems with the leading bogie became more frequent on the

---

[683] (Winkler, 2003), page 113

[684] (Winkler, 2003), page 142; (Weisbrod, et al., 2012), page 77

[685] From 1957 to 1962, the Reichsbahn procured special three-axle dust wagons for this purpose, each with three dust containers of 17 m³ capacity. Later, four-axle wagons with a capacity of 90 m³ were purchased.

[686] As the Reichsbahn was member of the UIC, it also introduced UIC codes locomotive numbers (cf. Chapter 10.9.4.).

class 52. This was due to the fact that the necessary material thicknesses, as well as essential spare parts, were not available. A close examination of the machines revealed that about half of them were affected by this problem. The Reichsbahn therefore decided to procure a total of 300 new bogies to equip the damaged machines. The other most pressing problems of the class, the axle bearing adjustment wedges[687] and the lack of feedwater heaters, should also be solved together with these repairs.

To put this all together the Reichsbahn presented in 1958 a 'Reconstruction and General Repair Programme for Steam Locomotives including the Construction of New Tenders'. The programme distinguished between 'General Repair' and 'Reconstruction'. 'General Repairs' involved replacing or overhauling major assemblies such as the boiler or the leading bogie. 'Reconstruction' involved the installation of a new, modern combustion chamber boilers and the elimination of wartime design flaws.

From an accounting point of view, this programme based on two budgets: General Repairs on the maintenance budget and Reconstructions on the investment budget.[688] While the utilisation of the maintenance budget had a full impact on the annual result, only the respective annual depreciation was used for investments.

Within the programme the design harmonisation was particularly important, especially the equipment with a feed water heater. In addition, the work included a number of other improvements. In many cases it involved a new welded boiler, wash-out plugs, sludge collectors[689], etc., the installation of a three-light signal[272] and the fitting of small smoke deflectors to the machines. As in West-Germany, some units received a replacement boiler from another class 52, which in turn was earmarked for Reconstruction.[690] The work on the class 50/50ÜK was carried out as part of normal maintenance, while the class 52s mostly underwent the General Repair Programme.[691]

In total about 70 units[692] of the class 52 had a general overhaul and were fitted with

---

[687] Axle bearing wedges can be used to adjust the clearance of the axles in the axle bearing. Correct adjustment protects the axle bearings and reduces the need for frequent replacement. In the war version (class 52, partly also 50ÜK) they were omitted as they were not considered necessary due to the expected short service life of the machine.

[688] (Weisbrod, et al., 2012), pages 71f

[689] As the boiler water accumulates minerals over time, it must be drained regularly and the boiler washed out. For this purpose, the boiler is equipped with washing plugs of different sizes in several places. In order to extend these maintenance intervals, the boiler is fitted with sludge collectors which allow the minerals to be drained daily. These measures are necessary because a steam locomotive cannot be operated with demineralised water for cost reasons.

[690] (Werner, 2019)

[691] (Weisbrod, et al., 2012), page 74

[692] Manfred Weisbrod reports 73 to 75 units (Weisbrod, et al., 2012), page 74; while Michael Reimer indicates only 69 units (Reimer, et al., 2001), page 23.

Fig. 113: Model of No. 52 5457 (Roco 62272), driver's side.
The original was part of the General Repair in 1960 and received a feedwater heater (at the top in front of the chimney). To make room for the mixing tank, a main air reservoir for the brakes was moved to the right-hand running board at the front of the driver's side near the steam inlet pipe. The model reproduces the 1968 condition.
Information on the historical model: Schichau 1943 → DRB 52 5457 (RBD Danzig) → 1945 DRo/DR 52 5457 → 1970 DR 52 5457-8 + 1977 Frankfurt (Oder)

an IfS/DR[693] type feedwater heater and axle bearing wedges[687]. The heater was an IfS development for the Reichsbahn. It was installed in the smokebox in front of the chimney and gave the repaired locomotives and later the rebuilt engines (cf. Chapter 10.10.8) their characteristic appearance with the typical, bulky looking box.

A total of 114 units went through the General Repair Programme between 1952 and 1964[694], with the emphasis on the years 1958 to 1962. Of these engines, about 70 units were fitted with the feedwater heater and about 100 machines with axle bearing adjustment wedges. In addition to these 114 units, the installation of a new boiler was verified on a further 45 units, although these were not officially counted as part of the General Repair Programme.[694]

10.10.6   New boilers for class 50/50ÜK (50³⁵⁻³⁷)

From the mid-1950s, the Reichsbahn also experienced increasing boiler damage. As with the Bundesbahn, the cause was the non-age-resistant boiler steel 'ST 47K'[598]. As more than 60 % of all class 50/50ÜK engines were fitted with boilers made from this steel, a quick solution was needed. Unfortunately, this was not as easy for the Reichsbahn as it was for the Bundesbahn, which had a large stock of class 52 units that had been decommissioned in the mid-1950s. At the Reichsbahn, all the existing

---

[693] IfS = Institut für Schienenfahrzeige, Berlin-Adlershof
[694] (Weisbrod, et al., 2012), page74

52s were needed for ongoing operations. Therefore they decided on a comprehensive 'Reconstruction Programme', which was also to include machines of other classes. Under this programme, all units were fitted with modern exchange boilers. At the same time, major repairs were carried out on parts subject to wear and tear. The replacement boilers were all fitted with the IfS/DR feedwater heaters, known from the General Repair, and were designed to burn domestic brown coal without damage.

The new boiler was built by 'VEB Lokomotivbau Karl Marx', the former 'Maschinenbau und Bahnbedarf AG, vorm. Orenstein & Koppel'[56], on the basis of Reichsbahn's new class 23^{10} and 50^{40} machines, but modified to suit the running gear of the twin-class. The result was the so-called boiler '50E', which was produced from 1957. The constructing VEB built 23 boilers, 32 boilers came from the Halberstadt repair workshop and 153 from SKL in Magdeburg.[695]

The '50E' boiler was a combustion chamber boiler (cf. Figure 2) in which the combustion chamber extended into the long boiler. Although the boiler had a smaller heating surface, it had an increased surface of the firebox. The operators described the boiler as 'evaporation-rich' and agile. And it was relatively easy for the fireman to maintain boiler pressure even with poor fuel.[696]

It also eliminated the problem of the old boiler's lack of overload capacity. With the old boiler, heating surface loads in excess of 57 kg/m²h sometimes caused considerable damage to the tube walls.[697]

Table 25 shows the main characteristics of the new boiler. The slightly reduced grate area is due to the installation of the combustion chamber. The front wall of the firebox is pushed forward, reducing the heating surface and the superheater surface. This allows the boiler to make better use of the much more effective radiant heat during heat transfer.

When the operating staff talked about 'evaporation-rich', they meant was that the boiler could convert more energy from the primary energy source (coal) into steam and was therefore more efficient. In operation, this was demonstrated by the fact that the engines with the old boiler reached their performance limits when pulling an 800 tons train at 70 km/h, while the units with the new boiler could pull heavy trains of up to 930 tons under the same conditions.[698]

---

[695] (Endisch, 2007), pages 34ff. SKL = VEB **S**chwermaschinenbau '**K**arl **L**iebknecht' (VEB Heavy Engineering „Karl Liebknecht")
[696] (Endisch, 2007), page 40
[697] (Endisch, 2007), page 32. See also early reports of water in superheated steam in Chapter 4.
[698] (Endisch, 2007), Seite 42

With this new boiler, which had already been discussed in a similar form when the engine was designed some 20 years earlier, the Reichsbahn had not only created a new replacement boiler, but also a significant improvement on the existing locomotive. In addition, the new boiler offered advantages in terms of long-term stability, as the rear tube wall was now further away from the fire, which meant that it was subject to less thermal stress, resulting in less wear.

Tab. 25: Comparison of the main dimensions of the boilers of the class 50 (pre-war) and the boiler '50E'[699]

			Boiler Class 50 (pre-war)	Boiler '50E'
Boiler				
Grate area	R	m^2	3.9	*3.71*
Pressure	p_K	bar	16	16
Firebox heating area	H_{vs}	m^2	15.9	*17.9*
Total heating area[369]	H_v	m^2	177.6	*172.3*
Superheater area	$H_{ü}$	m^2	64.1	*65.4*
Weight				
With supplies	G_{Ld}	t	88.2	88.2
Axle load		t	15.4	15.6

The installation of the 50E boilers began in 1957 and ended in 1962. During this time 208 units[695] were fitted with the new boiler. The remaining 129 units kept their original boilers until they were taken out of service.[700]

When the new boilers were installed, the machines were fitted with Trofimoff valves[446]. This relatively simple system was already known in 1928 by the Grunewald locomotive research institute. Although the results were positive, it was not considered any further by the former Reichsbahn. As the SŽD used this device on most of their engines, it came to East-Germany again via the ČSD in the mid-1950s.

All machines were also fitted with a running board and in the front the space between boiler and running gear was closed. They received a new bell and three front headlights. Later, some locomotives were fitted with a rear cab wall, a cab heater and a number of other minor modifications to improve the working conditions of the crew. A few weeks after the first rebuilds, the Reichsbahn decided to rename these units as sub-class 50[35-37]. The new service numbers consisted of a two-digit class designation ('50') separated by a four-digit number beginning with '35', '36' or '37'. The sequential

---

[699] cf. (Deutsche Reichsbahn, 1999)
[700] (Endisch, 2007), pages 19ff

number was completely new and had no relation to the former number. With the introduction of UIC-coded engine numbers, a control digit was added to the number, determined according to the Luhn-algorithm.

After the box-shaped tenders of 63 machines were worn out, at the end of the 1960s they were coupled with tenders of the decommissioned tenders of the 50^{40} (cf. Chapter 10.10.10).[701] Although the tenders carried 2 tons more coal and 2 m³ more water, they were unpopular with the operating staff because, unlike the earlier box tenders, they

Fig. 114: Model of No. 50 3632 (Roco 43360), driver's side.
The original was rebuilt in the late 1960s and fitted with a boiler from SKL. On top of the boiler there are two sand domes and a steam dome (centre). In front of the chimney there is a feed-water heater. The model is in the condition of 1966.
Information on the historical model: Cegielski 1942 → DRB 50 1959 (RBD Poznan) → 1945 DRo/DR 50 1959 → 1960 DR 50 3632 → 1970 DR 52 3632-2 + 1988 Halberstadt

Fig. 115: Model of No. 50 3646-2 (Roco 62168), fireman's side.
The model shows the condition in 1983. The historical engine was reconstructed in early 1961 and also received a new boiler from SKL.
Information on the historical model: Schwartzkopff 1941 → DRB 50 1831 (RBD Dresden) → 1945 DRo/DR 50 1831 → 1961 DR 50 3646 → 1970 DR 50 3646-2 + 1992 Chemnitz

---

[701] (Endisch, 2007), page 64

had no separator facing the cab, which was very uncomfortable when driving backwards, especially in winter.

The increased performance of the boiler was of course fully utilised in service, which led in the mid-1960s to problems as damages at the locomotive frames increased significantly. The frames were, of course, not designed for the loads that the new boiler had to cope with. Some could be repaired, but the frames of a total of eight engines had to be replaced.[702]

There were also problems with the cylinders. Some had to be replaced by cast cylinders from the late 1960s onwards. All these repairs led to a significant increase in maintenance costs, so it was decided to phase out maintenance from the early 1980s and replace the withdrawn units with class 110 diesel engines.

10.10.7 Cost reduction – from class 50^{35} to class 50^{50}/50^0

In countries with significant oil reserves, such as the USSR, Romania and the USA, work began early on the development of oil firing. In 1882, the Scottish engineer Thomas Urquhart, working for the former 'Грязе-Царицынская железная дорога' (Gryazo-Tsaritsyn railway)[703], presented a burner whose design was later used on the Soviet railways.[704] In the USA, the 'Atchison, Topeka and Santa Fe Railway' installed the first oil-fired locomotives in 1887.[705] The main driver for oil firing in both cases was that it was cheaper than coal firing.

After initial difficulties, the Reichsbahn's first trials with class 44 units produced good results, as the test locomotive was more powerful and more economical than the coal-fired original. It was shown that an oil-fired boiler reached its full steam-generating capacity within a short time. In addition, the maintenance work at the end of operation (removal of slag, cleaning of the smoke chamber) was considerably reduced.

The choice of oil firing was encouraged by the decision of the 'Council for Mutual Economic Assistance' (Comecon) in 1958 to build an oil pipeline from the Soviet Union to its western neighbours (Druzhba Pipeline, Pipeline of Friendship). This was completed in 1964 and delivered oil from the fields at Альме́тьевск (Almetyevsk) in

---

[702] (Endisch, 2007), page 82

[703] The Gryazo-Tsaritsyn Railway merged with the 'Юго-Восточные железные дороги' (Southeast Railway) in 1893 (Wikipedia046). Worth to know is that the city of Царицын (Tsaritsyn) was renamed to Сталинград (Stalingrad) in 1925 and to Волгоград (Volgograd) in 1961 (Wikipedia047).

[704] (Giesl-Gieslingen, 1986), page 128

[705] (Drury, 2015), page 57

Tatarstan to the transfer point at Schwedt (Oder), where it was processed directly at a petroleum processing plant (EVW Schwedt)[706]. The pipeline was later extended further to the east in the Soviet Union to the oil fields in Тюменская область (Tyumen Oblast) in the southern West Siberian basin.

The decision to use heavy oil for locomotive heating was facilitated by the accumulation of these fuels at EVW Schwedt, for which no other use was seen.

The Reichsbahn recognized the following advantages of oil firing:

- The heavy physical work of the fireman was made much easier as there was no need to shovel coal.
- The calorific value of the fuel was more than 9,500 kcal/kg[707] (in comparison: hard coal: 7,000 kcal/kg, brown coal: 4,500 kcal/kg)[77]. This meant that the same weight of fuel had a larger radius of action.
- The combustion of oil produced significantly less dust and soot particles, which was an advantage in stations and tunnels. There were also fewer flying sparks, which significantly reduced the number of embankment fires.
- The fuel supply could be better regulated and adapted to operational requirements. In particular, the fuel supply could be switched off for a certain time during idle periods, which led to fuel savings.

The Reichsbahn used heavy fuel oil known as 'HE-D'[707]. This is very viscous and has to be preheated to about 80 °C before it can be pumped. This was done in the oil tender by means of steam-heated coils. As there is no steam available to liquefy the oil of a cold locomotive, steam had to be generated from an external source (e.g. a heating locomotive). The oil was then fed to the burners, which used a jet of steam to atomise the oil and blow it into the firebox. Ignition was then provided by a fuse or a small wood fire in the firebox.[708]

The lower part of the firebox and the ash box were lined with fireclay to protect the steel and to store enough heat to reignite the oil on the hot walls during a stop.

Since the results of the conversion of the class 50/50ÜK to the class 50[35] were so successful, in 1964 the DR commissioned the Stendal workshop to convert some of the machines in this class to oil firing. With a few exceptions, the design of the experimental vehicle was adopted. Problems with the supply of certain components meant

---

[706] EVW = **E**rdö**l**verarbeitungs**w**erk (Petroleum Processing Plant), from 1970: VEB Petrolchemisches Kombinat (PCK), cf. also the situation in Czechoslovakia and Poland.

[707] See technical standard TGL 3667 of East-Germany (TGL = **T**echnische Normen, **G**ütevorschriften und **L**ieferbedingungen; Technical Standards, Quality Regulations and Delivery Conditions) (Universitätsbibliothek Universität Weimar).

[708] (Schwarze, et al., 1998), page 177ff

Fig. 116: Model of No. 50 0018-7 (Roco 62265), fireman's side
The original was converted to oil firing in 1966 from 50 3584, which itself had been rebuilt in
1959/1960 and fitted with an SKL boiler.
Information on the historical model: Orenstein&Koppel 1942 → DRB 50 2503 (RBD Hannover)
→ 1945 DRo/DR 52 2503 → 1960 DR 50 3584 → 1966 DR 50 5018 → 1970 DR 50 0018-7 +
1983 Wittenberge

that the first locomotive could not be completed until 1966.

An oil tank with a volume of 11.2 m^3 was installed in the coal box. This was thermally insulated to allow the heated heavy oil to flow freely. Heating coils were installed in the tank to preheat the oil.

When the first unit came into service, the class of the machine was changed to '50^{35} Oil', later it became the sub-class 50^{50}. Again, the old sequential numbers disappeared, for example the former machine No. 50 2503 (already renumbered to 50 **3584**) became 50 **5018**. After the introduction of UIC coded numbers, the sub-class 50^{50} was renumbered to 50^0, as all oil-fired locomotives had to have a '0' as their first digit. So, in our example became 50 **0018-7**.

The conversion was carried out in two runs, the first comprising 42 units and the second another 30 units.[709] The last machines delivered after 1970 were given the new UIC numbers right away.

This meant that about one third of all the 50^{35}s were now oil fired. They proved themselves very well in service. The further increase in power meant that they were also used for heavy freight service, which led to premature wear and tear on the engines. This affected not only the frame but also the boiler, which was loaded to or beyond its performance limits. The noise generated by the burner was also a problem, making acoustic communication within the locomotive crew very difficult and even causing

---

[709] (Endisch, 2007), pages 154f

permanent hearing damage to some of the crew. Over time, this led to some engines being fitted with noise-reducing firebox doors.

A second problem was the high temperatures at the superheater elements, which led to scaled tubes. This was solved by shortening the superheater tubes, which resulted in a temporary improvement, but eventually damaged the pressure compensators of the cylinders. Where this had not already been done, Trofimoff valves[446] or the old war locomotive compensators were fitted.

At the end of the 1970s, however, the fuel situation changed dramatically. Triggered by the Islamic Revolution in Iran and the Iraq Iran War, the price of oil rose dramatically from \$5/barrel Brent[710] to \$38/barrel in 1979/1980.[711] Due to the Comecon's price mechanism[712], there was a time lag before East-Germany felt this increase and it was foreseeable that the class 50^0 machines would become increasingly uneconomic. It was therefore decided to take all the class 50^0s out of service and close them down at the end of 1981. When prices began to fall again, diesel engines took over the tasks of the class 50^0s.

All units were scrapped by 1987. Only 50 0072-4 (ex-50 3502, ex-50 481) has been preserved as a museum locomotive in the Bavarian Railway Museum in Nördlingen (from 2021).

10.10.8   New boilers for class 52 (52⁸⁰)

As the new boilers for the 50/50ÜK class had been such a great success and the condition of the machines destined for General Repair was deteriorating, the Stendal Repair Workshop requested that the new boilers should also be installed in the machines that were originally intended for repair only. The background of this the consideration was the question whether it made sense to install new fireboxes in old boilers that might have to be replaced after some time anyway. The request was granted and the boiler replacement programme was extended to class 52 machines. Engines with a plate frame were selected for replacement, as this made the rebuild as uncomplicated as those of class 50.[713]

In addition to the replacement of the boilers, the corresponding general overhaul

---

[710] 1 Barrel = 159 litres. Brent is the most important type of crude oil for Europe.

[711] The all-time high for the Brent oil price is: 147 \$/barrel in July 2008 (as of 10/2023).

[712] Within the Eastern Bloc, the transfer price for crude oil was derived from the five-year average of the world market price. Therefore, the oil price crisis reached the Eastern bloc countries only with a certain delay (Wikipedia048).

[713] (Weisbrod, et al., 2012), page 85

Fig. 117: Model of No. 52 8105 (Gützold 49100), driver's side.
The original was reconstructed in 1964. The original tender was retained. This time angular sand tanks are placed in front of and after the steam dome. One of the main air reservoirs is attached to the top right of the running board like with the General Repair.
Information on the historical model: Schichau 1943 → DRB 52 614 (RBD Breslau) → 1945 DRo/DR 52 614 → 1964 DR 52 8105 → 1970 DR 52 8105-0 + 1991 Roßlau

work was also carried out, so that the Reichsbahn received engines identical in performance to the class 50[35-37]. This largely achieved standardisation meant that some boilers were exchanged between the 50/50ÜKs and the 52s,[714] and possibly not only these components. As a result, the two classes of locomotives became even more and more interlinked.

A total of 200 units of class 52 were fitted with the 50E boiler.[713] The sub-class 50[80-82] was created to distinguish them from the conventional class 52. The sequential numbers of the units were changed.

10.10.9   Acquisitions from the Soviet Union

During the advance to the West a number of German locomotives fell into the hands of the Soviet army, including those of the twin-class. After the war a number of machines, including the twin-class, were sent back to the Soviet Union as reparations.

When diesel traction became established in the Soviet Union, the USSR sold several hundred locomotives to its Eastern Bloc allies. Accordingly, the Reichsbahn also bought series ТЭ (ex-class 52) machines from the USSR. A total of 60 units were purchased.[715]

Most of the locomotives were delivered to the DR in early 1962. The transfer points

---

[714] (Weisbrod, et al., 2012), page 88
[715] (Weisbrod, et al., 2012), page 80. However, No. 52 3145 mentioned in this list was not in use in the USSR and ТЭ-6025 is said to have remained in the USSR (Paulsen, et al.); (Reimer, 1996); (Slaughter, et al., 1996).

were Polish-Soviet border stations. As the machines were used in the Soviet Union before they should have the Russian gauge (1,520 mm). The Polish railways however use the standard gauge. It is not known whether the engines had already been converted to standard gauge or weren't converted at all.

The machines could be recognised from the outside by the small opening in the smokebox. This was for inspection purposes only, as the German spark arrester mesh and baffle plate[507] had been removed from the locomotives. The cinder[716] in the smokebox could be removed by means of a built-in cinder pipe[717]. However, it can be assumed that most of the cinder was expelled through the chimney. This made the cleaning of the smokebox much easier.[718] Furthermore, like all Soviet units, they had only one large front lantern, similar to US engines.

After being handed over, the locomotives were taken to the Stendal workshop, where they were fitted with standard DR parts. Among other things, the Trofimoff valves[446] were replaced, axle bearing wedges[687] were fitted according to Reichsbahn's standards and the fittings in the cab were replaced with standard fittings.

A total of ten of the repurchased units were incorporated into the Reconstruction Programme and given 52[80] sequential numbers.

10.10.10 New production with new design (50[40])

In view of the age of its rolling stock, the DR began to consider the construction of a new, light steam locomotive for freight service. It should have a 1'E wheel arrangement and a maximum axle load of 15 tons. It was planned that this new engine would replace the old and worn out twin-classes.

The project planning was carried out from 1956 by the same institutions that had been involved in the development of the 50E boiler (IfS[693], VEB Lokomotivbau 'Karl Marx'[56]). During construction, the idea of the standard locomotive was taken up again, and as many parts as possible were harmonised with class 23[10], which was also under construction, as well as with other parts of the Reichsbahn's 'New Building

---

[716] Cinder is the residue of fly ash and unburnt coal particles that accumulates at the bottom of the smokebox and must be removed almost daily during operation.

[717] During operation, quantities of residues collect on the floor of the smoke box, which must be removed. If the smoke box is equipped with a cinder pipe, the residues can be swept into a cleaning opening at the bottom of the smoke box, where they fall down through the cinder pipe pipe between the rails into e.g. a slag pit.

[718] In the USA, special constructions ('self-cleaning smokebox', 'self-cleaning front end') were used to discharge the resulting cinder through the chimney. The reason for this was that cleaning to Central European standards was not possible with long locomotive runs, high loads or mechanical stoker feeding (Giesl-Gieslingen, 1986), page 161.

Programme'.[719]

A boiler similar to the 50E type boiler was used. It had a smaller heating area, due to a shorter boiler (tube length between the tube walls 4,200 mm instead of 4,700 mm). The boiler also used the same type of combustion chamber as the 50E boiler. The superheater area was slightly larger than with the 50E boiler.

The frame was designed as a plate frame, as it could be produced more cost-effective than other constructions thanks to the use of welding technology and better material utilisation. The designers also believed that a plate metal frame would have the same longitudinal rigidity as a bar frame. This proved to be a fatal error during operation as the frame was repeatedly damaged by cracks. Later reinforcements and modifications to the frame were able to mitigate the weaknesses, but this remained the locomotive's major problem, ultimately leading to its accelerated retirement.

The driving and running gear were similar to the class 50 and Trofimoff valves were fitted.

Tab. 26: Comparison of the main dimensions of the class 50, 50^{35} and the class 50^{40} of the New Building Programme[720]

			Class 50	Class 50³⁵	Class 50⁴⁰
Running gear					
Driving axles			5	5	5
Driving wheel diameter	D	mm	1,400	1,400	1,400
Leading axles			1	1	1
Leading wheel diameter	D_v	mm	850	850	850
Cylinders					
Number			2	2	2
Diameter	d	mm	600	600	600
Stroke	s	mm	660	660	660
Boiler					
Grate area	R	m²	3.90	3.71	3.71
Pressure	p_K	bar	16	16	16
Firebox heating area	H_{vs}	m²	15.9	*17.9*	*17.9*
Total heating area[369]	H_v	m²	177.6	*172.3*	*159.6*
Superheater area	$H_ü$	m²	64.1	*65.4*	*68.5*
Weight					
With supplies	G_{Ld}	t	88.2	88.2	85.9
Axle load		t	15.4	15.6	15.1ᵃ

ᵃ: The maximal axle load of the tender 2'2'T28 was 15,7 t

---

[719] The result of Reichbahn's 'New Building Programme' were the classes: 23¹⁰, 25/25¹⁰, 50⁴⁰, 65¹⁰, 83¹⁰, 99²³⁻²⁴ and 99⁷⁷⁻⁷⁹.
[720] (Deutsche Reichsbahn, 1999)

Fig. 118: Model of No. 50 4009-2 (Roco 62180), fireman's side
On the outside you can see the new boiler with two domes and the extended tender with five gusset plates on the coal box. The manufacturer (VEB Lokomotivbau 'Karl Marx' (LKM)[56]) is written on the cylinder. The last brake test is dated 30.9.70.
Information on the historical model: LKM 1959 → DRB 52 4009 (RBD Schwerin) → 1970 DR 50 400-2 + 1978 Wismar[721]

The locomotive was fitted with a newly designed tender that could hold 28 m³ of water and 10 tons of coal (2'2'T28). The declared power was the same as that of the class 50$^{35-37}$ machines, and the maximum speed was 80 km/h forward, but only 50 km/h reverse.

Due to the new boiler design with different main dimensions, these locomotives cannot be counted as part of the twin-class family.

10.10.11 Savings with the Giesl-Ejector

The Giesl-Ejector caused a great deal of interest at the Reichsbahn. Initial trials showed that savings of 6 - 12 % coal were possible, depending on the engine design and the boiler condition.

The ejector had the advantage that it required very little maintenance and did not take any additional power away from the locomotive for its operation. The simple and effective design was of interest to the Reichsbahn, which was short of primary fuel, and so a number of locomotives were fitted with a Giesl-Ejector. Sometimes this was done during general overhauls, sometimes when the 50E boiler was installed during Reconstruction.

A total of 59 units of class 50/50ÜK engines[722] and 76 class 50$^{35-37}$ machines were fitted

---

[721] Information about the historical model according to Mario Fliege (Fliege)
[722] Cf. (Habermann, 2014). Sebastian Werner gives a figure of 58 machines (Werner, 2019); while Andreas Knipping indicates

with the ejector[723]. With the class 52s, there were 160 machines[724], of which 97 units were of the class 52^{80} [725]. It cannot be excluded that some machines were counted twice due to boiler changes, so that the number of active licences for this technology at the Reichsbahn may have been considerably lower. The ejectors were all removed by 1980,[726] possibly because they were worn out and the new licence fees in foreign currency could not or would not be paid.[727]

Fig. 119: Model of No. 50 1815-5 (Roco 43293), fireman's side.
The model shows the locomotive as it was in 1972. The original model was fitted with a Giesl-Ejector in 1968. It is said to have received the tender of 52 6658.[728]
Information on the historical model: Schwartzkopff 1941 → DRB 50 1815 (RBD Hannover) → 1945 DRo/DR 50 1815 → 1970 DR 50 1815-5 + 1979 Dresden-Friedrichstadt

It is interesting to note that the ejector offered such clear advantages for the Reichsbahn that almost several hundred machines were fitted with it, whereas the Bundesbahn saw no particular benefit from this device.

The Reichsbahn did not pursue further improvements, for example in the direction of the Franco-Crosti technology, although its advantages were recognised. On the one hand, they feared that the construction and maintenance costs would not be worth the savings, and on the other hand, they were afraid that the locomotives would become too heavy. Another issue was the licence fees in foreign currency, which the Reichsbahn was not able to pay.

only 52 units (Knipping2, 2012). Josef Slezak on the other hand, states 101 units (Slezak, 1967), pages 25f.
[723] (Werner, 2019); (Endisch, 2007), page 52; Andreas Knipping indicates only 74 machines (Knipping2, 2012).
[724] Cf. (Habermann, 2014). Manfred Weisbrod and Andreas Knipping mention 163 units (Weisbrod, et al., 2012), page 82; (Knipping2, 2012). Josef Slezak indicates 290 machines (Slezak, 1967), pages 25f.
[725] Cf. (Habermann, 2014), (Knipping2, 2012)
[726] (Slaughter, et al., 1996), page 16
[727] (Sachsenstolz, 2006)
[728] (Fliege)

Fig. 120:   Model of No. 52 1006-7 (Gützold 45101), driver's side
A model of the standard version of the class 52 with a Giesl-Ejector installed in 1969.
Information on the historical model: Henschel 1942 → DRB 52 006 (RBD Halle (Saale)) → 1945
DRo/DR 52 006 → 1970 DR 52 1006-7 + 1977 Kamenz

Fig. 121:   Model of No. 52 8081 (Gützold 49400), fireman's side
The original was added to the Reconstruction Programme in 1963 and fitted with a Giesl-Ejector in 1968.[729] On the model the last brake test is dated 24.5.58, which does not correspond to the year of reconstruction.
Information on the historical model: Borsig 1944 → DRB 52 373 (RBD Posen) → 1945 DRo/DR
50 373 → 1963 DR 52 8081 → 1970 DR 52 8081-3 + 1983 Sangershausen

10.10.12 End of operation

Until 1970, the twin-class locomotives were typically painted in the pre-war Reichsbahn livery. The typeface and colour of the inscriptions were also retained. However, the water tank of the tender was given a pictogram (skull and crossbones) and the warning 'No drinking water'.[730] With the introduction of the UIC coded

---

[729] (Paulsen, et al.)
[730] (Diener, 2012), pages 144ff

numbers in 1970, the inscriptions of the locomotives were changed to standard type-face (TGL 0-16, TGL 0-17).[731] From 1970, the colours of the colour scheme were changed to the TGL standards used in East-Germany. However, despite the different designation, the colours were the same and essentially corresponded to the RAL standards.

The twin-class locomotives, especially classes 50^{35} and 50^{50}, were very popular from the start. Due to their low axle load, they were almost universal locomotives that could be used on all Reichsbahn lines. However, the time of operation of these loco-motives also took its toll on important components, especially the frame as a central component. As a result, from the mid-1970s onwards a number of locomotives were taken out of service because they were simply worn out and beyond repair. As the 50E boilers were relatively new, many locomotives could still be used as heating lo-comotives.

On the track, they were mainly replaced by Reichsbahn class V 100 (from 1970: class 110) diesel locomotives. These were much more economical because they were much easier to maintain and only one person was needed in the cab to operate them. However, the oil price shock of the late 1970s still had an impact, especially as the Soviet Union had also increased its prices. To prevent a possible shortage in the event of another oil price crisis, only machines that could not be repaired were released for scrapping until 1987. For all other machines that could not be repaired, the Reichsbahn set up the so-called 'MfV Reserve z-Park'[732] in 1986. This 'park' was used to mothball locomotives that could possibly be put back into service at a later date. The park included eleven class 50^{35-37} units. By the end of 1990s, all of these engines were scrapped with the exception of No. 50 3708 which was preserved as a museum machine. [733] A further seven class 52^{80} locomotives were transferred from the Reichsbahn to the Bundesbahn's numbering system in 1992, losing the '8' and retain-ing only the last three digits of the ordinal number. Of the class 50 units, only No. 50 3688 made it, after receiving the number 050 688-1 in 1992, it became 088 506-1 in 1994 before being retired in 1998.[734] It has been preserved at the DB Museum and is currently leased to the historic railroad depot in Arnstadt (as of 2023).

---

[731] The typefaces of these two East German standards were largely the same as the West German DIN 1451 standard font.
[732] MfV = **M**inisterium **f**ür **V**erkehrswesen der DDR (Ministry of Transport of the German Democratic Republic). The term 'z-Stellung' (deferred) was and still is used by the German Railways to describe the storage of unneeded rail vehicles.
[733] (Endisch, 2007), page 78
[734] (Fliege)

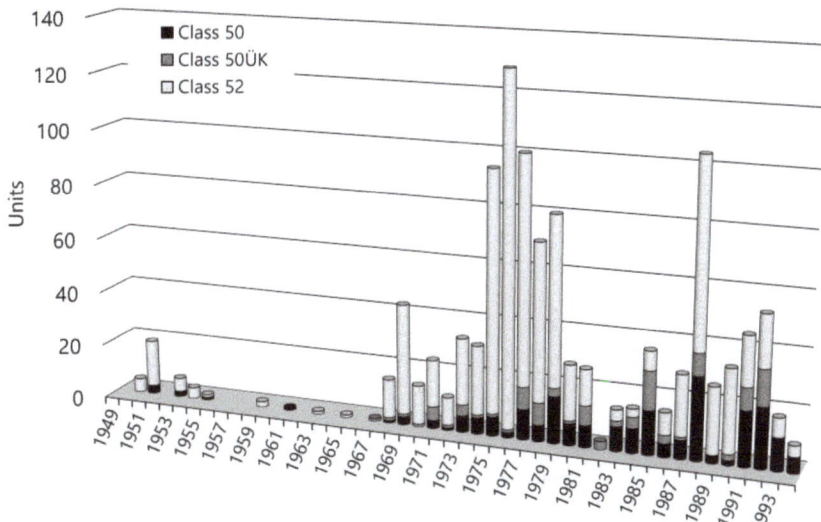

Fig. 122: Retirement of the twin-class machines from the DR operation[735]

If we consider that the class 52 engines in particular were designed for a five-year operational life and were still in service with the Reichsbahn for 30 to 40 years, this indicated the exceptional design of this 'consumable locomotive' and the good maintenance by the Reichsbahn.

Comparing the two German railways with their uneven stocks of twin-class units, it is interesting to see what the two railways have done with their heritage from the pre-war Reichsbahn. On the one hand, the Bundesbahn with a relatively large stock of engines after the war, and on the other, the Reichsbahn with a smaller stock and the best of which had already been shipped to the Soviet Union after the end of the loco-motive squad programme.

For Bundesbahn, the 52s were machines which had to be phased out quickly. The focus was mainly on class 50/50ÜK class, for which a number of different projects were started, only a few of which were eventually introduced across the entire fleet. The East-German Reichsbahn was under much greater economic pressure. After the war, it inherited the less favourable part of the twin-class (the class 52) from the pre-war Reichsbahn. With money and materials constantly in short supply, the change-over to new traction could only take place much more slowly than in West Germany. As a result, more emphasis was placed on maintaining and optimising the existing

---

[735] The use as a heating locomotive is considered as retirement.

locomotive stock. As the economy of East-Germany was much more dependent on the railways, the optimisation of the locomotive fleet had to be successful. Otherwise there were risks of negative repercussions for the socialist economic system.

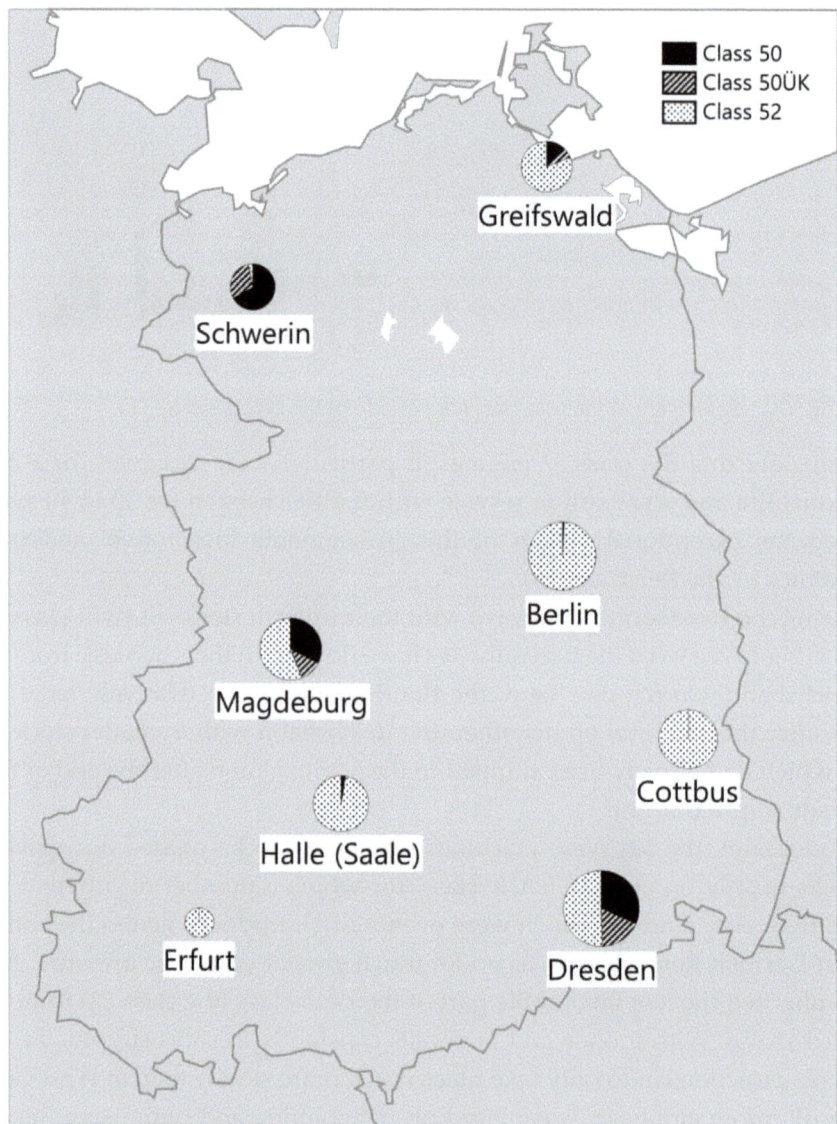

Fig. 123:   Last depots of the twin-class locomotives in East-Germany

10.11 Hungary

The railway network in Hungary came under the jurisdiction of the Hungarian government in 1867, following the establishment of the Austro-Hungarian Dual Monarchy. By the end of the 19th century, many of the existing private companies had been nationalised and were merged into the 'Magyar Államvasutak'[52] (MÁV). By 1919, the MÁV was one of the largest railway companies in Europe, both in terms of the length of its network and its financial situation.[736]

In 1911, MÁV introduced a new numbering system for its locomotives, which would remain in use until 2010. The first digit represented the number of driven axles, and the next two digits were an indication for the axle load of the locomotive. At MÁV, the serial number '520' for the class 52 is derived from five driven axles and the '20' from the axle load between 12.36 tons and 14.42 tons registered with MÁV.[737]

From 1933 on, Hungary politically moved closer to Nazi-Germany. After the occupation of Czechoslovakia by Nazi Germany, Hungary was granted territories in the south of the emerging Slovak vassal state, inhabited by a Hungarian population. At the same time, with the acceptance of the German Reich, Hungary was able to occupy the Carpathian Ukraine, which had previously belonged to Czechoslovakia. Parts of Romania were added in 1940 and, after the Balkan campaign in early 1941, also parts of Slovenia.

In return, Hungary sided with the Axis powers in the war against the Soviet Union. After suffering heavy losses of its own, the government sought a separate peace with the Western Allies, but this prompted Nazi Germany to occupy Hungary from early 1944 ('Operation Margaret') and install a puppet government. With the help of MÁV, this government immediately began to deport the Jews living on the Hungarian territory to concentration and extermination camps. After the capitulation of Romania, the Hungarian government negotiated an armistice with the Soviet Union in the autumn 1944. Again, at the instigation of Nazi Germany, the state leadership was deposed and replaced by the leader of the Arrow Cross fascist organisation ('Operation Panzerfaust'). The fighting and deportations continued, ending only with the complete occupation of Hungary by the Red Army in early April 1945. During this period much of the railway infrastructure and rolling stock in Hungary was destroyed.

---

[736] (Wikipedia049)
[737] (Wikipedia050)

During the war, MÁV hired some 530 locomotives from Italian and German stocks,[738] to fulfil its transport needs. At the end of the war, more than 100 twin-class machines remained on Hungarian territory or arrived in the country after the war, but by 1951 they had all left the country for the Soviet Union or Romania.

Interestingly, although Hungary had a recognised vehicle factory – MÁVAG – it was never included in the war locomotive building programme, unlike the Czech and Polish factories. Nor is there any evidence that German companies, particularly the 'Reichswerke', had any involvement in or influence over the MÁVAG. Although Henschel tried to win MÁVAG as a boiler supplier and placed an order for the supply of 100 boilers, it turned out that MÁVAG's expertise in the construction of welded boilers was too limited. As a result, only 25 boilers were delivered and no further orders were placed.

Although there was a severe shortage of engines, MÁVAG had to pay reparations to the Soviet Union, much of which consisted of the construction and delivery of the Soviet machine Эр (see Chapter 9.3). After the end of the reparations, the construction of units for the USSR continued, but this time on the basis of commercial contracts.[739] Although the Soviet Union offered MÁV the opportunity to sell some of its captured German trophy locomotives to reduce its locomotive shortage, MÁV decided to accept UNRRA's[740] offer and purchased 510 used USATC S160 units. The purchase was financed by a loan from the US government. The first deliveries were made in 1947 and these engines were incorporated into the MÁV fleet as series 411. This purchase was in no way in the interests of the Soviet Union, and it can be assumed that the show trial of MÁV president László Varga and his execution in 1950 were causally linked to it.[741]

In 1957, MÁV purchased a total of 19 units of class 52 from the Austrian Railways (ÖBB) at scrap value through the foreign trade company NIKEX. Unfortunately, not much is known about the whereabouts of these locomotives, nor whether they were refurbished and put into service like the German war class 42 (as MÁV series 501) bought the same time.

A few years after this deal, in 1963, MÁV bought a total of 100 engines of type ТЭ (ex-

---

[738] (Lányi, et al., 1984), Seite 24
[739] (Wikipedia051)
[740] UNRRA = United Nations Relief and Rehabilitation Administration, a UN humanitarian organisation whose aim was to provide relief in the form of food, clothing and medical care, and to assist in the production and transport of such goods in liberated areas. The aim was not to support long-term reconstruction (Wikipedia052).
[741] (Wikipedia053)

class 52) from the Soviet Union. 94 units of them were converted to standard gauge, while six engines were not re-gauged to handle traffic at the then Hungarian-Soviet border station at Záhony. Eight units were transferred to GySEV in the following years (see Chapter 10.11.1). The former Soviet machines were given the numbers 520.001 to 520.094[742] by MÁV according to the valid numbering system. The broad-gauge units were numbered 520.5001 to 520.5006.

The locomotives were mainly used in freight service, but could not be used everywhere due to their too high axle load for the Hungarian lines and their difficulties with the tight curve radii. Some were converted to oil main or auxiliary oil firing, but not much is known about the type and extent.

They were nicknamed 'Bumbardó' by the operating staff, and those converted to oil main or auxiliary firing were called 'Hruscsov-Dízelen' (Khrushchev diesel).[743]

Retirement began in the mid-1960s, not least because of the rapid switch to diesel engines. The last units were taken out of service in 1987. Unfortunately, little is known about their deployment and retirement. A few examples have been preserved as museum machines.

Fig. 124: Model of the No. 520.083 (EuroforceCZ 105200.16), driver's side
The model shows almost the original condition after the takeover from the Soviet Union: large headlight and steam outlet behind the chimney. The original was delivered to GySEV in the same year. The model does not yet have the GySEV ownership markings. The tender number is Y520.083.
Information on the historical model: Schichau 1943 → DRB 52 5595 (RBD ?) → 1945 SŽD ТЭ-5595 → 1963 MÁV 520.083 → 1963 GySEV 520.083 + 1981

---

[742] This includes the machines transferred to GySEV.
[743] (Wikipedia054)

10.11.1 GySEV

The 'Győr-Sopron-Ebenfurti Vasút'[52] (GySEV) is a private railway operating a network of about 520 km (as of 2017) in the Austro-Hungarian border region.

As parts of the railway network are located in Austria – a heritage of the separation of the Austro-Hungarian monarchy – the concession for operation on the Austrian side was confirmed after the First World War. After the Second World War, the Hungarian state nationalised the joint stock company, but did not touch its private-sector structure, especially in view of the preservation of the operating rights on the Austrian side.

In the 1960s, freight traffic on GySEV's lines increased significantly. As a result, the company took over four units of 520.0 series from MÁV in 1963 (buy-back units from the Soviet Union) and another four units in the early 1970s. In addition, the series 520 machines were regularly leased from MÁV during peak periods (e.g. autumn beet haulage).[744] The units kept their MÁV numbers, only the ownership mark was changed.

GySEV's steam locomotives were also replaced by diesel engines from the mid-1970s. The last of GySEVs' 520s were taken out of service in 1984.

Fig. 125: Model of No. 520.030 (EuroforceCZ 105200.15), fireman's side
Almost in the same condition as the MÁV model above, this model has a smaller headlight and different safety valves. The ownership mark is that of GySEV. The tender has the owner marking of the GySEV and the number of the locomotive on the coal box.
Information on the historical model: Krauss 1943 → DRB 52 3535 (RBD München) → 1945 DRo 52 3535 → 1947 SŽD ТЭ-3535 → 1963 MÁV 520.030 → 1976 GySEV 520.030 + 1984

---

[744] (Slaughter, et al., 1996), page 29

10.12 Italy

From 1922 on, Italy was ruled by the 'Partito Nazionale Fascista'[745] led by Benito Mussolini. Italy entered the Second World War in June 1940, declaring war on the United Kingdom and France and fighting with Germany. This was the result of a series of bi- and trilateral treaties (Italo-German protocol 1936, Pact of Steel 1939, Tripartite Pact 1940). When the Allies landed in Sicily in July 1943, Mussolini was deposed and arrested the next day. He was freed by German paratroopers and, with German help, attempted to regain power. Following the devastation of central Italy by heavy fighting and a number of German massacres of civilians, the southern Italian government declared war on the German Reich, whereupon the Western Allies recognised Italy as an ally.[746]

As a result of this change of affiliation, German troops immediately occupied the non-liberated part of Italy and managed to establish a defensive line south of Rome from coast to coast. In those parts of Italy not yet occupied by the Allies, German troops in Italy were from then on regarded as occupying forces. In order to ensure the operation of the railways in northern Italy, the Wehrmacht set up the 'Wehrmacht Transportdirektion Italien'[747] in Verona, with a subsidory in Florence.

As the Italian locomotives did not meet the Wehrmacht's expectations, 93 units of class 52 were brought to Italy to haul the supply trains,[748] according to other sources more than 100 engines were brought over.[749] With the withdrawal of the German troops, the machines were also withdrawn and none of the units brought to Italy by the Wehrmacht remained in the country.[750]

After the war, the Allies brought class 52 units back to Italy to provide transport from the ports of Venice and Trieste across the Brenner and the Pontebbana (Tarvisio-Udine railway) to their troops on the other side of the Alps. These locomotives were operated by Italian personnel and then temporarily handed over to the Italian railways for their own use.

During this time a total of 60 units returned to Italy, including 16 machines that had been confiscated by British troops in Austria for transport from Venice to Villach via

---

[745] National Fascist Party
[746] (Bundeszentrale für politische Bildung3, 2012)
[747] Wehrmacht Transport Directorate Italy
[748] (Reimer, 1996), page 48
[749] (Slaughter, et al., 1996), page 24
[750] (Riccardi, et al., 2021), pages 269ff

the Tarvisio–Udine railway.[751] There were 21 machines stationed at the Udine depot for service in the British Zone of Austria, and another at Tarvisio. For the Brenner line, the 37 machines were stationed in Verona and another in Trento.[750] With the reduction of Allied troops in Austria, the need for transport from the Italian ports was reduced and the number of machines in Italy decreased steadily until 1949.

Fig. 126: Model of No. 52 1545 (Liliput 5230), left side.
On the cab you can still see the Reichsbahn ownership plate with a slightly blurred imperial eagle. On the door you can see the registration number 'FS' and the inscriptions 'Peso reale T144' (real weight 144 tons) and 'Peso frenato 82T' (brake weight 82 tons).
The abbreviation 'GR. RIP. OFF. LOC. FOL. 27.8.46' (**Gr**ande **rip**arazione di **off**icina **loc**ale **Fo-l**igno 27.8.46).[752] The machine wears still its original livery (black grey).
The date of the last brake inspection is given on the tender: 20.5.43 (probably not the original tender or the right date), the water capacity is specified with 32m³. The side wall bears the inscription 'acqua non potabile' (no drinking water).
Information on the historical model: Esslingen 1944 → DRB 52 1545 (RBD Munich) → 1945 FS 52 1545 → 1949 DB 52 1545 + 1954 Freilassing

However, after the Allies no longer needed them, the locomotives were not taken into the FS fleet, but returned to Germany, although they could be used almost throughout the FS network due to their low axle load and good ability to run curves.[753] In addition to the German engines, machines of the Allies also came to Italy, among which the USATC S160 engines represented the largest group (248 units).

During their time in Italy, the locomotives retained their original German numbering and paint scheme. Only FS ownership markings and operational inscriptions were added.

---

[751] The British Zone in post-war Austria consisted of Carinthia, East Tyrol and Styria (excluding the Styrian Salzkammergut).
[752] Great repair of the local workshop in Foligno. After the war Foligno was a FS maintenance workshop under Allied management (trenoazzurro67).
[753] (trenoazzurro67)

It should be noted that 52 3810, which came from the Villach depot, was fitted with oil firing in the spring of 1946 at the Foligno maintenance facility[752]. A few test runs were made between Spoleto and Terni, but they did not seem to make a lasting impression. The machine was returned to Austria in the same year.[750]

Fig. 127: Deployments of class 52 in Italy after the war[750]

10.13 Japan

In 1978, the 'Hotel Orient Express' was opened in Kyoto next to the Hotel Koyo. This was a nine-car Orient Express train with an ÖBB 52.2436 with a caboose tender[754] that stood on a specially built bridge on the south-eastern shore of 琵琶湖 (Lake Biwa) in 大津市 (Otsu City). After some time, the hotel ran into financial difficulties and had to declare bankruptcy. In the 1990s, the layout must have been dismantled and two of the carriages were said to have been used as changing rooms in the 奈良県 (Nara prefecture).[755] Other cars were believed to be parked near 宇陀市 (Uda City) in the 奈良県 (Nara Prefecture).[756] The locomotive was reportedly dismantled in December 2009.[728]

The carriage preserved at the Lalique Museum in 箱根町, 神奈川県 (Hakone, Kanagawa Prefecture) was probably not part of the original display.[757]

Since then the site has been built over (coordinates of the former site: 35.022°N; 135.863°E).

History of the locomotive in service: Henschel 1943 → DRB 52 2436 (RBD Villach) → 1945 ÖBB 52 2436 → 1947 ÖBB 52.2436 + Straßhof 1977, then sold.

---

[754] (gingatetsudo); (oimactaka)
[755] (KDB, 2012)
[756] (tikz14684, 2017); (ijigenkuukann, 2018); (Pierre2427, 2021); (Wikipedia055)
[757] (Wikipedia056)

10.14 Luxembourg

The 'Société Royale Grand-Ducale des Chemins de Fer Guillaume-Luxembourg'[758], was a public limited company that granted concessions for the construction and operation of railways in Luxembourg. In 1857, it granted the concession for building and operation the railways to the French EST. After Alsace-Lorraine became German, the network in Luxembourg was isolated from the EST. During this period it was run by the German railway administration in Strasbourg, which had the control of the railways in Alsace-Lorraine. After the First World War, when Alsace-Lorraine rejoined France, the Luxembourg standard gauge network was taken over by the French company AL[52], which was later merged into SNCF in 1938. After the Second World War, in 1947 the 'Société Nationale des Chemins de Fer Luxembourgeois'[52] (CFL) was set up under a trilateral treaty between France, Belgium and Luxembourg and took over the concessions to operate the standard gauge and national narrow-gauge networks for 99 years. Today, 94 % of CFL's shares were held by the Luxembourg state, 4 % by Belgian and 2 % by French co-owners.[759]

At the end of the war, there were no twin-class units left in Luxembourg. As there was a relatively large fleet of new twin-class machines in Belgium, the CFL asked for machines to be supplied from Belgium to remedy the major shortage of engines. SNCB agreed to sell ten units to the CFL, which were delivered in 1946 (nine units) and 1947 (one unit). Half of them had been built by Tubize and had been in operation for a short time under the Belgian numbers 2612-2616. The other five came from Cockerill and were also almost brand new, bearing SNCB numbers 2642-2646. The rest came from the Bertix and Latour depots in south-east Belgium.[760] In Luxembourg, the machines were added to the fleet as class 56 under the numbers 56.01-56.10.

The SNCF was also prepared to supply a further ten units from the Graffenstaden factory. These were brand new and were delivered in 1946 and 1947. They were numbered 56.11-56.20. The locomotives were all fitted with the driver's position on the right-hand side of the engine, so the crew had to deal with the same problems as in Belgium, as Luxembourg also has left-hand traffic.

Efforts were made right from the beginning to optimise the economy of the machines.

---

[758] Royal Grand Ducal Railway Company Wilhelm Luxemburg. During the foundation of the company the Dutch King Wilem III was also Grand Duke of Luxembourg.
[759] (Groupe CFL, 2020), page 99
[760] (Federmeyer, 1984), page 449ff

An ACFI.RM feedwater heater[761] was therefore installed in all machines. The two characteristic tanks were located on each side of the chimney.

To treat the boiler feedwater, the CFL used the TIA process[762] developed by the SNCF. A mixture of soda (Na_2CO_3), sodium phosphate (Na_3PO_4), caustic soda ($NaOH$) and tannin is placed in a rectangular tank on the tender. Inside the tender, a device ensures that when the tender is filled, water rises into the TIA tank and the mixture is distributed in the tender's water tank.

The machines were stationed in changing formations at the Luxembourg and Ëlwen (Ulflingen) depots, and later at Péiteng (Petingen).[760] With the switch to diesel and electric machines, the engines were completely withdrawn from service in 1961. Some were used as reserve units for a few years, but were scrapped in 1964.

The colour scheme of the locomotives was black with red front and rear buffers and red-painted coupling rod notches.

Fig. 128: Model No. 5609 (Märklin 34158), right side.
The model represents the state of the unit in 1960 (last inspection: 30.8.60). On both sides of the chimney the are the reservoirs of the ACFI.RM feedwater heater. The related pumps are on the left side on the running board in front. At the rear of the tender is the tank for the water treatment system. The bar construction located there is for accident protection. The cab is marked with the engine number, the home depot (Luxembourg) and the manufacturer. The red dot indicates a steel firebox and the yellow marking indicates the TIA device.
Information on the historical model: Cockerill 1945 → SNCB 26.045 → 1946 CFL 5609 + 1961

---

[761] ACFI.RM is an open feedwater heater ('**R**échauffeur par **M**élange', mixing heater) from the French company 'l'**A**uxillaire des **C**hemins de **F**er et d'**I**ndustrie'. The main feature are two cylindrical tanks on the locomotive boiler just on each side of the chimney. One is the mixing chamber, which receives the cold water from the tender, which is then heated by the exhaust steam. The other tank serves as a reservoir for the heated water before it is pumped into the boiler (Giesl-Gieslingen, 1986), page 179.

[762] TIA = **T**raitement **I**ntégral **A**rmand is a process developed by Louis Armand at the SNCF to reduce boiler corrosion (Wikipedia057). Other railway companies also treated boiler water before consumption with other processes and ingredients.

10.15 The Netherlands

After the First World War, the two private railway companies in the Netherlands formed the 'Nederlandse Spoorwegen', in which the two companies merged their operations but remained legally independent entities. The government owned shares in both companies and in the following years repeatedly provided the companies with capital in exchange for company shares, which resulted that the private share was increasingly diluted.

In 1938, the government bought the remaining shares from the private investors and merged the two companies to form the public company 'Nederlandse Spoorwegen'[52] (NS), with the government as the sole shareholder. However, NS was run like a private company.

After the occupation of the Netherlands, the German occupiers set up the 'Dienststelle der Deutschen Bahnbevollmächtigten'[763] (Bbv) in Utrecht. This office was responsible for supervising the administration of the NS, which continued to be carried out by Dutch people, with the exception of employees of Jewish faith or known opponents of the system, who were dismissed in accordance with Nazi ideology. The NS itself remained intact as an independent company, but it had to comply with the wishes of the occupiers, for example by having to lease locomotives to the DRB or by following orders to use only the best engines for Wehrmacht transports in the Netherlands. However, unlike in the other Benelux countries or France, no machines were confiscated.

On the instructions of the Bbv, the Duch railways had to organise the deportations to the transit (and concentration) camp in Westerbork and to the German border. There the Reichsbahn took over the train and transported it to the extermination camps. When it was later discovered that the NS had made profit of about half a million guilders from the deportations, the NS offered compensation to the survivors and their relatives.

From 1941, a number of Reichsbahn locomotives were sent to the 'Hoofdwerkplaats Tilburg'[764], with the Reichsbahn workshop in Mühlheim-Speldorf acting as a spare parts supplier and service supervisor.

In 1943 there were strikes (also known as milkmen's or miners' strikes) against the occupiers' intention to use Dutch nationals as forced labourers. Despite calls from the

---

[763] Office of the German Railway Representative
[764] Tilburg main workshop

strikers, NS staff refused to take part. A year later, when another strike was called in support of the Allied advance, the NS staff took part. After this new strike, the entire railway infrastructure was placed under the direct control of the Reichsbahn and placed under the RBD Münster. As a result, all civilian traffic (passengers, goods) was banned in favour of military traffic.[765] In order to maintain Wehrmacht transports, some 4,500 military railway employees who were no longer needed in the east due to the retreat from Poland and the Soviet Union were transferred to the Netherlands. These personnel managed to keep the traffic running for the occupying force, despite the losses suffered by the railwaymen.

Fig. 129: Model of No. 4903 (Roco 63296), driver's side.
The model shows an ex-50ÜK. There is only one lantern at the front, although the NS normally had two lanterns at that time.[766] Not visible in the picture is the crossed out inscription '50 1680ÜK' on the smokebox door. The cab bears the NS ownership mark, the locomotive number and the place name 'Zwolle' (home depot). The black painted air tanks under the boiler were noticeable, as they did not match the DRB's colour scheme. This may have been done when the engine was rebuilt at the workshop in Zwolle.
Information on the historical model: Krauss 1942 → DRB 50 1680 (RBD Nürnberg) → 1945 NS 4903 → 1947 DRw/DB 52 1680 + 1965 Dortmund

After the liberation of the Netherlands, the damage to the railway infrastructure was enormous. Almost all the rolling stock had been taken to Germany and much of the infrastructure was destroyed by the German 'Scorched-Earth-Policy'[430].

Even before the surrender in 1944, the NS took two class 50 units (50 1964, 50 1586)

---

[765] (Muller, et al., 2005), pages 317ff

[766] Dutch engines used to have yellow headlights. It was not until the beginning of the 20th century that new locomotives were fitted with white headlights. From 1963, the so-called 'L-signal' was introduced. A third lamp was mounted on the driver's side. As this caused problems, a few months later the third lamp was mounted on the fireman's side ('inverted L-signal'). As this position also caused problems, the third lamp was finally placed in the middle ('A-signal'), corresponding to the German three-lamp headlights (Split).

into their fleet as series 4800¹ (4801, 4802).[767] After the German surrender, they got part of the fleed under the series 49 and were accordingly renumbered to 4904 and 4901.[768] Another four twin-class units, two 50s and two 50ÜKs, were added to the series 49 fleet by the NS after the war. Some of the locomotives were defective, e.g. 4902 was badly damaged and served as a spare part donor for 4903, which was rebuilt at the Central workshop in Zwolle. It also received the large smoke deflectors.[765]

The four remaining units were stationed at the depot in Eindhoven, where they mainly hauled coal trains from South Limburg to Belgium or Nijmegen. They were the most powerful engines on the Dutch railway network.

By 1947, all the machines were returned to the West-German railways and were used there.

During their operation with the NS, the Dutch railways did not paint them in the NS livery, because the corresponding materials were thought to be more urgently needed for other things than to paint these engines.

Until the introduction of a corporate design in 1968, inscriptions were made using in-house pattern sheets for letters and numbers[769] similar to the typeface 'Swift'.[770]

---

[767] The 4800ᴵᴵ series consisted of machines of the former German class 57 (van Wijck Jurriaanse, 1968), page 131.
[768] (Waldorp, 1986), page 268
[769] (Frans8800, 2014)
[770] (Vink)

10.16 Norway

At the beginning of the Second World War, Norway became in the German war machine's sights, as Swedish iron ore, vital to the German war economy, was shipped from Narvik in North Norway. Without this supply of raw materials, the German war industry would have been severely affected. The Germans were also concerned that Britain might pre-empt their occupation of Norway. In early April 1940, the German Reich attacked neutral Norway without declaring war.[771] As a result the Norwegian railways, which had been established long before the First World War as 'Norges Statsbaner'[52] (NSB), were placed under German command.

In order to provide the required transport services, the Reichsbahn initially loaned 15 units of class 52 to the NSB, ten of which were transferred to Trondheim via Saßnitz-Trelleborg at the beginning of August 1943. Another five followed at the beginning of October 1943.[772] From the summer of 1944, more class 52 units arrived in Norway, bringing the total to 74 units by the end of June 1945.[773]

Three of the units were originally ordered as class 50, but the order was changed to class 52. Two of the machines delivered were coupled with the box-shaped tender, 15 units with a rigid frame tender[774] and the remainder with a tub-shaped tender. The two box tenders were quickly rebuilt to a snow plough[775] and were used for snow clearance.

After the war, the German locomotives were taken over by the 'Direktoratet for fiendtlig eiendom'[776], which officially handed them over to 'Norges Statsbaner'[52] (NSB) in 1950. There they were quickly nicknamed 'Stortysker' (Big Germans).

The engines were well suited for use in Norway due to their winter equipment, but were prone to breakdowns due to their 'wartime' construction. A number of changes/improvements were therefore made to the machines after the war, including:

- Improvement of the working conditions for the locomotive crew: a double-insulated floor was installed and improvements were made to the roof hatch, the

---

[771] (Scriba)

[772] (Walinowski, 2014)

[773] Although the last deliveries arrived in Norway before the end of the war, they were unloaded in the port of Moss, as this was not possible in Oslo because the vessel's loading gear was not strong enough to put the locomotives ashore and the only suitable floating crane was sunk by a torpedo. It took until June for them to arrive in Oslo (Walinowski, 2014).

[774] (Bjerke, et al., 1987), page 210

[775] Photo of such a unit see (Norsk jernbanemuseum)

[776] Directorate for Enemy Property

windows and lighting.

- The safety valves were replaced with Norwegian standard valves.
- Axle bearing adjustment wedges[687] were fitted.
- After one boiler nearly burst due to lack of water, the fireboxes were fitted with fusible plugs[778].
- To protect the boilers from further damage, the boiler pressure was reduced from 16 to 14 bar[772].

Fig. 130: Last depots of series 63 in Norway[777]

---

[777] Cf. (Bjerke, et al., 1987)

[778] Fusible plugs are openings of the firebox filled with lead. When the firebox overheats, the lead melts and a mixture of water and steam enters the firebox to extinguish the fire.

After the handover, the locomotives were officially incorporated into the NSB fleet in 1950, where they were designated as series 63a, but retained their former sequential numbers. They were mainly used for heavy haulage.

In 1952, the so-called 'Vekk med dampen-programmet'[779] was passed with the aim of phasing out steam operations in the coming years. Therefore 50 % of the network, representing 80 % of the traffic, was electrified.

Diesel engines were used on the remaining part of the network. The conversion lasted until 1970, when the steam service was discontinued.

With the exception of three units taken out of service before 1955, the other engines terminated operation between the late 1950s and the late 1960s. Some machines were converted to oil firing, others were stored as strategic reserves.[777] Four locomotives were parked in a special tunnel[780] that was built in Drangsdalen in 1958: 1104, 2770, 5856 and 5865.[781]

Later machine 5856 became a museum locomotive in Great Britain, No. 2770 received the boiler of 5857 and the tender of 5858 and is in service as an operating museum locomotive.[782] The other engines were scrapped in 1972.

---

[779] Get Rid of Steam Programme
[780] Possibly in 'Stortunnelen' (58,482°N; 6,473°E)
[781] (Wikipedia058)
[782] (Gieseler03)

Fig. 131: Model of No. 52 324 (Gützold 32002), fireman's side.
The model shows the original state before the official takeover by NSB. It has red wheel rims, a red headstock and blue coupling rod notches. The painting of the notches was not unusual. As there were different colours for the coupling rod notches, there has been speculation whether there was a colour code for the different depots, but there is no evidence of this. Although NSB's main workshop had records of colour codes in its audit files, these were not transferred to the locomotives. It is more likely that the choice of colour was depending on the availability of the individual colours and the taste of the employees. This seems to have been tolerated by the NSB's management.[783]
The inscription on the cab has a white background and warns against driving under catenary. There is also a similar sign on the sand dome.
Information on the historical model: Floridsdorf 1943 → DRB 50 324 (RBD Posen) → 1945 NSB 52 324/324 + 1963 Trondheim

Fig. 132: Model of No. 2770 (Märklin 3417), driver's side.
On this model the coupling rod notches were also painted blue. The bar construction on the tender behind the coal box was for accident protection.
Information on the historical model: Henschel 1944 → DRB 52 2770 (Gedob) → 1945 NSB 2770 + 1958 Stavanger

---

[783] (Glasse)

10.17 Poland

After regaining independence after the First World War and the end of the Polish-Soviet War in 1921, the new Polish railway network faced a number of challenges. First of all, the network had to be rebuilt from the ground to integrate the various pre-war railway systems on the territory of Poland (former Prussian, Austro-Hungarian and Russian railway system) into a new whole. This was initially done under the direction of the newly established Ministry of Transport. A Ministry of Railways was created in 1919, and in 1926 the 'Polskie Koleje Państwowe'[52] (PKP) were established as a state-owned company with its own management.

After the occupation of Poland at the beginning of the Second World War, the railway passed into German and Soviet hands. In the German part, the railway network was operated according to the specifications of the Reichsbahn and the Ostbahn. In the Soviet part, the lines that had only been converted to standard gauge after the Polish-Soviet War were converted back to broad gauge (1,524 mm). Many of these lines were converted back to standard gauge (1,435 mm) by German railway troops a few months later, only to be converted back to broad gauge again a few years later during the Soviet advance.

The Second World War resulted in much destruction of the railway network, not least due to the 'Scorched-Earth-Policy'[430] of the retreating Germans. Abount 40 % of the tracks and half of the bridges were destroyed.[784]

In addition, even before the official end of the war, the Soviet army carried out dismantling operations in the former German territory east of the river Odra as it advanced westwards. It is estimated that about 5,400 km of standard gauge and 300 km of narrow-gauge lines were dismantled. The 'Трофейные Батальоные' (Trophy Battalions), under the direction of the Red Army's 'Трофейного Управления' (Trophy Office), often used German prisoners of war and civilians.[785] The dismantling continued until 1948,[786] even after the areas east of the river Odra had come under Polish administration under the Potsdam Agreement from 1945 and were no longer part of the Soviet Zone.[787] Reparation goods were transported through the ports of Świnoujście and Police. In accordance with the Potsdam Agreement, the entire outlet

---

[784] (Winek, 2017)
[785] (Taylor, 2007), pages 106f
[786] (Taylor, 2007), pages 114ff; (Mochocki, 1999)
[787] (Potsdam Agreement - Protocol of the Proceedings, August 1, 1945), part VIII, B

of the Odra (Oder) remained under Soviet sovereignty[788] and was not handed over to the Polish authorities until mid-October 1945.[789]

With the Soviet advance to the West, some main lines in Poland had been converted to broad gauge to meet the needs of the Red Army.[790] These lines were managed by the Soviet military, which employed Polish personnel. The lines not used by the Soviet military were reopened by the Poles. It is estimated that some of the lines dismantled by the Soviet troops, about 1,800 kilometres of standard gauge lines and about 130 kilometres of narrow-gauge lines, were rebuilt.[785]

In July 1945, the USSR handed over the administration of the Polish railways to the Polish Ministry of Railways.[791] A 'Generalna Dyrekcja Kolei' (General Directorate for the Railways) was established in 1948 and the Polish Railways were re-established a year later. By 1949, all private railways were gradually nationalised, including the 'Magistrala węglowa'[792] and the standard-gauge part of the 'Elektryczne Koleje Dojazdowe' (Electric Commuter Railways), which operated an electric regional railway network in the greater Warsaw area. At the same time, ten different regional directorates (DOKP)[793] were created, of which the DOKP Łódź and the DOKP Olsztyn were liquidated a few years later.

In 1945, the Polish railways had 57 engines of class 50, eight class 50ÜK machines, 1,091 class 52s and 13 units of class 52 with condensation tender. Post-war deliveries from the Polish locomotive factories included: four class 50 units (from Warsaw) and 150 class 52 engines (83 from Cegielski, 67 from Charnów). It should be noted, however, that a number of these locomotives were taken by the Soviet army as booty, although only a small part of it was really transferred to the Soviet Union and other countries.

The locomotives taken over were numbered according to the PKP numbering system introduced in 1922:

T   for a freight engine from 'Towary' (freight)

y   for a machine with five driving axles and one driving axle (1'E)

---

[788] (Mochocki, 1999)

[789] (Wikipedia059)

[790] (Kuhlmann, 2002), Seite 31

[791] (PRL, 2016)

[792] The Coal Main Line. Beginning of the 1930s i sovereignty t was built with French capital. The main purpose of the line was to connect the Upper Silesian coalfields with the port of Gdynia to promote exports. One of the shareholders of the joint-stock company set up for this purpose was the French group Schneider et Cie., which had already invested in the expansion of the port in Gdynia and in mines and metallurgical plants in Upper Silesia (Wikipedia060).

[793] DOKP = **D**yrekcja **O**kręgowa **K**olei **P**aństwowych (Regional Directorate of the State Railways)

2   for the ex-class 52 units built before the end of the war

5   for ex-class 50 locomotives

42   for class 52 engines delivered directly to the PKP after the war. These were machines that had been rebuilt from existing semi-finished products and/or from original layouts.[794]

Thus, the twin-class were given the Polish serial numbers Ty2, Ty42 and Ty5.[795] The condensation tender locomotives were numbered Ty2-1 to Ty2-13[796]. Their condensing units were removed in the mid-1950s.[797]

The numbers following the Ty2-1169 were mainly occupied by former Reichsbahn units, all the numbers above were reserved for locomotives of other origins.[796] These were arrivals from other countries, in particular the purchase of 200 units from the USSR in 1962/1963 (Ty2-1207 to 1406). They were in such good condition that they could be put into service immediately.[798]

The engines of the series Ty42 built by Cegielski were given the sequential numbers 29-81, 102-116 and 132-146, while those built by Charnów were given the numbers 1-28, 82-101, 117-131 and 147-150.

At the PKP, the tenders also had separate numbers. This was composed of the a series number for the tender and a sequential number:[799]

- First, there was a two-digit number indicating the capacity of the water tank, rounded off to the nearest m³, e.g. '26' for the German 2'2'T26 tender.
- A code letter followed indicating the number of axles of the tender (B for two axles, C for three axles, D for four axles, etc.), e.g. 26<u>D</u> for the 2'2'T26 tender.
- The letter was followed by a one-, two- or three-digit code that indicated the origin or the design of the tender (1-10: Prussian layout, from 11: Austrian layout, from 101: other layouts) For tenders built according to a PKP programme, the year of release for construction was coded. So, the German 2'2'T26 tender had the final number 26D<u>5</u>.

The series Ty2/42 thus had the following tender designations, although other tenders than the 'original tenders' (cf. Chapter 6.2.1) were also used:[800]

---

[794] (Piwowoński, 1978), pages 172f

[795] (Terczyński, 2003), pages 30f

[796] (Slaughter, et al., 1996), page 37

[797] (Paulsen, et al.)

[798] (Terczyński, 2020)

[799] (Terczyński, 2003), page 31

[800] (Terczyński, 2020), (Terczyński2, 2020)

Fig. 133: Model of No. Ty5-31 (Roco 63295), driver's side
A model of the original with large smoke deflectors, white wheel rims. The cab bears the PKP ownership mark with the Polish eagle of the Polish national emblem. The belonging to DOKP Poznań and the same 'Parowozownia' (steam locomotive depot) were inscribed. The engine's numbers were in white on a red background. The tender has the owner's mark and the tender identification '26D5' in the same way. The inscriptions on a yellow background were warnings for the catenary.
Information on the historical model: Henschel 1941 → DRB 50 1514 (RBD Dresden) → 1945 PKP Ty5-31 + 1978 Poznan

Fig. 134: Model of No. Ty2-1387 (UMF), fireman's side
Model of a Ty2 with small smoke deflectors, white wheel rims, large headlights and an orange painted buffer beam. Note, that the deflectors mounted here were flat. The machine's number, its belonging to the DOKP Olsztyn and the Lębork depot were written next to the owner's mark. The Lębork depot, however, belonged to the DOKP Gdańsk already from the 1950s.[801] The tender is marked 32D43. The yellow inscriptions were warnings for the catenary.
Information on the historical model: Henschel 1943 → DRB 52 2277 (RBD Poznan) → 1945 MÁV → 1948 CFR → 1950 SŽD TЭ-2277 → 1963 PKP Ty2-1387 + 1992 Chojnice

---

[801] (Wikipedia061)

26D5   2'2'T26, with '5' for 'Prussian' origin

30D42   K 4T30 (rigid frame tender), marked '42' for first built in 1942

32D43   K 2'2'T30(32) (tub-shaped tender), with '43' for the first built in 1943. The PKP gave a water capacity of 32 m³.

30D43   K 2'2'T30(32) (tub-shaped tender), with '43' for the first year of manufacture 1943. The PKP gives a water capacity of 30 m³. Possibly as result of lowering the filling mark

32D47   Tub-shaped tender, similar to 32D43, but Polish design for Ty45 (year of construction: 1947)

32D2   Former Prussian tender 2'2'T31,5, that was also used in the PKP series Pm2 (analogous to German Reichsbahn class 03)

34D44   Ex-2'2'T34, from Ty4 (ex-German class 44)

22D23   Polish type originally for the Polish series Ty23 (UIC code[36]: 2'2'T21,5)

After the signing of an agreement between Poland and the USSR in early September 1945 on the settlement of the Polish reparation claims,[802] which the USSR had committed to satisfy under the Potsdam Agreement,[803] the PKP was able to take over 60 units of class 50/50ÜK into its own fleet. There were some problems with the takeover, as some CFR series units (replicas of the G10/57[10-35], later PKP class Tw1) were causing confusion, as they were also running on PKP lines.[804]

A number of improvements were made to the Ty2s, some of which had already been carried out on the East-German Reichsbahn:[794] replacement or reinforcement of the boiler supports, replacement of the cylinder rupture discs[805] with safety valves, installation of axle bearing wedges[687], reconstruction of the boiler and the installation of water circulators[806].

The locomotives of the Ty2 series were fitted with small smoke deflectors, some of which were curved, similar to the German design, but also with flat plates. Some locomotives (e.g. Ty2-1049) have also been observed with stub smoke deflectors

---

[802] (Korzon, 1993)

[803] (Potsdam Agreement - Protocol of the Proceedings, August 1, 1945), Part III.2.

[804] (Terczyński, 2002)

[805] Class 50 had safety valves on each of its cylinders which were designed to open in the event of an overpressure (similar to boiler safety valves). For class 52 (and maybe parts of the 50ÜKs), these valves were replaced by rupture discs.

[806] Water circulation pipes or arch tubes were water pipes that ran through the firebox to ensure a better water circulation. and increased the firebox heating surface. These pipes connected the lower part of the firebox tube sheet and the space above the crown of the firebox. They were also often used to support the fire brick arch. With German steam engines they were rarely used, but were quite usual in other European and US layouts.

(cf. Figure 137).[807] It is not known whether these very small plates proved successful. Not many changes have been made to the Ty5 machines over the years. Worn components have been replaced and standard modifications have been made to some parts in accordance with PKP guidelines (e.g. installation of a combined steam jet pumps[808]). Some of the tenders were also replaced with 26D74 tenders in the 1970s.[809] In the mid-1960s, 59 engines of the Ty2 series were converted to oil firing.[810] The fuel used was 'Mazut'[477], obtained from crude oil transported to Poland via the 'Pipeline of Friendship'. The oil was processed in the Płock and Gdansk refineries.

The oil-fired locomotives were not popular with the staff as they required a greater degree of control over the water level and temperature in the firebox than coal-fired engines. In addition, staff training was incomplete as it was only theoretical and practical experience was only gained during operation, unfortunately often at the expense of the health or lives of the staff.[811] After some of the oil-fired units suffered boiler

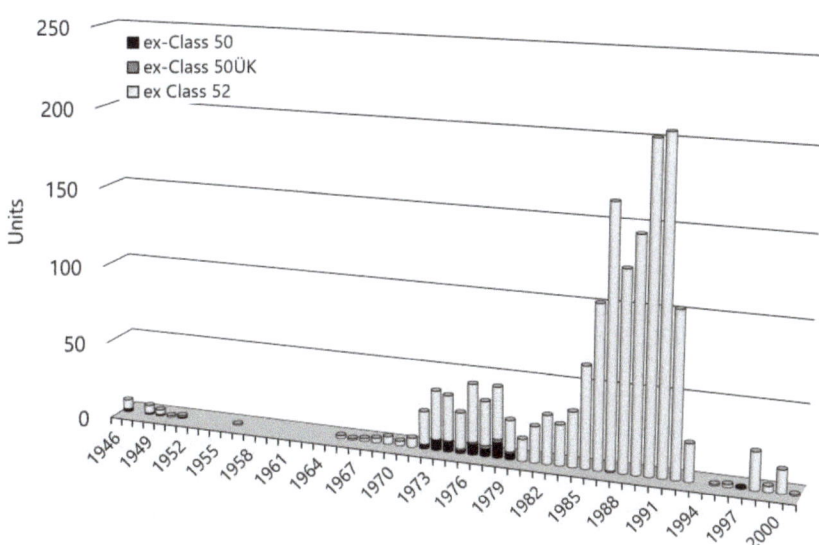

Fig. 135:   Retirements from service at PKP, by original class

---

[807] (Brutzer3, 2009)

[808] Combined steam jet pumps are a combination of a steam jet pump, a steam valve and a feed valve.

[809] Tenders with new bogies were developed for the Polish locomotive Pt47 series. From mid-1974 this design was also installed in the existing Ty5 tenders and at the same time their series was changed to 26D74 (Terczyński, 2002).

[810] (Czarnecki, et al.)

[811] (Stankiewicz, et al., 2013), pages 79f

explosions and the crude oil prices rose sharply, the machines were converted back to coal firing in the early 1970s.

From the beginning of the 1970s, the decline of steam locomotive operation also began in Poland due to the switch to diesel and electric transport. As in East-Germany, the phase-out was delayed by the oil price shock in the mid/late 1970s, but the number of units taken out of service continued to rise in the early 1980s, reaching a peak in 1991. Some Ty2 machines were still in service at the turn of the millennium.

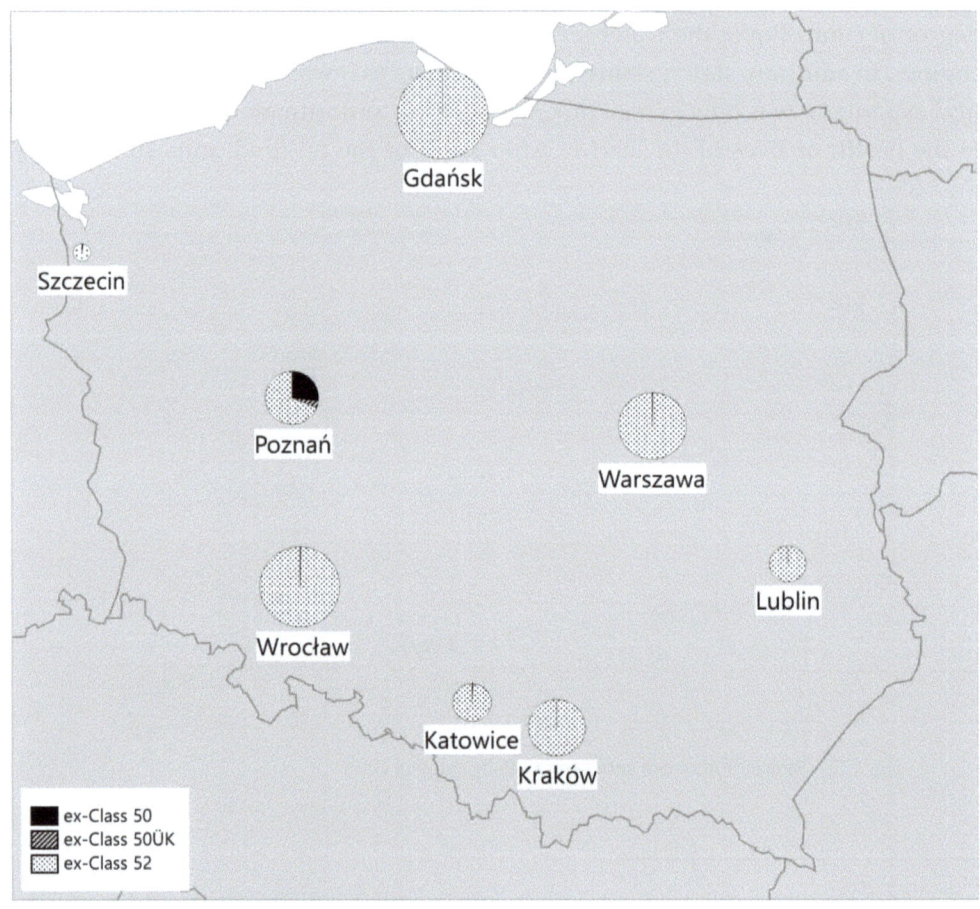

Fig. 136: Last depots by regional directorate (DOKP)

Fig. 137: Model of No. Ty2-911, driver's side
A model of a Ty2 with stub smoke deflectors fitted to the top of the boiler. It is unclear if, when and how long this equipment was fitted.
Information on the historical model: Cegielski 1944 → DRB 52 1346 (RBD Stettin) → 1945 PKP Ty2-911 → + 1999 Kraków

10.17.1 Przedsiębiorstwo Materiałów Podsadzkowych-Przemysłu Węglowego

In many cases, when coal or ore is mined underground, the empty beds are allowed to collapse. However, this leads to subsidences as the collapse continues to the surface over time. The results are sinkholes on the surface that cannot be drained. To avoid this, the seams have to be backfilled when mining is finished. Excavated material from the mine is used for backfilling, or additional sand and/or gravel is injected. This method was not used in the West-German coalfields (Ruhr, Saar), but in the Silesian coalfields.

Special plant railways, known as sand railways, were used to transport the backfill material, usually on special tracks approved for high axle loads.

The main sand railways in the Upper Silesian coalfield were operating on standard gauge and belonged to the following companies:

- Sand railway company of the Count of Ballestrem:
  This company was a joint venture between 'Borsigwerke AG' (50 %) and the Count of Ballestrem Group (50 %).[812]

---

[812] The Ballestrem Group was an Upper Silesian company (1798-1945) and was expropriated at the end of the war (Wikipedia062).

- Sand railway of the 'Schaffgott'sche Werke'

    This company owned a number of coal and calamine (zinc ore) mines in Upper Silesia.[813] There were connections on management level to the 'Vereinigte Oberschlesische Hüttenwerke AG', which was wholly owned by the Counts of Ballestrem from 1931.[814]

- Sand Railways of the 'Preußische Hütten- und Bergwerks AG' (Preussag)

    The Preussag was a company that grouped the former Prussian ownership of mines, smelters and other businesses from before the First World War into a public limited company. It was founded in 1923. When the Nazis came to power, the company was staffed by a management favourable to the regime. There were close links with the 'Reichswerke'.[815] After the war, the parts of the company located in the Eastern Bloc were nationalised.

The railway company 'Przedsiębiorstwo Materiałów Podsadzkowych-Przemysłu Węglowego'[52] (PMP-PW) was established at the end of 1950, bringing together the former sand railways and other industrial railways in the area. The company was headquartered in Katowice, with its operational centre at the depot in Pyskowice (near Katowice). The PMP-PW formed the second largest railway network in Poland and was under the control of the Polish Ministry of Mining, not the Ministry of Transport like the PKP.

A total of 29 units of Ty2 operated on this railway network, about 20 of which were bought back from the Soviet Union in 1963. The sequential numbers of the purchased locomotives were retained and the Soviet designation 'ТЭ' was replaced by the Polish designation 'Ty2'. The nine other units taken over from the PKP kept their PKP numbers. The steam engines were taken out of service in the course of the switch to electric machines.

---

[813] The Schaffgott'sche Werke was a family business in Upper Silesia (1815-1945) and was nationalised in 1945 (Wikipedia063).

[814] (Wikipedia064); (Graf von Ballestrem)

[815] The CEO of Preussag was also a member of the board of the 'Reichswerke' (Wikipedia065).

10.18 Romania

After the First World War, the regions of Transylvania, Bessarabia and Bukovina became part of Romania, forming 'Greater Romania'. With these territories, the railway lines that had previously belonged to Austria-Hungary or the Russian Empire also came under the administration of the 'Căile Ferate Române'[52] (CFR). With the territorial changes, important railway manufacturers such as the 'Uzinele de Fier și Domeniile Reșița'[56] (UDR) in Reșița and the 'ASTRA Prima Fabrica Romana de Vagoane si Motoare'[816] in Arad also became part of Romania. This enabled the Romanian railways to modernise its machinery extensively in the following years, without having to rely on imports.

Reșița, which had been run by the StEG[817] until the end of the First World War, became a joint stock company. In 1929, Max Auschnitt took over the management of the company. Under his leadership, Reșița developed into a national group of companies, including shareholdings in the Astra factories.[818] Reșița's position was so strong that Auschnitt was called the 'Iron King of Greater Romania' and was the dominant businessman in the Romanian defence, mining and metal industries.[819]

In 1928, Nicolae Malaxa founded the Malaxa Works in Bucharest, which was a strong competitor to Reșița, although Reșița was its supplier for many years. When Malaxa himself was appointed to the board of Reșița in 1931, he and Auschnitt set up the 'Compagnie Européenne de Participations Industrielles' (CEPI) in Monaco, through which they managed their shares in Reșița.

Unlike other industrial companies in Romania, Malaxa's company was not tied to the interests of foreign investors,[820] but maintained good (business) relations with Nazi-Germany.[821] He secretly cooperated with leading Nazis in confiscating the assets of Auschnitt, who had converted from Judaism to Catholicism but was still considered Jewish according the Nazi ideology.[819] In 1939, Auschnitt was accused of false charges and removed from the Reșița board.

---

[816] 'First Romanian Wagon and Engine Factory', name of the company from 1921. Astra was and is an important wagon manufacturer in Romania (gam3, 2013) and was a subsidiary of Grazer Maschinen- und Waggonbau-AG (Wikipedia066).

[817] StEG = k.k. privilegierte Österreichisch-ungarische **St**aats-**E**isenbahn-**G**esellschaft (Imperial-Royal privileged Austrian-Hungarian state railway company). This was a private railway company with lines in Austria and Hungary (1854-1920).

[818] (Perianu, 2000), page 98

[819] (Wikipedia067)

[820] One of the main shareholders of Reșița was the British 'Vickers-Armstrongs Limited', another major shareholder was the Czechoslovak 'Československá zbrojovka Brno' (Enciclopedia României).

[821] Malaxa had studied at the Polytechnic University in Karlsruhe.

After the occupation of Czechoslovakia in March 1939, the 'Československá zbrojovka Brno' was incorporated into the 'Reichswerke'. This meant that the Reşiţa shares of this company also passed into the hands of the 'Reichswerke'. The 'Reichswerke' used its new influence to ensure that a German was appointed to the board of directors of Reşiţa. Through further agreements with the Romanian government, the Reichswerke was able to increase its influence over Reşiţa, resulting in the Reichswerke taking over the commercial, financial, technical and administrative management of Reşiţa, in return for which the Reichswerke undertook to provide technical, administrative and commercial assistance.[822]

A further step in the takeover of Romanian industry was the establishment of the 'Societatea Româno – Germană pentru Industria şi Comerţul Fierului S.A.R. Rogifer'[823]. Under the terms of the agreement, the Malaxa leased his factories to Rogifer for a period of ten years.[824] After the Romanian King went into exile in 1940 and Romania became a fascist dictatorship. The Romanian state bought the shares from the Reichswerke and liquidated the company Rogifer in October 1943. However, the liquidation process was not completed until 1947.[825]

With the new government Romania joined the Axis powers in 1941 and took part in the attack on the Soviet Union and the Holocaust, which led to the murder of 287,000 Romanians of Jewish faith during the war.[826]

Active participation in the invasion of the Soviet Union led to an increase of the transport of the Romanian railways. This was helped by the fact that the Reichsbahn leased 100 units of class 57[10-35] (G10), class 50 and 52 engines to the CFR on favourable terms. The CFR was particularly pleased with the performance of the twin-class, and in 1943 further units were purchased and added to the CFR's fleet as series 150.000 (for class 50) and series 150.1000 (for class 52).[827]

After increasing casualties among the Romanian troops and the uncertain outcome of the war, Romania changed fronts following another coup d'état by the son of the exiled king and declared war on Germany in 1944. In September 1944, Romania signed an armistice with the Allies and contributed troops to the liberation of Hungary and Czechoslovakia.

---

[822] (Enciclopedia României)
[823] Romanian-German Company for Iron Industry and Trade S.A.R. Rogifer
[824] (Lacriţeanu, et al., 2007), pages 482ff
[825] (Arhivele Naţionale Române)
[826] (Bundeszentrale für politische Bildung2)
[827] (Lacriţeanu, et al., 2007), page 478

The armistice agreement stipulated that Romania had to pay reparations to the Soviet Union totalling $300 million (at 1938 prices), mainly in the form of industrial goods. Part of these reparations were the deliveries of Soviet Эр engines built in Romania (see Chapter 9.3).[828]

10.18.1 Replicas based on German plans (series 150.000)

After the Romanian state bought back Rogifer's shares in 1943, it decided to build its own locomotives instead of buying or leasing them from the Reich. To this end, in 1942 the CFR received the plans for the class 50 (or a version of a class 50ÜK?) from Rogifer and passed them on to Malaxa and Reșița[824]. A few months later, a contract was signed for the delivery of 100 machines from the series 150.000. The batch should be produced in equal parts by Reșița and Malaxa. In this context, there were indications that the lot for Malaxa included five class 50ÜK.[824]

Given the situation in Romania, the engines from these orders were not ready for delivery until 1945. It was planned to take over the lot under of Reșița under the numbers 150.001-150.050 and Malaxa's lot under 150.051-150.100.

However, Malaxa was nationalised as part of the Communist takeover in mid-1948, having been released from the liquidation process of the dissolved Rogifer company for a few months. Under the instructions of its new owner (the Romanian state), Malaxa had to give priority to Romania's reparation obligations to the Soviet Union, especially as the supply of parts and components from Germany had been exhausted. Accordingly, the construction of steam locomotives for the CFR was concentrated in Reșița. As Malaxa had already delivered 31 units, Reșița took over the construction of the remaining 19 machines.

Following a tragic boiler explosion in 1948, all locomotives were fitted with three test cocks to check the water level in deviation from the German blueprints.[829]

Machines with numbers 150.051-150.081 were fitted with special equipment that differed from the original design of the class 50:[830]

- From 1949, the engines were equipped with shaking grates[831] and 'Everlasting' blow-off cocks[832],

---

[828] (Perianu, 2000), pages 100f
[829] (Lacrițeanu, et al., 2007), page 497
[830] (Lacrițeanu, et al., 2007), page 490
[831] The original version of the class 50 was only equipped with a dumping grate.
[832] A blow-off cock is a plug valve at the lowest point of the boiler and is used to periodically drain the accumulated mud

- From 1952, the machines were equipped with an oil tank to spray coal with oil (additional oil firing),
- from 1958 they were fitted with Trofimoff valves[446],
- From 1961 a second Knorr air pump and a reinforced draw hook,
- from 1964, installation of water circulators[806] in the firebox (as a reaction of the purchase of such equipped machines from the Soviet Union?) and installation of double or flat chimneys and installation of a second fuel oil spraying device.

However, especially with heavy trains and/or on difficult routes, it became apparent that the steam generation of the engines with the previous equipment was inadequate. Comparison runs with the newly developed ČSD series 556 demonstrated the superior performance of this unit.[833] Improvements of the ČSD locomotive compared to the series 150.000 were:[834]

- mechanical coal loading (mechanical stoker)
- a firebox equipped with a water pocket[632] and a combustion chamber
- double 'Kylchap' exhaust system

Like the Giesl-Ejector, the 'Kylchap' exhaust system was a system of blast pipes in the smokebox designed to increase the pumping effect on the flue gases by means of the steam engine's exhaust. The system was designed to increase the draught in the boiler, which would lead to a higher fanning of the fire and thus a higher evaporation capacity of the boiler.

The Kylchap exhaust system consisted of two main parts: a spreading nozzle, which divided the steam engine's exhaust gases into four diverging jets, and cylindrical mixing nozzles, which drew in the flue gases at different heights in the smoke chamber.[835] The name 'Kylchap' is a combination of the names of the inventor of the spreading nozzle, the Finnish engineer Kyösti **Kyl**älä, and the designer of the mixing nozzle, the French steam locomotive engineer André **Chap**elon.

The first step in improving the draught in the smokebox was to install two blowpipes, each with its own chimney. The installation of two chimneys alone improved performance. The next step towards further improvements was the design of Kylälä, in

---

from the boiler. The mud is formed from water impurities, scale and residues of water treatment agents. Such a valve is also used to completely drain the boiler. 'Everlasting' is a US manufacturer of blow-off cocks (Everlasting Valve Company, South Plainfield, NJ).

[833] The ČSD 556 series was a 1'E axle arrangement freight steam engine with a maximum axle load of 16 tons. The machine was designed according to the latest findings in steam locomotive construction. It can be regarded as the crowning achievement of Czechoslovak steam locomotive construction and is considered a top European design.

[834] (Lacriţeanu, et al., 2007), pages 499f

[835] (Giesl-Gieslingen, 1986), pages 150f

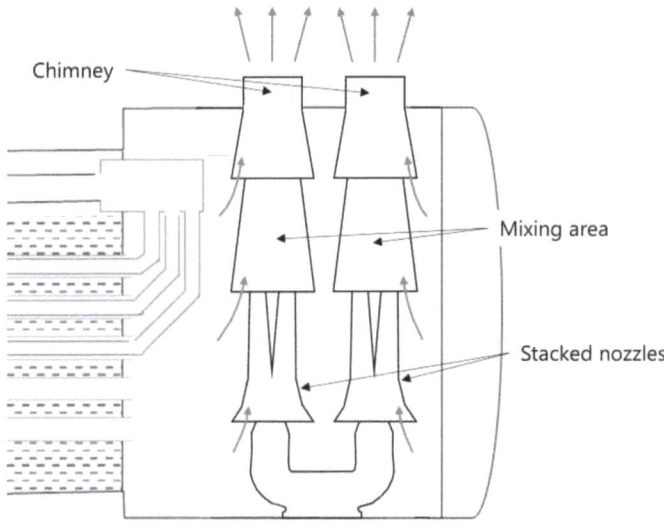

Fig. 138: Sketch of a double Kylchap exhaust system[837]

which the exhaust vapour from the cylinders was discharged through two blast pipes, each with four nozzles, and then reunited into two single jets as it travelled to the two chimneys. The Kylchap exhaust system already improved the pumping effect as a single system (one chimney); this effect was even greater in the double version (two chimneys). A further increase in the number of individual jets in the stacked nozzles eventually led to the Giesl-Ejector design.[836]

Of course, when installing such a design, that increased the draught in the firebox, the supply of fresh air has to be increased by means of additional openings as otherwise there would be insufficient air to fuel the fire.

On the basis of the findings from the Czech locomotive, two prototypes of the engine were built at Reșița: 150.241 (additional oil firing, water pocket, double Kylchap exhaust system) and 150.242 (like 150.241, but in addition with a new boiler with combustion chamber and a raised steam dome).

In tests, both units showed savings and improved performance (150.242 more than 150.241).[838] However, in order to limit investment costs, it was decided to equip all future machines with the features of 150.241. In the course of a general overhaul, the

---

[836] (Hartmann, 2011), pages 4ff
[837] See (Giesl-Gieslingen, 1986), pages 148ff
[838] (Perianu, 2000), pages 122ff

entire locomotive fleet should be equipped with these features.[839] An example of these engines, with equipment similar to that of 150.241, was exhibited at the Leipzig Spring Fair in 1960.[840] Furthermore, individual machines were said to be (temporarily?) fitted with a Giesl-Ejector.[841]

10.18.2 Acquisitions from the German Reich (series 150.1000)

In addition to the replicas, the CFR had ordered and purchased a number of machines from German companies during the war. These were delivered in 1943. The following engines were in CFR's stock as class 150.1000:[842]

Floridsdorf:	20 units	150.1001-150.1020	with tender 2'2'T26
Schwartzkopff	10 units	150.1021-150.1030	with tender 2'2'T26
Orenstein&Koppel	13 units	150.1031-150.1043	with tender 2'2'T30(32)

And in 1944:

Škoda	17 units	150.1044-150.1060	with tender 2'2'T30(32)
Henschel	40 units	150.1061-150.1100	with tender 2'2'T30(32)
	100 units		

Like the series 150.000, they remained in Romania at the end of the war as they were no longer German property and therefore not subject to the Soviet troops' spoils regulations. However, not all of the engines were in the CFR network at the end of the war. They were therefore initially classified and used by the Soviet troops as 'war trophy' and only returned to Romania after the war.

After the end of the war, a number of modifications were made to these machines, including the installation of axle bearing wedges[687], 'Everlasting' blow-off cocks[832], cylinder safety valves, shaking grates and oil burners for an auxiliary oil heating.

10.18.3 Remnants (series 150.1100)

All leased engines of the German Wehrmacht that remained in Romanian were confiscated as booty by the Soviet troops. After the war they were all taken to the USSR, except for 52 2498 (renumbered to 150.1117) and 50 2505 (taken over as 150.1115).

---

[839] It is not known to what extent the agreed changes from 150.241 have actually been implemented.

[840] (Lacrițeanu, et al., 2007), page 503

[841] No deliveries to the CFR are recorded in the delivery lists (Slezak, 1967), pages 25ff.

[842] (Lacrițeanu, et al., 2007), page 524

Nothing is known about the whereabouts of 50 1823, which was also said to be in Romania at the end of the war.

Over the next few years, 13 units of class 50/50ÜK and 14 units of class 52 came to Romania from the Soviet Union[843] and the East-Germany[844], respectively.

The CFR created the number range 150.1101-150.1134 for these locomotives, although it is uncertain whether all the numbers were actually assigned, as the existence of some engines is not confirmed by all sources.[845] The machines underwent the same modifications and improvements as the 150.000 and 150.1000 series.

Ten of these were converted to broad gauge for the transfer of trains to the Soviet broad-gauge network.

Fig. 139: Model of No. 150.1105 (EuroforceCZ 105200.17), driver's side.
Model of a CFR series 150.1100. Note the retrofitted wind deflectors and the large centre light, which may have been left over from its time with the SŽD. The cab is marked with the owner's mark and number, the maximum speed (centre) of 80 km/h and that it belonged to the depot 'Sib', for Sibiu.
The tender carries the owner's mark and number, but its home depot is 'Tim' for Timişoara. A tank for the auxiliary oil firing system can be seen behind the coal box.
Information on the historical model: Schwartzkopff 1943 → DRB 52 196 (RBD Poznan) → 1945 MÁV 52 196 → 1948 SŽD TЭ-196 → 1951 CFR 150.1105 + 1995 Craiova

[843] (Lacriţeanu, et al., 2007), page 549
[844] (Slaughter, et al., 1996), page 37
[845] (Lacriţeanu, et al., 2007), pages 566f

Fig. 140: Model of No. 150.1121 (EuroforceCZ 105200.19), fireman's side
The tender carries an oil tank behind the coal box. The tank consists of two compartments that can be filled individually. The tender is labelled with home depot 'Tim' for Timişoara.
A steam outlet is fitted between the chimney and the sandbox, as it was the case with the Soviet series 52 (ТЭ) engines.
Information on the historical model: Škoda 1944 → DRB 52 7468 (RBD Regensburg) → 1945 ÖBB 52 7468 → 1958 CFR 150.1121 + 1995 Petroşani

10.18.4 End of operation

With two exceptions, no engines were taken out of service until the 1980s. However, in Romania, too, the transformation of rail transport began, with steam locomotives being replaced by diesel and electric units, with the diesel machines being mainly built in Romania. Malaxa, renamed to 'Uzinele „23 August" '[846], had included the construction of diesel engines in its delivery programme after the end of reparations.[847] After the Romanian Revolution, there was a significant increase in the number of retirements, and in 1996/1997 the twin-class machines disappeared completely. It is not known whether these many simultaneous withdrawals were due to the cancellation of 'strategic reserves'.

---

[846] Factory 23 August. On 23nd August 1944 King Michael I of Romania led a coup d'état. One consequence of this was that the Romanian army declared a unilateral ceasefire with the Red Army.
[847] According to a decision of the Comecon, diesel locomotives with an axle load over 20 tons were built in the USSR as part of the division of labour in the Eastern Bloc, while diesel engines with an axle load up to 20 tons were built in Romania, e.g. the East-German Reichsbahn bought their class 119 diesels from Malaxa.

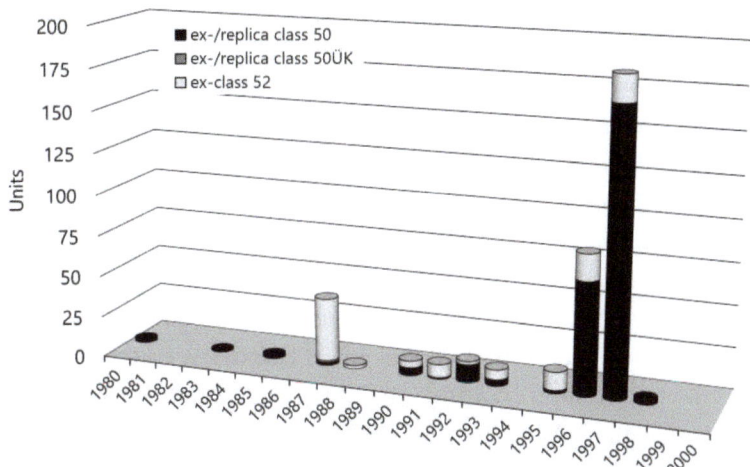

Fig. 141: Retirement of locomotives from the CFR twin-class, broken down by year of retirement and original class

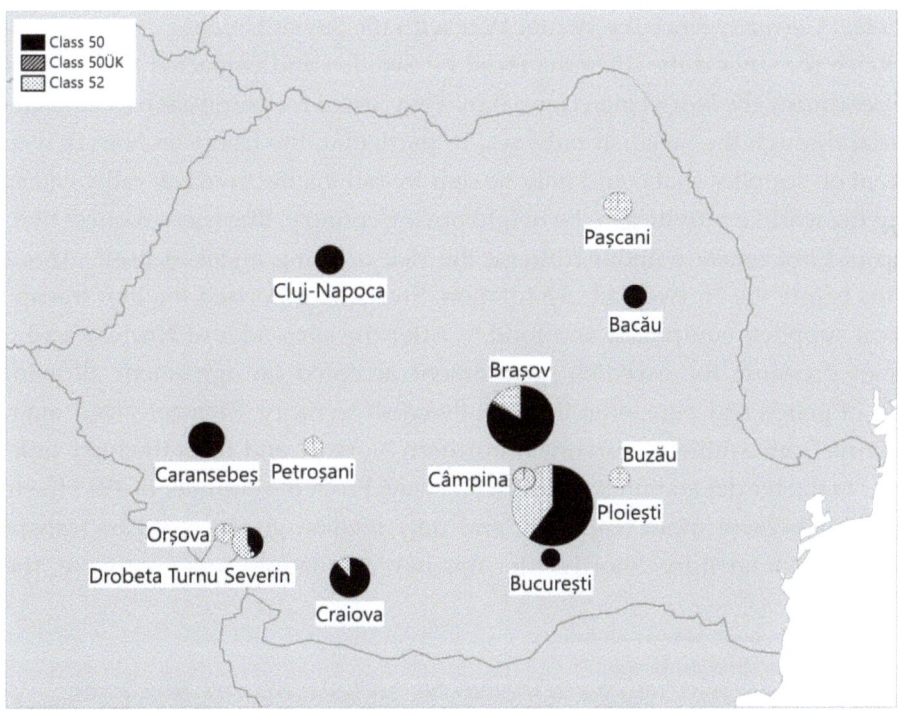

Fig. 142: Last depots of the twin-class and their replicas at the CFR

10.19 Sweden

Germany and Sweden have had close economic ties since the Hanseatic era. After the First World War, Swedish companies helped the German locomotive consortium to fulfil orders for the Soviet state railway (Locomotive Эⁱ). Swedish financiers were involved in the negotiations on the Dawes and Young Plan.[848] Through them, the German Reich obtained cheap loans in return for a monopoly on safety matches, which was abolished in Germany in 1983 with the last repayment of the Reich bond.[849]

At the outbreak of the Second World War, Sweden declared itself neutral. However, a senior Swedish government official described Sweden's course during the war as 'non-belligerent' rather than 'neutral'.[850] Sweden's course during this period was characterised by several phases designed to ensure that the Swedish model of society was preserved. Especially after the evacuation of British troops at Dunkirk, the Swedish government had the impression, at least for a short time, that Sweden would have to live in a Europe dominated by Nazi Germany. When the invasion of Denmark and Norway was added to this, Sweden was isolated, especially as Finland had sided with Nazi Germany since the Winter War with the Soviet Union.

The Reich recognised the dilemma faced by Sweden and contacted the Swedish authorities during the Norwegian campaign. They asked for permission to send German material through the Swedish railways. In particular, the troops in Narvik were dependent on supplies that could only be sent by rail via the Swedish railways. Recognizing the warlike activities in the neighbouring country, this was a request that Sweden could not refuse without running the risk of being attacked itself. About two months before the Norwegian capitulation, Sweden authorised the first transport of medical supplies, equipment and food.[851] After the surrender of Norway and under German pressure, the Swedish government accepted an agreement allowing the transit of goods and personnel through Swedish territory. This consisted mainly of transports from southern Norway to northern Norway and from the ferry link from Saßnitz to the border station Kornsjø in Norway. From the summer of 1943 the transit regulations became more restrictive and only civilian goods could be transported across Swedish territory. Shortly after this new regulation came into force, the first

---

[848] (Deutsch-Schwedische Handelskammer)
[849] cf. Zündwarenmonopolgesetz (Safety Matches Monopoly Law) (Reichsgesetzblatt, 1930), (Wikipedia068)
[850] (Levine, 1998), page 66
[851] (Kreidler, 2001), page 78

15 class 52 locomotives for the Norwegian State Railways arrived in Norway via Sweden. They were transported cold[852] from Sassnitz via Trelleborg to Trondheim.[853]

After the war, the Norwegian railways wanted to have a number of locomotives overhauled quickly. It used Swedish locomotive workshops for this purpose. NSB (63a) 5371 was sent to MV Motala[854] as the first test locomotive. After a test run, the result was satisfying,[855] so further locomotives were sent to MV Motala and also to ASJ Falun[856] for refurbishment. For this purpose, they were shipped to Sweden in cold[852] condition.[857] In this context, twin-class locomotives were also used on Swedish lines. However, they never operated for the Swedish State Railways or were part of its fleet.

---

[852] 'Cold' means hauled, unheated (cold) and with the connecting and coupling rods and other parts of the running gear removed.

[853] (Walinowski, 2014)

[854] MV = AB **M**otala **V**erkstad (Motala workshop LLC) is a Swedish industrial company.

[855] (Rehnberg, 1997)

[856] ASJ = **A**B **S**venska **J**ärnvägsverkstäderna (Swedish railway workshops LLC) was a Swedish engineering company.

[857] (Keller, 2010)

10.20 Switzerland

The 'Schweizerische Lokomotiv- und Maschinenfabrik'[858] (SLM) was a Swiss company from which the steam locomotive technology part was spun off in 1998 as 'Dampflokomotiv- und Maschinenfabrik'[859] (DLM). DLM develops and overhauls steam engines and steamships from an ecological and economic point of view. DLM was looking for an object to demonstrate the progress of its 'modern steam' concept. The Swiss company wanted to prove that modern technology can also be used to convert existing machines into much more economical, ecological and efficient machines by means of a 'gentle overhaul'.[860]

To this end, 52 8055, which was owned by the 'Eisenbahnfreunde Zollernbahn'[861] and only used as spare part donor, was rebuilt according to the latest criteria. The unit was converted to light oil firing and an oil tank was installed in the tender. The axle bearings and boiler tubes were completely overhauled, modernised and replaced. The boiler insulation was also significantly improved.

After completing test and load runs, the locomotive has been owned by DLM in Räterschen near Winterthur since 2003.[862] It is used in Switzerland for touristic trains. This means that a class 52 engine is also operating on Swiss tracks.[863] Beyond that, no machine of the twin-class were in operational service with SBB or any other railway company in Switzerland.

History of the locomotive in operational service: Graffenstaden 1943 → DRB 52 1649 (RBD Erfurt) → 1945 DR 52 1649 → 1962 DR 52 8055 → 1970 DR 52 8055-7 + 1992 Berlin-Schöneweide

---

[858] Swiss Locomotive and Machine Works
[859] Steam locomotive and machine factory
[860] (DLM)
[861] Friends of the Zollernbahn railway
[862] (Eisenbahnfreund Zollernbahn)
[863] At least one more engine is travelling on Swiss tracks for touristic trips: the 52 221 of the 'Association Vapeur Val-de-Travers' (Association Vapeur Val-de-Travers).

10.21 Soviet Union

Already with their advance to the West in 1943, engines of class 52 that fell into the hands of the Soviet army. Like all other German property, they were declared spoils of war and became Soviet property. This was also against the background that the Soviet Union had not only suffered the greatest population losses in the war, but its infrastructure had also been largely destroyed as a result of the German occupation policy and 'Scorched-Earth-Policy'[430].

The captured locomotives were initially used to transport supplies on the standard gauge lines in Central Europe. After the capitulation of the German Reich, they were in service of the Soviet Army and transported their troops and material. Some of them were temporarily left to national railway companies. All engines belonging to the Soviet Army were marked with a 'T' for Трофей (trophy) in front of their number. They were then provisionally regauged and repaired at railway stations near the border, such as Чоп (Čop), Годовиця (Hodovytsia), Мизове (Mizove), Брэст (Brest), Гродна (Grodno), Кёнигсберг (Königsberg) by so-called mobile repair teams[864].

For a provisional gauge change, the wheel bodies and tyres were pushed outwards by about 20 mm.[865] This increased the track width of the axles by about 80 mm, which was sufficient for the time being for running on the Russian broad gauge. The units were then driven in convoys of five at a maximum speed of 15 km/h to the appropriate workshops for final conversion. From mid-1946 on the locomotives were taken to the Унеча (Unecha) depot, where the gauge was first adjusted by moving the whole wheel outwards by about 40 mm.[866]

The further conversion began at the workshops at Івано-Франківськ (Ivano-Frankivsk), Львів (Lviv), Кёнигсберг/Калининград (Königsberg/Kaliningrad)[867], Vilinius, Liepāja, Daugavpils and Tallinn. Later, other suitably equipped workshops also carried out the gauge change work.

In the early autumn of 1946, more than 27 units of class 52 were said to have gone to the Soviet Union, bypassing the records of the NKPS, and to came directly into possession of the Ministry of the Interior. There they were marked with the number '004-7791'in front of the German number. Possibly they were used by railway militias of

---

[864] передвижные паровозно-ремонтные колонны (ППРК) (Mobile squads for the repair of steam locomotives, PPRC), in short: подремы (podremy, nap) (Васильев (Vasil'ev), 2010)

[865] (Макаров (Makarov), 2006)

[866] (Шаронин (Šaronin), 1945), pages 125f, there also Figure 78b

[867] The city was renamed in Kaliningrad on 4th July 1946.

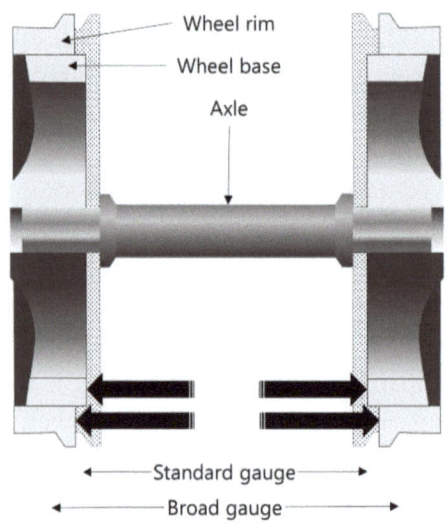

Wheel rim

Wheel base

Axle

Standard gauge

Broad gauge

Fig. 143: Procedure for provisional gauge changeover from standard to broad gauge[869]

the Transport Department for protection purposes of the railway infrastructure. All these locomotives later became part of the Soviet railway fleet.[868]

In 1947 the MPS (former NKPS) issued instructions to adapt the engines to the standards of the Soviet railways. In order to cope with the number of machines to be rebuilt, work was also carried out in workshops outside the Soviet Union starting end of the 1940s: in Česká Lípa, Česká Třebová, Ústí nad Labem in Czechoslovakia and Bucharest and Iași in Romania

The modifications made to the locomotives were (among others):[869]

- Installation of three water circulators[806] in the firebox
- Fitting of an extended chimney and a Kylchap exhaust system with appropriate geometric adjustments
- Mounting of a spark arrestor on the chimney
- Sealing of the large smokebox door and installation of a small inspection door and a cinder pipe[717] (diameter 160 - 200 mm).
- Installation of a Soviet-style shaking grate and modification of the air openings
- Replacement of existing safety valves with Soviet-design safety valves
- Installation of 'Everlasting' blow-off cocks[832]
- Installation of Soviet style injectors
- Installation of a five-tone whistle
- Installation of a Klinger water level gauge[870]

---

[868] (Васильев (Vasil'ev), 1995)

[869] (Про паровоз - pro parovoz)

[870] Klinger-type water level gauges were used by the Bavarian State Railways before the Reichsbahn was founded. They did not work with glass tubes as with the standard locomotives of the Reichsbahn, but with a tube open at the front and covered by a glass ((Niederstraßer, 1939) pages 139f). Similar water level gauges (Cardo-Reflexion-Water Gauges) were used in new engines of the East-German Reichsbahn (Schwarze, et al., 1998), pages 267f.

- Insulation of the boiler by filling the gap with asbestos compound
- Installation of new cast iron cylinders with cylinder safety valves and Trofimoff pressure compensators[446].
- Replacement of the draw hooks with an automatic coupler of the Soviet type CA-3 (SA-3)[871]
- Installation of wheelset bearings from a bronze alloy and axle bearing wedges[687]
- Installation of two turbo generators for the train lighting, the electrical operation of the Walschaert valve gear and the radio. As an alternative to the two turbo generators, a single generator with a higher output was installed.
- Installation of a large front light with a diameter of 450 mm
- Reinforcement of the tender suspension and elevation of the coal box side walls with wooden planks to allow 15 tons of coal to be stored.
- Installation of a Matrosov brake system[872]

All in all, this was a long series of modifications that not only changed the appearance of the class 52, but also its technology. However, it is not known whether all the items on this list were carried out on all the locomotives; it is conceivable that one or the other could not be carried out due to a lack of material. When the purchased engines were handed over to the East-German railways, some of the modifications mentioned above were documented in the handover protocol.[873]

As these were swag machines, they were marked 'T' for 'trophy'. 'Э' (i.e. 'TЭ') was chosen as the 2nd code letter as the locomotive was closest to the Soviet series 'Э' in terms of axle weight and power. Other German trophies were renumbered in a similar way: e.g. the German class 03 became 'TC', class 38 became 'TA' or '38', class 42 was called 'TЛ' and class 57 got the series code 'TЩ'.

Last but not least, the class 50 was given the new series designation 'TE'. The sequential numbers were adopted unchanged from the German engines, i.e.: 52 5293 → TЭ-5293 or: 50 486 → TE-486.

There were a number of nicknames for the former German engines of the TЭ series: The most common were: 'пятьдесят вторая' ('fifty-second'), 'фрау' (phonetic

---

[871] CA-3 = **C**оветская **a**втосцепка, **3**-й вариант (Soviet coupler, 3rd version). After an UIC initiative to introduce a standard for an European automatic coupler failed in 1922, the Soviet Union decided to go its own national way and further developed the British Willison coupler. The conversion of locomotives and wagons took from 1935 to 1957. The CA-3 coupler is considered to be very robust and resilient and is also used for example on the Kiruna-Narvik ore railway (Wikipedia069).

[872] This railway brake was developed in 1926 by Иван Матросов (Ivan Matrosov) and introduced at SŽD in 1931. It has been further developed to this day. It offered a number of advantages when braking heavy freight trains.

[873] (Weisbrod, et al., 2012), page 80

translation of the German word 'Frau' (woman)), 'немок' (German) or 'тэшка' (Belarusian for 'aunt').[874]

At the end of 1951, the Soviet Union had a total of 2,285 units of the twin-class: 36 units of the TE (ex-class 50) series, ten ex-class 50ÜK[875] machines, 2,216 units of the series ТЭ (ex-class 52) and 23 condensing locomotives. This includes the 37 machines of class 52 that were rebuilt from various damaged machines and were given the numbers ТЭ-8001 to ТЭ-8036.[876] Not included were three machines believed to be from a Romanian manufacturer (Malaxa?)[868] and numbered ТЭ-9101 to ТЭ-9103[876]. Other sources cite over 2,150 ex-class 52 units that were supposed to stay in the Soviet Union after closing all ownership discussions.[869]

Given the patchy nature of the sources on the whereabouts of the engines in the socialist countries, all figures on this can be only considered as an educated guess.

All the condensing locomotives were rebuilt and operated in the area of the city of Одеса (Odesa). Three were not rebuilt and used as heating locomotives.[869]

The ТЭ was mainly used in the western part of the Soviet Union in the 1950s, but could also be found in other parts of the USSR, e.g. Мурманск (Murmansk), Архангельск (Arkhangelsk), Воркута (Vorkuta) and also east of the Urals. The unit ТЭ-5200, for example, made it to the railway museum in Toshkent (Tashkent) in Uzbekistan.[877] As in other countries, the machine pulled freight and passenger trains. The trains the engines had to pull ranged from 1,500 to 2,000 tons. In some cases, however, trains weighing 4,000 tons were hauled, albeit at very low speeds.[878] Gradually, however, they were replaced by equivalent, usually more powerful, Soviet machines.

Some locomotives were converted to oil firing or additional oil firing. One focus was the former Estonian SSR, where oil shale was mined. Main air tanks from other decommissioned locomotives or welded boxes mounted on the tender were often used as oil tanks. In the case of a main oil firing system, a tank from a decommissioned two-axle tanker or a home-made welded construction was used for the oil, which was then fitted to the tender.[874]

---

[874] (Про паровоз - pro parovoz); (Макаров (Makarov), 2006)

[875] Whether the former class 50ÜK got the classification 'TE' or 'ТЭ' is not known.

[876] (Slaughter, et al., 1996), page 115

[877] (Königsmann, 2021), page 184

[878] (Васильев (Vasil'ev), 1995); (Про паровоз - pro parovoz), c.f. See also 'Dependence of tractive power on speed' (cf. Figure 7)

Fig. 144: Model of No. ТЭ-5293 (Märklin 34159), driver's side.
The model has a smokebox door with a small opening, a red star and a large headlight. Between the chimney and the sandbox, there is the Soviet version of a steam outlet. Behind the steam dome were the new safety valves and the new turbogenerator. The motor for the electrical control of the valve gear is unluckily not shown with the model (cf. Figure 66).
On the cab' side you can see a framed inscription. In the centre of the frame there is the coat of arms of the owner. 'МРС' (MPS) and 'ЛьВ ЖД'[879] on both sides of the coat of arms, the assignment to the corresponding railway company.
Information on the historical model: Chrzanów 1944 → DRB 52 5293 (RBD Dresden) → 1945 ČSD T52 5293? → 1952 SŽD ТЭ-5293 → 1984 SŽD 1042 3481 + 1987 Radviliškis

Fig. 145: Model of No. 1042 2830 (Märklin 37159), fireman's side
The model is equipped similar to ТЭ-5293. Here you can see a box (tools?) on the running board in front of the cab as well as a headlight on the cab to illuminate the tender when supplies have to be replenished.
The cab now shows the engine number only, all other elements were no longer labelled. This might be an indication the machines is now part of the strategic reserve. The locomotive's new series number is without a check digit, e.g. does not follow the UIC regulations, which might be interpreted that it was not in official operation.
Information on the historical model: Schwartzkopff 1944 → DRB 52 3915 (RBD Dresden) → 1945 ČSD (T?)52 3915 → 1950 SŽD ТЭ-3915 → 1984 SŽD 1042 28309 + 1993 Высокае (Vysokae)

---

[879] ЛьВ ЖД = **Льв**овская **ж**елезная **д**орога (Lviv Railway) was a regional railway company operating in western Ukraine. Today it is part of Ukrainian Railways (UZ) (Wikipedia070)

By the early 1960s there were so many Soviet replacements for the twin-class that over 500 units were sold to the socialist 'brother countries' in the West. A further 400 machines were sold to industry.[865] Many were parked heading west along the western border of the USSR as a strategic reserve.

Until the mid-1950s, SŽD locomotives were painted black above the running board and red below. The rims were painted white. The MPS emblem was usually placed on the side of the cab as a mark of ownership, with the inscription 'CCCP' and a crossed hammer and French Wrench underneath. The inscriptions on the side of the cab were often framed in red. A red star was often painted on the smokebox door.[869]

The ТЭ machines used for passenger service were often painted green above the running board (except for the smokebox and cab roof). However, some locomotives were painted blue instead of green. Colours were not standardised and could vary from depot to depot. Overall, the colour scheme depended to some extent on the wishes and tastes of the operating staff. Each crew tried to make their locomotive as individual and attractive as possible.[869]

In 1984, a total of 500 units were renumbered according to UIC numbering system. Instead of the designation 'ТЭ', they received the class designation '1042'[880] with the corresponding check digit according to UIC. This re-designation replaced the German sequential numbers with a continuous new numbering. The check digit was usually added without a hyphen or space. Whether the locomotives ever ran with this new number cannot be verified; it is possible that these were only the numbers used for the strategic reserve.[881] No renumbering is known for the TE series (ex-class 50).

The last known deployments were mainly on or near the western border of the Soviet Union. It can therefore be assumed that the majority of these designations were strategic reserve depots.

---

[880] (Slaughter, et al., 1996), page 119. You will also find a conversation table (old → new number) there.
[881] In the early 1990s the author saw locomotives marked in this way as part of the strategic reserve when he entered the Kaliningrad Oblast in Мамоново (Mamonovo). In some cases, the numbers on the tender were still written with 'ТЭ'.

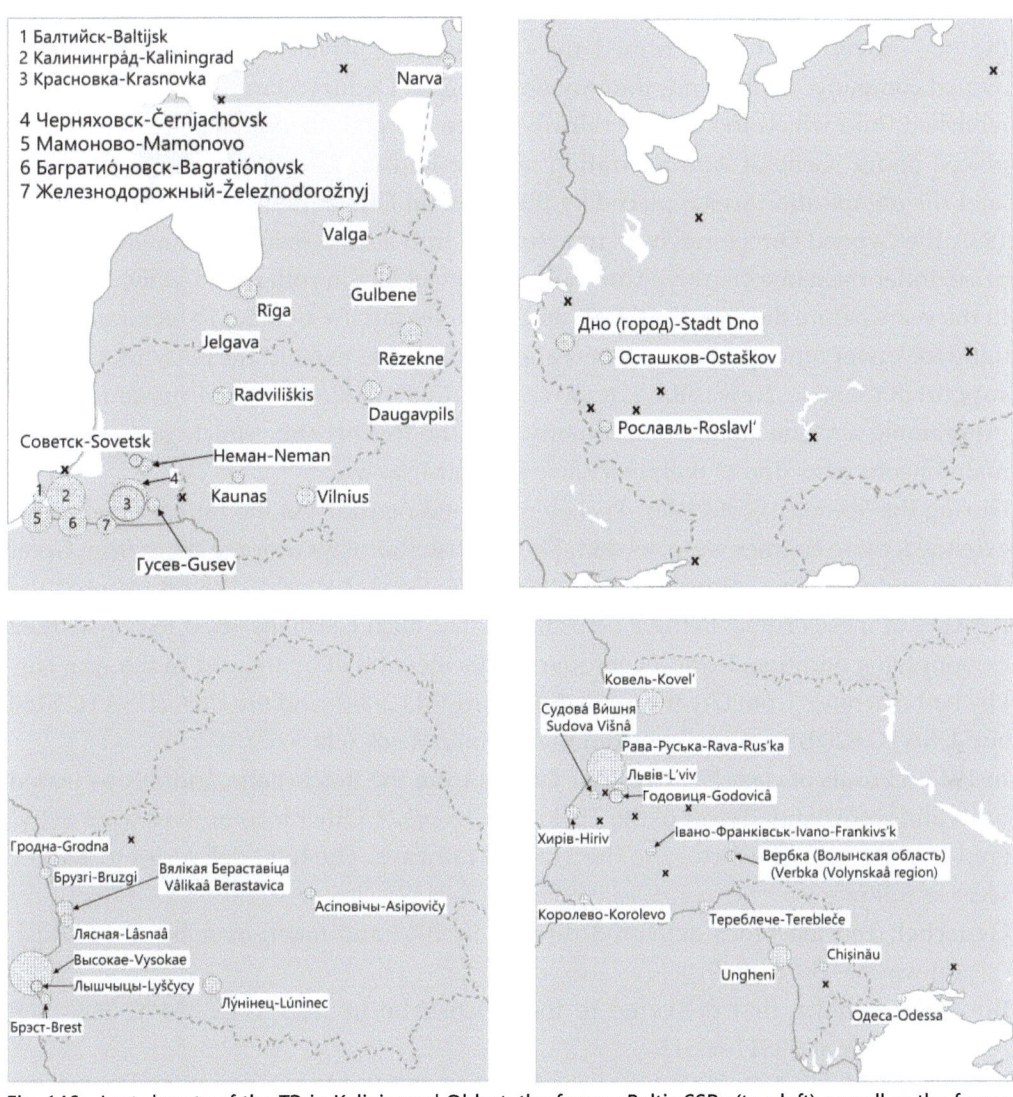

Fig. 146: Last depots of the ТЭ in Kaliningrad Oblast, the former Baltic SSRs (top left) as well as the former Russian RSFSR (top right), the former Belarusian SSR (bottom left) and the former Ukrainian and Moldovan SSR (bottom right) (only more than two deployments are included).[882]

---

[882] acc. (Зиновьев (Zinov'ev))

10.22 Turkey

After the establishment of the Turkish Republic in 1923 by Mustafa Kemal Atatürk, the new government transformed the Ottoman-era private railways into a state-owned company. To this end, the 'Anadolu-Bağdat Demiryolları'[52] (CFAB)[883] was established, into which the private railways were merged. In 1927, this company was placed under 'General Administration of State Railways and Ports'. and two years later the organisation was replaced by the 'General Directorate of State Railways'. In 1953, the General Directorate was transformed into a state-owned commercial enterprise under the name 'Türkiye Cumhuriyeti Devlet Demiryolları'[52] (TCDD).[884]

In the years before the war, the CFAB and its successor, the General Directorate, gradually took over other private railways and continued to expand the network with the support of the state. New rolling stock was acquired mainly from the Prussian railway programme and the standard locomotives of the Reichsbahn, which promised low maintenance costs due to their extensive standardisation.

During the Second World War, Turkey remained neutral. As the railway lines were extended, more engines were needed. The Turkish Railways ordered them from Great Britain and Germany. However, the start of the Second World War interrupted the delivery of these orders. Being a neutral country, Nazi Germany tried to win Turkey by supplying additional war locomotives. This meant that by the end of the war Turkey had machines from Great Britain (Standard WD 2-8-0) and the USA (USATC S160 and USATC S200)[885], as well as from the German Reich (class 52).

In 1943, 43 units of class 52 arrived in Turkey from the Reichsbahn, initially as leased units and were handed over to the Turkish railways.[886] Other locomotives were delivered directly from the factory to the Turkish railways. The total deliveries to Turkey were as follows:

Henschel: Ten machines delivered directly in 1943 and taken over by the Turkish railways as 56501-56510.

Borsig: Five units, first delivered to the Reichsbahn in 1943 as 52 364-52 368, then taken over as 56511-56515.

Orenstein&Koppel: Ten engines transferred to the Reichsbahn in 1943 as 52 4855-

---

[883] The abbreviation CFAB is derived from the French name of the company: **C**hemins de **f**er d'**A**natolie **B**aghdad
[884] (Wikipedia071)
[885] cf. Table 11
[886] (Talbot, 1981), page 103

52 4864 and classified by the railways as 56516-56525.

Schwartzkopff: Ten locomotives taken over by the Reichsbahn in 1943 as 52 6062-52 6073[887] and later taken over as 56526-56535.

Floridsdorf: 18 units with the numbers 52 7285-52 7434, first delivered to the Reichsbahn and then taken over as 56536-56553.

A number of changes were made at the Turkish railways as the locomotives did not meet its expectations in all respects:[888]

- Installation of a central locking for the smokebox door.
- Fitting a water drain pipe to the smokebox.
- Mounting the smokebox door with a large headlight.
- Fitting of a snow plough. On some engines, this was painted with white stripes.
- Removal of the frost protection of the pumps above the running board and the water pipes.

The locomotives from Germany had both rigid frame and tank shaped tenders. These were sometimes changed within a series, for example when a tender was damaged. On some tenders the coal box was enlarged by extending it to the rear over the water tank, creating additional loading space for an extra ton of coal. Some tenders were converted to oil main firing. For this purpose, an oil tank was installed in the coal box, which extended beyond the water tank. As Turkey's main energy base was hard and soft coal, the fuel for these machines had to be imported, creating an undesirable dependency.

In 1958 the TCDD received a Giesl-Ejector for the 56 series. It is not known whether any trials were made with it.[889]

The colour scheme of the locomotives was black, except for the counterbalances of the driving wheels, the headstock and the sides of the running board, some notches under the cab and the air reservoirs. These were painted red. Some wheel rims were painted white, as were the handrails on the cab and the locks on the smokebox door. The application of this special white decoration was the responsibility of the home depot. At some depots they were very pronounced, while at others did not use any decoration. The Turkish Railways did not explicitly specify type designations, but identical locomotives were numbered consecutively. The first number can therefore be used as a substitute for the class designation: '565'. Similarly, there is no separation in the

---

[887] 52 6064 and 52 6065 were not part of this deal and remained after the war in Poland resp. Austria
[888] (Trains of Turkey)
[889] (Slezak, 1967), page 26

Tab. 27: Configuration of the locomotives delivered to the Turkish State Railways[888]

Number	Frame type	Tender	Smoke deflectors
56501[890]		Tube-shaped	yes
56502-56504	Plate	Tube-shaped	yes
56505-56506			
56507-56510	Plate	Tube-shaped	yes
56511-56513	Plate	Tube-shaped	no
56514	Plate	Rigid-frame	no
56515			
56516	Bar	Rigid-frame	no
56517	Bar	Tube-shaped	no
56518-56519		Rigid-frame	no
56520-56523	Bar	Rigid-frame	no
56524	Plate	Rigid-frame	no
56525			
56526	Plate	Tube-shaped	no
56527	Plate	Tube-shaped	yes
56528-56531	Plate	Tube-shaped	no
56532			
56533	Plate	Tube-shaped	no
56534	Plate	Rigid-frame	no
56535-56536	Plate	Tube-shaped	no
56537			
56538	Plate	Tube-shaped	no
56539		Tube-shaped	no
56540			
56541-56542	Plate	Tube-shaped	no
56543		Tube-shaped	no
56544-56545	Plate	Rigid-frame	no
56546	Bar	Tube-shaped	no
56547	Plate	Tube-shaped	no
56548	Plate	Rigid-frame	no
56549-56551	Plate	Tube-shaped	no
56552		Tube-shaped	no
56553	Plate	Tube-shaped	no

numbers, which ran from 56501 to 56553.

The numbers were cast in brass. The background was red enamel. Above the number was the national emblem of Turkey (crescent and star), also as a brass plate with a red background. The national emblem was also applied to the sides of the tender.

---

[890] Starred in James Bond's 'From Russia with Love' from 1963

As elsewhere in Europe, the engine was used as an all-rounder in all parts of Turkey. This meant that they could be seen hauling both passenger and freight trains. The main advantage of these locomotives for the Turkish railway was their good performance together with a low axle load.

They were sometimes used in double heading in front of freight trains, often together with a British or American war locomotive. In later years, as diesel engines took over the operation of trains more and more, they were used on branch lines, replacing the

Fig. 147:   Model of No. 56547 (EuroforceCZ 105200.x), driver's side
This modell shows the changes that were made at the TCDD: snow plough, the large headlight and the extended coal box. The cab bears the national emblem, the name of the railway company and the locomotive number. The colour scheme of the model is intended to represent the standard colour scheme with white wheel rims and a striped snow plough in 'dirty condition'.
Information on the historical model: Floridsdorf 1944 → DRB 52 7428 (RBD Wien) → 1944 CAFB 56547 → 1953 TCDD 56547 + 1975 İzmir

Fig. 148:   Model of No. 56553 (EuroforceCZ 105200.x), fireman's side
This model represents the 'clean' condition. It is similar in construction to the model shown above.
Information on the historical model: Floridsdorf 1944 → DRB 52 7434 (RBD Wien) → 1944 CAFB 56566 → 1953 TCDD 56553 + 1984 Balıkesir

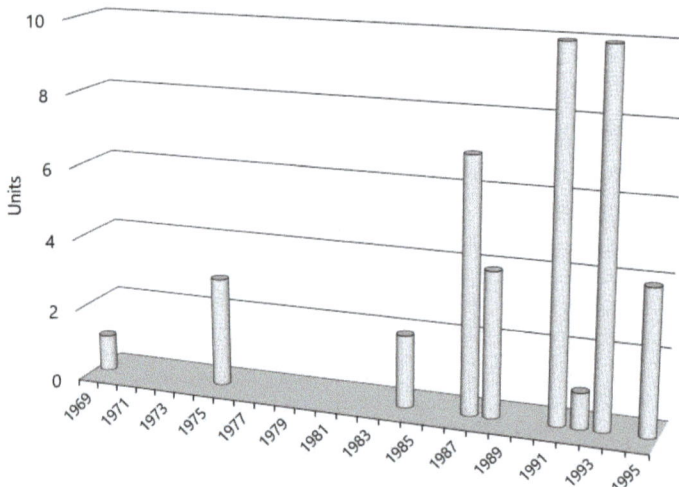

Fig. 149: Year of retirement of TCDD 565xx machines

old Prussian G8 machines, for example. By the mid-1990s, all German units were out of service.

Fig. 150: Last depots of the TCDD 556xx machines. ('x' is the base of a single machine)

10.23 United Kingdom

The twin-class were not used in Great Britain, where the clearance gauge[156] is much smaller than in continental Europe. A journey there would probably have ended very quickly at the next bridge, tunnel or oncoming train. Nevertheless, there were and probably are class 52 engines in the United Kingdom.

The 'Nene Valley Railway Ltd' in Peterborough, Cambridgeshire, bought the Polish Ty 2-7173 (ex-52 7173), which is said to have been in service at Nene between 1991 and 2001. As the line has several bridges, it is would be interesting under what circumstances it was used on the track.

The engine was sold to the 'Patrimoine Ferroviaire et Tourisme' (PFT) in Mons, Belgium, in 2013 and is now on display as a monument under the number 26.102 in front of a logistics centre in Oostmalle (coordinates: 51.285°N; 4.725°E), together with a SNCB/NMBS locomotive 8051[891]. Before being cosmetically restored, it supplied spare parts for the PFT's operational 26.101 (ex-52 3554).[892]

History of this machine in active service:
Built at Floridsdorf 1943 → DRB 52 7173 (RBD Dresden) → 1945 ČSD 52 7173 → 1950 SŽD TЭ-7173 → 1963 PMP-PW Ty2-7173 + 1990.

Another class 52 engine in England can be found at 'Bressingham Steam & Gardens' in Bressingham, Norfolk. This is a Norwegian NSB (63a) 5865 (ex-52 5865), which was parked as a strategic reserve in a tunnel in Drangsdalen in Norway at the end of the 1950s (see Chapter 10.16). It has been restored and is on display as the 'Peer Gynt' locomotive.[893]

History of this unit in active service:
Built at Schichau 1944 → DRB 52 5865 (RBD Königsberg) → 1945 NSB (63a) 5865 + 1958 Stavanger.

---

[891] The SNCB/NMBS series 80 diesel locomotives were largely comparable to the DB class V 60.
[892] (PFT, 2021)
[893] (Bressingham Steam Society, 2017)

10.24 USA

As early as January 1943, the British Ministry of Economic Warfare sent a report on the design of the class 52 to the military attaché at the US embassy in London.[894] It stated that this locomotive [class 52] would have a much stronger frame and supporting structure than the class 50, that the boiler would now be welded rather than riveted and it would no longer have a preheater. The frost protection equipment and the frameless (tub-shaped) tender of this new machine were mentioned. It was also noted that valuable metals had been saved and that a 20% saving in man-hours had been achieved during production. This should be the result of the new manufacturing process. As it was assumed that the new processes would only be used in the best-equipped locomotive factories and consequently it was thought that the new class 52 would only increase the production rate of engines by a maximum of 6 %.[894] This should prove to be a fallacy: It was not taken into account that the traditional production of a unit had been partially abandoned and reorganised, so that a machine was no longer completely manufactured in one factory, but the production of large assemblies (e.g. boilers or tenders) were outsourced to suppliers. This allowed the locomotive factories to concentrate on the more technologically advanced components.

As early as 1944, the 'Combined Intelligence Objectives Subcommittee' (CIOS)[895] was set up in London on the orders of the British and American chiefs of staff. CIOS organised teams of experts to travel around the liberated (Western) Europe in search of valuable technical and scientific objects. Later, the US set up the 'Technical Industrial Intelligence Committee' (TIIC) to assist government agencies in gathering information.

In early 1945, the CIOS was replaced by the 'Field Information Agency, Technical' (FIAT), whose mission was *"the securing of the major, and perhaps only, material reward of victory, namely, the advancement of science and the improvement of production and standards of living in the United Nations by proper exploitation of German methods in these fields".*[896] In this context, the US Army set up an 'Enemy Equipment Intelligence Service Teams' (EEIS), recruited from technically trained army personnel, to collect data and equipment from the enemy.

---

[894] (Clement, 2020), pages 177ff

[895] In addition to the CIOS, there was also the BIOS (British Intelligence Objective Sub-Committee), which was also interested in German technology. There is an interesting collection of documents on the subject at (Stg.C.D.V.& T.).

[896] (Wikipedia072)

US troops discovered the class 52 condensing locomotives already during their advance. The first evidence to date is a report in a troop newspaper about the 'christening' of the condensing unit 52 1960 as 'General Gray's Gull'.[268] The name 'Gull' was a reference to the engine's high-pitched whistle, which differed from that of the US locomotives. Due to its low water consumption, this series was nicknamed the 'Camel'. A little later, test runs were carried out with a condensing locomotive, the 52 2006, between Untertürkheim and Augsburg with a specially assembled 625-ton train. The results of the test run were considered so interesting that it was decided to transfer this engine to the USA.[898] In addition to other machines, wagons and railway equipment, 52 3674, was also to be transferred in order to study the new frameless tender, the special production method of the running gear and the design of the boiler.[899]

All machines confiscated by the US troops were given an 'L' before their number (e.g. 52 2006 → L52 2006), which is sometimes taken in the literature as an abbreviation for

Fig. 151:   Model of No. L52 2006
The model bears the USATC ownership mark: Seal and inscription 'Transportation Corps' on the tender. The cab shows the class designation and the instruction not to drive on marshalling humps. On the smokebox door is the abbreviation 'Au' (small picture), the abbreviation for its home depot Aulendorf. To make the locomotive's home depot easily recognisable from a distance, from 1944 on, the Recihsbahn painted it in white on the smokebox door and tender.[897] The engine was 'embellished' probably by the US-troops with white stripes and white wheel rims.
Information on the historical model: Henschel 1944 → DRB 52 2006 (RBD Berlin) → 1945 DRw 52 2006 → 1945 USATC L52 2006 + 1952 Fort Eustis

[897] (Diener, 2012), page 141
[898] (Clement, 2020), pages 54ff
[899] (Keil, et al., 2020); (Gottwaldt, 1967)

'lent'. However, it is more likely that the 'L' refers to the term 'levy'[900] or 'loot'. Accordingly, the locomotives to be transferred to the USA were marked with an 'L' in front of their number.

The units were grouped in a convoy and brought to Antwerp by the 743rd ROB.[901] After being unloaded, they were taken to Fort Monroe (Virginia) where they were overhauled and inspected by government and industry representatives. They were then taken to USATC headquarters at Fort Eustis, Virginia, for further testing. No test runs appear to have taken place there, as the interest was mainly in various individual parts. The examination of them was carried out with the participation of employees of the US steam locomotive industry.

However, just a month later, the head of the 'Steam Locomotive Research Institute' in New York declared that the engines were of no interest for either military or civilian purposes. This view was shared by the 'Association of American Railroads'.[902] The 'guest appearance' in the USA was soon over. The German machine L42 1597, which was also taken to the USA, had one more short appearance at the 'Chicago Railroad Fair' in 1948.[903] With no further use for the engines, they were scrapped in early 1952.[904]

---

[900] cf. 'compulsory levy'
[901] ROB = **R**ailway **O**perating **B**attalion. (Cunningham (Ed.), 1944-1945)
[902] (Clement, 2020), pages 72ff
[903] (Chicago Railroad Fair, 1948), (Unknown, 2018).
[904] (Unknown, 1952)

10.25 Vietnam

The railway network in Vietnam, with a gauge of 1,000 mm, is largely based on railways built during the French colonial period. After the French withdrew, the line to the Chinese border (from Hà Nội to Đồng Đăng) was renovated with Chinese help and connected to the Chinese standard gauge railway.[905] With the start of the Vietnam War in the mid-1950s, the North Vietnamese built a standard-gauge railway from the port of Hạ Long via Kép to Lưu Xá to secure Chinese supplies for the war. Soon after, a third rail was added to the metre-gauge line from Hà Nội via Kép to the Chinese border at Đồng Đăng. This allowed standard-gauge trains from China to travel directly to Hà Nội without changing gauge or reloading. Similarly, the line from Hà Nội to the important industrial centre around Thái Nguyên was also upgraded to three rails, allowing trains to travel directly with either the need of metre gauge or standard gauge from the port and from China.[905]

In 1965/1966, a standard gauge railway was built from Kép to Thái Nguyên by railway troops from the Chinese People's Liberation Army, who were helping the North Vietnamese to rebuild railway lines destroyed during the war.[906] The standard gauge was chosen because China was an important ally and supporter of North Vietnam during the Vietnam War and was able to replace war damage of railway material relatively easy from its comparatively large stock of standard gauge material.

Vietnam currently has a railway network of 401 km on which standard gauge material can be used, of which 163 km is pure standard gauge and 238 km of tracks with three rails. In addition to the lines mentioned above, there were a number of reports of other branch lines to industrial areas and/or strategic locations whose existence has not been officially confirmed or which were no longer in use but were held in strategic reserve.

After the end of the Vietnam War and Vietnam's invasion of Cambodia (December 1978), relations with China deteriorated to the point of war between the two countries. A month earlier, Vietnam had signed a treaty of friendship with the Soviet Union, under which they received support from the Soviet Union.

Probably as part of this contract the Soviet Union supplied ten TЭ-machines to Vietnam and three or four Ty2-machines were supplied from Poland. The number of

---

[905] (Schramm)
[906] (Wikipedia073), (Flo1979, 2010)

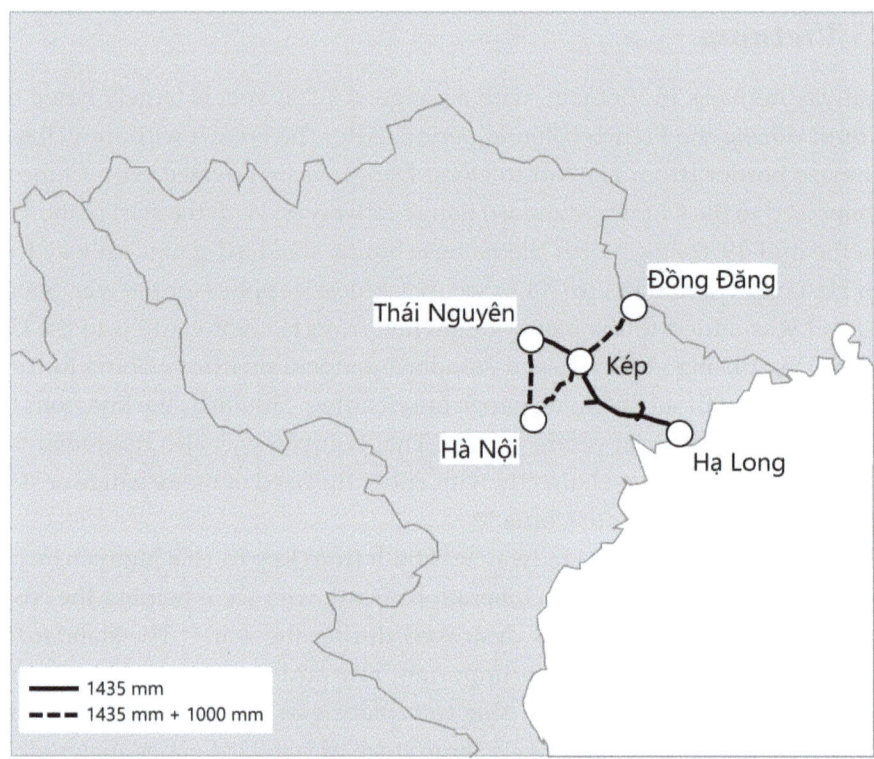

Fig. 152: Standard gauge railway lines in the north of Vietnam[912]

units delivered is not entirely clear and the figures vary between 13 and 16 units.[907] The locomotives probably arrived in Vietnam by ship via the port of Hạ Long.[908] They were unloaded there, but probably never put into operation. They have been parked at various locations around the country. According to sightings, there were seven units in Đông Anh (north of Hà Nội) and another five in Yên Viên (northeast of Hà Nội) and Kép.[909] There are reports of five TЭ units spotted in or near Kép in 1993.[910] The last units were said to have been scrapped in 1994,[909] others sources state that they were seen for the last time in spring 1995.[911]

---

[907] (Reimer, 1996), pages 52f; (Slaughter, et al., 1996), page 55; (Paulsen, et al.); (Gurnett)

[908] (Reimer, 1996), page 53 shows a photo of the loading of Ty 2-464 (ex 52 5240) in the harbour of Gdynia in 1985.

[909] (Slaughter, et al., 1996), page 55

[910] (Brutzer, 2009); (Brutzer2, 2009), (Gurnett)

[911] (Reimer, 1996), page 53

[912] (Wikipedia074)

10.26 Yugoslavia

After the First World War, the Kingdom of Serbs, Croats and Slovenes was established, which formally existed until the end of the Second World War. Accordingly, the new state took over the existing railway network and established the Yugoslav Railways, initially called 'Željeznice Kraljevine Srba, Hrvata i Slovenaca - Железнице Краљевине Срба, Хрвата и Словенаца'[52] (SHS-CXC). In 1929 they were renamed in 'Jugoslavenske Državne Željeznice'[52] (JDŽ). The company was headquartered in Belgrade with subdivisions in Ljubljana, Zagreb, Subotica, Belgrade and Sarajevo[913].

In early 1941, under German pressure the Kingdom of Yugoslavia joined the Tripartite Pact, only to leave it a few weeks later following a coup by Serbian generals. The German leadership wanted to bind the entire southern Balkans politically, militarily and economically to the German Reich in order to secure the 'southern flank' for the planned attack on the Soviet Union. The withdrawal of Yugoslavia destroyed their plans. A few days after Yugoslavia's withdrawal, German, Italian, Hungarian and Bulgarian armies invaded and occupied Yugoslavia. After the occupation, large parts of Yugoslavia were annexed. What was left were essentially three territories, each with puppet regimes: Croatia, Serbia and Montenegro. Accordingly, the lines and rolling stock of the JDŽ were taken over by the occupying forces and the rest was divided into the newly formed national railway companies, the'Hrvatske Državne Željeznice'[52] (HDŽ) in Croatia and the 'Српске државне железнице' (Srpske Državne Železnice)[52] (SDŽ) in Serbia.[914]

A total of 39 class 52s were delivered to the Croatian and Serbian railways to ensure transport on their routes: in 1944, Schwartzkopff delivered 15 and Henschel nine units of class 52 directly to HDŽ. There they were added to the fleet under the designation 30-001 to 30-024. A further 15 were delivered by Henschel in the same year directly to the SDŽ, where they were designated 33-001 to 33-015. Five SDŽ machines were left in the country during the German withdrawal, one of them (33-001) returned in 1951 (as 33-248).

The struggle for the liberation of Yugoslavia continued until the German capitulation. After that, a total of 139 class 52 units and two class 50 engines (50 010, 50 312) remained in Yugoslavia, which were transferred to the re-established JDŽ as 33-041 to

---

[913] The Serbo-Croatian language, as the national language of the former Yugoslavia, used the Serbian Cyrillic and Latin alphabets side by side. All place names are therefore given in the Latin alphabet.
[914] (Wikipedia075)

33-177. The two class 50 locomotives were also included in this numbering as 33-102 and 33-101, but were later renumbered to 33-179 and 33-178.

In 1952, the railway administration was reformed and henceforth called 'Jugoslavenske željeznice'[52] (JŽ). With the introduction of self-government in Yugoslavia, the railways were decentralised. The 'Zajednica Jugoslovenskih Železnica'[915] (ZJŽ) consisted of the general management in Belgrade and five railway companies with operational management in Titograd (today: Podgorica). Later, in the 1960s, the transport companies became increasingly more independent and the JŽ limited itself to drawing up timetables, setting tariffs and official representation abroad.[914]

In addition to the locomotives that existed in 1945, the JŽ's fleet was expanded by 144 units of class 52 and one 50ÜK by 1966. These came from many Eastern Bloc countries, mainly via the Soviet army. The Soviet army brought captured engines to Yugoslavia which they had used in other countries or given to local railways for use. Machines also came from the West, not least because Yugoslavia, as a non-aligned country, was a sought-after partner for both sides. The incoming engines were all classified as series 33 according to the existing plan, including 50 2881 (new: 33-230), which came from the CFR.

The majority of JŽ's series 33 engines had a tub-shaped tender. After the takeover, the machines got a sloping plate under the smokebox door. Machines 33-501-33-505 were delivered directly to the Kreka mine near Tuzla[916] and were no longer part of the JŽ fleet.[917] A further six machines were used temporarily at Kreka.[918]

The machines proved themselves well on the JŽ lines. In particular, their ability to cope with poor track was much appreciated. They were even used in front of passenger trains, as they had a maximum speed of 80 km/h.

In 1958, the JŽ was supplied with a Giesl-Ejector for the series 33. Whether this was installed and in which machine is not known.[919]

Unfortunately, due to the self-governing nature of the individual railways, it is difficult to determine retirement dates, which means that not much is known about the end of the locomotives.[920] What is known is that 32 units from the fleet were stored as

---

[915] Community of Yugoslav Railways

[916] Kreka is a group of mines that mine lignite (a type of brown coal). The deposits are among the largest in Europe. (Granić, et al., 2008).

[917] (Halliwell, 1973), page 119

[918] (Pospichal, 2015)

[919] (Slezak, 1967), page 26

[920] (Knipping, 2011)

Tab. 28: Origin of the class 33 locomotives of the JŽ[922]

Sequential number 33-...	Entry	Origin
001-015[a]	1944	SDŽ
016-039[a]	1944	HDŽ
040		?
041-100	1945	ex-DRB class 52
101-102	1945	ex-DRB class 50
103-137	1945	ex-DRB class 52
138	1948	ex-ÖBB class 52
139-177	1945	ex-DRB class 52
178-179	1954	rename of 33-101, 33-102
180-211	1947	ex-ÖBB series 52
212-214	1947	ex-BDŽ series 15 (ex-class 52)
213	1947	class 52 from soviet military units
214	1947	ex-BDŽ series 15 (ex-class 52)
215-217	1947	ex-ÖBB series 52
218-219	1948	ex-BDŽ series 15 (ex-class 52)
220	1948	class 52 from soviet military units
221-225	1948	ex-BDŽ series 15 (ex-class 52)
226-228	1948	class 52 from soviet military units
229	1948	ex-CFR series 150 (ex-class 52)
230	1945	ex-CFR series 150 (ex-class 50ÜK)
231-265	1952	ex-DB class 52
266-320	1964	ex-SŽD series TЭ (ex-class 52)
321-341	1966	ex-SŽD series TЭ (ex-class 52)
501-502	1960	ex-ČSD series 555 (ex-class 52)
503-505	1964	ex-SŽD series TЭ (ex-class 52)

[a]: some locomotives left the fleet after the war.

a strategic reserve at various locations in the country (Banovići, Doboj, Gračac, etc.) after being taken out of regular service.[921] This reserve was not liquidated until the collapse of the Yugoslav state in 1992.

The appearance of the units was inconsistent. Essentially, the Reichsbahn's colour scheme was not changed, but the locomotive number was applied to the red buffer beam in white paint. In some cases, the number was also applied to the smokebox door, and some units had red plates with white lettering. On some units, the hand rails on the boiler were painted in red and the wheel rims were painted white. The

---

[921] (Vlaki)
[922] (Halliwell, 1973), pages 113ff

smoke deflectors and tender water tank on some units had red stripes or a waving Yugoslavian flag was painted on the outside of the smoke deflectors. The cab sides had usually two plates each, one showing the owner's name and the other in red the number of the locomotive.

You could also find various smokebox doors: Original manufacturer's doors, doors of Soviet design or flat smokebox doors as replacements. Many machines had a small metal skirt behind the chimney to deflect smoke, although small smoke deflectors were also fitted.

11 Epilogue

Without the Second World War, the design of a 'light freight steam locomotive' of the Deutsche Reichsbahn would probably never have achieved the importance it has today in German steam locomotive construction. Nor would it have been built in such large numbers using the most modern production logistics of that time and would certainly not represent the work of an army of slave labourers who had to produce this machine and its sister, the war locomotive, under inhumane conditions.

The design of the engine is not very spectacular, some things could have been done better with the knowledge of the time, but it worked reliably. Its operational use was ambivalent: during the war it supported the Nazis' criminal war plans and helped to transport thousands of people to concentration and extermination camps. After the war, these machines remained in many European countries and were in some cases one of the most important engines for rebuilding the transport system of a war shaken countries and thus for dealing with the consequences of the war.

During all this time of war and destruction, only about 40 units can be considered as lost, with another 30 or so probably destroyed during the war. This is less than 1% of the total number of engines built. This is interesting because one would have expected more losses from a so-called war locomotive, which was used to transport goods close to the front.

The war machines were supposed to have an operational lifespan of about five years, but after stays in repair shops and retrofitting, they remained in service with some railway companies for up to 50 years after the end of the war. In some industrial companies, they were still hauling trains well into the new millennium. Of course, their lifespan and ultimate usefulness depended very much on the circumstances and decisions of the railway company concerned.

Particularly in the countries of the former 'Eastern Bloc' the class 52 was one of the most important traction units for the restart of their rail traffic and the reconstruction of their countries. This was also because the railways were the backbone of the socialist economy and passenger transport in these countries. The existing stock was looked after and maintained, and in some cases considerable efforts were made to maintain and optimise the fleet.

By contrast, in the western countries, where economic recovery was relatively rapid and the necessary capital was available, the switch to diesel or electric units took place

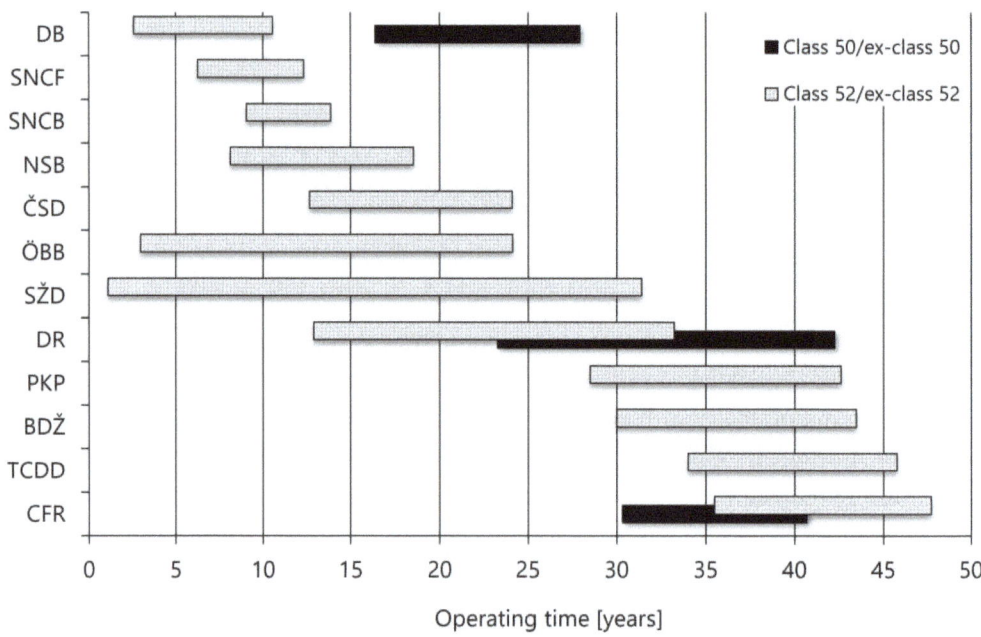

Fig. 153: Overview of the total operation time of the twin-class in European railway companies (by last railway company they served)

relatively early. Accordingly, also the war locomotives of the USATC and the British War Department, which had arrived in many continental European countries during and after the war, were quickly replaced. For some companies, such as the West-German Deutsche Bundesbahn, which had a relatively large fleet of war machines, the technically simple war engines were relatively quickly taken out of service and scrapped.

It is remarkable that just the simple war version of the class 50 design survived for so long in many countries. Its secret was probably its simple construction and the sheer number of units, which allowed even less well-equipped workshops or depots to use individual locomotives as spare part suppliers or to produce spare parts on their own to keep the remaining engines in service in times of great shortage. Much about the twin-class units were reminiscent of another famous design of that period: the 'Volkswagen Beetle'. Also there, the design was relatively simple and even amateur mechanics were able to repair it.

So, is the story of these machines ending here? Not at all, because their formative power can still be admired in more than 600 preserved examples: as monuments, objects of art or (operational) museum locomotives.

And in the world of model railways, the same design can be found in models of all scales. Only for the 1:87 scale (H0) it can be assumed that they were and are the most sold models ever on the market, currently with more than 140 different items of different originals for sale.

And if you come across one of these locomotives in the original state or as model, you might remember the history of its design and operation which has accompanied more than half a century of European railway history.

Annex

Romanization

For the purposes of this book, all place names have been used in their official Cyrillic names as of 1ˢᵗ January 2021, unless earlier/different names were deemed necessary for the historical context. To facilitate readability of the text, the English names of some well-known cities have been used.

Cyrillic names have been converted to the Latin alphabet according to ISO 9:1995[923].
Bulgarian names have been transliterated according to ISO 9:1986, as this is recommended for better readability.[924]

Chinese characters have been converted according to 汉语拼音方案 (Pinyin).[925]

Japanese characters have been romanised according to 訓令式ローマ字 (Kunrei-shiki, ISO 3602:1989).[926]

Railway companies

Abbreviation	Full Name	Translation
AL	Administration des chemins de fer d'Alsace et de Lorraine	Administration of the Railways of Alsace and Lorraine (1919-1937)
BBÖ	Österreichische Staatsbahn, Österreichische Bundesbahn	Austrian State Railway (1919-1921) Austrian Federal Railway (1921-1938)
BDŽ	Български държавни железници	Bulgarian State Railways (1888-)
BMB-ČMD	Protektoratsbahnen Böhmen und Mähren - Českomoravské dráhy	Protectorate Railways of Bohemia and Moravia - Czech-Moravian Railways (1939-1945)
BŽ	Белорусская железная дорога	Belarusian railway (1992-)
ČD	České dráhy	Czech Railways (1993-)
CFAB	Anadolu-Bağdat Demiryolları	Anatolia-Baghdad Railways (1924-1927)
CFL	Société Nationale des Chemins de Fer Luxembourgeois	Luxembourg national railway company (1946-)
CFM	Calea Ferată din Moldova	Railway of Moldova (1991-)
CFR	Căile Ferate Române	Romanian Railways (1880-1998)
CR	中国铁路	China Railways (1949-2019)

---

[923] (Wikipedia076)
[924] (Wikipedia077)
[925] (Wikipedia078).
[926] (Wikipedia079)

ČSD	Československé státní dráhy	Czechoslovakian State Railways (1918-1992)
DB	Deutsche Bundesbahn	German Federal Railway (1949-1994)
DOCF	Détachement d'Occupation des Chemins de fer Français	French Railways Occupation Detachment (1945 and 1946-1947)
DR	Deutsche Reichsbahn	Abbreviation used only for: Reichsbahn of the German Democratic Republic (1945-1993)
DRB	Deutsche Reichsbahngesellschaft	(1924-1937); the abbreviation is also used for the period 1920-1924 (Deutsche Reichseisenbahnen) and 1937-1945 (Deutsche Reichsbahn)
DRo	Deutsche Reichsbahn Ost	Remaining organisation of the DRB active in the Soviet Zone after the capitulation until the founding of the German Democratic Republic in 1949
DRw	Deutsche Reichsbahn West	General description of the remaining organisations of the DRB active in the three western zones after the capitulation (in various organisations, except SEB/EdS) until the founding of the Federal Republic of Germany in 1949
DSB	Danske Statsbaner	Danish State Railways (1885-)
EB	Chemins de fer de l'État belge, short: L'État belge	Belgian State Railways (1832-1926)
EdS	Eisenbahnen des Saarlandes	Railway company of the Saarland (1951-1957)
EST	Chemin de fer de l'Est	Eastern Railway (1853-1938)
ETAT	Chemins de fer de l'État	State Railways (1878-1938)
FS	Ferrovie dello Stato Italiane	Italian State Railways (1905-)
GySEV	Győr-Sopron-Ebenfurti Vasút	Raaberbahn (1875-)
GKB	Graz-Köflacher Eisenbahn- und Bergbau Gesellschaft	Graz-Köflach railway and mining company (1945-1998)
HDŽ	Hrvatske Državne Željeznice	Croatian National Railways (1942-1945)
HVE	Hauptverwaltung der Eisenbahnen des amerikanischen und britischen Besatzungsgebiets	Headquarters of the Railways of the American and British Occupied Territories (1946-1948)
HVR	Deutsche Reichsbahn im Vereinigten Wirtschaftsgebiet	German Reichsbahn in the United Economic Zone (1948-1949)
JDŽ	Jugoslovenske Državne Železnice - Југословенске Државне Железнице	Yugoslav State Railways (1929-1942 and 1945-1952)
JŽ	Jugoslovenske Železnice - Југословенске Железнице	Yugoslav Railways (1952-2004)
kkStB	kaiserlich-königliche Staatsbahnen	Imperial and Royal State Railways (railway company in the Austrian half of the Austro-Hungarian Empire) (until 1918)
K.P.St.E.	Königlich Preußische Staatseisenbahnen	Royal Prussian State Railways (until 1897)
K.P.u.G.H.St.E.	Königlich Preußische und Großherzoglich Hessische Staatseisenbahn	Royal Prussian and Grand-Ducal Hessian State Railways (1898-1918)
LG	Lietuvos geležinkeliai	Lithuanian Railways (1992-)
MÁV	Magyar Államvasutak	Hungarian State Railways (1868-)
MPS	Министерство путей сообщения СССР	USSR Ministry of Railways (railway administration) (1946-1992)
NKPS	Народный комиссариат путей сообщения РСФСР (Наркомпуть)	People's Commissariat for Roads of the RSFSR, (Narkomput) (1917-1923)

	Наро́дный комиссариа́т путе́й сообще́ния СССР (Наркомпуть)	People's Commissariat for Roads of the USSR, (Narkomput) (1923-1946) (both railway administration)
NORD	Compagnie des Chemins de fer du Nord	Northern Railways (1845-1938)
NS	Nederlandse Spoorwegen	Dutch Railways (1938-)
NSB	Norges Statsbaner	Norwegian State Railways (1883-)
ÖBB	Österreichische Bundesbahnen	Austrian Federal Railways (1947-)
ODE	Oberdirektion der Deutschen Eisenbahnen in der französisch besetzten Zone	Chief Directorate of the German Railways in the French-Occupied Zone (1945/1946)
OBL USZ	Oberbetriebsleitung US Zone	Chief Operational Management US Zone (1945-1946)
RGBD	Reichsbahngeneraldirektion in der britischen Besatzungszone	Reichsbahn General Directorate in the British Occupation Zone (1945-1946)
PKP	Polskie Koleje Państwowe	Polish State Railways (1926-)
PLM	Compagnie des Chemins de fer de Paris à Lyon et à la Méditerranée	Railway Company from Paris to Lyon and the Mediterranean (1857-1938)
PMPPW	Przedsiębiorstwo Materiałów Podsadzkowych Przemysłu Węglowego	Company for Backfill Materials-Coal Industry (1951-1992)
PO-MIDI	Chemin de fer de Paris à Orléans et du Midi	Railway from Paris to Orléans and the South (1933-1938)
RŽD	Российские железные дороги	Russian Railways (2003-)
SDŽ	Српске државне железнице	Serbian State Railways (1942-1945)
SEB	Saarländische Eisenbahn	Saarland railway (1947-1951)
SNCB/NMBS	Société Nationale des Chemins de Fer Belges/ Nationale Maatschappij der Belgische Spoor-wegen	National Railway Company of Belgium (1926-)
SHS-CXC	Željeznice Kraljevine Srba, Hrvata i Slove-наса - Железнице Краљевине Срба, Хрвата и Словенаца	Railways of the Kingdom of Serbia, Croatia and Slovenia (1920-1929)
SNCF	Société Nationale des Chemins de Fer Français	National Company of French Railways (1938-)
SWDE	Betriebsvereinigung der Südwestdeutschen Eisenbahnen	Association of operation of the Southwest German Railways (1947-1951)
SŽ	Slovenské Železnice	Slovak Railways (1939-1945)
SŽD	Советские железные дороги	Soviet Railways (1922-2003)
TCDD	Türkiye Cumhuriyeti Devlet Demiryolları	State Railways of the Republic of Turkey (1927-)
UZ	Українські залізниці	Ukrainian Railways (1991-)
ŽSR	Železnice Slovenskej republiky	Railways of the Sloavak Republic (1993-)

Locomotive works

IAL-code[927]	IAL-Keyword	Manufacturer	Translation	Location
Bors	Borsig	Borsig Lokomotiv-Werke GmbH	Borsig locomotive works Ltd.	(Berlin-) Hennigsdorf
Bp	MÁVAG	Magyar Királyi Állami Vas-, Acél- és Gépgyárak	Royal Hungarian state iron, steel and machine works	Budapest
Brja	Brjansk	Брянский машиностроительный завод	Bryansk machine building plant	Брянск (Bryansk)
Ceg	Cegielski	H. Cegielski Spółka Akcyjna w Poznaniu	H. Cegielski plc. in Poznań	Poznań
Chark	Charkow	Харьковский завод транспортного машиностроения имени В. А. Малышева	V. A. Malyshev Kharkov transport machine building plant	Харків (Kharkiv)
Chrz	Chrzanów	Pierwsza Fabryka Lokomotyw w Polsce S.A.	First locomotive factory in Poland plc.	Chrzanów
ČKD	ČKD	Českomoravská-Kolben-Daněk	Czech-Moravian-Kolben-Daněk	Praha
Cock	Cockerill	Société pour l'Exploitation des Etablissements John Cockerill	Company for the exploitation of John Cockerill plants	Seraing
Energ	Énergie	Société Anonyme Énergie	Energy plc	Charleroi-Marcinelle
Essl	Esslingen	Maschinenfabrik Esslingen	Machine factory Esslingen	Esslingen
Flor	Floridsdorf	Wiener Lokomotivfabrik	Vienna locomotive works	(Wien-) Floridsdorf
FUF	Haine	Société Anonyme des Forges, Usines et Fonderies	Public limited company of blacksmiths, factories and foundries	Haine-Saint-Pierre
Haint	Hainaut	Société Anonyme des Usines Métallurgiques du Hainaut	Public limited company of the metallurgical plants of Hainaut	Couillet
He	Henschel	Henschel & Sohn	Henschel & Son	Kassel
Jung	Jung	Arnold Jung Lokomotivfabrik	Arnold Jung locomotive work	Kirchen-Jungenthal/Sieg
Kolom	Kolomna	Коломенский машиностроительный завод им. В. В. Куйбышева	Kolomna machine-building plant named after V. V. Kuibyshev	Коломна (Kolomna)
KrMa	Krauss	Krauss-Maffei AG	Krauss-Maffei plc.	München
Krupp	Krupp	Fried. Krupp Maschinenfabriken, Abt. Lokomotivbau	Friedrich Krupp machine factories, locomotive construction department	Essen
LHB	Linke-Hofmann	Linke-Hofmann-Busch		Wrocław
Lug	Lugansk	Локомотивный завод Октябрьская Революция	Locomotive plant October Revolution	Луганськ (Luhansk)
Malax	Malaxa	Uzinele Malaxa	Malaxa factories	București

---

[927] according (Slezak, 1962). Non-European locomotive factories are not covered by this source

MBA	Orenstein& Koppel	Maschinenbau und Bahnbedarf AG vorm. Orenstein & Koppel	Orenstein&Koppel (till 1939), Mechanical engineering and railway supplies (1939-1945), VEB[649] Locomotive building Karl Marx Babelsberg (LKM), (1945-1992)	Berlin
Meuse	Meuse	Société Anonyme des Ateliers de Construction de la Meuse	Public limited company of Meuse construction workshops	Liège-Sclessin
NyHo	Nidqvist & Holm	Nidqvist & Holm	Nidqvist & Holm	Trollhättan
PFW	PAFAWAG	Państwowa Fabryka Wagonów	State wagon factory (formerly LHB)	Wrocław
Resit	Reșița	Uzinele de Fier și Domeniile din Reșița Societate Anonimă	Iron works and estates of Reșița plc.	Reșița
SACM	Graffenstaden	SACM-Société Alsacienne de Constructions Mécaniques	Alsatian company for mechanical constructions	Graffenstaden
SAFB	Anglo-Franco-Belge	Société Anglo-Franco-Belge des Ateliers de la Croyère	English-French-Belgian society of the workshop of Croyère	Seneffe, Godarville
Schi	Schichau	Maschinenbauanstalt F. Schichau	Mechanical engineering company F. Schichau	Elbląg
Schk	Schwartzkopff	Berliner Maschinenbau-Actien-Gesellschaft, vormals L. Schwartzkopff	Berlin machine building plc, formerly L. Schwartzkopff	Berlin
Škoda	Škoda	Škoda	Škoda	Plzeň
Sorm	Sormowo	Гос. завод Красное Сормово	State-owned plant Red Sormovo	Сормово (Sormovo)
Tubi	Tubize	Les Ateliers Métallurgiques	The metallurgical workshops	Nivelles, Tubize, La Sambre
Warsz	Warszawa	Warszawska Spółka Akcyjna Budowy Parowozów	Warsaw steam locomotive construction plc.	Warszawa
	Changchun	中车长春轨道客车	Changchun railway vehicles	长春市 (Chángchūn)
	Dalian	大连机车车辆厂	Dalian locomotive & rolling stock company	大连市 (Dàlián)
	Datong	大同机车厂	Datong locomotive works (for short-time: Factory 428)	大同市 (Dàtóng)

Boiler suppliers for war locomotive production

This is certainly not a complete list of suppliers. All factories are known that they did not produce engines, but boilers for the twin-class.[928]

Code	Name	Location
B&V	Fa. Blohm & Voss	Hamburg
BrünM	Československá zbrojovka Brno	Brno
DanzW	Danziger Werft und Eisenbahnwerkstätten	Gdańsk
Dupuis	D. Dupuis & Co.	Mönchengladbach
EAWSt	Eisenbahn-Ausbesserungswerk Straßburg	Strasbourg
Ferrum	Aktiengesellschaft Ferrum, vorm. Rhein & Co.	Sosnowiec
Franck	Francke Werke	Bremen
Frichs	Frichs Maskinfabrik og Kedelsmedie	Aarhus
Germ	Maschinenfabrik Germania vorm. J. S. Schwalbe & Sohn	Chemnitz
Howalt	Howaldtswerke	Hamburg
MAN	MAN Werk Gustavsburg	Mainz-Gustavsburg
MÁVAG	Magyar Királyi Állami Vas-, Acél- és Gépgyárak	Budapest
MJahr	Moritz Jahr	Gera
Na&Eb	Natorp & Eberhard	Hohenturm/Halle
OtEis	Ottensener Eisenwerk	Hamburg-Ottensen
Pölten	Reichsbahnausbesserungswerk St. Pölten	St. Pölten
Walther	Walther & Cie.	Köln-Dellbrück
Wilhel	Wilhelmshütte Eisen- und Emaillierwerke	Szprotawa
	Ateliers et Chantiers de la Loire (ACL)	Nantes
	Bahnbedarf-Rodberg	Darmstadt
	Chantiers Navals & Chaudronneries du Midi	Marseille
	Deutsche Werft	Hamburg
	Deutsche Werke	Kiel
	Dinglerwerke Aktiengesellschaft Zweibrücken	Zweibrücken
	F. L. Oschatz	Meerane
	Friedrich Krupp Germaniawerft	Kiel
	Herzoglich Schleswig-Holstein'sches Eisenhütten- und Emaillierwerk Henriettenhütte	Przemków
	Reichsbahnausbesserungswerk Stendal	Stendal

---

[928] according (Reimer, 1996), page 239; (Hütter, 2012), pages 160ff; (Ebel2, et al., 1988), page 13; (Wikipedia080)

References

Ambros, Jiří, Mrkos, Jiří und Kotrman, Jiří. Organizace dráhy. [online] [Accessed 01. 03. 2022] Available from: https://www.brnak.net/index.php?id=org1_pro.

Arhivele Naţionale Române. Societatea Româno-Germană Pentru Industria Şi Comterţul Fierului S.A.R. ROGIFER Anii 1930-1947. [online] [Accessed 01. 01. 2024] Available from: https://arhivelenationale.ro/site/download/inventare/Societatea-Romano-Germana-pentru-Industria-si-Comertul-Fierului-S.A.R.-ROGIFER-1930-1947-Inv-3502.pdf

Association Vapeur Val-de-Travers. Vapeur Val-de-Travers. [online] [Accessed 01. 03. 2022] Available from: https://www.vvt.ch/.

Bähr, Johannes, et al. 2008. *Der Flick-Konzern im Dritten Reich.* München : Oldenbourg Wissenschaftsverlag GmbH, 2008. ISBN 9783486586831.

Banko, Jan. 1986. Tabulky s označením lokomotiv. *Modelář.* 1 1986, page 26.

Bastisch, Andre. 2000. Arbeitsbeschaffungsmaßnahmen im Dritten Reich von 1933-1936. *Masterthesis.* München : s.n., 2000. Available from: https://www.grin.com/document/1560.

Baumann, Hans, [Ed.]. 1931. *Deutsches Verkehrsbuch.* Berlin : Deutsche Verlagsgesellschaft m.b.H., 1931.

Bek, Zdeněk und Bek, Jindřich. 2000. *Encyklopedie železnice - Parní lokomotivy ČSD (3).* Praha : Nakladatelství Corona, s.r.o., 2000. ISBN 9788086116204.

Berkenkopf, Paul. 1942/1943. Verkehrsprobleme der Sowjet-Union. *Zeitschrift für Verkehrswissenschaft.* 1942/1943, pages 233-256.

Bjerke, Thor, et al. 1987. *Damplokomotiver i Norge.* Lillehammer : Norsk jernbaneklubb, 1987. ISBN 8290286090.

Borel, Victor. 1943. *Kriegslokomotiven.* Universum-Film AG (UFA) (Berlin), 1943.

Bossig, Klaus. 2017. "Gardinenzüge" und "EVR-Pendel" DDR-UdSSR. *Eisenbahnkurier-Special 126.* 2017, S. 90-95.

Bressingham Steam Society. 2017. [online] 28. 2 2017. [Accessed 01. 03. 2022] Available from: http://bressinghamsteamsociety.org/repaint-of-german-kreigslok-peer-gynt/.

Bruce, A. W. 1952. *The Steam Locomotive in America.* New York : Bonanza Books, 1952.

Brutzer, Hansjörg. 2009. TE 2727 + TE 6775 Kep 26.02.93. [online] 26. 09. 2009. [Accessed 01. 03. 2022] Available from: https://www.bahnbilder.de/bild/Vietnam~Dampfloks~Sonstige/338427/te-2727--te-6775-kep.html.

Brutzer2, Hansjörg. 2009. TE 1390 + TE 5096 + TE 5470 Kep 26.02.93. [online] 26. 09. 2009. [Accessed 01. 03. 2022] Available from: https://www.bahnbilder.de/bild/Vietnam~Dampfloks~Sonstige/338426/te-1390--te-5096-.html.

Brutzer3, Werner. 2009. Ty2 1049 Chabowka 03.06.77. [online] 27. 01. 2009. [Accessed 01. 03. 2022] Available from: https://www.bahnbilder.de/bild/polen~dampfloks~ty2-dr-baureihe-52/257040/ty2-1049-chabowka-030677.html.

Budde, Ulrich. Die Bundesbahnzeit. *Bauartunterschiede Baureihe 50.* [online] [Accessed 01. 03. 2022] Available from: https://www.bundesbahnzeit.de/seite.php?id=602.

Buggeln, Marc. 2015. Die Zwangsarbeit im Deutschen Reich 1939–1945 und die Entschädigung vormaliger Zwangsarbeiter nach dem Kriegsende: Eine weitgehend statistische Übersicht. [Ed.] Unabhängige Historikerkommission zur Aufarbeitung der Geschichte des Reichsarbeitsministeriums in der Zeit des Nationalsozialismus. *Konferenz "Regimenting Unfree Labour in Europe During the Second World War".* Working Papers Series A, No. 4, 2015.

Bundesarchiv. Die "Allgemeinen Bestimmungen" über Arbeitskräfte aus den besetzten Gebieten im Osten von 1942. [online] [Accessed 01. 03. 2022] Available from: https://www.bundesarchiv.de/zwangsarbeit/dokumente/texte/00357/index.html.

Bundesgesetzblatt. 1957. Verordnung zur Änderung der Eisenbahnsignalordnung und der vereinfachten Eisenbahnsignalordnung sowie zur Einführung eines einheitlichen Spitzsignals für Eisenbahnen des nichtöffentlichen Verkehrs. 29. 8 1957, Bd. 25, Teil II, Pages 1269-1271.

Bundeszentrale für politische Bildung. 2.1. Entstehung der Bundesrepublik Deutschland (BRD). *29. Mai 1947.* [online] [Accessed 01. 03. 2022] Available from: https://www.bpb.de/geschichte/zeitgeschichte/deutschland-chronik/131216/29-mai-1947.

Bundeszentrale für politische Bildung2. Unter der NS-Herrschaft ermordete Juden nach Land. [online] [Accessed 01. 03. 2022] Available from: https://www.bpb.de/fsd/centropa/ermordete_juden_nach_land.php.

Bundeszentrale für politische Bildung3. 2012. Vor 90 Jahren: Benito Mussolini kommt an die Macht. [online]

29. 10. 2012. [Accessed 01. 03. 2022] Available from: https://www.bpb.de/politik/hintergrund-aktuell/147468/benito-mussolini-kommt-an-die-macht-30-10-2012.

Chester (Ed.), Keith R. 2000. *Russian and Soviet Steam Locomotives.* Skipton, North Yorkshire, England : Trackside Publications, 2000.

Chicago Railroad Fair. 1948. *Official Guide Book.* Chicago : s.n., 1948.

CIA. 1952. *The Russian Steam Locomotives in the last 50 Years.* Moscow Leningrad : CIA, 1952. Declassified in Part - Sanitized Copy Approved for Release 2012/03/15. CIA-RDP82-00039R000200130002-4.

Clement, H. K,. War Diaries *1939-1945.* s.l. : not published.

Clement, Marc, [Ed.]. 2020. *Die Fort Eustis Files.* Norderstedt : Books on Demand, 2020. ISBN 9783757820473.

Coinnews Media Group LLC. US Inflation Calculator. [online] [Accessed 01. 03. 2022] Available from: https://www.usinflationcalculator.com/.

Creydt, Detlef und Meyer, August. 1993. *Zwangsarbeit für die Wunderwaffen in Südniedersachsen 1943-1945, Band 1.* Braunschweig : Steinweg-Verlag, 1993. ISBN 3925151575.

Cunningham (Ed.), Nancy. 1944-1945. *Thomas D. Murphy's photo albums.* s.l. : private communication, 1944-1945.

Cunningham, Nancy. 2020. *The Men of the 743rd ROB - Privat communication.* 2020.

Czarnecki, Tomisław und Szponder, Jan. Parowozy PKP opalane ropą naftową. [online] [Accessed 01. 03. 2022] Available from: http://www.polskieparowozy.pl/index2.php?wykaz=mazut.

Dambly, Phil. Numérotation et classification. [online] [Accessed 01. 03. 2022] Available from: https://www.rixke.tassignon.be/spip.php?article454&lang=fr.

—. **1994.** *Vapeur en Belgique.* Brussel - Bruxelles : Blanchart & Cie., 1994. ISBN 2872020136.

Danmarks Jernbanemuseum. 2021. *Locomotive numbering.* 2021. private communication.

Davie, H. G. W. . 2018. Logistics of the Combined-Arms Army – Motor Transport. *The Journal of Slavic Military Studies.* 2018, Bd. 31, 4, Pages 474-501.

Davie, H. G. W. 2020. Logistics of the Tank Army: The Uman-Botoşani Operation, 1944. *The Journal of Slavic Military Studies.* 2020, Bd. 33, 3, Pages 420-441.

—. **2017.** The Influence of Railways on Military Operations in the Russo-German War 1941-1945. *Journal of Slavic Military Studies.* 2017, Bd. 30, 2, Pages 321-346.

Dejanow, Dimiter. 1990. *Die Lokomotiven der Bulgarischen Staatsbahnen.* Wien : Verlag Josef Otto Slezak, 1990. ISBN 3854161506.

Dejanow2, Dimiter. Цветова схема на БДЖ парни локомотиви (Colour scheme of BDZ steam locomotives). *Railway Passion.* [online] [Accessed 01. 03. 2022] Available from: http://www.railwaypassion.com/forums/index.php/topic,1669.90.html.

Denzin, Paul. 2009. *Die Dampflokomotive - Aufsätze für den Lokomotivführer.* Stuttgart : transpress Verlag, 2009. ISBN 9783613713604.

Deutsche Bundesbahn . 1953. *Merkbuch für die Schienenfahrzeuge der Deutschen Bundesbahn - DV 939a.* Minden : Bundesbahn-Zentralamt Minden (Westf.), 1953.

Deutsche Bundesbank. Kaufkraftvergleiche historischer Geldbeträge. [online] [Accessed 01. 03. 2022] Available from: https://www.bundesbank.de/de/statistiken/konjunktur-und-preise/erzeuger-und-verbraucherpreise/kaufkraftvergleiche-historischer-geldbetraege-775308.

Deutsche Reichsbahn. 1999. *Die Dampflokomotiven der Deutschen Reichsbahn - Merkbuch für Triebfahrzeuge.* Holzminden : Reprint-Verlag-Leipzig, 1999. ISBN 3826200128.

Deutsch-Schwedische Handelskammer. Meilensteine deutsch-schwedischer Innovationen seit dem 19. Jahrhundert. [online] [Accessed 01. 03. 2022] Available from: https://www.handelskammer.se/de/nyheter/meilensteine-deutsch-schwedischer-innovationen.

Diener, Wolfgang. 2012. *Anstrich und Bezeichnung von Lokomotiven.* Fürstenfeldbruck : VGB Verlagsgruppe Bahn GmbH, 2012. ISBN 9783837508215.

DLM. Modernisierte Dampflokomotiven. [online] [Accessed 01. 03. 2022] Available from: https://dlm-ag.ch/modernised-steam-locomotives/.

Donat, Gerhard. 1964. Der Munitionsverbrauch der deutschen Wehrmacht im Feldzug gegen Sowjetrussland 1941 bis 1945. *Allgemeine schweizerische Militärzeitschrift.* 1964, Bd. 130, Pages 31- 34.

Drury, George H. 2015. *Guide to North American Steam Locomotives.* Waukesha, WI : Kalmbach Books, 2015. ISBN

9781627002592.

Dufrenoy, Christophe. Railcolor. [online] [Accessed 01. 03. 2022] Available from: https://www.amf87.fr/peintures.htm.

Ebel, Jürgen U. und Wenzel, Hansjürgen. 1988. *Die Baureihe 50, Band 1: Deutsche Reichsbahn.* Freiburg : Eisenbahn-Kurier Verlag, 1988. ISBN 3882555459.

Ebel, Jürgen-Ulrich und Gänsfuß, Rüdiger. 2002. *Franco-Crosti: Die Baureihen 42 90 und 50 40.* Freiburg : EK-Verlag GmbH, 2002. ISBN 388255150X.

Ebel2, Jürgen U. und Wenzel, Hansjürgen. 1988. *Die Baureihe 50, Band 2: Deutsche Bundesbahn.* Freiburg : Eisenbahn-Kurier Verlag, 1988. ISBN 3882555467.

Eckhardt, Friedrich Wilhelm. 2009. *Die Konstruktion der Dampflokomotive und ihre Berechnung.* Stuttgart : transpress Verlag, 2009. ISBN 9783613713482.

Eichholtz, Dietrich. 1999. *Geschichte der deutschen Kriegswirtschaft - Band I.* München : K. G. Saur Verlag GmbH & Co KG, 1999. ISBN 3598114281.

Eichholtz2, Dietrich. 1999. *Geschichte der deutschen Kriegswirtschaft 1939-1945, Band II: 1941-1943, Teil 2.* München : K. G. Saur Verlag GmbH & Co. KG, 1999. ISBN 3598114281.

Eisenbahnfreund Zollernbahn. Geschichte der 52 8055. [online] [Accessed 01. 03. 2022] Available from: https://www.eisenbahnfreunde-zollernbahn.de/loks/152ng.htm.

Enciclopedia României. Uzinele şi Domeniile Reşiţa. [online] [Accessed 01. 03. 2022] Available from: http://enciclopediaromaniei.ro/wiki/Uzinele_%C8%99i_Domeniile_Re%C8%99i%C8%9Ba.

Endisch, Dirk. 2007. *Baureihen 50.35 und 50.50.* Korntal-Münchingen : Verlag Dirk Endisch, 2007. ISBN 9783936893441.

Engwert, Andreas. 2009. Die Zusammenarbeit von Reichssicherheitshauptamt und Reichsverkehrsministerium. [Buchverf.] Andreas Engwert und Susanne Kill. *Sonderzüge in den Tod - Die Deportationen mit der Deutschen Reichsbahn.* Köln : Böhlau Verlag GmbH & Cie, 2009, pages 50-54.

Epkenhans, Michael. 2020. *Der Deutsch-Französische Krieg 1870/1871.* Ditzingen : Philipp Reclam jun. Verlag GmbH, 2020. ISBN 9783150112717.

erinnern. 2020. Vorabdruck des Kapitels KZ und Zwangsarbeit aus Nationalsozialismus in Wien. *Arbeitsmaterialien: KZ und Zwangsarbeit in Wien.* Wien : Agentur für Bildung und Internationalisierung, 2020.

Federmeyer, Ed. 1984. *Eisenbahnen in Luxemburg.* Freiburg : Eisenbahn-Kurier Verlag, 1984. ISBN 3882554002.

Fliege, Mario. Datenbank Triebfahrzeuge. [online] [Accessed 01. 03. 2022] Available from: https://revisionsdaten.de/tfzdatenbank/index.php.

Flo1979. 2010. [VN]13.000 km im Zug: Viele versch. V-Loktypen - Die Eisenbahn in Vietnam [27B]. [online] 10. 9. 2010. [Accessed 01. 03. 2022] Available from: https://www.drehscheibe-online.de/foren/read.php?30,4999332.

Forschner, Dirk. 2017. *German Steam Locomotives in China.* 北京 (Peking) : China Railway Publishing House, 2017. ISBN 9787113238018.

Forstmeier, Friedrich und Volkmann, Hans-Erich. 1981. *Wirtschaft und Rüstung am Vorabend des Zweiten Weltkrieges.* Düsseldorf : Droste Verlag, 1981. ISBN 3770003993.

Frans8800. 2014. Lettertype NS nummerplaat. [online] 29. 09. 2014. [Accessed 01. 03. 2022] Available from: https://forum.beneluxspoor.net/index.php?topic=60786.0.

Friedrich, Klaus-Peter. 2013. *Polen: Generalgouvernement August 1941-1945.* München : Oldenbourg Wissenschaftsverlag, 2013. Available from: https://doi.org/10.1524/9783486735987.

Frister, Thomas (verantw.). 2014. *EK Special 113: 1945-1949.* Freiburg : EK-Verlag GmbH, 2014. ISBN 9783844670066.

FXTOP. Historische Wechselkurse. [online] [Accessed 15. 10. 2021] Available from: https://fxtop.com/de/historische-wechselkurse.php?A=1000&C1=DKK&C2=DEM&DD1=01&MM1=01&YYYY1=1953&B=1&P=&I=1&DD2=01&MM2=12&YYYY2=1953&btnOK=Gehen.

Gall, Lothar und Pohl, Manfred. 1999. *Die Eisenbahn in Deutschland.* München : Verlag C. H. Beck, 1999. ISBN 9783406453342.

gam3. 2013. Fabrici Romanesti constructoare de vagoane. [online] 22. 10 2013. [Accessed 01. 03. 2022] Available from: https://forum.lokomotiv.ro/threads/fabrici-romanesti-constructoare-de-vagoane.11912/.

Garbe, Robert. 1980/81. *Die zeitgemässe Heissdampflokomotive - Nachdruck.* Moers : Steiger Verlag, 1980/81. ISBN 3921564344.

Gerteis, Adolf. 1949. *Fünf Jahre Ostbahn.* Berlin-Lichterfelde : Bundesarchiv, 1949. Signatur R 5 ANH. I/120.

Gesetzblatt der Deutschen Demokratischen Republik. 1956. Anordnung zur Änderung der Eisenbahn-

Verkehrsordnung. [Ed.] Bundesarchiv ZB 20049 a /6. 6. 2 1956, Bd. 6, Teil 2.

Gibbons, Robin. 2017. *Locomotives of China - The QJ Class.* Plumtree, Nottinghamshire/GB : Tynedale Publishing, 2017. ISBN 9780993419225.

Gieseler01, Albert. Aktiengesellschaft Ferrum. [online] [Accessed 01. 03. 2022] Available from: http://www.albert-gieseler.de/dampf_de/firmen0/firmadet6340.shtml.

Gieseler02, Albert. August Borsig. [online] [Accessed 01. 03. 2022] Available from: http://www.albert-gieseler.de/dampf_de/firmen0/firmadet769.shtml.

Gieseler03, Albert. Dampflokomotive 52 2770. [online] [Accessed 01. 03. 2022] Available from: http://www.albert-gieseler.de/dampf_de/lokdaten14/lokdet148905.shtml.

Gieseler04, Albert. H. Cegielski Akt.-Ges., Maschinenbauanstalt und Eisengießerei. [online] [Accessed 01. 03. 2022] Available from: http://www.albert-gieseler.de/dampf_de/firmen0/firmadet6308.shtml.

Gieseler05, Albert. Société Alsacienne de Constructions Mécaniques, Werk Graffenstaden. [online] [Accessed 01. 03. 2022] Available from: http://www.albert-gieseler.de/dampf_de/firmen5/firmadet51934.shtml.

Gieseler06, Albert. Société Anonyme des Usines Métallurgiques de Hainaut. [online] [Accessed 01. 03. 2022] Available from: http://www.albert-gieseler.de/dampf_de/firmen0/firmadet3996.shtml.

Gieseler07, Albert. Wiener Lokomotivfabrik-Aktien-Gesellschaft. [online] [Accessed 01. 03. 2022] Available from: http://www.albert-gieseler.de/dampf_de/firmen1/firmadet16958.shtml.

Gieseler08, Albert. Aktien-Gesellschaft der Lokomotivfabrik vorm. G. Sigl. [online] [Accessed 01. 03. 2022] Available from: http://www.albert-gieseler.de/dampf_de/firmen4/firmadet40127.shtml.

Gieseler09, Albert. Oberschlesische Lokomotivwerke AG Kattowitz, Werk Krenau. [online] [Accessed 01. 03. 2022] Available from: http://www.albert-gieseler.de/dampf_de/firmen5/firmadet51539.shtml.

Giesl-Gieslingen, Adolph. 1986. *Anatomie der Dampflokomotive international.* Wien : Verlag Josef Otto Slezak, 1986. ISBN 9783854160892.

Gillot, Jean. 1985. *Les Locomotives à Vapeur de la S.N.C.F. - Région Est.* Levallots-Perret : Éditions Picador, 1985.

gingatetsudo. びわ湖畔のオリエント急行 (Orient Express by Lake Biwa). [online] [Accessed 01. 03. 2022] Available from: http://jijiganko.web.fc2.com/sub2112.htm.

Glasse, Andrew. Kobbelstenger 236. [online] [Accessed 01. 03. 2022] Available from: https://medlem.njk.no/forum/forum.php?modul=traad&toppinnlegg=22736&rom=24.

Goshen, Seev. 1981. Eichmann und die Nisko-Aktion im Oktober 1939. *Vierteljahreshefte für Zeitgeschichte.* 29, 1981, Bd. 1, Pages 74-96.

Gottwaldt, Alfred B. 1978. *Geschichte der deutschen Einheitslokomotiven.* Stuttgart : Franckh'sche Verlagshandlung, 1978. ISBN 9783440079414.

Gottwaldt, Alfred B. 2016. *Deutsche Kriegslokomotiven.* Stuttgart : transpress Verlag, 2016. ISBN 9783613715332.

Gottwaldt, Alfred. 1967. Deutsche Lokomotiven in den USA. *Lok Magazin.* 1967, Bd. 27, Dezember 1967, Pages 39-42.

—. 2009. *Dorpmüllers Reichsbahn.* Freiburg : EK-Verlag GmbH, 2009. ISBN 9783882557268.

—. 2001. Neuartige Dampflokomotiven von Henschel in Kassel: Das Lebenswerk des Ingenieurs Richard Roosen. *Zeitschrift des Vereins für hessische Geschichte (ZHG).* 2001, Bd. 106, Pages 299-330.

—. 2013. Warum war die Reichsbahn nicht auf der Wannsee-Konferenz vertreten ? [Buchverf.] Norbert Kampe und Peter Klein. *Die Wannsee-Konferenz am 20. Januar 1942.* Köln : Böhlau Verlag GmbH & Cie, 2013, Pages 341-354.

Gottwaldt2, Alfred. 2009. Die Logistik des Holocaust als mörderische Aufgabe der Deutschen Reichsbahn im europäischen Raum. [Ed.] Ralf Roth und Karl Schlögel. *Neue Wege in ein neues Europa.* 2009, Pages 261-280.

Gottwaldt3, Alfred. 2009. *Eisenbahner gegen Hitler.* Wiesbaden : Matrixverlag GmbH, 2009. ISBN 9783865392046.

Grabe, Georg. 1942. Die russische Verkehrswirtschaft unter dem Sowjetregime. *Archiv für Eisenbahnwesen.* 1942, Pages 697-720.

Grace's Guide. Superheater Corporation. [online] [Accessed 01. 03. 2022] Available from: https://www.gracesguide.co.uk/Superheater_Corporation.

Graf von Ballestrem, Nikolaus. Ballestremsches Firmen- und Familienarchiv. [online] [Accessed 01. 03. 2022] Available from: https://ballestrem.de/firmen-und-orte/einzelfirmen/vereinigte-oberschlesische-huettenwerke-ag/.

Granić, Goran und et. al. 2008. *Final report: Energy Sector Study in BIH.* Zagreb : Energy Institute Hrvoje Požar, 2008. Projekt no. BHP3-EES-TEPRP-Q-04/05 WB.

Grenier Ferroviaire - Spoorse Zolder. Fontes SNCB - NMBS Lettertype. [online] [Accessed 01. 03. 2022] Available from:

https://trains.tassignon.be/documentation/documentation.php#Fontes.

Griebl, Helmut und Wenzel, Hansjürgen. 1971. *Geschichte der deutschen Kriegslokomotiven.* Wien : Verlag Josef Otto Slezak, 1971. ISBN 3900134030.

Groß, Gerhard P. 2012. *Mythos und Wirklichkeit.* Paderborn : Ferdinand Schöningh, 2012. ISBN 9783506775542.

Groupe CFL. 2020. *Rapport Annuel.* Luxembourg : Société Nationale des Chemins de Fer Luxembourgeois, 2020.

Gurnett, David. Railways in Vietnam. *TE/TY2/BR52/Kriegslokomotive.* [online] [Accessed 01. 03. 2022] Available from: http://railwaysinvietnam.com/TE.html.

Habermann, Klaus. 2014. Giesl-Ejektoren bei der DR. [online] 18. 08. 2014. [Accessed 01. 02. 2022] Available from: https://www.drehscheibe-online.de/foren/read.php?17,2921504.

Hahn, Karl Eugen. 1954. *Eisenbahner im Krieg und Frieden.* Frankfurt (M) : Lanzenreiter Verlag, 1954.

Halliwell, C. J. 1973. *The Locomotives of Jugoslavia.* Malmö/S : Frank Stenvalls Förlag, 1973. ISBN 9172660120.

Harris, T. E. und Ross, F. S. 1955. *Fundamental of a Method for Evaluating Rail Net Capacities.* Santa Monica, CA : The Rand Corporation, 1955. US Air Force Project Research Memorandum, RM1573, unclassified.

Hartmann, Jan. 2011. Die Dampflokomotive am Ende ihrer Entwicklung. [online] 17. 11. 2011. [Accessed 04. 05. 2021] Available from: https://www.technikgeschichte.org/2011-a/.

Hengst, Matthias. 2021. Rettet die Nation. *Eisenbahn Geschichte.* 2021, 6, Pages 30-43.

Henschel & Sohn GmbH. 1944. *Beschreibung und Betriebsanweisung der 1'E-Henschel Kondenslokomotive der BR 52.* Kassel : Henschel & Sohn GmbH, 1944.

Henschel-Werke GmbH. 1960. *Henschel Lokomotiv-Taschenbuch.* Düsseldorf : VDI-Verlag GmbH, 1960.

Heywood, Anthony J. und Button, Ian D. C. 1995. *Soviet Locomotive Types : The Union Legacy.* Malmö/S : Frank Stenvalls Förlag, 1995. ISBN 9172661321.

Heywood, Anthony. 1999. *Modernising Lenin's Russia.* Cambridge/GB : Cambridge University Press, 1999. ISBN 9780521621786.

Hilberg, Raul. 1987. *Sonderzüge nach Ausschwitz.* Frankfurt (M), Berlin : Ullstein Taschenbuch, 1987. ISBN 9783548330853.

Hildebrandt, Roland. 2021. Die 10 meistgebauten Autos aller Zeiten: Könige des Fließbands. [online] 07. 02. 2021. [Accessed 01. 03. 2022] Available from: https://www.motorsport-total.com/auto/news/die-10-meistgebauten-autos-aller-zeiten-koenige-des-fliessbands-21020701.

Holding BDZ EAD. 2021. Private communication 03. 12. 2021.

Hucho, Wolf-Heinrich. 2002. *Aerodynamik der stumpfen Körper.* Braunschweig : Friedr. Vieweg & Sohn Verlagsgesellschaft mbH, 2002. ISBN 9783663077596.

Hütter, Ingo. Beiträge zur Lokomotiv- und Eisenbahngeschichte. *Lokomotivdatenbank.* [online] [Accessed 01. 03. 2022] Available from: https://www.beitraege.lokomotive.de/datenbank/d_datenbank.html.

—. 2012. *Die Dampflokomotiven der Baureihe 50 bis 53 der DRG, DRB, DB und DR - Band 2.* Hövelhof : DGEG und DGEG Medien GmbH, 2012. ISBN 9783937189635.

ijigenkuukann. 2018. [online] 5. 6 2018. [Accessed 01. 03. 2022] Available from: https://twitter.com/ijigenkuukann/status/1003994121424363521.

Jernbanen.dk. DSB damplokomotiver Litra N (III). *DSB N 206.* [online] [Accessed 01. 03. 2022] Available from: https://www.jernbanen.dk/damp_solo.php?s=1&lokid=813.

Josten, Elmar. 2013. *Die Deutsche Reichsbahn - die Ostbahn - im Generalgouvernement 1939-1945.* Berlin : Morgana-Edition, 2013. ISBN 9783943844283.

Karlsch, Rainer. 1993. *Allein bezahlt?* Berlin : Christoph Links Verlag, 1993. ISBN 3861530546.

KDB. 2012. [online] 12. 07. 2012. [Accessed 01. 03. 2022] Available from: https://maerklin-kiste.blog.ss-blog.jp/2012-07-11.

Keil, Uwe und Wunderlich, Karl-Heinz. 2020. Beutefahrzeuge in den USA. [Ed.] EK-Verlag GmbH. *Eisenbahnkurier Nr. 579.* 2020, Pages 48-52.

Keller, Hans B. 2010. Tyska lok på svenska spår, BR 52, 57 och 89. [online] 30. 9. 2010. [Accessed 01. 03. 2022] Available from: https://www.jvmv2.se/forum/index.php?mode=thread&id=63059 (deleted or moved).

Kevers, Paul. Lijst van Belgische spoorwegstations met telegrafische afkortingen. [online] [Accessed 01. 03. 2022] Available from: http://users.telenet.be/pk/stations.htm.

King, Charles R. 1907. The first steam superheaters. *Railroad Gazette.* 1907, Bd. 43, 18.

Kittel, Theodor. 1954. Die Deutsche Reichsbahn-Gesellschaft. [Ed.] Verkehrs-Verlag J. Fischer GmbH & Co. KG. *Zeitschrift für Verkehrswissenschaft.* 1954, Bd. 2, Pages 125-143.

Knipping, Andreas. 2011. Die Baureihe 52 in Jugoslawien: Bis heute im Einsatz. *Lok Magazin.* 2011, 4.

—. 2012. Glückloser Giesl - Teil 1. *EisenbahnKurier Nr. 479.* 2012, Pages 64-68.

Knipping, Andreas und Schulz, Reinhard. 2015. *Deutsche Reichsbahn 1939-1945.* Stuttgart : transpress Verlag, 2015. ISBN 9783613715059.

Knipping2, Andreas. 2012. Glückloser Giesl - Teil 2. *EisenbahnKurier Nr. 480.* 2012, Pages 64-68.

Kommerell, Otto. 1925. Das neue Achsdruckverzeichnis (A.V.). *Organ für die Fortschritte des Eisenbahnwesens.* 1925, Bd. 80, 4, Pages 57-63.

Kommunist, Moskau. 1964. Comecon 1949-1963: Realitäten und Probleme. *Ost-Probleme.* 16. Jg., 24. 07 1964, Nr. 15, Pages 434-444.

Königsmann, Bastian. 2021. *Das deutsche Dampflokerbe.* Erlangen : BoD - Books on Demand, 2021. ISBN 9783753419992.

Korzon, Andrzej. 1993. Niektóre problemy polsko-radzieckich stosunków gospodarczych w latach 1945-1957. [Ed.] Zakład Narodowy im. Ossolińskich - Wydawnictwo Polskiej Akademii Nauk. *Studia z Dziejów Rosji i Europy Środkowo-Wschodniej.* 28, 1993, Pages 135-153.

KPZS. Přečíslování řady T334.0. [online] [Accessed 01. 03. 2022] Available from: http://kpzs.logout.cz/t334/historie/precislovani.html.

Kreidler, Eugen. 2001. *Die Eisenbahnen im Zweiten Weltkrieg.* Hamburg : Nikol Verlagsgesellschft mbH & Co. KG, 2001. ISBN 393320352X.

Kuczynski, Thomas. 2009. Dem Regime dienen – nicht Geld verdienen. *Zeitschrift für Geschichtswissenschaft.* 2009, Bd. 57, 6, Pages 510-528.

Kuhlmann, Bernd. 2002. *Russische Züge auf deutschen Schienen 1945 bis 1994.* Berlin : Gesellschaft für Verkehrspolitik und Eisenbahnwesen (GVE) e.V., 2002. ISBN 3892180768.

Lacrițeanu, Șerban und Popescu, Ilie. 2007. *Istoricul Tracțiunii Feroviare Din România.* București : Editura ASAB, 2007. Bd. 2. ISBN 9789737725295.

Lange, Andreas. 2005. Lackierungen und Farbgebungen. *1. Die Farbliste.* [online] 2005. [Accessed 16. 05. 2021] Available from: http://www.rbd-breslau.de/71-tips/106-lackierung/lack.html.

Lányi, Ernö, et al. 1984. *Nagyvasúti Vontatójármüvek Magyarorsszágon.* Budapest : Közlekedési Dokumentációs Vállalat, 1984. ISBN 9635521618.

LC. DSB damplokomotiver. *DSB Litra N (III).* [online] [Accessed 01. 03. 2022] Available from: https://www.jernbanen.dk/damp.php?s=1&litra=N&typenr=3.

Le Fleming, H M und Price, J H. 1969. *Russian Steam Locomotives.* New York : Augustus M. Kelley, Publishers, 1969. Library of Congress No. 69-12831.

Le forum de N belge. Liste des couleurs SNCB/Lijst van kleuren NMBS. [online] [Accessed 01. 03. 2022] Available from: https://forum.trains-160.be/viewtopic.php?f=32&t=493&hilit=lijst+van+kleuren.

Lévi, Robert. 1935. Étude relative au Contact des Roues sur le Rail. [Ed.] Elsevier (Paris). *Revue Générale de Chémin de Fer.* 2, 1935.

Levine, Paul A. 1998. *From Indifference to Activism.* Uppsala : Uppsala University Library,, 1998. ISBN 9155442498.

Lichtenstein, Heiner. 1985. *Mit der Reichsbahn in den Tod.* Köln : Bund-Verlag GmbH, 1985. ISBN 9783766308092.

Luckow, Jan. 2021. *Die Deutsche Reichsbahn und das "Unternehmen Barbarossa".* Berlin : Verlag Bernd Neddermeyer, 2021. ISBN 9783941712751.

Luhn, Hans P. 1960. *Computer for verifying numbers. US2950048* USA, 23. 08 1960.

Mallet, M. A. 1908. Évolution Pratique de la Machine a Vapeur, Troisième Partie, Surchauffe de la Vapeur. *Mémoires et Compte Rendu des Travaux de la Société des Ingénieurs Civils des France.* Paris : Société des Ingénieurs Civils de France, 1908.

Matthäus, Stefan. 2004. Die kondensierenden Kriegslokomotiven. [offline] 2004. [Accessed 04. 04. 2015] Available from: http://kondenslok.de.

mdr. Deutsche Vertriebene im Zweiten Weltkrieg. [online] [Accessed 01. 03. 2022] Available from: https://www.mdr.de/zeitreise/deutsche-vertriebene-zweiter-weltkrieg100.html.

Mehrl, Andreas. Die Farbgebung österreichischer Dampflokomotiven. [online] [Accessed 01. 03. 2022] Available from:

http://www.laenderbahn-forum.de/journal/farbgebung_dampfloks_oesterreich/farbgebung_dampfloks_oesterreich.html.

Meineke, F. und Röhrs, Fr. 1949. *Die Dampflokomotive.* Göttingen : Springer-Verlag OHG, 1949. ISBN 9783642862304.

Messerschmidt, Wolfgang. 1987. *Dampflokomotiven und ihre Tender.* Stuttgart : Franckh'sche Verlagshandlung, 1987. ISBN 9783440057780.

Meszároš, Peter. Písma ČSD. [online] [Accessed 16. 01. 2022] Available from: https://www.railnet.sk/view.php?cisloclanku=2004051001.

Meyer, August. 1999. *Hilters Holding: Die Reichswerke "Hermann Göring".* München : Europa Verlag GmbH, 1999. ISBN 3203800357.

Michaels, Conrad. 2020. *Rüstungsmanagement der Ministerien Todt und Speer.* Münster : Aschendorff Verlag GmbH & Co KG, 2020. ISBN 9783402246221.

Mierzejewski, Alfred C. 2000. *The Most Valuable Asset of the Reich.* Chapel Hill and London : The University of North Carolina Press, 2000. Bde. 2 1933-1945. ISBN 9781469613963.

—. 1999. *The Most Valuable Asset of the Reich.* Chapel Hill and London : The University of North Carolina Press, 1999. Bde. 1 1920-1932. ISBN 9780807824962.

Mierzejewski, Alfred. 2005. *Hitler's Trains.* Strout (UK) : Tempus Publishing Limited, 2005. ISBN 9780752429816.

Military Government. 1947. [Ed.] U.S. Control Office APO 742 U.S. Army. s.l. : Office of Military Government for Germany, 03. 02 1947, Weekly Information Bulletin, Bd. 78.

Milward, Alan S. 1966. Fritz Todt als Minister für Bewaffnung und Munition. *Vierteljahreshefte für Zeitgeschichte.* 14, 1966, Bd. 1, Pages 40-58.

Mochocki, Władysław. 1999. Die Sowjetarmee in Polen: Die wirtschaftliche Ausbeutung der wiedergewonnenen Gebiete durch die Sowjetische Armee 1945 bis 1947. *Osteuropa.* 1999, Bd. 49, 2, Pages 195-207.

Moll, Martin. 1997. *Führer-Erlasse 1939-1945.* Stuttgart : Franz Steiner Verlag, 1997. ISBN 35150688732.

Moroz, George. 1945. "Camel" Locomotive liked by G.I. Crews. *The Yankee Boomer.* 1945, Bd. 2, 37.

Mosch-Wicke, Klaus. 1985. *Nationalsozialismus in Nordhessen.* Kassel : Verlag Gesamthochschulbibliothek Kassel, 1985. ISBN 3881222545.

Motyčka, Josef. 2001. *Encyklopedie železnice - Parní lokomotivy ČSD (5).* Praha : Nakladatelství Corona, s.r.o., 2001. ISBN 9788086116235.

Muller, R.C. Statius, Veenendaal jr., A.J. und Waldorp, H. 2005. *De Nederlandse Stoomlocomotieven.* Alkmaar : De Alk bv, 2005. ISBN 9060132629.

Nerdinger, Winfried. 2018. *Zwangsarbeit in München - Das Lager der Reichsbahn in Neuaubing.* Berlin : Metropol-Verlag, 2018. ISBN 9783863314040.

Niederstraßer, Leopold. 1939. *Leitfaden für den Dampflokomotivdienst.* Leipzig : Verkehrswissenschaftliche Lehrmittelgesellschaft m.b.H., 1939.

Norsk jernbanemuseum. Roterende snøplog nr 6 foran to damplokomotiver type 63a. [online] [Accessed 01. 03. 2022] Available from: https://digitaltmuseum.org/021016957027/roterende-snoplog-nr-6-foran-to-damplokomotiver-type-63a.

Noßke, Thomas. 2006. Einteilung der Züge. [offline] 2006. [Accessed 01. 03. 2022] Available from: https://epoche2.modellbahnfrokler.de/dd/e2d_4801.html.

—. Fahrdienstvorschriften (FV), eingeführt durch Verfügung der Hauptverwaltung 24 Bavfu 58 vom 27. 04.1933, gültig vom 01.09.1933, unter Berücksichtigung der bis zum 31.12.1938 eingetretenen Änderungen. [offline] [Accessed 01. 03. 2022] Available from: https://epoche2.modellbahnfrokler.de/dv/e2d_3310.html.

Oatley, Henry B. 1921. *Locomotive Draft Appliance.* New York : s.n., 1921. US Patent 1,372,976.

oimactaka. [offline] [Accessed 24. 10. 2014] Available from: http://oimactaka.blog.hobidas.com/archives/article/101524.html.

Pagenstecher, Cord. Begriffe: Fremdarbeiter - Zwangsarbeiter - Slavenarbeiter. [online] Bundeszentrale für politische Bildung. [Accessed 01. 03. 2022] Available from: https://www.bpb.de/geschichte/nationalsozialismus/ns-zwangsarbeit/227269/begriffe.

Paulsen, Patrick, et al. dampflokomotivarchiv.de. [online] [Accessed 01. 03. 2022] Available from: https://www.dampflokomotivarchiv.de.

Perianu, Dan Gh. 2000. *Istoria locomotivelor şi a căilor ferate din Banatul Montan.* Reşiţa : Editura Timpul, 2000. ISBN 9739249361.

Peters, Jan-Henrik. 2005. Kassel - Schöneweide - Ostfront. *Eisenbahngeschichte.* 2005, Bd. 3, Nr. 12, Pages 8-25.

Pfleiderer, Doris. Volksbegehren und Volksentscheid gegen den Youngplan. [online] [Accessed 18. 02. 2021] Available from: https://www.landesarchiv-bw.de/media/full/43143.

PFT. 2021. private communication. 14. 01. 2021.

Picker, Henry. 1963. *Hitlers Tischgespräche im Führerhauptquartier 1941-1942.* Stuttgart : Seewald Verlag, 1963.

Pierre2427. 2021. 2427junction. [online] 27. 06. 2021. [Accessed 01. 03. 2022] Available from: https://twitter.com/nwKEdpnlsDoqRRm/status/1409728054214025216?s=20.

Pierson, Kurt. 1967. *Kohlenstaublokomotiven.* Stuttgart : Franckh'sche Verlagshandlung, W. Keller & Co., 1967.

Piwowoński, Jan. 1978. *Parowozy kolei Polskich.* Warszawa : Wydawnictwa Komunikacji i Łączności, 1978.

Pospichal, Josef. 2015. Dampflokomotiven Bosnien und Herzegowina, zuletzt ergänzt 27. 10 2015. [Accessed 01. 03. 2022] Available from: https://www.pospichal.net/lokstatistik/20901-bih2003.htm.

Potsdam Agreement. *Potsdam Agreement - Protocol of the Proceedings, August 1, 1945.* Potsdam : Department of State, Washington DC.

Pottgiesser, Hans. 1975. *Die Deutsche Reichsbahn im Ostfeldzug.* 2nd extended Edition. Neckargemünd : Kurt Vowinckel Verlag, 1975.

Pritchard, R. N. 1996. *Industrial Locomotives of the People's Republic of China.* Oakham : Industrial Railway Society, 1996. ISBN 0901096962.

PRL. 2016. Kalendarium powojennej Polski. 1945 r. [online] 24. 12. 2016. [Accessed 01. 03. 2022] Available from: https://historia.interia.pl/prl/news-kalendarium-powojennej-polski-1945-r,nId,2342083.

Rahlf, Thomas. 2015. Dokumentation zum Zeitreihendatensatz für Deutschland, 1834-2012. *Historical Social Research, Transition (online Supplement).* 26v1, 2015.

Rakow, W. A. 1986. *Russische und sowjetische Dampflokomotiven.* Berlin : transpress VEB Verlag für Verkehrswesen, DDR, 1986. ISBN 3344004131.

Rees, E. A. 1995. *Stalinism and Soviet Rail Transport, 1928-1941.* London : Palgrave Macmillan, 1995. ISBN 9780333524152.

Rehnberg, Bertil. 1997. Krigslok i Sverige. [Ed.] Järnvägarnas Museiförening och Östergötlands Järnvägsmuseum. *Tåg och Spår.* 1997, 106, Pages 8-9.

Reichsgesetzblatt. 1930. *Zündwarenmonopolgesetz.* Berlin : s.n., 1930. Bd. 3.

Reimer, Michael. 1996. *Die Lokomotiven der Baureihe 52.* Gülzow : Lokrundschau Verlag GmbH, 1996. ISBN 393164703X.

—. 1999. *Lokomotiven für die Ostfront.* München : GeraMond Verlag, 1999. ISBN 3932785355.

Reimer, Michael und Endisch, Dirk. 2001. *Baureihe 52.80 - Die rekonstruierte Kriegslokomotive.* München : GeraMond Verlag, 2001. ISBN 3765471011.

Reimer, Michael und Kubitzki, Volkmar. 2004. *Eisenbahn in Polen 1939-1945.* Stuttgart : transpress Verlag, 2004. ISBN 978361371213X.

Reimer, Michael, Meyer, Lothar und Kubitzki, Volkmar. 1998. *Kolonne.* Stuttgart : transpress Verlag, 1998. ISBN 3613710803.

Riccardi, Aldo und Grillo, Marcello. 2021. *Locomotive di guerra, Vol. 2.* Firenze : Edizioni Pegaso Firenze, 2021. ISBN 9791280191076.

Rinn, Georg M. 2008. *Das Automobil als nationales Identifikationssymbol.* Humboldt-Universität Berlin, Philosophische Fakultät I : Dissertation, 2008.

Rollo. 2017. Die Metamorphose der DRG 98 674 zu einer ÖBB-Lok [online] 16. 02. 2017. [Accessed 01. 03. 2022] Available from: https://forum.spurnull-magazin.de/thread/14263-die-metamorphose-der-drg-98-674-zu-einer-%C3%B6bb-lok/?postID=111066.

Rubeš, Václav. 2018. 1948: DO RUDA! [Ed.] a.s. České dráhy. *ČD Pro Vás.* 2018, Bd. 6, Pages 12-13.

Ruyters, Dr. F. 1953. *Erlebnisbericht über den Kriegseinsatz im Osten 1939-1944.* Berlin-Lichterfelde : Bundesarchiv, 1953. Signatur R 5-ANH. I/120.

Sachsenstolz. 2006. Giesl-Ejektoren bei der DR [online] 23. 05. 2006. [Accessed 01. 03. 2022] Available from: https://www.drehscheibe-online.de/foren/read.php?17,2921504,2925081.

Sammlung Sarter. Berlin-Lichterfelde : Bundesarchiv. Signatur R 5-ANH. I.

Sarter, Adolf und Kittel, Theodor. 1953. *Was jeder von der Deutschen Bundesbahn wissen muss.* Frankfurt/M. : Verkehrswissenschaftliche Lehrmittelgesellschaft m.b.H., 1953.

Sawodny, Wolfgang. 1996. *Die Panzerzüge des Deutschen Reiches 1904-1945.* Freiburg : EK-Verlag GmbH, 1996. ISBN

3882556781.

Schaefer, Hans. Description of the QJ type steam locomotive. [Accessed 01. 03. 2022] Available from: http://web.archive.org/web/20020416163204/, Available from: http://home.c2i.net/schaefer/qjdetails/qjhistory.html.

Scharf, Hans-Wolfgang. 1981. *Eisenbahnen zwischen Oder und Weichsel.* Freiburg : Eisenbahn-Kurier Verlag GmbH, 1981. ISBN 3882555432.

Scheibinger, Mathias. 2012. *Die Lokomotivindustrie im Dritten Reich (1933 - 1945) am Beispiel der Wiener Lokomotivfabrik Floridsdorf (WLF).* Wien : Universität Wien - Diploma Thesis, 2012. ISBN 9783950354348.

Schnell, Rainer. 2017. Terra Incognita. *Modelleisenbahner.* 2017, 4, Pages 44-48.

Schoenberg, Robert. PRR Steam Locomotive diagrams. [online] [Accessed 01. 03. 2022] Available from: http://prr.railfan.net/diagrams/PRRdiagrams.html?sel=ste&sz=lg&fr=.

Schramm, Gerhard. 1952. Eisenbahnschwellen. *Jahrbuch des Eisenbahnwesens.* 1952, Bd. 3.

Schramm, Sébastien. Description du Résau. [online] [Accessed 01. 03. 2022] Available from: http://chfervietnam.free.fr/Reseau%20Vietnam/Reseau.html.

Schüler, Klaus A. Friedrich. 1987. *Logistik im Rußlandfeldzug.* s.l. : Verlag Peter Lang GmbH, 1987. ISBN 9783820409505.

Schulz, Joachim. Oberbauzeichnungen Preussen Normalspur. [online] [Accessed 01. 03. 2022] Available from: http://www.laenderbahn-forum.de/zeichnungen/oberbau/josch/PreussenL1-Z.jpg.

Schwarze, Johannes, et al. 1998. *Die Dampflokomotive.* Stuttgart : transpress Verlag, 1998. ISBN 3344707914.

Scriba, Arnulf. Die Besetzung von Norwegen 1940. [online] [Accessed 01. 03. 2022] Available from: https://www.dhm.de/lemo/kapitel/der-zweite-weltkrieg/kriegsverlauf/besetzung-von-norwegen-1940.html.

Service, Robert. 2003. *A history of modern Russia from Nicholas II to Vladimir Putin.* Cambridge, Massachusetts : Harvard University Press, 2003. ISBN: 067401801X.

Slaughter, Peter, Wasssiljew, Alexander und Beier, Roland. 1996. *Kurze Geschichte der Kriegslokomotiven Baureihe 52 und ihr Verbleib in Ost und West.* Malmö : Verlag Frank Stenvall, 1996. ISBN 9789172661394.

Slezak, Josef Otto. 1962. *Internationales Archiv für Lokomotivgeschichte IAL 1 - Die Lokomotivfabriken Europas.* Wien : Verlag Josef Otto Slezak, Wien XIX, 1962.

—. 1967. *Internationales Archiv für Lokomotivgeschichte IAL 7 - Der Giesl-Ejektor.* Wien : Verlag Josef Otto Slezak, 1967.

Smith, Jonathan D. H. Pennsylvania Railroad 19th C. steam locomotives. [offline] [Accessed 01. 08. 2019] Available from: https://jdhsmith.math.iastate.edu/term/slusprr0.htm.

Split, Nico. Treinseinbeelden. [online] [Accessed 01. 03. 2022] Available from: https://www.nicospilt.com/index_treinseinbeelden.htm.

Stankiewicz, Ryszard und Garbacik, Roman. 2013. *Ty2 - wojenna lokomotywa na pokojowe czasy.* Rybnik : Wydawn ictwo Eu rospri nter, 2013. ISBN 9788363652036.

Statistisches Reichsamt. 1923. *Statistisches Jahrbuch für das Deutsche Reich.* Berlin : Verlag für Politik und Wirtschaft, 1923.

—. 1930. *Statistisches Jahrbuch für das Deutsche Reich.* Berlin : Verlag von Reimar Hobbing, 1930.

—. 1926. *Statistisches Jahrbuch für das Deutsche Reich.* Berlin : Verlag von Reimar Hobbing, 1926.

—. 1932. *Statistisches Jahrbuch für das Deutsche Reich.* Berlin : Verlag von Reimar Hobbing, 1932.

—. 1934. *Statistisches Jahrbuch für das Deutsche Reich.* Berlin : Verlag von Reimar Hobbing GmbH, 1934.

—. 1936. *Statistisches Jahrbuch für das Deutsche Reich.* Berlin : Verlag für Sozialpolitik, Wirtschaft und Statistik GmbH, 1936.

—. 1938. *Statistisches Jahrbuch für das Deutsche Reich.* Berlin : Verlag für Sozialpolitik, Wirtschaft und Statistik, 1938.

—. 1940. *Statistisches Jahrbuch für das Deutsche Reich.* Berlin : s.n., 1940.

Stg.C.D.V.& T. Foundation for German communication and related technologies. [online] [Accessed 01. 03. 2022] Available from: https://www.cdvandt.org/index.htm.

Stockklausner, Hanns. 1950. *25 Jahre deutsche Einheitslokomotive.* Nürnberg : Miba-Verlag, 1950.

Stroner, Dominik. 2002. Drehen und Wenden. *Bahn Extra.* Dezember/Januar, 2002, Bd. 6.

Talbot, E. 1981. *Steam In Turkey.* Kenton, Harrow, Middlesex : The Continental Railway Circle, 1981. ISBN 9780950346960.

Taylor, Zbigniew. 2007. *Rozwój i regres sieci kolejowej w Polsce.* Warszawa : Instytut Geografii i Przestrzennego Zagospodarowania, 2007. ISBN 9788387954799.

Terczyński, Paweł. 2003. *Atlas parowozów.* Poznań : Poznań Klub Modelarzy Kolejowych, 2003. ISBN 8390190281.

Terczyński, Paweł. 2002. Nasz portret Parowóz serii Ty 5. *Świat Kolei.* 6, 2002, Pages 10-17.

—. 2020. Portret parowozu serii Ty2. [online] 15. 05. 2020. [Accessed 01. 03. 2022] Available from: https://eraparowozow.org.pl/portret-parowozu-serii-ty2/.

Terczyński2, Paweł. 2020. Portret parowozu serii Ty42. [online] 10. 09. 2020. [Accessed 01. 03. 2022] Available from: https://eraparowozow.org.pl/portret-parowozu-serii-ty42/.

The Babcock & Wilcox Co. 1914. *Steam Superheaters.* New York : Bartlett-Orr Press, 1914.

tikz14684. 2017. の猫 (no neko). [online] 20. 03. 2017. [Accessed 01. 03. 2022] Available from: https://twitter.com/tikz14684/status/843822722194923520.

Tourret, R. 1995. *Allied Military Locomotives of the Second World War.* 3rd Edition. Abingdon : Tourret Publishing, 1995. ISBN 090587806X.

Train World Heritage. Private communication NMBS - Stations / B-ST.0411 -Train World Heritage - Charters & Collection Modelbouw.

Trains of Turkey. 56501 to 56553. [online] [Accessed 01. 03. 2022] Available from: http://www.trainsofturkey.com/pmwiki.php/Steam/56501.

Traintamarre. Les locomotives Type 25, 26, 27, 28 et 29. [online] [Accessed 01. 03. 2022] Available from: https://traintamarre.tassignon.be/textes/25-26-29.htm.

trenoazzurro67. Loco preda bellica BR 52. [online] [Accessed 16. 01. 2022] Available from: http://www.forum-duegieditrice.com/viewtopic.php?f=21&t=32207&start=30.

Treue, Wilhelm. 1955. Dokumentation "Hitlers Denkschrift zum Vierjahresplan 1936". *Vierteljahreshefte für Zeitgeschichte.* 1955, Bd. 2, Pages 184-210.

U.S. Department of Commerce. 1939. *Statistical Abstract of the United States 1939.* Washington, DC : United States Printing Office, 1939.

UIC. 2017. *L'UIC - L'Organisation Ferroviaire Mondiale.* Paris : UIC, 2017. ISBN 9782746125858.

Ullrich, Volker. 2019. *Die Rede, in der er die Vernichtung der Juden ankündigte.* Hamburg : Zeitverlag Gerd Bucerius GmbH & Co. KG, 30. 01. 2019, Die Zeit.

United States Holocaust Memorial Museum. Wer waren die Opfer des Holocaust? [online] [Accessed 01. 03. 2022] Available from: https://encyclopedia.ushmm.org/content/de/article/mosaic-of-victims-an-overview.

Universitätsbibliothek Universität Weimar. TGL-Verzeichnis, Liste digitalisierter TGL. [online] [Accessed 01. 03. 2022] Available from: https://katalog.ub.uni-weimar.de/tgl/TGL_3667+1.%C3%84nderung_11-1982.pdf.

Unknown. 1945. A Profile of the 757th Railway Shop Battalion. [Ed.] Milwaukee, St. Paul and Pacific Railroad Chicago. *The Milwaukee Magazine.* 1945, 10.

—. 1952. Post to Scrap Captured, Foreign Rail Equipment. *The Fort Eustis Sentinel.* 1952, April 11, 1952.

—. 1998. Der Heinl-Mischvorwärmer bei den ÖBB. *Eisenbahn Kurier Themen.* 1998, Bd. 29, Pages 80-87.

—. 2018. The Fair. [online] 15. 12. 2018. [Accessed 01. 03. 2022] Available from: http://www.rgusrail.com/ilcrf.html.

USATC. 1945. Historical Report of the Transportation Corps in the European Theater of Operations. Paris. Pap. Du Sentier, 1945 [online] [Accessed 01. 03. 2022] Available from: https://asu.army.mil/library/special_collections/Documents/Transportation%20Corp%20V.%205%20Part%20II.pdf

van Wijck Jurriaanse, N. J. 1968. *Geschiedkundig overzicht der stoomlocomotieven van de Nederlandse spoorwegmaatschappijen over de periode 1839-1958.* Culemborg : H. Stam Nederland N.V., 1968.

Vandenberghen, J. 1991. *XIV. La Société Nationale des Chemins de Fer Belges 1926-1939.* Bruxelles : s.n., 1991.

Vink, René F. Belettering NS Stoomlocomotieven (bij benadering). [online] [Accessed 01. 03. 2022] Available from: https://www.modelrailroading.nl/Projects/NS4300%20bachmann/pdf/Belettering%20NS%20Stoomlocomotieven%20Geel.pdf.

Vlaki. Teritorijalni razpored lokomotiv po nekdanji Jugoslaviji. [offline] [Accessed 29. 03. 2013] Available from: http://www.vlaki.net/dodatno/lok-33.html.

Waldorp, H. 1986. *Onze Nederlandse stoomlocomotieven in woord en beeld.* Alkmaar : De Alk bv, 1986. ISBN 906013947X.

Walinowski, Mario. 2014. Kriegslok hilft beim Aufbau. *LokMagazin.* 2014, Bd. 5, Pages 2-7.

Webster, Ian. CPI Inflation Calculator. [online] [Accessed 01. 03. 2022] Available from: https://www.in2013dollars.com/us/inflation/1923?amount=77549.

Weisbrod, Manfed und Obermayer, Horst J. 2012. *Baureihe 52.* Fürstenfeldbruck : Verlagsgruppe Bahn GmbH, 2012.

Bd. 1, Eisenbahn-Journal Extra-Ausgabe 1/2012. ISBN 9783896103598.

Weisbrod, Manfred. 1991. *Tender*. Berlin : Transpress Verlagsgesellschaft mbH, 1991. ISBN 334470723X.

Wenzel, Hans-Jürgen. 2019. Bauartänderungen bei der DB - Die Vielfalt wird noch größer. *Eisenbahn-Kurier Special 132.* 2019, Pages 60-67.

Wenzel, Hansjürgen. 1979. *Die Baureihe 55*. Freiburg : Eisenbahn-Kurier Verlag GmbH, 1979. ISBN 9783882551556.

Wenzel, Hans-Jürgen. 2014. Die deutsche Reichsbahn in der Britischen und US-Besatzungszone 1945-1949. *Eisenbahn-Kurier Special 113.* 2014, Pages 10-21.

Wenzel2, Hansjürgen. 1979. *Die Baureihe 57*. Freiburg : Eisenbahn-Kurier Verlag GmbH, 1979. ISBN 9783882551570.

Wenzel2, Hans-Jürgen. 2014. Die Deutsche Reichsbahn in der Französischen Besatzungszone 1945-1949. *Eisenbahn-Kurier Special 113.* 2014.

—. **2019.** Franco-Crosti-Kessel-Reihe 5040 - Der Versuch einer modernen Dampflok. *Eisenbahn-Kurier Special 132.* 2019, Pages 52-55.

Wenzel3, Hans-Jürgen. 2014. Die Deutsche Reichsbahn in der Sowjetischen Besatzungszone 1945-1949. *Eisenbahn-Kurier Special 113.* 2014, Pages 46-67.

—. **2019.** Rahmentausch in Bremen und Schwerte - Eindeutiges und Rätselhaftes. *Eisenbahn-Kurier Special 132.* 2019, Pages 48-51.

Werner, Sebastian. 2019. Aus einer werden drei. *Eisenbahn-Kurier Special 132.* 2019, Pages 74-95.

—. **2017.** Kolonnenzüge - Reparationstransporte für Stalin. *Eisenbahn-Kurier Special 126.* 2017, Pages 44-47.

White Jr., John H. 1979. *A History of the American Locomotive, Its Development: 1830-1880*. New York : Dover Publications Inc., 1979. ISBN 0486238180.

Wikipedia001. Wheel arrangement. [online] [Accessed 01. 03. 2022] Available from: https://en.wikipedia.org/wiki/Wheel_arrangement.

Wikipedia002. 240 PO 4701 à 4712. [online] [Accessed 04. 05. 2021] Available from: https://fr.wikipedia.org/wiki/240_PO_4701_%C3%A0_4712.

Wikipedia003. Nisko-Plan. [online] [Accessed 01. 03. 2022] Available from: https://en.wikipedia.org/wiki/Nisko_Plan.

Wikipedia004. Herman Haupt. [online] [Accessed 01. 03. 2022] Available from: https://en.wikipedia.org/wiki/Herman_Haupt.

Wikipedia005. Breitspurbahn. [online] [Accessed 01. 03. 2022] Available from: https://en.wikipedia.org/wiki/Breitspurbahn.

Wikipedia006. No Frills. [online] [Accessed 01. 03. 2022] Available from: https://en.wikipedia.org/wiki/No_frills.

Wikipedia007. Rheinmetall. [online] [Accessed 01. 03. 2022] Available from: https://de.wikipedia.org/wiki/Rheinmetall#Zweiter_Weltkrieg.

Wikipedia008. Fablok. [online] [Accessed 01. 03. 2022] Available from: https://pl.wikipedia.org/wiki/Fablok.

Wikipedia009. Konrad Gamper. [online] [Accessed 01. 03. 2022] Available from: https://pl.wikipedia.org/wiki/Konrad_Gamper.

Wikipedia010. Aktion T4. [online] [Accessed 01. 03. 2022] Available from: https://en.wikipedia.org/wiki/Aktion_T4.

Wikipedia011. P (Nazi symbol). [online] [Accessed 01. 03. 2022] Available from: https://en.wikipedia.org/wiki/P_(Nazi_symbol).

Wikipedia012. Heuaktion. [online] [Accessed 01. 03. 2022] Available from: https://en.wikipedia.org/wiki/Heuaktion.

Wikipedia013. Forced labour under German rule during World War II. [online] [Accessed 01. 03. 2022] Available from: https://en.wikipedia.org/wiki/Forced_labour_under_German_rule_during_World_War_II.

Wikipedia014. Berliner Maschinenbau. [online] [Accessed 01. 03. 2022] Available from: https://en.wikipedia.org/wiki/Berliner_Maschinenbau.

Wikipedia015. Schichau-Werke. [online] [Accessed 01. 03. 2022] Available from: https://en.wikipedia.org/wiki/Schichau-Werke.

Wikipedia016. Cessna 172. [online] [Accessed 01. 03. 2022] Available from: https://en.wikipedia.org/wiki/Cessna_172.

Wikipedia017. Class (locomotive). [online] [Accessed 01. 03. 2022] Available from: https://en.wikipedia.org/wiki/Class_(locomotive).

Wikipedia018. DRG locomotive classification. [online] [Accessed 01. 03. 2022] Available from: https://en.wikipedia.org/wiki/DRG_locomotive_classification.

Wikipedia019. Паровоз. [online] [Accessed 01. 03. 2022] Available from:

https://ru.wikipedia.org/wiki/%D0%9F%D0%B0%D1%80%D0%BE%D0%B2%D0%BE%D0%B7.

Wikipedia020. Pennsylvania Railroad. [online] [Accessed 01. 03. 2022] Available from:
https://en.wikipedia.org/wiki/Pennsylvania_Railroad.

Wikipedia021. Юго-Восточная железная дорога (Ûgo-Vostočnaâ železnaâ doroga). [online] [Accessed 01. 03. 2022]
Available from: https://ru.wikipedia.org/wiki/%D0%AE%D0%B3%D0%BE-
%D0%92%D0%BE%D1%81%D1%82%D0%BE%D1%87%D0%BD%D0%B0%D1%8F_%D0%B6%D0%B5%D0%BB%D0%B5%
D0%B7%D0%BD%D0%B0%D1%8F_%D0%B4%D0%BE%D1%80%D0%BE%D0%B3%D0%B0.

Wikipedia022. Gölsdorf axle. [online] [Accessed 01. 03. 2022] Available from:
https://en.wikipedia.org/wiki/G%C3%B6lsdorf_axle.

Wikipedia023. Владикавказская железная дорога (Vladikavkazskaâ železnaâ doroga). [В Интернете] [Accessed
01. 03. 2022] Available from:
https://ru.wikipedia.org/wiki/%D0%92%D0%BB%D0%B0%D0%B4%D0%B8%D0%BA%D0%B0%D0%B2%D0%BA%D0%B0
%D0%B7%D1%81%D0%BA%D0%B0%D1%8F_%D0%B6%D0%B5%D0%BB%D0%B5%D0%B7%D0%BD%D0%B0%D1%8F_
%D0%B4%D0%BE%D1%80%D0%BE%D0%B3%D0%B0.

Wikipedia024. Северо-Донецкая железная дорога (Severo-Doneckaâ železnaâ doroga). [В Интернете] [Accessed
01. 03. 2022] Available from: https://ru.wikipedia.org/wiki/%D0%A1%D0%B5%D0%B2%D0%B5%D1%80%D0%BE-
%D0%94%D0%BE%D0%BD%D0%B5%D1%86%D0%BA%D0%B0%D1%8F_%D0%B6%D0%B5%D0%BB%D0%B5%D0%B7%
D0%BD%D0%B0%D1%8F_%D0%B4%D0%BE%D1%80%D0%BE%D0%B3%D0%B0.

Wikipedia025. Liste russischer und sowjetischer Triebfahrzeuge. [online] [Accessed 15. 07. 2019] Available from:
https://de.wikipedia.org/wiki/Liste_russischer_und_sowjetischer_Triebfahrzeuge#G%C3%BCterzuglokomotiven_ab_1925.

Wikipedia026. Колонны паровозов особого резерва (Kolonny parovozov osobogo rezerva). [online] [Accessed
01. 03. 2022] Available from:
https://ru.wikipedia.org/wiki/%D0%9A%D0%BE%D0%BB%D0%BE%D0%BD%D0%BD%D1%8B_%D0%BF%D0%B0%D1%80
%D0%BE%D0%B2%D0%BE%D0%B7%D0%BE%D0%B2_%D0%BE%D1%81%D0%BE%D0%B1%D0%BE%D0%B3%D0%BE_%
D1%80%D0%B5%D0%B7%D0%B5%D1%80%D0%B2%D0%B0.

Wikipedia027. Konferenz von Moskau. [online] [Accessed 01. 03. 2022] Available from:
https://de.wikipedia.org/wiki/Konferenz_von_Moskau.

Wikipedia028. Yalta Conference. [online] [Accessed 01. 03. 2022] Available from:
https://en.wikipedia.org/wiki/Yalta_Conference.

Wikipedia029. ARLZ-Maßnahmen. [online] [Accessed 01. 03. 2022] Available from: https://de.wikipedia.org/wiki/ARLZ-
Ma%C3%9Fnahmen.

Wikipedia030. Nero Decree. [online] [Accessed 01. 03. 2022] Available from: https://en.wikipedia.org/wiki/Nero_Decree.

Wikipedia031. Scorched earth. [online] [Accessed 01. 03. 2022] Available from:
https://en.wikipedia.org/wiki/Scorched_earth.

Wikipedia032. Allied-occupied Austria. [online] [Accessed 01. 03. 2022] Available from:
https://en.wikipedia.org/wiki/Allied-occupied_Austria.

Wikipedia033. Österreichische Bundesbahnen. [online] [Accessed 01. 03. 2022] Available from:
https://de.wikipedia.org/wiki/%C3%96sterreichische_Bundesbahnen.

Wikipedia034. Klima-Schneepflug. [online] [Accessed 01. 03. 2022] Available from: https://de.wikipedia.org/wiki/Klima-
Schneepflug.

Wikipedia035. Rettung der bulgarischen Juden. [online] [Accessed 01. 03. 2022] Available from:
https://de.wikipedia.org/wiki/Rettung_der_bulgarischen_Juden.

Wikipedia036. Strategic steam reserve. [online] [Accessed 01. 03. 2022] Available from:
https://en.wikipedia.org/wiki/Strategic_steam_reserve.

Wikipedia037. Janney coupler. [online] [Accessed 01. 01. 2024] Available from:
https://en.wikipedia.org/wiki/Janney_coupler.

Wikipedia038. Kryšpínovo označení lokomotiv. [online] [Accessed 01. 03. 2022] Available from:
https://cs.wikipedia.org/wiki/Kry%C5%A1p%C3%ADnovo_ozna%C4%8Den%C3%AD_lokomotiv.

Wikipedia039. Farver på tog. [online] [Accessed 01. 03. 2022] Available from:
https://da.wikipedia.org/wiki/Farver_p%C3%A5_tog.

Wikipedia040. London Protocol (1944). [online] [Accessed 01. 01. 2024] Available from:

https://en.wikipedia.org/wiki/London_Protocol_(1944).

Wikipedia041. Kriegsgefangene des Zweiten Weltkrieges. [online] [Accessed 01. 03. 2022] Available from: https://de.wikipedia.org/wiki/Kriegsgefangene_des_Zweiten_Weltkrieges.

Wikipedia042. Displaced Person. [online] [Accessed 01. 03. 2022] Available from: https://de.wikipedia.org/wiki/Displaced_Person.

Wikipedia043. Marshall Plan. [online] [Accessed 01. 03. 2022] Available from: https://en.wikipedia.org/wiki/Marshall_Plan.

Wikipedia044. CARE Package. [online] [Accessed 01. 03. 2022] Available from: https://en.wikipedia.org/wiki/CARE_Package.

Wikipedia045. Золотник Трофимова (Zolotnik Trofimova). [online] [Accessed 01. 03. 2022] Available from: https://ru.wikipedia.org/wiki/%D0%97%D0%BE%D0%BB%D0%BE%D1%82%D0%BD%D0%B8%D0%BA_%D0%A2%D1%80%D0%BE%D1%84%D0%B8%D0%BC%D0%BE%D0%B2%D0%B0.

Wikipedia046. Грязе-Царицынская железная дорога (Grâze-Caricynskaâ železnaâ doroga). [online] [Accessed 01. 03. 2022] Available from: https://ru.wikipedia.org/wiki/%D0%93%D1%80%D1%8F%D0%B7%D0%B5-%D0%A6%D0%B0%D1%80%D0%B8%D1%86%D1%8B%D0%BD%D1%81%D0%BA%D0%B0%D1%8F_%D0%B6%D0%B5%D0%BB%D0%B5%D0%B7%D0%BD%D0%B0%D1%8F_%D0%B4%D0%BE%D1%80%D0%BE%D0%B3%D0%B0.

Wikipedia047. Volgograd. [online] [Accessed 01. 03. 2022] Available from: https://en.wikipedia.org/wiki/Volgograd.

Wikipedia048. 1970s energy crisis. [online] [Accessed 01. 03. 2022] Available from: https://en.wikipedia.org/wiki/1970s_energy_crisis.

Wikipedia049. Hungarian State Railways. [online] [Accessed 01. 03. 2022] Available from: https://en.wikipedia.org/wiki/Hungarian_State_Railways.

Wikipedia050. MÁV mozdonysorozatok. [online] [Accessed 01. 03. 2022] Available from: https://hu.wikipedia.org/wiki/M%C3%81V_mozdonysorozatok.

Wikipedia051. Magyar Királyi Állami Vas-, Acél- és Gépgyárak. [online] [Accessed 01. 03. 2022] Available from: https://hu.wikipedia.org/wiki/Magyar_Kir%C3%A1lyi_%C3%81llami_Vas-,_Ac%C3%A9l-_%C3%A9s_G%C3%A9pgy%C3%A1rak.

Wikipedia052. United Nations Relief and Rehabilitation Administration. [online] [Accessed 01. 03. 2022] Available from: https://en.wikipedia.org/wiki/United_Nations_Relief_and_Rehabilitation_Administration.

Wikipedia053. Varga László (gépészmérnök, 1891–1950). [online] [Accessed 01. 03. 2022] Available from: https://hu.wikipedia.org/wiki/Varga_L%C3%A1szl%C3%B3_(g%C3%A9p%C3%A9szm%C3%A9rn%C3%B6k,_1891%E2%80%931950).

Wikipedia054. DRB 52 sorozat. [online] [Accessed 01. 03. 2022] Available from: https://hu.wikipedia.org/wiki/DRB_52_sorozat.

Wikipedia055. びわ湖パラダイス (Biwako paradaisu). [online] [Accessed 01. 03. 2022] Available from: https://ja.wikipedia.org/wiki/%E3%81%B3%E3%82%8F%E6%B9%96%E3%83%91%E3%83%A9%E3%83%80%E3%82%A4%E3%82%B9.

Wikipedia056. オリエント・エクスプレス '88 (oriento ekusupuresu 88). [online] [Accessed 01. 03. 2022] Available from: https://ja.wikipedia.org/wiki/%E3%82%AA%E3%83%AA%E3%82%A8%E3%83%B3%E3%83%88%E3%83%BB%E3%82%A8%E3%82%AF%E3%82%B9%E3%83%97%E3%83%AC%E3%82%B9_%2788#%E3%83%A8%E3%83%BC%E3%83%AD%E3%83%E3%83%91%E3%81%B8%E8%BF%94%E5%8D%B4.

Wikipedia057. Traitement intégral Armand. [online] [Accessed 01. 03. 2022] Available from: https://fr.wikipedia.org/wiki/Traitement_int%C3%A9gral_Armand.

Wikipedia058. Drangsdalen. [online] [Accessed 01. 03. 2022] Available from: https://no.wikipedia.org/wiki/Drangsdalen.

Wikipedia059. Свиноуйсьце (Svinoujs'ce). [online] [Accessed 01. 03. 2022] Available from: https://ru.wikipedia.org/wiki/%D0%A1%D0%B2%D0%B8%D0%BD%D0%BE%D1%83%D0%B9%D1%81%D1%8C%D1%86%D0%B5.

Wikipedia060. Polish Coal Trunk-Line. [online] [Accessed 01. 03. 2022] Available from: https://en.wikipedia.org/wiki/Polish_Coal_Trunk-Line.

Wikipedia061. Lębork (stacja kolejowa). [online] [Accessed 01. 03. 2022] Available from: https://pl.wikipedia.org/wiki/L%C4%99bork_(stacja_kolejowa).

Wikipedia062. Ballestrem (Adelsgeschlecht). [online] [Accessed 01. 03. 2022] Available from:

https://de.wikipedia.org/wiki/Ballestrem_(Adelsgeschlecht).

Wikipedia063. Gräflich Schaffgotsch'sche Werke. [online] [Accessed 01. 03. 2022] Available from: https://de.wikipedia.org/wiki/Gr%C3%A4flich_Schaffgotsch%E2%80%99sche_Werke.

Wikipedia064. Franz Pieler (Bergbauingenieur, 1869). [online] [Accessed 01. 03. 2022] Available from: https://de.wikipedia.org/wiki/Franz_Pieler_(Bergbauingenieur,_1869).

Wikipedia065. Heinrich Wisselmann. [online] [Accessed 16. 12. 2021] Available from: https://de.wikipedia.org/wiki/Heinrich_Wisselmann.

Wikipedia066. Grazer Maschinen- und Waggonbau-Aktiengesellschaft. [online] [Accessed 01. 03. 2022] Available from: https://de.wikipedia.org/wiki/Grazer_Maschinen-_und_Waggonbau-Aktiengesellschaft.

Wikipedia067. Max Auschnitt. [online] [Accessed 01. 03. 2022] Available from: https://en.wikipedia.org/wiki/Max_Auschnitt.

Wikipedia068. Zündwaren monopoly. [online] [Accessed 01. 03. 2022] Available from: https://en.wikipedia.org/wiki/Z%C3%BCndwaren_monopoly.

Wikipedia069. SA3 coupler. [online] [Accessed 01. 03. 2022] Available from: https://en.wikipedia.org/wiki/SA3_coupler.

Wikipedia070. Львівська залізниця (L'vivs'ka zaliznicâ). [online] [Accessed 01. 03. 2022] Available from: https://uk.wikipedia.org/wiki/%D0%9B%D1%8C%D0%B2%D1%96%D0%B2%D1%81%D1%8C%D0%BA%D0%B0_%D0%B7%D0%B0%D0%BB%D1%96%D0%B7%D0%BD%D0%B8%D1%86%D1%8F.

Wikipedia071. Türkiye Cumhuriyeti Devlet Demiryolları. [online] [Accessed 01. 03. 2022] Available from: https://tr.wikipedia.org/wiki/T%C3%BCrkiye_Cumhuriyeti_Devlet_Demiryollar%C4%B1#1923_-_1940_D%C3%B6nemi.

Wikipedia072. Field Information Agency, Technical. [online] [Accessed 01. 03. 2022] Available from: https://en.wikipedia.org/wiki/Field_Information_Agency,_Technical.

Wikipedia073. List of railway lines in Vietnam. [online] [Accessed 01. 03. 2022] Available from: https://en.wikipedia.org/wiki/List_of_railway_lines_in_Vietnam#Hanoi-ThaiNguyen.

Wikipedia074. Đường sắt Việt Nam. [online] [Accessed 01. 03. 2022] Available from: https://vi.wikipedia.org/wiki/%C4%90%C6%B0%E1%BB%9Dng_s%E1%BA%AFt_Vi%E1%BB%87t_Nam.

Wikipedia075. Jugoslavenske željeznice. [online] [Accessed 01. 03. 2022] Available from: https://hr.wikipedia.org/wiki/Jugoslavenske_%C5%BEeljeznice.

Wikipedia076. ISO 9. [online] [Accessed 01. 03. 2022] Available from: https://de.wikipedia.org/wiki/ISO_9.

Wikipedia077. Wiktionary: Bulgarisch/Umschrift. [online] [Accessed 01. 03. 2022] Available from: https://de.wiktionary.org/wiki/Wiktionary:Bulgarisch/Umschrift.

Wikipedia078. Pinyin. [online] [Accessed 01. 03. 2022] Available from: https://en.wikipedia.org/wiki/Pinyin.

Wikipedia079. Kunrei-System. [online] [Accessed 01. 03. 2022] Available from: https://de.wikipedia.org/wiki/Kunrei-System.

Wikipedia080. Ateliers et chantiers de la Loire. [online] [Accessed 01. 03. 2022] Available from: https://fr.wikipedia.org/wiki/Ateliers_et_chantiers_de_la_Loire.

Winek, Włodzimierz. 2017. Jaką infrastrukturę kolejową odziedziczyła Polska po II wojnie światowej? [online] 03. 12. 2017. [Accessed 01. 03. 2022] Available from: https://www.rynek-kolejowy.pl/mobile/jaka-infrastrukture-kolejowa-odziedziczyla-polska-po-ii-wojnie-swiatowej-84690.html.

Winkler, Dirk. 2003. *Kohlenstaublokomotiven der Deutschen Reichsbahn: Entwicklung, Technik und Einsatzgeschichte der Bauarten AEG, STUG und Wendler.* Freiburg/Breisgau : EK-Verlag GmbH, 2003. ISBN 3882551798.

Wolf, Gerd. 2015. Verschleppt und ausgebeutet: Zwangsarbeiter bei der Deutschen Reichsbahn 1939-1945. [online] 28. 02. 2015. [Accessed 01. 03. 2022] Available from: https://www.forum-der-wehrmacht.de/index.php?thread/42829-verschleppt-und-ausgebeutet-zwangsarbeiter-bei-der-deutschen-reichsbahn-1939-194/.

Wolmar, Christian. 2010. *Engines of War.* London (GB) : Atlantic Books, 2010. ISBN 9781848871731.

Wulfert, Gustav. 1942. *Der neue Oberbau der Deutschen Reichsbahn und der Oberbau der Gruppe Preußen.* Mühlheim/Ruhr : Selbstverlag des Verfassers, 1942.

Wysoki, Gerd. 1992. *Arbeit für den Krieg.* Braunschweig : Steinweg Verlag, 1992. ISBN 3925151516.

Zander, Peter. 2012. Mitbringsel von Maffei. *EisenbahnGeschichte.* 2012, Bd. 53, Pages 54-60.

Ziegler, Michael. 2012. Dokumentation zur Bauartreihe 52, Fortsetzung (mit vielen Bildern). [online] 30. 03. 2012. [Accessed 04. 04. 2015] Available from: https://www.drehscheibe-online.de/foren/read.php?17,5840522.

—. 2009. Drehscheibe-online. *04 - Historisches Forum - Der Bau der Kriegslokomotive R52 kann auf vollen Touren laufen* *(denkste...).* [online] 07. 02. 2009. [Accessed 14. 05. 2021] Available from: https://www.drehscheibe-online.de/foren/read.php?17,4154988.

Zug der Erinnerung. Was Reich-Ranicki nicht erwähnte. [online] [Accessed 01. 03. 2022] Available from: http://www.zug-der-erinnerung.eu/aktuell20120206.html.

Васильев (Vasil'ev), A. (A.). 1995. Никаких Чудес Техники (No Miracles of Engineering). *Железнодорожный курьер (Railway Courier).* 1, 1995, Pages 22-28.

—. 2010. Паровоз 1-5-0 серии ТЭ (BR 52) (Steam locomotive 1-5-0 series TÈ (Class 52)). [online] 18. 02. 2010. [Accessed 01. 03. 2022] Available from: https://scaletrainsclub.com/board/viewtopic.php?f=42&t=1921&start=20.

Вольфсон (Vol''fson), Л. (L.), Корнеев (Korneev), A. (A.) и Шильников (Šil''nikov), H. (N.). 1939. *Развитие ЖЕЛЕЗНЫХ ДОРОГ СССР (Razvitie ŽELEZNYH DOROG SSSR).* Москва (Moskva) : Государственное Транспортное Железнодорожное Издательство (Gosudarstvennoe Transportnoe Železnodorožnoe Izdatel''stvo), 1939.

Зиновьев (Zinov'ev), Д. (D.). Сбор статистики по паровозам железных дорогах СНГ, Прибалтики и Монголии *(Sbor statistiki po parovozam železnyh dorogah SNG, Pribaltiki i Mongolii).* [online] [Accessed 29. 06. 2020] Available from: https://www.parovoz.com/history/existing/index.php?ID=1586&LOC=&NUMBER=&BUILDER=*&STATUS=*&GAUGE=*&SERIES=%D0%A2%D0%AD&REGION=*.

Ковалев (Kovalev), Иван Владимирович (Ivan Vladimirovič). 1981. *Транспорт в ВЕЛИКОЙ ОТЕЧЕСТВЕННОЙ ВОЙНЕ (1941-1945 гг.) (Transport v VELIKOJ OTEČESTVENNOJ VOJNE (1941-1945 gg.)).* Москва (Moskva) : Наука (Nauka), 1981.

Макаров (Makarov), Леонид (Leonid). 2006. ФРАУ (FRAU). *Техника-молодежи (Tehnika-molodeži).* 8 2006, Bd. 8, Pages 48-49.

Про паровоз - pro parovoz. ТЭ (BR52) – грузовой паровоз *(TÈ (BR52) – gruzovoj parovoz).* [offline] [Accessed 01. 03. 2022] Available from: https://pro-parovoz.ru/index.php/component/k2/889-te-br52-gruzovoj-parovoz.

Раков (Rakov), В. А. (V. A.). 1995. *Локомотивы отечественных железных дорог (1845—1955 гг.) (Lokomotivy otečestvennyh železnyh dorog (1845—1955 gg.)).* 2nd revised and amended Edition. Москва (Moskva) : Транспорт (Transport), 1995. ISBN 5277008217.

Российский государственный архив экономики (Rossijskij gosudarstvennyj arhiv èkonomiki). Статистические динамические ряды за 1913-1951 годы *(Statističeskie dinamičeskie râdy za 1913-1951 gody).* [online] [Accessed 01. 03. 2022] Available from: https://istmat.org/node/40054.

Соколов (Sokolov), Вячеслав (Vâčeslav). S.C.A.D.O. ОТЕЧЕСТВЕННЫЕ ЛОКОМОТИВЫ, Товарные и грузовые паровозы *(S.C.A.D.O. OTEČESTVENNYE LOKOMOTIVY, Tovarnye i gruzovye parovozy).* [online] [Accessed 21. 06. 2021] Available from: http://scado.narod.ru/rail/r_0p.html.

Соколов2 (Sokolov), Вячеслав (Vâčeslav). Семейство Э *(Semejstvo È).* [online] [Accessed 01. 03. 2022] Available from: http://e917964x.beget.tech/catalog/r_p_ae.htm.

Центральное Статистическом Уравление (Central''noe Statističeskow Uravlenie). 1957. Транспорт И Связь СССР Статистический Сборник *(Transport I Svâz'' SSSR Statističeskij Sbornik).* [online] 1957. [Accessed 01. 03. 2022] Available from: https://istmat.org/node/29521.

Центральное управление народнохозяйственного учёта (ЦУНХУ) Госплана СССР (Central'noe upravlenie narodnohozâjstvennogo učëta (CUNHU) Gosplana SSSR). 1936. Транспорт и связь СССР в цифрах (1936) *(Transport i svâz' SSSR v cifrah (1936)).* [online] 1936. [Accessed 01. 03. 2022] Available from: https://istmat.org/node/22113.

Шаронин (Šaronin), В. С. (V. S.). 1945. *Транспортировка И Переделка Трофейных Паровозов (Transportirovka I Peredelka Trofejnyh Parovozov).* Москва (Moskva) : Государственное Транспортное Железнодорожное Издательство (Gosudarstvennoe Transportnoe Železnodorožnoe Izdatel''stvo), 1945.